The Life and Voyages of Christopher Columbus, Volume 1

THE

LIFE AND VOYAGES

OF

CHRISTOPHER COLUMBUS.

BY

WASHINGTON IRVING.

Venient annis
Sæcula seris, quibus Oceanus
Vincula rerum laxet, et ingens
Pateat tellus, Typhisque novos
Detegat Orbes, nec sit terris
Ultima Thule.
SENECA: *Medea.*

AUTHOR'S REVISED EDITION.

VOL. I.

PHILADELPHIA:
DAVID McKAY, PUBLISHER,
23 SOUTH NINTH STREET.
1893.

4 CONTENTS.

BOOK VI.

BOOK VII.

BOOK VIII.

BOOK IX.

PREFACE.

Being at Bordeaux, in the winter of 1825–6, I received a letter from Mr. Alexander Everett, Minister Plenipotentiary of the United States at Madrid, informing me of a work then in the press, edited by Don Martin Fernandez de Navarrete, Secretary of the Royal Academy of History, &c., &c., containing a collection of documents relative to the voyages of Columbus, among which were many of a highly important nature, recently discovered. Mr. Everett, at the same time, expressed an opinion that a version of the work into English, by one of our own country, would be peculiarly desirable. I concurred with him in the opinion; and, having for some time intended a visit to Madrid, I shortly afterwards set off for that capital, with an idea of undertaking, while there, the translation of the work.

Soon after my arrival, the publication of M. Navarrete made its appearance. I found it to contain many documents, hitherto unknown, which threw additional lights on the discovery of the New World; and which reflected the greatest credit on the industry and activity of the learned editor. Still the whole presented rather a mass of rich materials for history, than a history itself. And invaluable as such stores may be to the laborious inquirer, the

sight of disconnected papers and official documents is apt
to be repulsive to the general reader, who seeks for clear
and continued narrative. These circumstances made me
hesitate in my proposed undertaking; yet the subject was
of so interesting and national a kind, that I could not willingly abandon it.

On considering the matter more maturely, I perceived
that, although there were many books, in various languages, relative to Columbus, they all contained limited
and incomplete accounts of his life and voyages; while
numerous valuable tracts on the subject existed only in
manuscript or in the form of letters, journals, and public
muniments. It appeared to me that a history, faithfully
digested from these various materials, was a desideratum in
literature, and would be a more satisfactory occupation to
myself, and a more acceptable work to my country, than
the translation I had contemplated.

I was encouraged to undertake such a work, by the great
facilities which I found within my reach at Madrid. I was
resident under the roof of the American Consul, O. Rich,
Esq., one of the most indefatigable bibliographers in
Europe, who, for several years, had made particular researches after every document relative to the early history
of America. In his extensive and curious library, I found
one of the best collections extant of Spanish colonial history, containing many documents for which I might search
elsewhere in vain. This he put at my absolute command,
with a frankness and unreserve seldom to be met with
among the possessors of such rare and valuable works;
and his library has been by main resource throughout the
whole of my labors.

I found also the Royal Library of Madrid, and the library of the Jesuits' College of San Isidro, two noble and extensive collections, open to access, and conducted with great order and liberality. From Don Martin Fernandez de Navarrete, who communicated various valuable and curious pieces of information, discovered in the course of his researches, I received the most obliging assistance; nor can I refrain from testifying my admiration of the self-sustained zeal of that estimable man, one of the last veterans of Spanish literature, who is almost alone, yet indefatigable in his labors, in a country where, at present, literary exertion meets with but little excitement or reward.

I must acknowledge, also, the liberality of the Duke of Veraguas, the descendant and representative of Columbus, who submitted the archives of his family to my inspection, and took a personal interest in exhibiting the treasures they contained. Nor, lastly, must I omit my deep obligations to my excellent friend Don Antonio de Uguina, treasurer of the Prince Francisco, a gentleman of talents and erudition, and particularly versed in the history of his country and its dependencies. To his unwearied investigations, and silent and unavowed contributions, the world is indebted for much of the accurate information, recently imparted, on points of early colonial history. In the possession of this gentleman are most of the papers of his deceased friend, the late historian Muños, who was cut off in the midst of his valuable labors. These, and various other documents, have been imparted to be by Don Antonio, with a kindness and urbanity which greatly increased, yet lightened the obligation.

With these, and other aids incidentally afforded me by

my local situation, I have endeavored, to the best of my abilities, and making the most of the time which I could allow myself during a sojourn in a foreign country, to construct this history. I have diligently collated all the works that I could find relative to my subject, in print and manuscript; comparing them, as far as in my power, with original documents, those sure lights of historic research; endeavoring to ascertain the truth amid those contradictions which will inevitably occur, where several persons have recorded the same facts, viewing them from different points, and under the influence of different interests and feelings.

In the execution of this work I have avoided indulging in mere speculations or general reflections, excepting such as rose naturally out of the subject, preferring to give a minute and circumstantial narrative, omitting no particular that appeared characteristic of the persons, the events, or the times; and endeavoring to place every fact in such a point of view, that the reader might perceive its merits, and draw his own maxims and conclusions.

As many points of the history required explanations, drawn from contemporary events and the literature of the times, I have preferred, instead of incumbering the narrative, to give detached illustrations at the end of the work. This also enabled me to indulge in greater latitude of detail, where the subject was of a curious or interesting nature, and the sources of information such as not to be within the common course of reading.

After all, the work is presented to the public with extreme diffidence. All that I can safely claim is, an earnest desire to state the truth, an absence from prejudices respecting the nations mentioned in my history, a strong interest in my subject, and a zeal to make up by assiduity for many deficiencies of which I am conscious.

WASHINGTON IRVING.

Madrid, 1827.

P. S. I have been surprised at finding myself accused by some American writer of not giving sufficient credit to Don Martin Fernandez de Navarrete for the aid I had derived from his collection of documents. I had thought I had sufficiently shown, in the preceding preface, which appeared with my first edition, that his collection first prompted my work and subsequently furnished its principal materials; and that I had illustrated this by citations at the foot of almost every page. In preparing this revised edition, I have carefully and conscientiously examined into the matter, but find nothing to add to the acknowledgments already made.

To show the feelings and opinions of M. Navarrete himself with respect to my work and myself, I subjoin an extract from a letter received from that excellent man; and a passage from the introduction to the third volume of his collection. Nothing but the desire to vindicate myself on this head would induce me to publish extracts so laudatory.

From a letter dated Madrid, April 1st, 1831.

I congratulate myself that the documents and notices which I published in my collection about the first occurrences in the history of America, have fallen into hands so able to appreciate their authenticity, to examine them critically, and to circulate them in all directions; establishing fundamental truths which hitherto have been adulterated by partial or systematic writers.

Yo me complazeo en que los documentos y noticias que publico en mi coleccion sobre los primeros acontacimientos de la historia de America, hayan recaido en manos tan habiles para apreciar su autenticidad, para examinar las con critica y propagarlas por todos partes echando los fundamentos de la verdad que hasta ahora há sido tan adulterada par los escritores parciales ó sistematicos.

In the introduction to the third volume of his Collection of Spanish Voyages, Mr. Navarrete cites various testimonials he has received since the publication of his two first volumes, of the utility of his work to the republic of letters.

"A signal proof of this," he continues, "is just given us by Mr. Washington Irving in the History of the Life and Voyages of Christopher Columbus, which he has published with a success as general as it is well merited. We said in our introduction that we did not propose to write the history of the admiral, but to publish notes and materials that it might be written with veracity; and it is fortunate that the first person to profit by them, should be a literary man, judicious and erudite, already known in his own country and in Europe by other works of merit. Resident in Madrid, exempt from the rivalries which have influenced some European natives with respect to Columbus and his discoveries; having an opportunity to examine excellent books and precious manuscripts; to converse with persons

instructed in these matters, and having always at hand the
authentic documents which we had just published, he has
been enabled to give to his history that fullness, impartiality, and exactness, which make it much superior to
those of the writers who preceded him. To this he adds
his regular method and convenient distribution; his style
animated, pure, and elegant; the notice of various personages who mingled in the concerns of Columbus; and
the examination of various questions, in which always
shine sound criticism, erudition, and good taste."

Insigne prueba de esto mismo acaba de darnos el Senor
Washington Irving en la Historia de la Vida y de los
Viages de Cristóbal Colon que ha publicado con una
aceptacion tan general como bien merecida. Digimos en
nuestra introduccion (1 § 56 pag. lxxxii.) que no nos
proponiamos escribir la historia de aqual almirante, sino
publicar noticias y materiales para que se escribiese con
veracidad, y es una fortuna que el primero que se haya
aprovechado de ellas sea un literato juicioso y erudito,
conocido ya en su patria y en Europa por otras obras
apreciables. Colocado en Madrid, exento de las rivalidades
que han dominado entre algunas naciones Europeas sobre
Colon y sus descubrimientos; con la proporcion de examinar
excelentes libros y preciosos manuscritos, de tratar á per-
sonas instruidas en estas materias, y teniendo siempre á la
mano los autenticos documentos que acabamos de publicar,
ha logrado dar á su historia aquella extension imparcialidad
y exactitud que la hacen muy superior á las de los escritores
que le precedieron. Agrégate á esto su metodico arreglo y
conveniente distribucion; su estilo animado, puro y ele-

gante; la noticia de varios personages que intervenieron en los sucesos de Colon, y el exámen de varias cuestiones en que luce siempre la mas sana critica, la erudicion y buen gusto.—*Prologo to 3d volume.*

LIFE AND VOYAGES OF COLUMBUS.

BOOK I.

WHETHER in old times, beyond the reach of history or
tradition, and in some remote period of civilization, when,
as some imagine, the arts may have flourished to a degree
unknown to those whom we term the Ancients, there existed
an intercourse between the opposite shores of the Atlantic;
whether the Egyptian legend, narrated by Plato, respecting
the island of Atalantis was indeed no fable, but the obscure
tradition of some vast country, ingulfed by one of those
mighty convulsions of our globe, which have left traces of
the ocean on the summits of lofty mountains, must ever
remain matters of vague and visionary speculation. As
far as authenticated history extends, nothing was known
of terra firma, and the islands of the western hemisphere,
until their discovery towards the close of the fifteenth century. A wandering bark may occasionally have lost sight
of the landmarks of the old continents, and been driven by
tempests across the wilderness of waters long before the
invention of the compass, but never returned to reveal the
secrets of the ocean. And though, from time to time, some
document has floated to the shores of the old world, giving
to its wondering inhabitants evidences of land far beyond
their watery horizon; yet no one ventured to spread a sail,

2   17

and seek that land enveloped in mystery and peril. Or if
the legends of the Scandinavian voyagers be correct, and
their mysterious Vinland was the coast of Labrador, or the
shore of Newfoundland, they had but transient glimpses
of the new world, leading to no certain or permanent knowledge, and in a little time lost again to mankind.[1] Certain
it is that at the beginning of the fifteenth century, when
the most intelligent minds were seeking in every direction
for the scattered lights of geographical knowledge, a profound ignorance prevailed among the learned as to the
western regions of the Atlantic; its vast waters were
regarded with awe and wonder, seeming to bound the
world as with a chaos, into which conjecture could not
penetrate, and enterprise feared to adventure. We need
no greater proofs of this than the description given of
the Atlantic by Xerif al Edrisi, surnamed the Nubian, an
eminent Arabian writer, whose countrymen were the boldest
navigators of the middle ages, and possessed all that was
then known of geography.

"The ocean," he observes, "encircles the ultimate bounds
of the inhabited earth, and all beyond it is unknown. No one
has been able to verify anything concerning it, on account
of its difficult and perilous navigation, its great obscurity,
its profound depth, and frequent tempests; through fear of
its mighty fishes, and its haughty winds; yet there are many
islands in it, some peopled, others uninhabited. There is
no mariner who dares to enter into its deep waters; or if
any have done so, they have merely kept along its coasts,
fearful of departing from them. The waves of this ocean,
although they roll as high as mountains, yet maintain themselves without breaking; for if they broke, it would be
impossible for ship to plough them."[2]

[1] See Illustrations at the end of this work, article SCANDINAVIAN
DISCOVERIES.
[2] Description of Spain, by Xerif al Edrisi: Conde's Spanish translation, Madrid, 1799.

It is the object of the following work, to relate the deeds and fortunes of the mariner who first had the judgment to divine, and the intrepidity to brave the mysteries of this perilous deep; and who, by his hardy genius, his inflexible constancy, and his heroic courage, brought the ends of the earth into communication with each other. The narrative of his troubled life is the link which connects the history of the old world with that of the new.

CHAPTER I.

BIRTH, PARENTAGE AND EARLY LIFE OF COLUMBUS.

CHRISTOPHER COLUMBUS, or Columbo, as the name is written in Italian,[1] was born in the city of Genoa, about the year 1435. He was the son of Dominico Columbo, a wool comber, and Susannah Fontanarossa, his wife, and it would seem that his ancestors had followed the same handicraft for several generations in Genoa. Attempts have been made to prove him of illustrious descent, and several noble houses have laid claim to him since his name has become so renowned as to confer rather than receive distinction. It is possible some of them may be in the right, for the feuds in Italy in those ages had broken down and scattered many of the noblest families, and while some branches remained in the lordly heritage of castles and domains, others were confounded with the humblest popula-

[1] Columbus Latinized his name in his letters according to the usage of the time, when Latin was the language of learned correspondence. In subsequent life when in Spain he recurred to what was supposed to be the original Roman name of the family, Colonus, which he abbreviated to Colon, to adapt it to the Castilian tongue. Hence he is known in Spanish history as Christoval Colon. In the present work the name will be written Columbus, being the one by which he is most known throughout the world.

tion of the cities. The fact, however, is not material to his
fame; and it is a higher proof of merit to be the object of
contention among various noble families, than to be able to
substantiate the most illustrious lineage. His son Fernando
had a true feeling on the subject. "I am of opinion," says
he, "that I should derive less dignity from any nobility of
ancestry, than from being the son of such a father."[1]

Columbus was the oldest of four children; having two
brothers, Bartholomew and Giacomo, or James (written
Diego in Spanish), and one sister, of whom nothing is
known but that she was married to a person in obscure life
called Giacomo Bavarello. At a very early age Columbus
evinced a decided inclination for the sea; his education,
therefore, was mainly directed to fit him for maritime life,
but was as general as the narrow means of his father would
permit. Besides the ordinary branches of reading, writing, grammar and arithmetic, he was instructed in the
Latin tongue, and made some proficiency in drawing and
design. For a short time, also, he was sent to the university of Pavia, where he studied geometry, geography,
astronomy and navigation. He then returned to Genoa,
where, according to a contemporary historian, he assisted
his father in his trade of wool combing.[2] This assertion is
indignantly contradicted by his son Fernando, though there
is nothing in it improbable, and he gives us no information
of his father's occupation to supply its place. He could
not, however, have remained long in this employment, as,
according to his own account, he entered upon a nautical
life when but fourteen years of age.[3]

---

[1] The reader will find the vexed questions about the age, birth-
place and lineage of Columbus severally discussed in the Appendix.

[2] Agostino Giustiniani, Ann. de Genova. His assertion has been
echoed by other historians, viz., Anton Gallo de Navigatione Co-
lombi, &c., Muratori, tom. 23, Barta Senaraga, de rebus Genuensibus,
Muratori, tom. 24.

[3] Hist. del. Almirante, cap. 4.

In tracing the early history of a man like Columbus, whose actions have had a vast effect on human affairs, it is interesting to notice how much has been owing to external influences, how much to an inborn propensity of the genius. In the latter part of his life, when, impressed with the sublime events brought about through his agency, Columbus looked back upon his career with a solemn and superstitious feeling, he attributed his early and irresistible inclination for the sea, and his passion for geographical studies, to an impulse from the Deity preparing him for the high decrees he was chosen to accomplish.[1]

The nautical propensity, however, evinced by Columbus in early life, is common to boys of enterprising spirit and lively imagination brought up in maritime cities; to whom the sea is the high road to adventure and the region of romance. Genoa, too, walled in and straitened on the land side by rugged mountains, yielded but little scope for enterprise on shore, while an opulent and widely extended commerce, visiting every country, and a roving marine, battling in every sea, naturally led forth her children upon the waves, as their propitious element. Many, too, were induced to emigrate by the violent factions which raged within the bosom of the city, and often dyed its streets with blood. A historian of Genoa laments this proneness of its youth to wander. They go, said he, with the intention of returning when they shall have acquired the means of living comfortably and honorably in their native place; but we know from long experience, that of twenty who thus depart scarce two return; either dying abroad, or taking to themselves foreign wives, or being loth to expose themselves to the tempest of civil discords which distract the republic.[2]

The strong passion for geographical knowledge, also, felt by Columbus in early life, and which inspired his after ca-

---

[1] Letter to the Castilian Sovereigns, 1501.
[2] Foglieta, Istoria de Genova, lib. ii.

reer, was incident to the age in which he lived. Geographical discovery was the brilliant path of light which was
forever to distinguish the fifteenth century. During a long
night of monkish bigotry and false learning, geography,
with the other sciences, had been lost to the European nations. Fortunately it·had not been lost to mankind: it
had taken refuge in the bosom of Africa. While the
pedantic schoolmen of the cloisters were wasting time and
talent, and confounding erudition by idle reveries and so-
phistical dialectics, the Arabian sages, assembled at Senaar,
were taking the measurement of a degree of latitude, and
calculating the circumference of the earth, on the vast
plains of Mesopotamia.

True knowledge, thus happily preserved, was now making its way back to Europe. The revival of science accompanied the revival of letters. Among the various
authors which the awakening zeal for ancient literature
had once more brought into notice, were Pliny, Pomponius,
Mela, and Strabo. From these was regained a fund of geographical knowledge, which had long faded from the
public mind. Curiosity was aroused to pursue this forgotten path, thus suddenly reopened. A translation of the
work of Ptolemy had been made into Latin, at the commencement of the century, by Emanuel Chrysoleras, a
noble and learned Greek, and had thus been rendered more
familiar to the Italian students. Another translation had
followed, by James Angel de Scarpiaria, of which fair and
beautiful copies became common in the Italian libraries.[1]
The writings also began to be sought after of Averroes,
Alfraganus, and other Arabian sages, who had kept the
sacred fire of science alive, during the interval of European
darkness.

The knowledge thus reviving was limited and imperfect;
yet, like the return of morning light, it seemed to call a
new creation into existence, and broke, with all the charm

[1] Andres, Hist. B. Let., lib. iii. cap. 2.

of wonder, upon imaginative minds. They were surprised
at their own ignorance of the world around them. Every
step was discovery, for every region beyond their native
country was in a manner terra incognita.

Such was the state of information and feeling with respect
to this interesting science, in the early part of the fifteenth
century. An interest still more intense was awakened by
the discoveries which began to be made along the Alantic
coasts of Africa; and must have been particularly felt
among a maritime and commercial people like the Genoese.
To these circumstances may we ascribe the enthusiastic devotion which Columbus imbibed in his childhood for cosmographical studies, and which influenced all his after
fortunes.

The short time passed by him at the university of Pavia
was barely sufficient to give him the rudiments of the necessary sciences; the familiar acquaintance with them,
which he evinced in after life, must have been the result
of diligent self-schooling, in casual hours of study amid
the cares and vicissitudes of a rugged and wandering life.
He was one of those men of strong natural genius, who,
from having to contend at their very outset with privations
and impediments, acquire an intrepidity in encountering
and a facility in vanquishing difficulties, throughout their
career. Such men learn to effect great purposes with small
means, supplying this deficiency by the resources of their
own energy and invention. This, from his earliest commencement, throughout the whole of his life, was one of the
remarkable features in the history of Columbus. In every
undertaking, the scantiness and apparent insufficiency of
his means enhance the grandeur of his achievements.

CHAPTER II.

EARLY VOYAGES OF COLUMBUS.

COLUMBUS, as has been observed, commenced his nautical career when about fourteen years of age. His first voyages were made with a distant relative named Colombo, a hardy veteran of the seas, who had risen to some distinction by his bravery, and is occasionally mentioned in old chronicles; sometimes as commanding a squadron of his own, sometimes as an admiral in the Genoese service. He appears to have been bold and adventurous; ready to fight in any cause, and to seek quarrel wherever it might lawfully be found.

The seafaring life of the Mediterranean, in those days, was hazardous and daring. A commercial expedition resembeled a warlike cruise, and the maritime merchant had often to fight his way from port to port. Piracy was almost legalized. The frequent feuds between the Italian states; the cruisings of the Catalonians; the armadas fitted out by private noblemen, who exercised a kind of sovereignty in their own domains, and kept petty armies and navies in their pay; the roving ships and squadrons of private adventurers, a kind of naval Condottieri, sometimes employed by hostile governments, sometimes scouring the seas in search of lawless booty; these, with the holy wars waged against the Mahometan powers, rendered the narrow seas, to which navigation was principally confined, scenes of hardy encounters and trying reverses.

Such was the rugged school in which Columbus was reared, and it would have been deeply interesting to have marked the early development of his genius amidst its stern adversities. All this instructive era of his history, however, is covered with darkness. His son Fernando, who could have best elucidated it, has left it in obscurity, or has now and then perplexed us with cross lights; perhaps unwilling, from a principle of mistaken pride, to reveal the indigence and obscurity from which his father so gloriously emerged.

The first voyage in which we have any account of his being engaged was a naval expedition, fitted out in Genoa in 1459 by John of Anjou, Duke of Calabria, to make a descent upon Naples, in the hope of recovering that kingdom for his father King Reinier, or Renato, otherwise called René, Count of Provence. The republic of Genoa aided him with ships and money. The brilliant nature of the enterprise attracted the attention of daring and restless spirits. The chivalrous nobleman, the soldier of fortune, the hardy corsair, the desperate adventurer, the mercenary partisan, all hastened to enlist under the banner of Anjou. The veteran Colombo took a part in this expedition, either with galleys of his own, or as a commander of the Genoese squadron, and with him embarked his youthful relative, the future discoverer.

The struggle of John of Anjou for the crown of Naples lasted about four years, with varied fortune, but was finally unsuccessful. The naval part of the expedition, in which Columbus was engaged, signalized itself by acts of intrepidity; and at one time, when the Duke was reduced to take refuge in the island of Ischia, a handful of galleys scoured and controlled the bay of Naples.[1]

In the course of this gallant but ill-fated enterprise, Columbus was detached on a perilous cruise, to cut out a galley from the harbor of Tunis. This is incidentally mentioned by himself in a letter written many years afterwards. It happened to me, he says, that King Reinier (whom God has taken to himself) sent me to Tunis, to capture the galley Fernandina, and when I arrived off the island of St. Pedro, in Sardinia, I was informed that there were two ships and a carrack with the galley; by which intelligence my crew were so troubled that they determined to proceed

[1] Colenuccio, Istoria de Nap., lib. vii. cap. 17.

no further, but to return to Marseilles for another vessel and more people; as I could not by any means compel them, I assented apparently to their wishes, altering the point of the compass and spreading all sail. It was then evening, and next morning we were within the Cape of Carthagena, while all were firmly of opinion that they were sailing towards Marseilles.[1]

We have no further record of this bold cruise into the harbor of Tunis; but in the foregoing particulars we behold early indications of that resolute and persevering spirit which insured him success in his more important undertakings. His expedient to beguile a discontented crew into a continuation of the enterprise, by deceiving them with respect to the ship's course, will be found in unison with a stratagem of altering the reckoning, to which he had recourse in his first voyage of discovery.

During an interval of many years we have but one or two shadowy traces of Columbus. He is supposed to have been principally engaged on the Mediterranean and up the Levant; sometimes in commercial voyages; sometimes in the warlike contests between the Italian states; sometimes in pious and predatory expeditions against the Infidels. Historians have made him in 1474 captain of several Genoese ships, in the service of Louis XI of France, and endangering the peace between that country and Spain by running down and capturing Spanish vessels at sea, on his own responsibility, as a reprisal for an irruption of the Spaniards into Roussillon.[2] Again, in 1475, he is represented as brushing with his Genoese squadron in ruffling bravado by a Venetian fleet stationed off the island of Cyprus, shouting "Viva San Georgio!" the old war-cry of Genoa, thus endeavoring to pique the jealous pride of the

---

[1] Letter of Columbus to the Catholic sovereigns, vide Hist. del Almirante, cap. 4.

[2] Chaufepie, Suppl. to Bayle, vol. ii. article "Columbus."

Venetians and provoke a combat, though the rival republics were at peace at the time.

These transactions, however, have been erroneously attributed to Columbus. They were the deeds, or misdeeds, either of his relative the old Genoese admiral, or of a nephew of the same, of kindred spirit, called Colombo the Younger, to distinguish him from his uncle. They both appear to have been fond of rough encounters, and not very scrupulous as to the mode of bringing them about. Fernando Columbus describes this Colombo the Younger as a famous corsair, so terrible for his deeds against the Infidels, that the Moorish mothers used to frighten their unruly children with his name. Columbus sailed with him occasionally as he had done with his uncle, and, according to Fernando's account, commanded a vessel in his squadron on an eventful occasion.

Colombo the Younger, having heard that four Venetian galleys richly laden were on their return voyage from Flanders, laid in wait for them on the Portuguese coast, between Lisbon and Cape St. Vincent. A desperate engagement took place; the vessels grappled each other, and the crews fought hand to hand, and from ship to ship. The battle lasted from morning until evening, with great carnage on both sides. The vessel commanded by Columbus was engaged with a huge Venetian galley. They threw hand-grenades and other fiery missiles, and the galley was wrapped in flames. The vessels were fastened together by chains and grappling irons, and could not be separated; both were involved in one conflagration, and soon became a mere blazing mass. The crews threw themselves into the sea; Columbus seized an oar, which was floating within reach, and being an expert swimmer, attained the shore, though full two leagues distant. It pleased God, says his son Fernando, to give him strength, that he might preserve him for greater things. After recovering from his exhaustion he repaired to Lisbon, where he found many of his Genoese countrymen, and was induced to take up his residence.[1]

Such is the account given by Fernando of his father's first arrival in Portugal; and it has been currently adopted by modern historians; but on examining various histories of the times, the battle here described appears to have happened several years after the date of the arrival of Columbus in that country. That he was engaged in the contest is not improbable; but he had previously resided for some time in Portugal. In fact, on referring to the history of that kingdom, we shall find, in the great maritime enterprises in which it was at that time engaged, ample attractions for a person of his inclinations and pursuits; and we shall be led to conclude, that his first visit to Lisbon was not the fortuitous result of a desperate adventure, but was undertaken in a spirit of liberal curiosity, and in the pursuit of honorable fortune.

CHAPTER III.

PROGRESS OF DISCOVERY UNDER PRINCE HENRY OF PORTUGAL.

THE career of modern discovery had commenced shortly before the time of Columbus, and at the period of which we are treating was prosecuted with great activity by Portugal. Some have attributed its origin to a romantic incident in the fourteenth century. An Englishman of the name of Macham, flying to France with a lady of whom he was enamored, was driven far out of sight of land by stress of weather, and after wandering about the high seas, arrived at an unknown and uninhabited island, covered

---

[1] Hist. del. Almirante, cap. 5. See Illustrations at the end of this work, article "Capture of the Venetian Galleys."

with beautiful forests, which was afterwards called Madeira.[1]
Others have treated this account as a fable, and have pronounced the Canaries to be the first fruits of modern discovery. This famous group, the Fortunate Islands of the
ancients, in which they placed their garden of the Hesperides, and whence Ptolemy commenced to count the longitude,
had been long lost to the world. There are vague accounts,
it is true, of their having received casual visits, at wide
intervals, during the obscure ages, from the wandering bark
of some Arabian, Norman, or Genoese adventurer; but all
this was involved in uncertainty, and led to no beneficial
result. It was not until the fourteenth century that they
were effectually rediscovered, and restored to mankind.
From that time they were occasionally visited by the hardy
navigators of various countries. The greatest benefit produced by their discovery was, that the frequent expeditions
made to them emboldened mariners to venture far upon
the Atlantic, and familiarized them, in some degree, to its
dangers.

The grand impulse to discovery was not given by chance,
but was the deeply meditated effort of one master mind.
This was Prince Henry of Portugal, son of John the First,
surnamed the Avenger, and Philippa of Lancaster, sister
of Henry the Fourth of England. The character of this
illustrious man, from whose enterprises the genius of Columbus took excitement, deserves particular mention.

Having accompanied his father into Africa, in an expedition against the Moors, at Ceuta he received much
information concerning the coast of Guinea, and other
regions in the interior, hitherto unknown to Europeans,
and conceived an idea that important discoveries were to
be made by navigating along the western coast of Africa.
On returning to Portugal, this idea became his ruling
thought. Withdrawing from the tumult of a court to a
country retreat in the Algarves, near Sagres, in the neigh-

[1] See Illustrations, article "Discovery of Madeira."

borhood of Cape St. Vincent, and in full view of the
ocean, he drew around him men eminent in science, and
prosecuted the study of those branches of knowledge connected with the maritime arts. He was an able mathema-
tician, and made himself master of all the astronomy
known to the Arabians of Spain.

On studying the works of the ancients, he found what
he considered abundant proofs that Africa was circumnavigable. Eudoxus of Cyzicus was said to have sailed
from the Red Sea into the ocean, and to have continued on
to Gibraltar; and Hanno the Carthaginian, sailing from
Gibraltar with a fleet of sixty ships, and following the
African coast, was said to have reached the shores of
Arabia.[1] It is true these voyages had been discredited by
several ancient writers; and the possibility of circumnavigating Africa, after being for a long time admitted by
geographers, was denied by Hipparchus, who considered
each sea shut up and land-bound in its peculiar basin; and
that Africa was a continent continuing onward to the south
pole, and surrounding the Indian sea, so as to join Asia
beyond the Ganges. This opinion had been adopted by
Ptolemy, whose works, in the time of Prince Henry, were
the highest authority in geography. The prince, however,
clung to the ancient belief, that Africa was circumnavigable,
and found his opinion sanctioned by various learned men
of more modern date. To settle this question, and achieve
the circumnavigation of Africa, was an object worthy the
ambition of a prince, and his mind was fired with the idea
of the vast benefits that would arise to his country should
it be accomplished by Portuguese enterprise.

The Italians, or Lombards, as they were called in the
north of Europe, had long monopolized the trade of Asia.
They had formed commercial establishments at Constanti-
nople and in the Black Sea, where they received the rich

[1] See Illustrations, article " Circumnavigation of Africa by the
Ancients."

produce of the Spice Islands, lying near the Equator; and
the silks, the gums, the perfumes, the precious stones, and
other luxurious commodities of Egypt and southern Asia,
and distributed them over the whole of Europe. The
republics of Venice and Genoa rose to opulence and power
in consequence of this trade. They had factories in the
most remote parts, even in the frozen regions of Moscovy
and Norway. Their merchants emulated the magnificence
of princes. All Europe was tributary to their commerce.
Yet this trade had to pass through various intermediate
hands, subject to the delays and charges of internal navigation, and the tedious and uncertain journeys of the
caravan. For a long time, the merchandise of India was
conveyed by the Gulf of Persia, the Euphrates, the Indus,
and the Oxus, to the Caspian and the Mediterranean seas;
thence to take a new destination for the various marts of
Europe. After the Soldan of Egypt had conquered the
Arabs, and restored trade to its ancient channel, it was
still attended with great cost and delay. Its precious commodities had to be conveyed by the Red Sea; thence on
the backs of camels to the banks of the Nile, whence they
were transported to Egypt to meet the Italian merchants.
Thus, while the opulent traffic of the East was engrossed
by these adventurous monopolists, the price of every article
was enhanced by the great expense of transportation.

It was the grand idea of Prince Henry, by circumnavigating Africa to open a direct and easy route to the source
of this commerce, to turn it in a golden tide upon his
country. He was, however, before the age in thought, and
had to counteract ignorance and prejudice, and to endure
the delays to which vivid and penetrating minds are subjected, from the tardy co-operations of the dull and the
doubtful. The navigation of the Atlantic was yet in its
infancy. Mariners looked with distrust upon a boisterous
expanse, which appeared to have no opposite shore, and
feared to venture out of sight of the landmarks. Every

bold headland, and far-stretching promontory, was a wall
to bar their progress. They crept timorously along the
Barbary shores, and thought they had accomplished a
wonderful expedition when they had ventured a few degrees beyond the Straits of Gibraltar. Cape Non was long
the limit of their daring; they hesitated to double its
rocky point, beaten by winds and waves, and threatening
to thrust them forth upon the raging deep.

Independent of these vague fears, they had others,
sanctioned by philosophy itself. They still thought that
the earth, at the equator, was girdled by a torrid zone,
over which the sun held his vertical and fiery course,
separating the hemispheres by a region of impassive heat.
They fancied Cape Bojador the utmost boundary of secure
enterprise, and had a superstitious belief, that whoever
doubled it would never return.[1] They looked with dismay
upon the rapid currents of its neighborhood, and the furious
surf which beats upon its arid coast. They imagined that
beyond it lay the frightful region of the torrid zone,
scorched by a blazing sun; a region of fire, where the
very waves, which beat upon the shores, boiled under the
intolerable fervor of the heavens.

To dispel these errors, and to give a scope to navigation,
equal to the grandeur of his designs, Prince Henry established a naval college, and erected an observatory at Sagres,
and he invited thither the most eminent professors of the
nautical faculties; appointing as president James of Mallorca, a man learned in navigation, and skillful in making
charts and instruments.

The effects of this establishment were soon apparent.
All that was known relative to geography and navigation
was gathered together and reduced to system. A vast
improvement took place in maps. The compass was also
brought into more general use, especially among the Portuguese, rendering the mariner more bold and venturous,

[1] Mariana, Hist. Esp., lib. ii. cap. 22.

by enabling him to navigate in the most gloomy day; and in the darkest night. Encouraged by these advantages, and stimulated by the munificence of Prince Henry, the Portuguese marine became signalized for the hardihood of its enterprises, and the extent of its discoveries. Cape Bojador was doubled; the region of the tropics penetrated, and divested of its fancied terrors; the greater part of the African coast, from Cape Blanco to Cape de Verde, explored; and the Cape de Verde and Azore islands, which lay three hundred leagues distant from the continent, were rescued from the oblivious empire of the ocean.

To secure the quiet prosecution and full enjoyment of his discoveries, Henry obtained the protection of a papal bull, granting to the crown of Portugal sovereign authority over all the lands it might discover in the Atlantic, to India inclusive, with plenary indulgence to all who should die in these expeditions; at the same time menacing, with the terrors of the church, all who should interfere in these Christian conquests.[1]

Henry died on the 13th of November, 1473, without accomplishing the great object of his ambition. It was not until many years afterwards, that Vasco de Gama, pursuing with a Portuguese fleet the track he had pointed out, realized his anticipations by doubling the Cape of Good Hope, sailing along the southern coast of India, and thus opening a highway for commerce to the opulent regions of the East. Henry, however, lived long enough to reap some of the richest rewards of a great and good mind. He beheld, through his means, his native country in a grand and active career of prosperity. The discoveries of the Portuguese were the wonder and admiration of the fifteenth century, and Portugal, from being one of the least among nations, suddenly rose to be one of the most important.

All this was effected, not by arms, but by arts; not by

[1] Vasconcelos, Hist. de Juan II.

the stratagems of a cabinet, but by the wisdom of a college.
It was the great achievement of a prince, who has well
been described "full of thoughts of lofty enterprise, and
acts of generous spirit:" one who bore for his device the
magnanimous motto, "The talent to do good," the only
talent worthy the ambition of princes.[1]

Henry, at his death, left it in charge to his country to
prosecute the route to India. He had formed companies
and associations, by which commercial zeal was enlisted in
the cause, and it was made a matter of interest and compe-
tition to enterprising individuals.[2] From time to time
Lisbon was thrown into a tumult of excitement by the
launching forth of some new expedition, or the return of a
squadron with accounts of new tracts explored, and new
kingdoms visited. Every thing was confident promise, and
sanguine anticipation. The miserable hordes of the African
coast were magnified into powerful nations, and the voyagers
continually heard of opulent countries farther on. It was
as yet the twilight of geographic knowledge; imagination
went hand in hand with discovery, and as the latter groped
its slow and cautious way, the former peopled all beyond
with wonders. The fame of the Portuguese discoveries,
and of the expeditions continually setting out, drew the
attention of the world. Strangers from all parts, the
learned, the curious, and the adventurous, resorted to
Lisbon to inquire into the particulars or to participate in
the advantages of these enterprises. Among these was
Christopher Columbus, whether thrown there, as has been
asserted, by the fortuitous result of a desperate adventure,
or drawn thither by liberal curiosity, and the pursuit of
honorable fortune.[3]

[1] Joam de Barros, Asia, decad. i.
[2] Lafitau, Conquêtes des Portugais, tom. i. lib. i.
[3] Herrera, decad. i. lib. i.

CHAPTER IV.

RESIDENCE OF COLUMBUS AT LISBON.—IDEAS CONCERNING
ISLANDS IN THE OCEAN.

COLUMBUS arrived at Lisbon about the year 1470. He was
at that time in the full vigor of manhood, and of an engaging presence. Minute descriptions are given of his person
by his son Fernando, by Las Casas, and others of his contemporaries.[1] According to these accounts, he was tall,
well-formed, muscular, and of an elevated and dignified
demeanor. His visage was long, and neither full nor
meagre; his complexion fair and freckled and inclined to
ruddy; his nose aquiline; his cheek-bones were rather high,
his eyes light gray, and apt to enkindle; his whole countenance had an air of authority. His hair, in his youthful
days, was of a light color; but care and trouble, according
to Las Casas, soon turned it gray, and at thirty years of age
it was quite white. He was moderate and simple in diet
and apparel, eloquent in discourse, engaging and affable
with strangers, and his amiableness and suavity in domestic
life strongly attached his household to his person. His
temper was naturally irritable;[2] but he subdued it by the
magnanimity of his spirit, comporting himself with a courteous and gentle gravity, and never indulging in any intem-
perance of language. Throughout his life he was noted for
strict attention to the offices of religion, observing rigorously
the fasts and ceremonies of the church; nor did his piety con-
sist in mere forms, but partook of that lofty and solemn enthusiasm with which his whole character was strongly tinctured.

While at Lisbon, he was accustomed to attend religious
service at the chapel of the convent of All Saints. In this
convent were certain ladies of rank, either resident as board-

[1] Hist. del Almirante, cap. 3. Las Casas, Hist. Ind., lib. i. cap.
2, MS.
[2] Illescas, Hist. Pontifical, lib. vi.

ers, or in some religious capacity. With one of these, Columbus became acquainted. She was Doña Felipa, daughter of Bartolomeo Moñis de Perestrello, an Italian cavalier, lately deceased, who had been one of the most distinguished navigators under Prince Henry, and had colonized and governed the island of Porto Santo. · The acquaintance soon ripened into attachment, and ended in marriage. It appears to have been a match of mere affection, as the lady was destitute of fortune.

. The newly married couple resided with the mother of the bride. The latter, perceiving the interest which Columbus took in all matters concerning the sea, related to him all she knew of the voyages and expeditions of her late husband, and brought him all his papers, charts, journals, and memorandums.[1] In this way he became acquainted with the routes of the Portuguese, their plans and conceptions; and having, by his marriage and residence, become naturalized in Portugal, he sailed occasionally in the expeditions to the coast of Guinea. When on shore, he supported his family by making maps and charts. His narrow circumstances obliged him to observe a strict economy; yet we are told that he appropriated a part of his scanty means to the succor of his aged father at Genoa,[2] and to the education of his younger brothers.[3]

. The construction of a correct map or chart, in those days, required a degree of knowledge and experience sufficient to entitle the possessor to distinction. Geography was but just emerging from the darkness which had enveloped it for ages. Ptolemy was still a standard authority. The maps of the fifteenth century display a mixture of truth and .error, in which facts handed down from antiquity, and others revealed by recent discoveries, are confused with popular fables, and extravagant conjectures. At such a

[1] Oviedo, Cronica de las Indias, lib. ii. cap. 2.
[2] Ibid.
[3] Muñoz, Hist. del N. Mundo, lib. ii.

period, when the passion for maritime discovery was seeking every aid to facilitate its enterprises, the knowledge and skill of an able cosmographer, like Columbus, would be properly appreciated, and the superior correctness of his maps and charts would give him notoriety among men of science.[1] We accordingly find him, at an early period of his residence in Lisbon, in correspondence with Paulo Toscanelli, of Florence, one of the most scientific men of the day, whose communications had great influence in inspiriting him to his subsequent undertakings.

While his geographical labors thus elevated him to a communion with the learned, they were peculiarly calculated to foster a train of thoughts favorable to nautical enterprise. From constantly comparing maps and charts, and noting the progress and direction of discovery, he was led to perceive how much of the world remained unknown, and to meditate on the means of exploring it. His domestic concerns, and the connections he had formed by marriage, were all in unison with this vein of speculation. He resided for some time at the recently discovered island of Porto Santo, where his wife had inherited some property, and during his residence there she bore him a son, whom

[1] The importance which began to be attached to cosmographical knowledge is evident from the distinction which Mauro, an Italian friar, obtained from having projected an universal map, esteemed the most accurate of the time. A fac-simile of this map, upon the same scale as the original, is now deposited in the British Museum, and it has been published, with a geographical commentary, by the learned Zurla. The Venetians struck a medal in honor of him, on which they denominated him Cosmographus incomparabilis (Colline del Bussol. Naut., p. 2. c. 5). Yet Ramusio, who had seen this map in the monastery of San Michele de Murano, considers it merely an improved copy of a map brought from Cathay by Marco Polo (Ramusio, t. ii. p. 17. Ed. Venet. 1606). We are told that Americus Vespucius paid one hundred and thirty ducats (equivalent to five hundred and fifty-five dollars in our time) for a map of sea and land, made at Mallorca, in 1439, by Gabriel de Valseca (Barros, D. l. i. c. 15. Derroto por Tofino, Introd. p. 25).

he named Diego. This residence brought him, as it were,
on the very frontier of discovery. His wife's sister was married to Pedro Correo, a navigator of note, who had at one
time been governor of Porto Santo. Being frequently
together in the familiar intercourse of domestic life, their
conversation naturally turned upon the discoveries prosecuting in their vicinity along the African coasts; upon the
long sought for route to India; and upon the possibility of
some unknown lands existing in the west.

In their island residence, too, they must have been frequently visited by the voyagers going to and from Guinea.
Living thus, surrounded by the stir and bustle of discovery,
communing with persons who had risen by it to fortune and
honor, and voyaging in the very tracks of its recent triumphs, the ardent mind of Columbus kindled up to enthusiasm in the cause. It was a period of general excitement
to all who were connected with maritime life, or who resided
in the vicinity of the ocean. The recent discoveries had
inflamed their imaginations, and had filled them with
visions of other islands, of greater wealth and beauty, yet
to be discovered in the boundless wastes of the Atlantic.
The opinions and fancies of the ancients on the subject were
again put in circulation. The story of Antilla, a great
island in the ocean, discovered by the Carthaginians, was
frequently cited, and Plato's imaginary Atalantis once more
found firm believers. Many thought that the Canaries
and Azores were but wrecks which had survived its sub-
mersion, and that other and larger fragments of that
drowned land might yet exist, in remoter parts of the
Atlantic.

One of the strongest symptoms of the excited state of
the popular mind at this eventful era, was the prevalence
of rumors respecting unknown islands casually seen in the
ocean. Many of these were mere fables, fabricated to feed
the predominant humor of the public; many had their
origin in the heated imaginations of voyagers, beholding

islands in those summer clouds which lie along the horizon, and often beguile the sailor with the idea of distant lands.

On such airy basis, most probably, was founded the story told to Columbus by one Antonio Leone, an inhabitant of Madeira, who affirmed that sailing thence westward one hundred leagues, he had seen three islands at a distance. But the tales of the kind most positively advanced and zealously maintained, were those related by the people of the Canaries, who were long under a singular optical delusion. They imagined that, from time to time, they beheld a vast island to the westward, with lofty mountains and deep valleys. Nor was it seen in cloudy and dubious weather, but in those clear days common to tropical climates, and with all the distinctness with which distant objects may be discerned in their pure, transparent atmosphere. The island, it is true, was only seen at intervals: while at other times, and in the clearest weather, not a vestige of it was to be descried. When it did appear, however, it was always in the same place, and under the same form. So persuaded were the inhabitants of the Canaries of its reality, that application was made to the king of Portugal for permission to discover and take possession of it; and it actually became the object of several expeditions. The island, however, was never to be found, though it still continued occasionally to cheat the eye.

There were all kinds of wild and fantastic notions concerning this imaginary land. Some supposed it to be the Antilla mentioned by Aristotle; others, the Island of Seven Cities, so called from an ancient legend of seven bishops, who, with a multitude of followers, fled from Spain at the time of its conquest by the Moors, and, guided by Heaven to some unknown island in the ocean, founded on it seven splendid cities. While some considered it another legendary island, on which, it was said, a Scottish priest of the name of St. Brandan had landed, in the sixth century. This last legend passed into current belief. The fancied island was called by the name of St. Brandan, or St. Borondon, and long continued to be actually laid down in maps far to the west of the Canaries.[1] The same was done with the fabulous island of Antilla; and these erroneous maps, and phantom islands, have given rise at various times to assertions, that the New World had been known prior to the period of its generally reputed discovery.

Columbus, however, considers all these appearances of land as mere illusions. He supposes that they may have been caused by rocks lying in the ocean, which, seen at a distance, under certain atmospherical influences, may have assumed the appearance of islands; or that they may have been floating islands, such as are mentioned by Pliny and Seneca and others, formed of twisted roots, or of a light and porous stone, and covered with trees, and which may have been driven about the ocean by the winds.

The islands of St. Brandan, of Antilla, and of the Seven Cities, have long since proved to be fabulous tales, or atmospherical delusions. Yet the rumors concerning them derive interest, from showing the state of public thought with respect to the Atlantic, while its western regions were yet unknown. They were all noted down with curious care by Columbus, and may have had some influence over his imagination. Still, though of a visionary spirit, his penetrating genius sought in deeper sources for the aliment of its meditations. Aroused by the impulse of passing events, he turned anew, says his son Fernando, to study the geographical authors which he had read before, and to consider the astronomical reasons which might corroborate the theory gradually forming in his mind. He made himself acquainted with all that had been written by the ancients, or discovered by the moderns, relative to geography. His own voyages enabled him to correct many of their errors, and appreciate many of their theories. His genius having thus taken its decided bent, it is interesting to notice from what a mass

[1] See Illustrations, article " Island of St. Brandan."

of acknowledged facts, rational hypotheses, fanciful narrations, and popular rumors, his grand project of discovery was wrought out by the strong workings of his vigorous mind.

CHAPTER V.

GROUNDS ON WHICH COLUMBUS FOUNDED HIS BELIEF OF THE EXISTENCE OF UNDISCOVERED LANDS IN THE WEST.

It has been attempted, in the preceding chapters, to show how Columbus was gradually kindled up to his grand design by the spirit and events of the times in which he lived. His son Fernando, however, undertakes to furnish the precise data on which his father's plan of discovery was founded.[1] "He does this," he observes, "to show from what slender argument so great a scheme was fabricated and brought to light; and for the purpose of satisfying those who may desire to know distinctly the circumstances and motives which led his father to undertake this enterprise."

As this statement was formed from notes and documents found among his father's papers, it is too curious and interesting not to deserve particular mention. In this memorandum he arranged the foundation of his father's theory under three heads: 1. The nature of things. 2. The authority of learned writers. 3. The reports of navigators.

Under the first head, he set down as a fundamental principle, that the earth was a terraqueous sphere or globe, which might be traveled round from east to west, and that men stood foot to foot, when on opposite points. The circumference from east to west, at the equator, Columbus divided, according to Ptolemy, into twenty-four hours of

[1] Hist. del Almirante, cap. 6, 7, 8.

fifteen degrees each, making three hundred and sixty
degrees. Of these he imagined, comparing the globe of
Ptolemy with the earlier map of Marinus of Tyre, that
fifteen hours had been known to the ancients, extending
from the Straits of Gibraltar, or rather from the Canary
Islands, to the city of Thinæ in Asia, a place set down as
at the eastern limits of the known world. The Portuguese
had advanced the western frontier one hour more by the
discovery of the Azores and Cape de Verde Islands. There
remained, then, according to the estimation of Columbus,
eight hours, or one-third of the circumference of the earth,
unknown and unexplored. This space might, in a great
measure, be filled up by the eastern regions of Asia, which
might extend so far as nearly to surround the globe, and
to approach the western shores of Europe and Africa.
The tract of ocean, intervening between these countries,
he observes, would be less than might at first be supposed,
if the opinion of Alfraganus, the Arabian, were admitted,
who, by diminishing the size of the degrees, gave to the
earth a smaller circumference than did other cosmographers; a theory to which Columbus seems at times to have
given faith. Granting these premises, it was manifest, that,
by pursuing a direct course from east to west, a navigator
would arrive at the extremity of Asia, and discover any
intervening land.

Under the second head, are named the authors whose
writings had weight in convincing him that the intervening ocean could be but of moderate expanse, and easy
to be traversed. Among these, he cites the opinion of
Aristotle, Seneca, and Pliny, that one might pass from
Cadiz to the Indies in a few days; of Strabo, also, who
observes, that the ocean surrounds the earth, bathing on
the east the shores of India; on the west, the coasts of
Spain and Mauritania; so that it is easy to navigate from
one to the other on the same parallel.[1]

[1] Strab. Cos., lib. i. ii.

In corroboration of the idea, that Asia, or, as he always terms it, India, stretched far to the east, so as to occupy the greater part of the unexplored space, the narratives are cited of Marco Polo and John Mandeville. These travelers had visited, in the thirteenth and fourteenth centuries, the remote parts of Asia, far beyond the regions laid down by Ptolemy; and their accounts of the extent of that continent to the eastward, had a great effect in convincing Columbus that a voyage to the west, of no long duration, would bring him to its shores, or to the extensive and wealthy islands which lie adjacent. The information concerning Marco Polo, is probably derived from Paulo Toscanelli, a celebrated doctor of Florence, already mentioned, with whom Columbus corresponded in 1474, and who transmitted to him a copy of a letter which he had previously written to Fernando Martinez, a learned canon of Lisbon. This letter maintains the facility of arriving at India by a western course, asserting the distance to be but four thousand miles, in a direct line from Lisbon to the province of Mangi, near Cathay, since determined to be the northern coast of China. Of this country he gives a magnificent description, drawn from the work of Marco Polo. He adds, that in the route lay the islands of Antilla and Cipango, distant from each other only two hundred and twenty-five leagues, abounding in riches, and offering convenient places for ships to touch at, and obtain supplies on the voyage.

Under the third head, are enumerated various indications of land in the west, which had floated to the shores of the known world. It is curious to observe, how, when once the mind of Columbus had become heated in the inquiry, it attracted to it every corroborating circumstance, however vague and trivial. He appears to have been particularly attentive to the gleams of information derived from veteran mariners, who had been employed in the recent voyages to the African coasts; and also from the inhabitants of lately discovered islands, placed, in a manner, on the frontier posts of geographical knowledge. All these are carefully noted down among his memorandums, to be collocated with the facts and opinions already stored up in his mind.

Such, for instance, is the circumstance related to him by Martin Vicenti, a pilot in the service of the king of Portugal; that, after sailing four hundred and fifty leagues to the west of Cape St. Vincent, he had taken from the water a piece of carved wood, which evidently had not been labored with an iron instrument. As the winds had drifted it from the west, it might have come from some unknown land in that direction.

Pedro Correa, brother-in-law of Columbus, is likewise cited, as having seen, on the island of Porto Santo, a similar piece of wood, which had drifted from the same quarter. He had heard also from the king of Portugal, that reeds of an immense size had floated to some of those islands from the west, in the description of which, Columbus thought he recognized the immense reeds said by Ptolemy to grow in India.

Information is likewise noted, given him by the inhabitants of the Azores, of trunks of huge pine trees, of a kind that did not grow upon any of the islands, wafted to their shores by the westerly winds; but especially of the bodies of two dead men, cast upon the island of Flores, whose features differed from those of any known race of people.

To these is added the report of a mariner of the port of St. Mary, who asserted that, in the course of a voyage to Ireland, he had seen land to the west, which the ship's company took for some extreme part of Tartary. Other stories, of a similar kind, are noted, as well as rumors concerning the fancied islands of St. Brandan, and of the Seven Cities, to which, as has already been observed, Columbus gave but little faith.

Such is an abstract of the grounds, on which, according to Fernando, his father proceeded from one position to another, until he came to the conclusion, that there was undiscovered land in the western part of the ocean; that it was attainable; that it was fertile; and finally, that it was inhabited.

It is evident, that several of the facts herein enumerated, must have become known to Columbus after he had formed his opinion, and merely served to strengthen it; still, every thing that throws any light upon the process of thought, which led to so great an event, is of the highest interest; and the chain of deductions here furnished, though not perhaps the most logical in its concatenation, yet, being extracted from the papers of Columbus himself, remains one of the most interesting documents in the history of the human mind.

On considering this statement attentively, it is apparent that the grand argument which induced Columbus to his enterprise, was that placed under the first head, namely, that the most eastern part of Asia known to the ancients, could not be separated from the Azores by more than a third of the circumference of the globe; that the intervening space must, in a great measure, be filled up by the unknown residue of Asia; and that, if the circumference of the world was, as he believed, less than was generally supposed, the Asiatic shores could easily be attained by a moderate voyage to the west.

It is singular how much the success of this great undertaking depended upon two happy errors, the imaginary extent of Asia to the east, and the supposed smallness of the earth; both, errors of the most learned and profound philosophers, but without which Columbus would hardly have ventured upon his enterprise. As to the idea of finding land by sailing directly to the west, it is at present so familiar to our minds, as in some measure to diminish the merits of the first conception, and the hardihood of the first

attempt : but in those days, as has well been observed, the
circumference of the earth was yet unknown; no one
could tell whether the ocean were not of immense extent,
impossible to be traversed; nor were the laws of specific
gravity and of central gravitation ascertained, by which,
granting the rotundity of the earth, the possibility of making the tour of it would be manifest.[1] The practicability,
therefore, of finding land by sailing to the west, was one of
those mysteries of nature which are considered incredible
whilst matters of mere speculation, but the simplest things
imaginable when they have once been ascertained.

  When Columbus had formed his theory, it became fixed
in his mind with singular firmness, and influenced his entire
character and conduct. He never spoke in doubt or hesitation, but with as much certainty as if his eyes had beheld
the promised land. No trial nor disappointment could
divert him from the steady pursuit of his object. A deep
religious sentiment mingled with his meditations, and gave
them at times a tinge of superstition, but it was of a sublime and lofty kind : he looked upon himself as standing in
the hand of Heaven, chosen from among men for the
accomplishment of its high purpose; he read, as he supposed, his contemplated discovery foretold in Holy Writ,
and shadowed forth darkly in the mystic revelations of the
prophets. The ends of the earth were to be brought together, and all nations and tongues and languages united
under the banners of the Redeemer. This was to be the
triumphant consummation of his enterprise, bringing the
remote and unknown regions of the earth into communion
with Christian Europe; carrying the light of the true
faith into benighted and Pagan lands, and gathering their
countless nations under the holy dominion of the church.

  The enthusiastic nature of his conceptions gave an elevation to his spirit, and a dignity and loftiness to his whole

[1] Malte-Brun, Géographie Universelle, tom. xiv. Note sur le Dé-
couverte de l'Amérique.

demeanor. He conferred with sovereigns almost with a feeling of equality. His views were princely and unbounded; his proposed discovery was of empires; his conditions were proportionally magnificent; nor would he ever, even after long delays, repeated disappointments, and under the pressure of actual penury, abate what appeared to be extravagant demands for a mere possible discovery.

Those who could not conceive how an ardent and comprehensive genius could arrive, by presumptive evidence, at so firm a conviction, sought for other modes of accounting for it. When the glorious result had established the correctness of the opinion of Columbus, attempts were made to prove that he had obtained previous information of the lands which he pretended to discover. Among these, was an idle tale of a tempest-tossed pilot, said to have died in his house, bequeathing him written accounts of an unknown land in the west, upon which he had been driven by adverse winds. This story, according to Fernando Columbus, had no other foundation than one of the popular tales about the shadowy island of St. Brandan, which a Portuguese captain, returning from Guinea, fancied he had beheld beyond Madeira. It circulated for a time in idle rumor, altered and shaped to suit their purposes, by such as sought to tarnish the glory of Columbus. At length, it found its way into print, and has been echoed by various historians, varying with every narration, and full of contradictions and improbabilities.[1]

An assertion has also been made, that Columbus was preceded in his discoveries by Martin Behem, a contemporary cosmographer, who, it was said, had landed accidentally on the coast of South America, in the course of an African expedition; and that it was with the assistance of a map, or globe, projected by Behem, on which was laid down the

[1] See Illustrations, article "Rumor concerning the Pilot who died in the House of Columbus."

newly-discovered country, that Columbus made his voyage. This rumor originated in an absurd misconstruction of a Latin manuscript, and was unsupported by any documents; yet it has had its circulation, and has even been revived not many years since, with more zeal than discretion; but is now completely refuted and put to rest. The land visited by Behem was the coast of Africa beyond the equator; the globe he projected was finished in 1492, while Columbus was absent on his first voyage: it contains no trace of the New World, and thus furnishes conclusive proof, that its existence was yet unknown to Behem.[1]

There is a certain meddlesome spirit, which, in the garb of learned research, goes prying about the traces of history, casting down its monuments, and marring and mutilating its fairest trophies. Care should be taken to vindicate great names from such pernicious erudition. It defeats one of the most salutary purposes of history, that of furnishing examples of what human genius and laudable enterprise may accomplish. For this purpose, some pains have been taken in the preceding chapters, to trace the rise and progress of this grand idea in the mind of Columbus; to show that it was the conception of his genius, quickened by the impulse of the age, and aided by those scattered gleams of knowledge, which fell ineffectually upon ordinary minds.

CHAPTER VI.

CORRESPONDENCE OF COLUMBUS WITH PAULO TOSCANELLI. —EVENTS IN PORTUGAL RELATIVE TO DISCOVERIES.— PROPOSITION OF COLUMBUS TO THE PORTUGUESE COURT. —DEPARTURE FROM PORTUGAL.

IT is impossible to determine the precise time when Columbus first conceived the design of seeking a western route to India. It is certain, however, that he meditated it as early

[1] See Illustrations, article " Behem."

PART OF A TERRESTRIAL GLOBE

MADE AT NUREMBERG, IN THE YEAR 1492, BY MARTIN BEHEM.

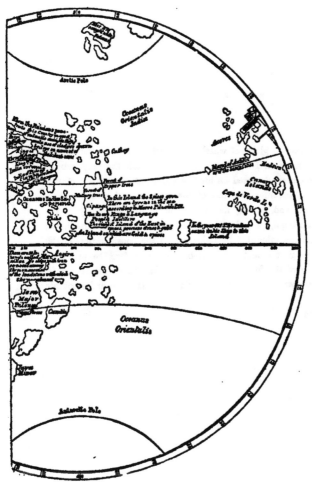

For description see reverse page.

4   49

The terrestrial globe, of which a segment is given on the reverse page, was made at Nuremberg in the year 1492, the very year in which Columbus departed on his first voyage of discovery. Martin Behem, the inventor, was one of the most learned cosmographers of the time, and, having resided at Lisbon in the employ of the king of Portugal, he had probably seen the map of Toscanelli, and the documents submitted by Columbus to the consideration of the Portuguese government. His globe may, therefore, be presumed illustrative of the idea entertained by Columbus of the islands in the ocean near the extremity of Asia, at the time he undertook his discovery.

as the year 1474, though as yet it lay crude and unmatured
in his mind. This fact, which is of some importance, is
sufficiently established by the correspondence already mentioned with the learned Toscanelli of Florence, which took
place in the summer of that year. The letter of Toscanelli
is in reply to one from Columbus, and applauds the design
which he had expressed of making a voyage to the west.
To demonstrate more clearly the facility of arriving at
India in that direction, he sent him a map, projected partly
according to Ptolemy, and partly according to the descriptions of Marco Polo, the Venetian. The eastern coast of
Asia was depicted in front of the western coasts of Africa
and Europe, with a moderate space of ocean between them,
in which were placed at convenient distances Cipango, Antilla, and the other islands.[1] Columbus was greatly animated
by the letter and chart of Toscanelli, who was considered
one of the ablest cosmographers of the day. He appears to
have procured the work of Marco Polo, which had been
translated into various languages, and existed in manuscript
in most libraries. This author gives marvelous accounts of
the riches of the realms of Cathay and Mangi, or Mangu,
since ascertained to be Northern and Southern China, on
the coast of which, according to the map of Toscanelli, a
voyager sailing directly west would be sure to arrive. He
describes in unmeasured terms the power and grandeur of
the sovereign of these countries, the Great Khan of Tartary,
and the splendor and magnitude of his capitals of Cambalu
and Quinsai, and the wonders of the island of Cipango or
Zipangi, supposed to be Japan. This island he places opposite Cathay, five hundred leagues in the ocean. He repre-

[1] This map, by which Columbus sailed on his first voyage of discovery, Las Casas (lib. i. cap. 12) says he had in his possession at the
time of writing his history. It is greatly to be regretted that so interesting a document should be lost. It may yet exist among the cha-
otic lumber of the Spanish archives. Few documents of mere curiosity would be more precious.

sents it as abounding in gold, precious stones, and other
choice objects of commerce, with a monarch whose palace
was roofed with plates of gold instead of lead.   The narrations of this traveler were by many considered fabulous;
but though full of what appear to be splendid exaggerations, they have since been found substantially correct.
They are thus particularly noted, from the influence they
had over the imagination of Columbus.   The work of Marco Polo is a key to many parts of his history.   In his applications to the various courts, he represented the countries
he expected to discover as those regions of inexhaustible
wealth which the Venetian had described.   The territories
of the Grand Khan were the objects of inquiry in all his
voyages; and in his cruisings among the Antilles, he was
continually flattering himself with the hopes of arriving at
the opulent island of Cipango, and the coasts of Mangi and
Cathay.[1]

While the design of attempting the discovery in the west
was maturing in the mind of Columbus, he made a voyage
to the north of Europe.   Of this we have no other memorial
than the following passage, extracted by his son from one
of his letters:—"In the year 1477, in February, I navigated
one hundred leagues beyond Thule, the southern part of
which is seventy-three degrees distant from the equator, and
not sixty-three, as some pretend; neither is it situated within the line which includes the west of Ptolemy, but is much
more westerly.   The English, principally those of Bristol,
go with their merchandise to this island, which is as large
as England.   When I was there, the sea was not frozen, and
the tides were so great as to rise and fall twenty-six fathom."[2]

The island thus mentioned is generally supposed to have
been Iceland, which is far to the west of the Ultima Thule
of the ancients, as laid down in the map of Ptolemy.

[1] A more particular account of Marco Polo and his writings is
given among the Illustrations.
[2] Hist. del Almirante, cap. 4.

Several more years elapsed, without any decided efforts on the part of Columbus to carry his design into execution. He was too poor to fit out the armament necessary for so important an expedition. Indeed, it was an enterprise only to be undertaken in the employ of some sovereign state, which could assume dominion over the territories he might discover, and reward him with dignities and privileges commensurate to his services. It is asserted that he at one time endeavored to engage his native country, Genoa, in the undertaking, but without success. No record remains of such an attempt, though it is generally believed, and has strong probability in its favor. His residence in Portugal placed him at hand to solicit the patronage of that power, but Alphonso, who was then on the throne, was too much engrossed in the latter part of his reign with a war with Spain, for the succession of the Princess Juana to the crown of Castile, to engage in peaceful enterprises of an expensive nature. The public mind, also, was not prepared for so perilous an undertaking. Notwithstanding the many recent voyages to the coast of Africa and the adjacent islands, and the introduction of the compass into more general use, navigation was still shackled with impediments, and the mariner rarely ventured far out of sight of land.

Discovery advanced slowly along the coasts of Africa, and the mariners feared to cruise far into the southern hemisphere, with the stars of which they were totally unacquainted. To such men, the project of a voyage directly westward, into the midst of that boundless waste, to seek some visionary land, appeared as extravagant as it would be at the present day to launch forth in a balloon into the regions of space, in quest of some distant star.

The time, however, was at hand, that was to extend the sphere of navigation. The era was propitious to the quick advancement of knowledge. The recent invention of the art of printing enabled men to communicate rapidly and extensively their ideas and discoveries. It drew forth

learning from libraries and convents, and brought it fa-
miliarly to the reading-desk of the student. Volumes of
information, which before had existed only in costly manuscripts, carefully treasured up, and kept out of the reach
of the indigent scholar and obscure artist, were now in every
hand. There was, henceforth, to be no retrogression in
knowledge, nor any pause in its career. Every step in advance was immediately, and simultaneously, and widely
promulgated, recorded in a thousand forms, and fixed for
ever. There could never again be a dark age; nations
might shut their eyes to the light, and sit in willful darkness, but they could not trample it out; it would still shine
on, dispensed to happier parts of the world, by the diffusive
powers of the press.

At this juncture, in 1481, a monarch ascended the throne
of Portugal, of different ambition from Alphonso. John II,
then in the twenty-fifth year of his age, had imbibed the
passion for discovery from his grand-uncle, Prince Henry,
and with his reign all its activity revived. His first care
was to build a fort at St. George de la Mina, on the coast
of Guinea, to protect the trade carried on in that neighborhood for gold dust, ivory, and slaves.

The African discoveries had conferred great glory upon
Portugal, but as yet they had been expensive rather than
profitable. The accomplishment of the route to India, however, it was expected would repay all cost and toil, and
open a source of incalculable wealth to the nation. The
project of Prince Henry, which had now been tardily prosecuted for half a century, had excited a curiosity about the
remote parts of Asia, and revived all the accounts, true
and fabulous, of travelers.

Beside the work of Marco Polo, already mentioned, there
was the narrative of Rabbi Benjamin ben Jonah, of Tudela,
a Spanish Jew, who set out from Saragossa in 1173, to
visit the scattered remnants of the Hebrew tribes. Wandering with unwearied zeal on this pious errand, over most

parts of the known world, he penetrated China, and passed thence to the southern islands of Asia.[1] There were also the narratives of Carpini and Ascelin, two friars, dispatched, the one in 1246, the other in 1247, by Pope Innocent IV, as apostolic ambassadors, for the purpose of converting the Grand Khan of Tartary; and the journal of William Rubruquis (or Ruysbroek), a celebrated Cordelier, sent on a similar errand in 1253, by Louis IX of France, then on his unfortunate crusade into Palestine. These pious but chimerical missions had proved abortive; but the narratives of them being revived in the fifteenth century, served to inflame the public curiosity respecting the remote parts of Asia.

In these narratives we first find mention made of the renowned Prester John, a Christian king, said to hold sway in a remote part of the East, who was long an object of curiosity and research, but whose kingdom seemed to shift its situation in the tale of every traveler, and to vanish from the search as effectually as the unsubstantial island of St. Brandan. All the speculations concerning this potentate and his oriental realm were again put in circulation. It was fancied that traces of his empire were discovered in the interior of Africa, to the east of Benin, where there was a powerful prince, who used a cross among the insignia of royalty. John II partook largely of the popular excitement produced by these narrations. In the early part of his reign he actually sent missions in quest of Prester John, to visit whose dominions became the romantic desire of many a religious enthusiast.[2] The magnificent idea he had formed of the remote parts of the East, made him extremely anxious that the splendid project of Prince Henry

[1] Bergeron, Voyages en Asia, tom. i. The work of Benjamin of Tudela, originally written in Hebrew, was so much in repute, that the translation went through sixteen editions. Andres, Hist. B. Let., ii. cap. 6.

[2] See Illustrations, article "Prester John."

should be realized, and the Portuguese flag penetrate to the Indian seas. Impatient of the slowness with which his discoveries advanced along the coast of Africa, and of the impediments which every cape and promontory presented to nautical enterprise, he called in the aid of science to devise some means by which greater scope and certainty might be given to navigation. His two physicians, Roderigo and Joseph, the latter a Jew, the most able astronomers and cosmographers of his kingdom, together with the celebrated Martin Behem, entered into a learned consultation on the subject. The result of their conferences and labors was the application of the astrolabe to navigation, enabling the seaman, by the altitude of the sun, to ascertain his distance from the equator.[1] This instrument has since been improved and modified into the modern quadrant, of which, even at its first introduction, it possessed all the essential advantages.

It is impossible to describe the effect produced upon navigation by this invention. It cast it loose at once from its long bondage to the land, and set it free to rove the deep. The mariner now, instead of coasting the shores like the ancient navigators, and, if driven from the land, groping his way back in doubt and apprehension by the uncertain guidance of the stars, might adventure boldly into unknown seas, confident of being able to trace his course by means of the compass and the astrolabe.

It was shortly after this event, which had prepared guides for discovery across the trackless ocean, that Columbus made the first attempt, of which we have any clear and indisputable record, to procure royal patronage for his enterprise. The court of Portugal had shown extraordinary liberality in rewarding nautical discovery. Most of those who had succeeded in her service had been appointed to the government of the islands and countries they had discovered, although many of them were foreign-

[1] Barros, decad. 1, lib. iv. cap. 2. Maffei, lib. vi. pp. 6 and 7.

ers by birth. Encouraged by this liberality, and by the anxiety evinced by King John II to accomplish a passage by sea to India, Columbus obtained an audience of that monarch, and proposed, in case the king would furnish him with ships and men, to undertake a shorter and more direct route than that along the coast of Africa. His plan was to strike directly to the west, across the Atlantic. He then unfolded his hypothesis with respect to the extent of Asia, describing also the immense riches of the island of Cipango, the first land at which he expected to arrive. Of this audience we have two accounts, written in somewhat of an opposite spirit; one by his son Fernando, the other by Joam de Barros, the Portuguese historiographer. It is curious to notice the different views taken of the same transaction by the enthusiastic son, and by the cool, perhaps prejudiced, historian.

The king, according to Fernando, listened to his father with great attention, but was discouraged from engaging in any new scheme of the kind, by the cost and trouble already sustained in exploring the route by the African coast, which as yet remained unaccomplished. His father, however, supported his proposition by such excellent reasons, that the king was induced to give his consent. The only difficulty that remained was the terms; for Columbus, being a man of lofty and noble sentiments, de-demanded high and honorable titles and rewards, to the end, says Fernando, that he might leave behind him a name and family worthy of his deeds and merits.[1]

Barros, on the other hand, attributes the seeming acquiescence of the king merely to the importunities of Columbus. He considered him, says the historian, a vainglorious man, fond of displaying his abilities, and given to fantastic fancies, such as that respecting the island of Cipango.[2] But in fact, this idea of Columbus being vain,

[1] Hist. del. Almirante, cap. 10.
[2] Barros, Asia, decad. 1, lib. iii., cap, 2.

was taken up by the Portuguese writers in after years; and as to the island of Cipango, it was far from being considered chimerical by the king, who, as has been shown by his mission in search of Prester John, was a ready believer in these travelers' tales concerning the East. The reasoning of Columbus must have produced an effect on the mind of the monarch, since it is certain that he referred the proposition to a learned junto, charged with all matters relating to maritime discovery.

This junto was composed of two able cosmographers, masters Roderigo and Joseph, and the king's confessor, Diego Ortiz de Cazadilla, bishop of Ceuta, a man greatly reputed for his learning, a Castilian by birth, and generally called Cazadilla, from the name of his native place. This scientific body treated the project as extravagant and visionary.

Still the king does not appear to have been satisfied. According to his historian Vasconcelos,[1] he convoked his council, composed of prelates and persons of the greatest learning in the kingdom, and asked their advice, whether to adopt this new route of discovery, or to pursue that which they had already opened.

It may not be deemed superfluous to notice briefly the discussion of the council on this great question. Vasconcelos reports a speech of the bishop of Ceuta, in which he not only objected to the proposed enterprise, as destitute of reason, but even discountenanced any further prosecution of the African discoveries. "They tended," he said, "to distract the attention, drain the resources, and divide the power of the nation, already too much weakened by recent war and pestilence. While their forces were thus scattered abroad on remote and unprofitable expeditions, they exposed themselves to attack from their active enemy the king of Castile. The greatness of monarchs," he continued, "did not arise so much from the extent of their dominions,

---

[1] Vasconcelos, Vida del Rey Don Juan II., lib. iv.

as from the wisdom and ability with which they governed. In the Portuguese nation it would be madness to launch into enterprises without first considering them in connection with its means. The king had already sufficient undertakings in hand of certain advantage, without engaging in others of a wild, chimerical nature. If he wished employment for the active valor of the nation, the war in which he was engaged against the Moors of Barbary was sufficient, wherein his triumphs were of solid advantage, tending to cripple and enfeeble those neighboring foes, who had proved themselves so dangerous when possessed of power."

This cool and cautious speech of the bishop of Ceuta, directed against enterprises which were the glory of the Portuguese, touched the national pride of Don Pedro de Meneses, count of Villa Real, and drew from him a lofty and patriotic reply. It has been said by an historian that this reply was in support of the proposition of Columbus; but that does not clearly appear. He may have treated the proposal with respect, but his eloquence was employed for those enterprises in which the Portuguese were already engaged.

"Portugal," he observed, "was not in its infancy, nor were its princes so poor as to lack means to engage in discoveries. Even granting that those proposed by Columbus were conjectural, why should they abandon those commenced by their late Prince Henry, on such solid foundations, and prosecuted with such happy prospects? Crowns," he observed, "enriched themselves by commerce, fortified themselves by alliance, and acquired empires by conquest. The views of a nation could not always be the same; they extended with its opulence and prosperity. Portugal was at peace with all the princes of Europe. It had nothing to fear from engaging in an extensive enterprise. It would be the greatest glory for Portuguese valor to penetrate into the secrets and horrors of the ocean sea, so formidable to

the other nations of the world. Thus occupied, it would
escape the idleness engendered in a long interval of peace
—idleness, that source of vice, that silent file, which, little
by little, wore away the strength and valor of a nation.
It was an affront," he added, "to the Portuguese name to
menace it with imaginary perils, when it had proved itself
so intrepid in encountering those which were most certain
and tremendous. Great souls were formed for great enterprises. He wondered much, that a prelate, so religious as
the bishop of Ceuta, should oppose this undertaking; the
ultimate object of which was to augment the Catholic faith,
and spread it from pole to pole; reflecting glory on the
Portuguese nation, and yielding empire and lasting fame
to its princes." He concluded by declaring that, "although
a soldier, he dared to prognosticate, with a voice and spirit
as if from heaven, to whatever prince should achieve this
enterprise, more happy success and durable renown, than
had ever been obtained by sovereign the most valorous and
fortunate." [1] The warm and generous eloquence of the
count overpowered the cold-spirited reasonings of the
bishop as far as the project of circumnavigating Africa
was concerned, which was prosecuted with new ardor and
triumphant success: the proposition of Columbus, however,
was generally condemned by the council.

Seeing that King John still manifested an inclination
for the enterprise, it was suggested to him by the bishop of
Ceuta, that Columbus might be kept in suspense while a
vessel secretly dispatched in the direction he should point
out might ascertain whether there were any foundation for
his theory. By this means all its advantages might be
secured, without committing the dignity of the crown by
formal negotiations about what might prove a mere chimera.
King John, in an evil hour, had the weakness to permit a
stratagem so inconsistent with his usual justice and magnanimity. Columbus was required to furnish for the consider-

[1] Vasconcelos, lib. iv. La Clede, Hist. Portugal, lib. xiii. tom. iii.

ation of the council a detailed plan of his proposed voyage, with the charts and documents according to which he intended to shape his course. These being procured, a caravel was dispatched with the ostensible design of carrying provisions to the Cape de Verde islands; but with private instructions to pursue the designated route. Departing from those islands, the caravel stood westward for several days, until the weather became stormy; when the pilots, seeing nothing but an immeasurable waste of wild tumbling waves still extending before them, lost all courage and put back, ridiculing the project of Columbus as extravagant and irrational.[1]

This unworthy attempt to defraud him of his enterprise roused the indignation of Columbus, and he declined all offers of King John to renew the negotiation. The death of his wife, which had occurred some time previously, had dissolved the domestic tie which bound him to Portugal; he determined, therefore, to abandon a country where he had been treated with so little faith, and to look elsewhere for patronage. Before his departure, he engaged his brother Bartholomew to carry proposals to the king of England, though he does not appear to have entertained great hope from that quarter; England by no means possessing at the time the spirit of nautical enterprise which has since distinguished her. The great reliance of Columbus was on his own personal exertions.

It was towards the end of 1484 that he left Lisbon, taking with him his son Diego. His departure had to be conducted with secrecy, lest, as some assert, it should be prevented by King John; but lest, as others surmise, it should be prevented by his creditors.[2] Like many other

---

[1] Hist. del Almirante, cap. 8. Herrera, decad. 1, lib. i. cap. 7.

[2] This surmise is founded on a letter from King John to Columbus, written some years afterwards, inviting him to return to Portugal, and insuring him against arrest on account of any process, civil or

great projectors, while engaged upon schemes of vast benefit to mankind, he had suffered his own affairs to go to ruin, and was reduced to struggle hard with poverty; nor is it one of the least interesting circumstances in his eventful life, that he had, in a manner, to beg his way from court to court, to offer to princes the discovery of a world.

criminal, which might be pending against him.   See Navarrete, Collec., tom. ii. doc. 3.

BOOK II.

CHAPTER I.

PROCEEDINGS OF COLUMBUS AFTER LEAVING PORTUGAL.—
HIS APPLICATIONS IN SPAIN.— CHARACTERS OF FERDI-
NAND AND ISABELLA.

[1485.]

THE immediate movements of Columbus on leaving
Portugal are involved in uncertainty. It is said that about
this time he made a proposition of his enterprise, in person,
as he had formerly done by letter, to the government of
Genoa. The republic, however, was in a languishing decline, and embarrassed by a foreign war. Caffa, her great
deposit in the Crimea, had fallen into the hands of the
Turks, and her flag was on the point of being driven from
the Archipelago. Her spirit was broken with her fortunes;
for with nations, as with individuals, enterprise is the child
of prosperity, and is apt to languish in evil days when
there is most need of its exertion. Thus Genoa, disheartened by her reverses, shut her ears to the proposition of
Columbus, which might have elevated her to tenfold
splendor, and perpetuated within her grasp the golden
wand of commerce. While at Genoa, Columbus is said
to have made arrangements, out of his scanty means, for
the comfort of his aged father. It is also affirmed, that
about this time he carried his proposal to Venice, where it
was declined on account of the critical state of national
affairs. This, however, is merely traditional, and unsupported by documentary evidence. The first firm and

indisputable trace we have of Columbus after leaving
Portugal is in .the south of Spain, in 1485, where we find
him seeking his fortune among the Spanish nobles, several
of whom had vast possessions, and exercised almost independent sovereignty in their domains.

Foremost among these were the dukes of Medina Sidonia
and Medina Celi, who had estates like principalities lying
along the sea-coast, with ports and shipping and hosts of
retainers at their command. They served the crown in its
Moorish wars more as allied princes than as vassals, bringing armies into the field led by themselves, or by captains
of their own appointment. Their domestic establishments
were on almost a regal scale; their palaces were filled with
persons of merit, and young cavaliers of noble birth, to be
reared under their auspices, in the exercise of arts and arms.

Columbus had many interviews with the duke of Medina
Sidonia, who was tempted for a time by the splendid
prospects held out; but their very splendor threw a coloring of improbability over the enterprise, and he finally
rejected it as the dream of an Italian visionary.

The duke of Medina Celi was likewise favorable at the
outset. He entertained Columbus for some time in his
house, and was actually on the point of granting him three
or four caravels which lay ready for sea in his harbor of
Port St. Mary, opposite Cadiz, when he suddenly changed
his mind, deterred by the consideration that the enterprise,
if successful, would involve discoveries too important to be
grasped by any but a sovereign power, and that the Spanish government might be displeased at his undertaking it
on his own account. Finding, however, that Columbus
intended to make his next application to the king of
France, and loth that an enterprise of such importance
should be lost to Spain, the duke wrote to Queen Isabella
recommending it strongly to her attention. The queen
made a favorable reply, and requested that Columbus
might be sent to her. He accordingly set out for the

Spanish court, then at Cordova, bearing a letter to the queen from the duke, soliciting that, in case the expedition should be carried into effect, he might have a share in it, and the fitting out of the armament from his port of St. Mary, as a recompense for having waived the enterprise in favor of the crown.[1]

The time when Columbus thus sought his fortunes at the court of Spain coincided with one of the most brilliant periods of the Spanish monarchy. The union of the kingdoms of Arragon and Castile, by the marriage of Ferdinand and Isabella, had consolidated the Christian power in the Peninsula, and put an end to those internal feuds, which had so long distracted the country, and insured the domination of the Moslems. The whole force of united Spain was now exerted in the chivalrous enterprise of the Moorish conquest. The Moors, who had once spread over the whole country like an inundation, were now pent up within the mountain boundaries of the kingdom of Granada. The victorious armies of Ferdinand and Isabella were continually advancing, and pressing this fierce people within narrower limits. Under these sovereigns, the various petty kingdoms of Spain began to feel and act as one nation, and to rise to eminence in arts as well as arms. Ferdinand and Isabella, it has been remarked, lived together not like man and wife, whose estates are common, under the orders of the husband, but like two monarchs strictly allied.[2] They

[1] Letter of the duke of Medina Celi to the grand cardinal. Navarrete, Collect., vol. ii. p. 20.

N. B. In the previous editions of this work, the first trace we have of Columbus in Spain is at the gate of the convent of La Rabida, in Andalusia. Subsequent investigations have induced me to conform to the opinion of the indefatigable and accurate Navarrete, given in his third volume of documents, that the first trace of Columbus in Spain was his application to the dukes of Medina Sidonia and Medina Celi, and that his visit to the convent of La Rabida was some few years subsequent.

[2] Voltaire, Essai sur les Mœurs, &c.

5

had separate claims to sovereignty, in virtue of their respective kingdoms; they had separate councils, and were often distant from each other in different parts of their empire, each exercising the royal authority. Yet they were so happily united by common views, common interests, and a great deference for each other, that this double administration never prevented a unity of purpose and of action. All acts of sovereignty were executed in both their names; all public writings were subscribed with both their signatures; their likenesses were stamped together on the public coin; and the royal seal displayed the united arms of Castile and Arragon.

Ferdinand was of the middle stature, well proportioned, and hardy and active from athletic exercise. His carriage was free, erect, and majestic. He had a clear, serene forehead, which appeared more lofty from his head being partly bald. His eyebrows were large and parted, and, like his hair, of a bright chestnut; his eyes were clear and animated; his complexion was somewhat ruddy, and scorched by the toils of war; his mouth moderate, well formed, and gracious in its expression; his teeth white, though small and irregular; his voice sharp; his speech quick and fluent. His genius was clear and comprehensive; his judgment grave and certain. He was simple in dress and diet, equable in his temper, devout in his religion, and so indefatigable in business, that it was said he seemed to repose himself by working. He was a great observer and judge of men, and unparalleled in the science of the cabinet. Such is the picture given of him by the Spanish historians of his time. It has been added, however, that he had more of bigotry than religion; that his ambition was craving rather than magnanimous; that he made war less like a paladin than a prince, less for glory than for mere dominion; and that his policy was cold, selfish, and artful. He was called the wise and prudent in Spain; in Italy, the pious; in France and England, the ambitious and per-

fidious.[1] He certainly was one of the most subtle states-
men, but one of the most thorough egotists, that ever sat
upon a throne.

While giving his picture, it may not be deemed imperti-
nent to sketch the fortunes of a monarch whose policy had
such an effect upon the history of Columbus and the destinies of the New World. Success attended all his measures.
Though a younger son, he had ascended the throne of Arragon by inheritance; Castile he obtained by marriage;
Granada and Naples by conquest; and he seized upon
Navarre as appertaining to any one who could take possession of it, when Pope Julius II excommunicated its
sovereigns, Juan and Catalina, and gave their throne to the
first occupant.[2] He sent his forces into Africa, and subjugated, or reduced to vassalage, Tunis, Tripoli, Algiers, and
most of the Barbary powers. A new world was also given
to him, without cost, by the discoveries of Columbus, for
the expense of the enterprise was born exclusively by his
consort Isabella. He had three objects at heart from the
commencement of his reign, which he pursued with bigoted
and persecuting zeal; the conquest of the Moors, the expulsion of the Jews, and the establishment of the Inquisition in his dominions. He accomplished them all, and was
rewarded by Pope Innocent VIII with the appellation of
Most Catholic Majesty—a title which his successors have
tenaciously retained.

Contemporary writers have been enthusiastic in their descriptions of Isabella, but time has sanctioned their eulogies. She is one of the purest and most beautiful characters in the pages of history. She was well formed, of the
middle size, with great dignity and gracefulness of deportment, and a mingled gravity and sweetness of demeanor.

[1] Voltaire, Essai sur les Mœurs, ch. 14.
[2] Pedro Salazar di Mendoza, Monarq. de Esp., lib. iii. cap. 5.
(Madrid, 1770, tom. i. p. 402.)—Gonzalo de Illescas, Hist. Pontif.,
lib. vi. cap. 23, § 3.

Her complexion was fair; her hair auburn, inclining to
red; her eyes were of a clear blue, with a benign expression, and there was a singular modesty in her countenance,
gracing, as it did, a wonderful firmness of purpose, and
earnestness of spirit. Though strongly attached to her
husband, and studious of his fame, yet she always maintained her distinct rights as an allied prince. She exceeded
him in beauty, in personal dignity, in acuteness of genius,
and in grandeur of soul.[1] Combining the active and resolute qualities of man with the softer charities of woman,
she mingled in the warlike councils of her husband, engaged personally in his enterprises,[2] and in some instances
surpassed him in the firmness and intrepidity of her measures; while, being inspired with a truer idea of glory, she
infused a more lofty and generous temper into his subtle
and calculating policy.

It is in the civil history of their reign, however, that the
character of Isabella shines most illustrious. Her fostering
and maternal care was continually directed to reform the
laws, and heal the ills engendered by a long course of internal wars. She loved her people, and while diligently
seeking their good, she mitigated, as much as possible, the
harsh measures of her husband, directed to the same end,
but inflamed by a mistaken zeal. Thus, though almost
bigoted in her piety, and perhaps too much under the influence of ghostly advisers, still she was hostile to every
measure calculated to advance religion at the expense of
humanity. She strenuously opposed the expulsion of the
Jews, and the establishment of the Inquisition, though,
unfortunately for Spain, her repugnance was slowly vanquished by her confessors. She was always an advocate for
clemency to the Moors, although she was the soul of the

---

[1] Garibay, Hist. de España, tom. ii. lib. xviii. cap. 1.

[2] Several suits of armor cap-a-pié, worn by Isabella, and still preserved in the royal arsenal at Madrid, show that she was exposed to
personal danger in her campaigns

war against Granada. She considered that war essential to protect the Christian faith, and to relieve her subjects from fierce and formidable enemies. While all her public thoughts and acts were princely and august, her private habits were simple, frugal, and unostentatious. In the intervals of state-business, she assembled round her the ablest men in literature and science, and directed herself by their counsels, in promoting letters and arts. Through her patronage, Salamanca rose to that height which it assumed among the learned institutions of the age. She promoted the distribution of honors and rewards for the promulgation of knowledge; she fostered the art of printing, recently invented, and encouraged the establishment of presses in every part of the kingdom; books were admitted free of all duty, and more, we are told, were printed in Spain, at that early period of the art, than in the present literary age.[1]

It is wonderful how much the destinies of countries depend at times upon the virtues of individuals, and how it is given to great spirits, by combining, exciting, and directing the latent powers of a nation, to stamp it, as it were, with their own greatness. Such beings realize the idea of guardian angels, appointed by Heaven to watch over the destinies of empires. Such had been Prince Henry for the kingdom of Portugal; and such was now for Spain the illustrious Isabella.

CHAPTER II.

COLUMBUS AT THE COURT OF SPAIN.

WHEN Columbus arrived at Cordova he was given in charge to Alonzo de Quintanilla, comptroller of the treasury of Castile, but was disappointed in his expectation of re-

[1] Elogio de la Reina Catholica, por Diego Clemencin. Madrid, 1821.

ceiving immediate audience from the queen. He found the city in all the bustle of military preparation. It was a critical juncture of the war. The rival kings of Granada, Muley Boabdil the uncle, and Mohammed Boabdil the nephew, had just formed a coalition, and their league called for prompt and vigorous measures.

All the chivalry of Spain had been summoned to the field; the streets of Cordova echoed to the tramp of steed and sound of trumpet, as day by day the nobles arrived with their retainers, vieing with each other in the number of their troops and the splendor of their appointments. The court was like a military camp; the king and queen were surrounded by the flower of Spanish chivalry; by those veteran cavaliers who had distinguished themselves in so many hardy conflicts with the Moors; and by the prelates and friars who mingled in martial council, and took deep interest and agency in this war of the Faith.

This was an unpropitious moment to urge a suit like that of Columbus. In fact, the sovereigns had not a moment of leisure throughout this eventful year. Early in the spring, the king marched off to lay siege to the Moorish city of Loxa; and though the queen remained at Cordova, she was continually employed in forwarding troops and supplies to the army, and, at the same time, attending to the multiplied exigencies of civil government. On the 12th of June, she repaired to the camp, then engaged in the siege of Moclin, and both sovereigns remained for some time in the Vega of Granada, prosecuting the war with unremitting vigor. They had barely returned to Cordova to celebrate their victories by public rejoicings, when they were obliged to set out for Gallicia, to suppress a rebellion of the count of Lemos. Thence they repaired to Salamanca for the winter.

During the summer and autumn of this year Columbus remained at Cordova, a guest in the house of Alonzo de Quintanilla, who proved a warm advocate of his theory.

Through his means he became acquainted with Antonio Geraldini, the pope's nuncio, and his brother, Alexander Geraldini, preceptor to the younger children of Ferdinand and Isabella; both valuable friends about court. Wherever he obtained a candid hearing from intelligent auditors, the dignity of his manners, his earnest sincerity, the elevation of his views, and the practical shrewdness of his demonstrations, commanded respect even where they failed to produce conviction.

While thus lingering in idle suspense in Cordova, he became attached to a lady of the city, Beatrix Euriquez by name, of a noble family, though in reduced circumstances. Their connection was not sanctioned by marriage; yet he cherished sentiments of respect and tenderness for her to his dying day. She was the mother of his second son, Fernando, born in the following year (1487), whom he always treated on terms of perfect equality with his legitimate son Diego, and who, after his death, became his historian.

In the winter, Columbus followed the court to Salamanca. Here his zealous friend, Alonzo de Quintanilla, exerted his influence to obtain for him the countenance of the celebrated Pedro Gonzalez de Mendoza, archbishop of Toledo and grand cardinal of Spain. This was the most important personage about the court; and was facetiously called by Peter Martyr, the "third king of Spain." The king and queen had him always by their side, in peace and war. He accompanied them in their campaigns, and they never took any measure of consequence without consulting him. He was a man of sound judgment and quick intellect, eloquent in conversation and able in the dispatch of business. His appearance was lofty and venerable; he was simple yet curiously nice in his apparel, and of gracious and gentle deportment. Though an elegant scholar, yet, like many learned men of his day, he was but little skilled in cosmography. When the theory of Columbus was first men-

tioned to him, it struck him as involving heterodox opinions,
incompatible with the form of the earth as described in the
Sacred Scriptures. Further explanations had their force
with a man of his quick apprehension and sound sense.
He perceived that at any rate there could be nothing irre-
ligious in attempting to extend the bounds of human knowledge, and to ascertain the works of creation : his scruples
once removed, he permitted Columbus to be introduced to
him, and gave him a courteous reception. The latter knew
the importance of his auditor, and that a conference with
the grand cardinal was almost equivalent to a communication with the throne; he exerted himself to the utmost,
therefore, to explain and demonstrate his proposition. The
clear-headed cardinal listened with profound attention. He
was pleased with the noble and earnest manner of Columbus, which showed him to be no common schemer; he felt
the grandeur, and, at the same time, the simplicity of his
theory, and the force of many of the arguments by which
it was supported. He determined that it was a matter
highly worthy of the consideration of the sovereigns, and
through his representations Columbus at length obtained
admission to the royal presence.[1]

We have but scanty particulars of this audience, nor can
we ascertain whether Queen Isabella was present on the
occasion; the contrary seems to be most probably the case.
Columbus appeared in the royal presence with modesty, yet
self-possession, neither dazzled nor daunted by the splendor
of the court or the awful majesty of the throne. He unfolded his plan with eloquence and zeal, for he felt himself,
as he afterwards declared, kindled as with a fire from on
high, and considered himself the agent chosen by Heaven
to accomplish its grand designs.[2]

Ferdinand was too keen a judge of men not to appreciate
the character of Columbus. He perceived that, however

[1] Oviedo, lib. ii. cap. 4. Salazar, Cron. G. Cardinal, lib. i. cap. 62.
[2] Letter to the Sovereigns in 1501.

soaring might be his imagination, and vast and visionary his views, his scheme had scientific and practical foundation. His ambition was excited by the possibility of discoveries far more important than those which had shed such glory upon Portugal; and perhaps it was not the least recommendation of the enterprise to this subtle and grasping monarch, that, if successful, it would enable him to forestall that rival nation in the fruits of their long and arduous struggle, and by opening a direct course to India across the ocean, to bear off from them the monopoly of oriental commerce.

Still, as usual, Ferdinand was cool and wary, and would not trust his own judgment in a matter that involved so many principles of science. He determined to take the opinion of the most learned men in the kingdom, and to be guided by their decision. Fernando de Talavera, prior of the monastery of Prado and confessor of the queen, one of the most erudite men of Spain, and high in the royal confidence, was commanded to assemble the most learned astronomers and cosmographers for the purpose of holding a conference with Columbus, and examining him as to the grounds on which he founded his proposition. After they had informed themselves fully on the subject, they were to consult together and make a report to the sovereign of their collective opinion.[1]

CHAPTER III.

COLUMBUS BEFORE THE COUNCIL AT SALAMANCA.

[1486.]

THE interesting conference relative to the proposition of Columbus took place in Salamanca, the great seat of learning in Spain. It was held in the Dominican convent

[1] Hist. del Almirante, cap. xi.

of St. Stephen, in which he was lodged and entertained
with great hospitality during the course of the examination.[1]

Religion and science were at that time, and more especially in that country, closely associated. The treasures of
learning were immured in monasteries, and the professors'
chairs were exclusively filled from the cloister. The domination of the clergy extended over the state as well as the
church, and posts of honor and influence at court, with the
exception of hereditary nobles, were almost entirely confined to ecclesiastics. It was even common to find cardinals
and bishops in helm and corslet at the head of armies; for
the crosier had been occasionally thrown by for the lance,
during the holy war against the Moors. The era was distinguished for the revival of learning, but still more for the
prevalence of religious zeal, and Spain surpassed all other
countries of Christendom in the fervor of her devotion.
The Inquisition had just been established in that kingdom,
and every opinion that savored of heresy made its owner
obnoxious to odium and persecution.

Such was the period when a council of clerical sages was
convened in the collegiate convent of St. Stephen, to investigate the new theory of Columbus. It was composed of
professors of astronomy, geography, mathematics, and other
branches of science, together with various dignitaries of the
church, and learned friars. Before this erudite assembly,
Columbus presented himself to propound and defend his
conclusions. He had been scoffed at as a visionary by the
vulgar and the ignorant; but he was convinced that he only
required a body of enlightened men to listen dispassionately
to his reasonings, to insure triumphant conviction.

The greater part of this learned junto, it is very probable,
came prepossessed against him, as men in place and dignity are apt to be against poor applicants. There is always
a proneness to consider a man under examination as a kind

[1] Hist. de Chiapa por Remesal, lib. ii. cap. 27.

of delinquent, or impostor, whose faults and errors are to
be detected and exposed. Columbus, too, appeared in a
most unfavorable light before a scholastic body: an obscure
navigator, a member of no learned institution, destitute of
all the trappings and circumstances which sometimes give
oracular authority to dullness, and depending upon the
mere force of natural genius. Some of the junto entertained the popular notion that he was an adventurer, or at
best a visionary; and others had that morbid impatience
of any innovation upon established doctrine, which is apt to
grow upon dull and pedantic men in cloistered life.

What a striking spectacle must the hall of the old convent have presented at this memorable conference! A simple mariner, standing forth in the midst of an imposing
array of professors, friars, and dignitaries of the church;
maintaining his theory with natural eloquence, and, as it
were, pleading the cause of the new world. We are told
that when he began to state the grounds of his belief, the
friars of St. Stephen alone paid attention to him;[1] that convent being more learned in the sciences than the rest of the
university. The others appear to have intrenched themselves behind one dogged position; that, after so many profound philosophers and cosmographers had been studying
the form of the world, and so many able navigators had
been sailing about it for several thousand years, it was
great presumption in an ordinary man to suppose that there
remained such a vast discovery for him to make.

Several of the objections proposed by this learned body
have been handed down to us, and have provoked many a
sneer at the expense of the university of Salamanca; but
they are proofs, not so much of the peculiar deficiency of
that institution, as of the imperfect state of science at the
time, and the manner in which knowledge, though rapidly
extending, was still impeded in its progress by monastic
bigotry. All subjects were still contemplated through the

[1] Remesal, Hist. de Chiapa, lib. xi. cap. 7.

obscure medium of those ages when the lights of antiquity
were trampled out and faith was left to fill the place of
inquiry. Bewildered in a maze of religious controversy,
mankind had retraced their steps, and receded from the
boundary line of ancient knowledge. Thus, at the very
threshold of the discussion, instead of geographical objections, Columbus was assailed with citations from the Bible
and the Testament: the book of Genesis, the psalms of
David, the prophets, the epistles, and the gospels. To these
were added the expositions of various saints and reverend
commentators: St. Chrysostom and St. Augustine, St. Je-
rome and St. Gregory, St. Basil and St. Ambrose, and
Lactantius Firmianus, a redoubted champion of the faith.
Doctrinal points were mixed up with philosophical discussions, and a mathematical demonstration was allowed no
weight, if it appeared to clash with a text of Scripture, or a
commentary of one of the fathers. Thus the possibility of
antipodes, in the southern hemisphere, an opinion so generally maintained by the wisest of the ancients, as to be pronounced by Pliny the great contest between the learned
and the ignorant, became a stumbling-block with some of
the sages of Salamanca. Several of them stoutly contradicted this fundamental position of Columbus, supporting
themselves by quotations from Lactantius and St. Augustine, who were considered in those days as almost evangel-
ical authority. But, though these writers were men of consummate erudition, and two of the greatest luminaries of
what has been called the golden age of ecclesiastical learning, yet their writings were calculated to perpetuate darkness in respect to the sciences.

The passage cited from Lactantius to confute Columbus,
is in a strain of gross ridicule, unworthy of so grave a theo-
logian. "Is there any one so foolish," he asks, "as to believe that there are antipodes with their feet opposite to
ours; people who walk with their heels upward, and their
heads hanging down? That there is a part of the world in

which all things are topsy-turvy; where the trees grow with their branches downward, and where it rains, hails and snows upward? The idea of the roundness of the earth," he adds, " was the cause of inventing this fable of the antipodes, with their heels in the air; for these philosophers, having once erred, go on in their absurdities, defending one with another."

Objections of a graver nature were advanced on the authority of St. Augustine. He pronounces the doctrine of antipodes to be incompatible with the historical foundations of our faith; since, to assert that there were inhabited lands on the opposite side of the globe, would be to maintain that there were nations not descended from Adam, it being impossible for them to have passed the intervening ocean. This would be, therefore, to discredit the Bible, which expressly declares, that all men are descended from one common parent.

Such were the unlooked for prejudices which Columbus had to encounter at the very outset of his conference, and which certainly relish more of the convent than the university. To his simplest proposition, the spherical form of the earth, were opposed figurative texts of Scripture. They observed that in the Psalms the heavens are said to be extended like a hide,[1] that is, according to commentators, the curtain or covering of a tent, which, among the ancient pastoral nations, was formed of the hides of animals; and that St. Paul, in his Epistle to the Hebrews, compares the heavens to a tabernacle, or tent, extended over the earth, which they thence inferred must be flat.

Columbus, who was a devoutly religious man, found that he was in danger of being convicted not merely of error, but of heterodoxy. Others more versed in science admitted the globular form of the earth, and the possibility of an opposite and habitable hemisphere; but they brought up

[1] Extendens cœlum sicut pellem. Psal. 103. In the English translation it is Psal. 104, ver. 3.

the chimera of the ancients, and maintained that it would
be impossible to arrive there, in consequence of the insupportable heat of the torrid zone.   Even granting this could
be passed, they observed that the circumference of the
earth must be so great as to require at least three years to
the voyage, and those who should undertake it must perish
of hunger and thirst, from the impossibility of carrying
provisions for so long a period.   He was told, on the
authority of Epicurus, that admitting the earth to be
spherical, it was only inhabitable in the northern hemisphere, and in that section only was canopied by the heavens;
that the opposite half was a chaos, a gulf, or a mere waste
of water.   Not the least absurd objection advanced was,
that should a ship even succeed in reaching, in this way,
the extremity of India, she could never get back again; for
the rotundity of the globe would present a kind of mountain, up which it would be impossible for her to sail with
the most favorable wind.[1]

Such are specimens of the errors and prejudices, the
mingled ignorance and erudition, and the pedantic bigotry,
with which Columbus had to contend throughout the examination of his theory.   Can we wonder at the difficulties
and delays which he experienced at courts, when such
vague and crude notions were entertained by the learned
men of a university?   We must not suppose, however,
because the objections here cited are all which remain on
record, that they are all which were advanced; these only
have been perpetuated on account of their superior absurd-
ity.   They were probably advanced by but few, and those
persons immersed in theological studies, in cloistered retire-
ment; where the erroneous opinions derived from books
had little opportunity of being corrected by the experience
of the day.

There were no doubt objections advanced more cogent
in their nature, and more worthy of that distinguished

[1] Hist. del Almirante, cap. 11.

university. It is but justice to add, also, that the replies
of Columbus had great weight with many of his learned
examiners. In answer to the Scriptural objections, he
submitted that the inspired writers were not speaking
technically as cosmographers, but figuratively, in language
addressed to all comprehensions. The commentaries of
the fathers he treated with deference as pious homilies,
but not as philosophical propositions which it was necessary
either to admit or refute. The objections drawn from
ancient philosophers he met boldly and ably upon equal
terms; for he was deeply studied on all points of cosmography. He showed that the most illustrious of those sages
believed both hemispheres to be inhabitable, though they
imagined that the torrid zone precluded communication;
and he obviated conclusively that difficulty; for he had
voyaged to St. George la Mina in Guinea, almost under
the equinoctial line, and had found that region not merely
traversable, but abounding in population, in fruits and
pasturage.

When Columbus took his stand before this learned body,
he had appeared the plain and simple navigator; somewhat
daunted, perhaps, by the greatness of his task, and the
august nature of his auditory. But he had a degree of
religious feeling which gave him a confidence in the execution of what he conceived his great errand, and he was of
an ardent temperament that became heated in action by
its own generous fires. Las Casas, and others of his contemporaries, have spoken of his commanding person, his
elevated demeanor, his air of authority, his kindling eye,
and the persuasive intonations of his voice. How must
they have given majesty and force to his words, as, casting
aside his maps and charts, and discarding for a time his
practical and scientific lore, his visionary spirit took fire at
the doctrinal objections of his opponents, and he met them
upon their own ground, pouring forth those magnificent
texts of Scripture, and those mysterious predictions of the

prophets, which, in his enthusiastic moments, he considered
as types and annunciations of the sublime discovery which
he proposed !

Among the number who were convinced by the reasoning,
and warmed by the eloquence of Columbus, was Diego de
Deza, a worthy and learned friar of the order of St. Dom-
inick, at that time professor of theology in the convent of
St. Stephen, but who became afterwards archbishop of
Seville, the second ecclesiastical dignitary of Spain. This
able and erudite divine was a man whose mind was above
the narrow bigotry of bookish lore; one who could appreciate the value of wisdom even when uttered by unlearned
lips. He was not a mere passive auditor; he took a generous interest in the cause, and by seconding Columbus with
all his powers, calmed the blind zeal of his more bigoted
brethren, so as to obtain for him a dispassionate, if not an
unprejudiced hearing. By their united efforts, it is said,
they brought over the most learned men of the schools.[1]
One great difficulty was to reconcile the plan of Columbus
with the cosmography of Ptolemy, to which all scholars
yielded implicit faith. How would the most enlightened
of those sages have been astonished, had any one apprised
them that the man, Copernicus, was then in existence,
whose solar system should reverse the grand theory of
Ptolemy, which stationed the earth in the centre of the
universe!

Notwithstanding every exertion, however, there was a
preponderating mass of inert bigotry, and learned pride,
in this erudite body, which refused to yield to the demonstrations of an obscure foreigner, without fortune or connections, or any academic honors. "It was requisite,"
says Las Casas, "before Columbus could make his solutions
and reasonings understood, that he should remove from his
auditors those erroneous principles on which their objections
were founded; a task always more difficult than that of

[1] Remesal, Hist. de Chiapa, lib. xi. cap. 7.

teaching the doctrine." Occasional conferences took place, but without producing any decision. The ignorant, or what is worse, the prejudiced, remained obstinate in their opposition, with the dogged perseverance of dull men; the more liberal and intelligent felt little interest in discussions wearisome in themselves, and foreign to their ordinary pursuits; even those who listened with approbation to the plan, regarded it only as a delightful vision, full of probability and promise, but one which never could be realized. Fernando de Talavera, to whom the matter was especially intrusted, had too little esteem for it, and was too much occupied with the stir and bustle of public concerns, to press it to a conclusion; and thus the inquiry experienced continual procrastination and neglect.

CHAPTER IV.

FURTHER APPLICATIONS AT THE COURT OF CASTILE.— COLUMBUS FOLLOWS THE COURT IN ITS CAMPAIGNS.

THE Castilian court departed from Salamanca early in the spring of 1487 and repaired to Cordova, to prepare for the memorable campaign against Malaga. Fernando de Talavera, now bishop of Avila, accompanied the queen as her confessor, and as one of her spiritual counselors in the concerns of the war. The consultations of the board at Salamanca were interrupted by this event, before that learned body could come to a decision, and for a long time Columbus was kept in suspense, vainly awaiting the report that was to decide the fate of his application.

It has generally been supposed that the several years which he wasted in irksome solicitation, were spent in the drowsy and monotonous attendance of antechambers; but it appears, on the contrary, that they were often passed amidst scenes of peril and adventure, and that, in following

6

up his suit, he was led into some of the most striking
situations of this wild, rugged, and mountainous war.
Several times he was summoned to attend conferences in
the vicinity of the sovereigns, when besieging cities in the
very heart of the Moorish dominions; but the tempest of
warlike affairs, which hurried the court from place to place
and gave it all the bustle and confusion of a camp, prevented those conferences from taking place, and swept
away all concerns that were not immediately connected
with the war.   Whenever the court had an interval of
leisure and repose, there would again be manifested a disposition to consider his proposal, but the hurry and tempest would again return and the question be again swept
away.

The spring campaign of 1487, which took place shortly
after the conference at Salamanca, was full of incident and
peril.   King Ferdinand had nearly been surprised and
cut off by the old Moorish monarch before Velez Malaga,
and the queen and all the court at Cordova were for a
time in an agony of terror and suspense until assured of his
safety.

When the sovereigns were subsequently encamped before
the city of Malaga, pressing its memorable siege, Columbus
was summoned to the court.   He found it drawn up in
its silken pavilions on a rising ground, commanding the
fertile valley of Malaga; the encampments of the warlike
nobility of Spain extended in a semicircle on each side, to
the shores of the sea, strongly fortified, glittering with the
martial pomp of that chivalrous age and nation, and closely
investing that important city.

The seige was protracted for several months, but the
vigorous defence of the Moors, their numerous stratagems,
and fierce and frequent sallies, allowed but little leisure in
the camp.   In the course of this siege, the application of
Columbus to the sovereigns was nearly brought to a violent
close; a fanatic Moor having attempted to assassinate

Ferdinand and Isabella. Mistaking one of the gorgeous pavilions of the nobility for the royal tent, he attacked Don Alvaro de Portugal, and Doña Beatrix de Bobadilla, marchioness of Moya, instead of the king and queen. After wounding Don Alvaro dangerously, he was foiled in a blow aimed at the marchioness, and immediately cut to pieces by the attendants.[1] The lady here mentioned was of extraordinary merit and force of character. She eventually took a great interest in the suit of Columbus, and had much influence in recommending it to the queen, with whom she was a particular favorite.[2]

Malaga surrendered on the 18th of August, 1487. There appears to have been no time during its stormy siege to attend to the question of Columbus, though Fernando de Talavera, the bishop of Avila, was present, as appears by his entering the captured city in solemn and religious triumph. The campaign being ended, the court returned to Cordova, but was almost immediately driven from that city by the pestilence.

For upwards of a year the court was in a state of continual migration; part of the time in Saragossa, part of the time invading the Moorish territories by the way of Murcia, and part of the time in Valladolid and Medina del Campo. Columbus attended it in some of its movements, but it was vain to seek a quiet and attentive hearing from a court surrounded by the din of arms, and continually on the march. Wearied and discouraged by these delays, he began to think of applying elsewhere for patronage, and appears to have commenced negotiations with King John II for a return to Portugal. He wrote to that monarch on the subject, and received a letter in reply, dated 20th of March, 1488, inviting him to return to his court, and assuring him of protection from any suits of either a civil or criminal nature, that might be pending against

[1] Pulgar, Cronica, cap. 87. P. Martyr.
[2] Retrato del Buen Vassallo, lib. ii. cap. 16.

him. He received, also, a letter from Henry VII of England, inviting him to that country, and holding out promises of encouragement.

There must have been strong hopes, authorized about this time by the conduct of the Spanish sovereigns, to induce Columbus to neglect these invitations; and we find ground for such a supposition in a memorandum of a sum of money paid to him by the treasurer Gonzalez, to enable him to comply with a summons to attend the Castilian court. By the date of this memorandum, the payment must have been made immediately after Columbus had received the letter of the king of Portugal. It would seem to have been the aim of King Ferdinand to prevent his carrying his proposition to another and a rival monarch, and to keep the matter in suspense, until he should have leisure to examine it, and, if advisable, to carry it into operation.

In the spring of 1489, the long-adjourned investigation appeared to be on the eve of taking place. Columbus was summoned to attend a conference of learned men, to be held in the city of Seville; a royal order was issued for lodgings to be provided for him there; and the magistrates of all cities and towns through which he might pass, on his way, were commanded to furnish accommodations gratis, for himself and his attendants. A provision of the kind was necessary in those days, when even the present wretched establishments, called posadas, for the reception of travelers, were scarcely known.

The city of Seville complied with the royal command, but as usual the appointed conference was postponed, being interrupted by the opening of a campaign, " in which," says an old chronicler of the place, " the same Columbus was found fighting, giving proofs of the distinguished valor which accompanied his wisdom and his lofty desires." [1]

[1] Diego Ortiz de Zuñiga. Ann. de Sevilla, lib. xii., anno 1489, p. 404.

' The campaign in which Columbus is here said to have borne so honorable a part, was one of the most glorious of the war of Granada. Queen Isabella attended with all her court, including as usual a stately train of prelates and friars, among whom is particularly mentioned the procrastinating arbiter of the pretensions of Columbus, Fernando de Talavera. Much of the success of the campaign is ascribed to the presence and counsel of Isabella. The city of Baza, which was closely besieged and had resisted valiantly for upwards of six months, surrendered soon after her arrival; and on the 22d of December, Columbus beheld Muley Boabdil, the elder of the two rival kings of Granada, surrender in person all his remaining possessions, and his right to the crown, to the Spanish sovereigns.

· During this siege a circumstance took place which appears to have made a deep impression on the devout and enthusiastic spirit of Columbus. Two reverend friars arrived one day at the Spanish camp, and requested admission to the sovereigns on business of great moment. They were two of the brethren of the convent established at the holy sepulchre at Jerusalem. They brought a message from the Grand Soldan of Egypt, threatening to put to death all the Christians in his dominions, to lay waste their convents and churches, and to destroy the sepulchre, if the sovereigns did not desist from the war against Granada. The menace had no effect in altering the purpose of the sovereigns, but Isabella granted a yearly and perpetual sum of one thousand ducats in gold,[1] for the support of the monks who had charge of the sepulchre; and sent a veil, embroidered with her own hands, to be hung up at its shrine.[2]

The representations of these friars of the sufferings and indignities to which Christians were subjected in the Holy Land, together with the arrogant threat of the Soldan,

[1] Or 1423 dollars, equivalent to 4269 dollars in our time.
[2] Garabay, Compend. Hist., lib. xviii. cap. 36.

roused the pious indignation of the Spanish cavaliers, and
many burned with ardent zeal once more to revive the contests of the faith on the sacred plains of Palestine. It was
probably from conversation with these friars, and from the
pious and chivalrous zeal thus awakened in the warrior
throng around him, that Columbus first conceived an enthusiastic idea, or rather made a kind of mental vow,
which remained more or less present to his mind until the
very day of his death. He determined that, should his
projected enterprise be successful, he would devote the
profits arising from his anticipated discoveries, to a crusade
for the rescue of the holy sepulchre from the power of the
Infidels.

If the bustle and turmoil of this campaign prevented the
intended conference, the concerns of Columbus fared no
better during the subsequent rejoicings. Ferdinand and
Isabella entered Seville in February, 1490, with great
pomp and triumph. There were then preparations made
for the marriage of their eldest daughter, the Princess
Isabella, with the Prince Don Alonzo, heir apparent of
Portugal. The nuptials were celebrated in the month of
April, with extraordinary splendor. Throughout the whole
winter and spring the court was in a continual tumult of
parade and pleasure, and nothing was to be seen at Seville
but feasts, tournaments, and torch-light processions. What
chance had Columbus of being heard amid these alternate
uproars of war and festivity?

During this long course of solicitation he supported himself, in part, by making maps and charts, and was occasionally assisted by the purse of the worthy friar Diego de
Deza. It is due to the sovereigns to say, also, that whenever he was summoned to follow the movements of the
court, or to attend any appointed consultation, he was attached to the royal suite, and lodgings were provided for
him and sums issued to defray his expenses. Memorandums of several of these sums still exist in the book of ac-

counts of the royal treasurer, Francisco Gonzalez, of Seville, which has lately been found in the archives of Simancas; and it is from these minutes that we have been enabled, in some degree, to follow the movements of Columbus during his attendance upon this rambling and war- like court.

During all this time he was exposed to continual scoffs and indignities, being ridiculed by the light and ignorant as a mere dreamer, and stigmatized by the illiberal as an adventurer. The very children, it is said, pointed to their foreheads as he passed, being taught to regard him as a kind of madman.

The summer of 1490 passed away, but still Columbus was kept in tantalizing and tormenting suspense. The subsequent winter was not more propitious. He was lingering at Cordova in a state of irritating anxiety, when he learnt that the sovereigns were preparing to depart on a campaign in the Vega of Granada, with a determination never to raise their camp from before that city, until their victorious banners should float upon its towers.

Columbus was aware that when once the campaign was opened and the sovereigns were in the field, it would be in vain to expect any attention to his suit. He was wearied, if not incensed, at the repeated postponements he had experienced, by which several years had been consumed. He now pressed for a decisive reply with an earnestness that would not admit of evasion. Fernando de Talavera, therefore, was called upon by the sovereigns to hold a definitive conference with the scientific men to whom the project had been referred, and to make a report of their decision. The bishop tardily complied, and at length reported to their majesties, as the general opinion of the Junto, that the proposed scheme was vain and impossible, and that it did not become such great princes to engage in an enterprise of the kind on such weak grounds as had been advanced.[1]

[1] Hist. del Almirante, cap. 2.

Notwithstanding this unfavorable report, the sovereigns were unwilling to close the door upon a project which might be productive of such important advantages. Many of the learned members of the Junto also were in its favor, particularly Fray Diego de Deza, tutor to Prince Juan, who from his situation and clerical character had access to the royal ear, and exerted himself strenuously in counteracting the decision of the board. A degree of consideration, also, had gradually grown up at court for the enterprise, and many men, distinguished for rank and merit, had become its advocates. Fernando de Talavera, therefore, was commanded to inform Columbus, who was still at Cordova, that the great cares and expenses of the wars rendered it impossible for the sovereigns to engage in any new enterprise; but that when the war was concluded they would have both time and inclination to treat with him about what he proposed.[1]

This was but a starved reply to receive after so many days of weary attendance, anxious expectation, and deferred hope; Columbus was unwilling to receive it at second hand, and repaired to the court at Seville to learn his fate from the lips of the sovereigns. Their reply was virtually the same, declining to engage in the enterprise for the present, but holding out hopes of patronage when relieved from the cares and expenses of the war.

Columbus looked upon this indefinite postponement as a mere courtly mode of evading his importunity, and supposed that the favorable dispositions of the sovereigns had been counteracted by the objections of the ignorant and bigoted. Renouncing all further confidence, therefore, in vague promises, which had so often led to disappointment, and giving up all hopes of countenance from the throne, he turned his back upon Seville, indignant at the thoughts of having been beguiled out of so many precious years of waning existence.

[1] Hist. del Almirante, cap. 2.

CHAPTER V.

COLUMBUS AT THE CONVENT OF LA RABIDA.

ABOUT half a league from the little sea-port of Palos de Moguer in Andalusia there stood, and continues to stand at the present day, an ancient convent of Franciscan friars, dedicated to Santa Maria de Rabida. One day a stranger on foot, in humble guise, but of a distinguished air, accompanied by a small boy, stopped at the gate of the convent, and asked of the porter a little bread and water for his child. While receiving this humble refreshment, the prior of the convent, Juan Perez de Marchena, happening to pass by, was struck with the appearance of the stranger, and observing from his air and accent that he was a foreigner, entered into conversation with him, and soon learned the particulars of his story. That stranger was Columbus.[1] He was on his way to the neighboring town of Huelva, to seek his brother-in-law, who had married a sister of his deceased wife.[2]

The prior was a man of extensive information. His attention had been turned in some measure to geographical and nautical science, probably from his vicinity to Palos, the inhabitants of which were among the most enterprising navigators of Spain, and made frequent voyages to the recently discovered islands and countries on the African

---

[1] "Lo dicho Almirante Colon veniendo á la Rabida, que es un monastério de frailes en esta villa, el qual demandó á la porteria que le diesen para aquel niñico, que era niño, pan i agua que bebiese." The testimony of Garcia Fernandez exists in manuscript among the multifarious writings of the Pleito or lawsuit, which are preserved at Seville. I have made use of an authenticated extract, copied for the late historian, Juan Baut. Muñoz.

[2] Probably Pedro Correa, already mentioned, from whom he had received information of signs of land in the west, observed near Puerto Santo.

coast. He was greatly interested by the conversation of
Columbus, and struck with the grandeur of his views. It
was a remarkable occurrence in the monotonous life of the
cloister, to have a man of such singular character, intent
on so extraordinary an enterprise, applying for bread and
water at the gate of his convent.

When he found, however, that the voyager was on the
point of abandoning Spain to seek patronage in the court
of France, and that so important an enterprise was about
to be lost for ever to the country, the patriotism of the
good friar took the alarm. He detained Columbus as his
guest, and, diffident of his own judgment, sent for a scientific friend to converse with him. That friend was Garcia
Fernandez, a physician, resident in Palos, the same who
furnishes this interesting testimony. Fernandez was equally
struck with the appearance and conversation of the stranger;
several conferences took place at the convent, at which several of the veteran mariners of Palos were present. Among
these was Martin Alonzo Pinzon, the head of a family of
wealthy and experienced navigators of the place, celebrated
for their adventurous expeditions. Facts were related by
some of these navigators in support of the theory of Columbus. In a word, his project was treated with a deference
in the quiet cloisters of La Rabida, and among the seafaring men of Palos, which had been sought in vain among
the sages and philosophers of the court. Martin Alonzo
Pinzon, especially, was so convinced of its feasibility that
he offered to engage in it with purse and person, and to
bear the expenses of Columbus in a renewed application to
the court.

Friar Juan Perez was confirmed in his faith by the
concurrence of those learned and practical councilors.
He had once been confessor to the queen, and knew that
she was always accessible to persons of his sacred calling.
He proposed to write to her immediately on the subject,
and entreated Columbus to delay his journey until an

answer could be received. The latter was easily persuaded,
for he felt as if, in leaving Spain, he was again abandoning
his home. He was also reluctant to renew, in another
court, the vexations and disappointments experienced in
Spain and Portugal.

The little council at the convent of La Rabida now cast
round their eyes for an ambassador to depart upon this
momentous mission. They chose one Sebastian Rodriguez,
a pilot of Lepe, one of the most shrewd and important
personages in this maritime neighborhood. The queen
was, at this time, at Santa Fé, the military city which had
been built in the Vega before Granada, after the conflagration of the royal camp. The honest pilot acquitted himself
faithfully, expeditiously, and successfully, in his embassy.
He found access to the benignant princess, and delivered
the epistle of the friar. Isabella had always been favorably
disposed to the proposition of Columbus. She wrote in reply to Juan Perez, thanking him for his timely services,
and requesting that he would repair immediately to the
court, leaving Christopher Columbus in confident hope
until he should hear further from her. This royal letter
was brought back by the pilot at the end of fourteen days,
and spread great joy in the little junto at the convent. No
sooner did the warm-hearted friar receive it, than he saddled
his mule, and departed privately, before midnight, for the
court. He journeyed through the conquered countries of
the Moors, and rode into the newly-erected city of Santa
Fé, where the sovereigns were superintending the close
investment of the capital of Granada.

The sacred office of Juan Perez gained him a ready entrance in a court distinguished for religious zeal; and, once
admitted to the presence of the queen, his former relation,
as father confessor, gave him great freedom of counsel. He
pleaded the cause of Columbus with characteristic enthusiasm, speaking, from actual knowledge, of his honorable
motives, his professional knowledge and experience, and his

perfect capacity to fulfill the undertaking; he represented
the solid principles upon which the enterprise was founded,
the advantage that must attend its success, and the glory
it must shed upon the Spanish crown. It is probable that
Isabella had never heard the proposition urged with such
honest zeal and impressive eloquence. Being naturally
more sanguine and susceptible than the king, and more
open to warm and generous impulses, she was moved by the
representations of Juan Perez; which were warmly seconded
by her favorite, the Marchioness of Moya, who entered into
the affair with a woman's disinterested enthusiasm.[1] The
queen requested that Columbus might be again sent to her,
and, with the kind considerateness which characterized her,
bethinking herself of his poverty, and his humble plight,
ordered that twenty thousand maravedies[2] in florins should
be forwarded to him, to bear his traveling expenses, to
provide him with a mule for his journey, and to furnish
him with decent raiment, that he might make a respectable
appearance at the court.

The worthy friar lost no time in communicating the
result of his mission; he transmitted the money, and a
letter, by the hands of an inhabitant of Palos, to the physician Garcia Fernandez, who delivered them to Columbus.
The latter complied with the instructions conveyed in the
epistle. He exchanged his threadbare garb for one more
suited to the sphere of a court, and, purchasing a mule, set
out once more, reanimated by hopes, for the camp before
Granada.[3]

[1] Retrato del Buen Vasallo, lib. ii. cap. 16.
[2] Or 72 dollars, and equivalent to 216 dollars of the present day.
[3] Most of the particulars of this visit of Columbus to the convent
of La Rabida are from the testimony rendered by Garcia Fernandez
in the lawsuit between Diego, the son of Columbus, and the crown.

CHAPTER VI.

APPLICATION TO THE COURT AT THE TIME OF THE SUR-
RENDER OF GRANADA.

[1492.]

WHEN Columbus arrived at the court, he experienced a favorable reception, and was given in hospitable charge to his steady friend Alonzo de Quintanilla, the accountant-general. The moment, however, was too eventful for his business to receive immediate attention. He arrived in time to witness the memorable surrender of Granada to the Spanish arms. He beheld Boabdil, the last of the Moorish kings, sally forth from the Alhambra, and yield up the keys of that favorite seat of Moorish power; while the king and queen, with all the chivalry, and rank, and magnificence of Spain, moved forward in proud and solemn procession, to receive this token of submission. It was one of the most brilliant triumphs in Spanish history. After near eight hundred years of painful struggle, the crescent was completely cast down, the cross exalted in its place, and the standard of Spain was seen floating on the highest tower of the Alhambra. The whole court and army were abandoned to jubilee. The air resounded with shouts of joy, with songs of triumph, and hymns of thanksgiving. On every side were beheld military rejoicings and religious oblations; for it was considered a triumph, not merely of arms, but of Christianity. The king and queen moved in the midst, in more than common magnificence, while every eye regarded them as more than mortal; as if sent by Heaven for the salvation and building up of Spain.[1] The court was thronged by the most illustrious of that warlike country, and stirring era; by the flower of its nobility, by the most dignified of its prelacy, by bards and minstrels,

[1] Mariana, Hist. de Espana, lib. xxv. cap. 18.

and all the retinue of a romantic and picturesque age. There was nothing but the glittering of arms, the rustling of robes, the sound of music and festivity.

Do we want a picture of our navigator during this brilliant and triumphant scene? It is furnished by a Spanish writer. "A man obscure and but little known followed at this time the court. Confounded in the crowd of importunate applicants, feeding his imagination in the corners of antechambers with the pompous project of discovering a world, melancholy and dejected in the midst of the general rejoicing, he beheld with indifference, and almost with contempt, the conclusion of a conquest which swelled all bosoms with jubilee, and seemed to have reached the utmost bounds of desire. That man was Christopher Columbus."[1]

The moment had now arrived, however, when the monarchs stood pledged to attend to his proposals. The war with the Moors was at an end, Spain was delivered from its intruders, and its sovereigns might securely turn their views to foreign enterprise. They kept their word with Columbus. Persons of confidence were appointed to negotiate with him, among whom was Fernando de Talavera, who, by the recent conquest, had risen to be archbishop of Granada. At the very outset of their negotiation, however, unexpected difficulties arose. So fully imbued was Columbus with the grandeur of his enterprise, that he would listen to none but princely conditions. His principal stipulation was, that he should be invested with the titles and privileges of admiral and viceroy over the countries he should discover, with one-tenth of all gains, either by trade or conquest. The courtiers who treated with him were indignant at such a demand. Their pride was shocked to see one, whom they had considered as a needy adventurer, aspiring to rank and dignities superior to their own. One observed with a sneer that it was a shrewd arrangement which he

[1] Clemencin, Elogio de la Reina Catolica, p. 20.

proposed, whereby he was secure, at all events, of the honor of a command, and had nothing to lose in case of failure. To this Columbus promptly replied, by offering to furnish one-eighth of the cost, on condition of enjoying an eighth of the profits. To do this, he no doubt calculated on the proffered assistance of Martin Alonzo Pinzon, the wealthy navigator of Palos.

His terms, however, were pronounced inadmissible. Fernando de Talavera had always considered Columbus a dreaming speculator, or a needy applicant for bread; but to see this man, who had for years been an indigent and threadbare solicitor in his antechamber, assuming so lofty a tone, and claiming an office that approached to the awful dignity of the throne, excited the astonishment as well as the indignation of the prelate. He represented to Isabella, that it would be degrading to the dignity of so illustrious a crown to lavish such distinguished honors upon a nameless stranger. Such terms, he observed, even in case of success, would be exorbitant; but in case of failure, would be cited with ridicule, as evidence of the gross credulity of the Spanish monarchs.

Isabella was always attentive to the opinions of her ghostly advisers, and the archbishop, being her confessor, had peculiar influence. His suggestions checked her dawning favor. She thought the proposed advantages might be purchased at too great a price. More moderate conditions were offered to Columbus, and such as appeared highly honorable and advantageous. It was all in vain; he would not cede one point of his demands, and the negotiation was broken off.

It is impossible not to admire the great constancy of purpose and loftiness of spirit displayed by Columbus, ever since he had conceived the sublime idea of his discovery. More than eighteen years had elapsed since his correspondence with Paulo Toscanelli of Florence, wherein he had announced his design. The greatest part of that time had

been consumed in applications at various courts. During
that period, what poverty, neglect, ridicule, contumely, and
disappointment had he not suffered! Nothing, however,
could shake his perseverance, nor make him descend to
terms which he considered beneath the dignity of his enterprise. In all his negotiations he forgot his present obscurity, he forgot his present indigence; his ardent imagination realized the magnitude of his contemplated discoveries, and he felt himself negotiating about empire.

Though so large a portion of his life had worn away in
fruitless solicitings; though there was no certainty that the
same weary career was not to be entered upon at any other
court; yet so indignant was he at the repeated disappointments he had experienced in Spain, that he determined to
abandon it for ever, rather than compromise his demands.
Taking leave of his friends, therefore, he mounted his mule,
and sallied forth from Santa Fé in the beginning of February, 1492, on his way to Cordova, whence he intended to
depart immediately for France.

When the few friends who were zealous believers in the
theory of Columbus saw him really on the point of abandoning the country, they were filled with distress, considering his departure an irreparable loss to the nation. Among
the number was Luis de St. Angel, receiver of the ecclesiastical revenues in Arragon. Determined if possible to
avert the evil, he obtained an immediate audience of the
queen, accompanied by Alonzo de Quintanilla. The exigency of the moment gave him courage and eloquence. He
did not confine himself to entreaties, but almost mingled
reproaches, expressing astonishment that a queen who had
evinced the spirit to undertake so many great and perilous
enterprises, should hesitate at one where the loss could be
so trifling, while the gain might be incalculable. He reminded her how much might be done for the glory of God,
the exaltation of the church, and the extension of her own
power and dominion. What cause of regret to herself, of

triumph to her enemies, of sorrow to her friends, should this enterprise, thus rejected by her, be accomplished by some other power! He reminded her what fame and dominion other princes had acquired by their discoveries; here was an opportunity to surpass them all. He entreated her majesty not to be misled by the assertions of learned men, that the project was the dream of a visionary. He vindicated the judgment of Columbus, and the soundness and practicability of his plans. Neither would even his failure reflect disgrace upon the crown. It was worth the trouble and expense to clear up even a doubt upon a matter of such importance, for it belonged to enlightened and magnanimous princes to investigate questions of the kind, and to explore the wonders and secrets of the universe. He stated the liberal offer of Columbus to bear an eighth of the expense, and informed her that all the requisites for this great enterprise consisted but of two vessels, and about three thousand crowns.

These and many more arguments were urged with that persuasive power which honest zeal imparts, and it is said the Marchioness of Moya, who was present, exerted her eloquence to persuade the queen. The generous spirit of Isabella was enkindled. It seemed as if, for the first time, the subject broke upon her mind in its real grandeur, and she declared her resolution to undertake the enterprise.

There was still a moment's hesitation. The king looked coldly on the affair, and the royal finances were absolutely drained by the war. Some time must be given to replenish them. How could she draw on an exhausted treasury for a measure to which the king was adverse! St. Angel watched this suspense with trembling anxiety. The next moment reassured him. With an enthusiasm worthy of herself, and of the cause, Isabella exclaimed, "I undertake the enterprise for my own crown of Castile, and will pledge my jewels to raise the necessary funds." This was the proudest moment in the life of Isabella; it stamped her

7

renown for ever as the patroness of the discovery of the New World.

St. Angel, eager to secure this noble impulse, assured her majesty that there would be no need of pledging her jewels, as he was ready to advance the necessary funds. His offer was gladly accepted; the funds really came from the coffers of Arragon; seventeen thousand florins were advanced by the accountant of St. Angel out of the treasury of King Ferdinand. That prudent monarch, however, took care to have his kingdom indemnified some few years afterwards; for in remuneration of this loan, a part of the first gold brought by Columbus from the New World was employed in gilding the vaults and ceilings of the royal saloon in the grand palace of Saragoza, in Arragon, anciently the Aljaferia, or abode of the Moorish kings.[1]

Columbus had pursued his lonely journey across the Vega and reached the bridge of Pinos, about two leagues from Granada, at the foot of the mountain of Elvira; a pass famous in the Moorish wars for many a desperate encounter between the Christians and Infidels. Here he was overtaken by a courier from the queen, spurring in all speed, who summoned him to return to Santa Fé. He hesitated for a moment, being loth to subject himself again to the delays and equivocations of the court; when informed, however, of the sudden zeal for the enterprise excited in the mind of the queen, and the positive promise she had given to undertake it, he no longer felt a doubt, but, turning the reins of his mule, hastened back, with joyful alacrity, to Santa Fé, confiding in the noble probity of that princess.

[1] Argensola, Anales de Arragon, lib. i. cap. 10.

CHAPTER VII.

**ARRANGEMENT WITH THE SPANISH SOVEREIGNS.—PREP-
ARATIONS FOR THE EXPEDITION AT THE PORT OF
PALOS.**

[1492.]

ON arriving at Santa Fé, Columbus had an immediate
audience of the queen, and the benignity with which she
received him atoned for all past neglect.   Through deference to the zeal she thus suddenly displayed, the king
yielded his tardy concurrence, but Isabella was the soul of
this grand enterprise.   She was prompted by lofty and
generous enthusiasm, while the king proved cold and calculating in this as in all his other undertakings.

A perfect understanding being thus effected with the
sovereigns, articles of agreement were ordered to be drawn
out by Juan de Coloma, the royal secretary.   They were
to the following effect:—

1. That Columbus should have, for himself during his
life, and his heirs and successors forever, the office of admiral in all the lands and continents which he might discover or acquire in the ocean, with similar honors and prerogatives to those enjoyed by the high admiral of Castile
in his district.

2. That he should be viceroy and governor-general over
all the said lands and continents; with the privilege of
nominating three candidates for the government of each
island or province, one of whom should be selected by the
sovereigns.

3. That he should be entitled to reserve for himself one-
tenth of all pearls, precious stones, gold, silver, spices, and
all other articles and merchandises, in whatever manner
found, bought, bartered, or gained within his admiralty,
the costs being first deducted.

4. That he, or his lieutenant, should be the sole judge in all causes and disputes arising out of traffic between those countries and Spain, provided the high admiral of Castile had similar jurisdiction in his district.

. 5. That he might then, and at all after times, contribute an eighth part of the expense in fitting out vessels to sail on this enterprise, and receive an eighth part of the profits.

The last stipulation, which admits Columbus to bear an eighth of the enterprise, was made in consequence of his indignant proffer, on being reproached with demanding ample emoluments while incurring no portion of the charge. He fulfilled this engagement, through the assistance of the Pinzons of Palos, and added a third vessel to the armament. Thus one-eighth of the expense attendant on this grand expedition, undertaken by a powerful nation, was actually borne by the individual who conceived it, and who likewise risked his life on its success.

The capitulations were signed by Ferdinand and Isabella, at the city of Santa Fé, in the Vega or plain of Granada, on the 17th of April, 1492. A letter of privilege or commission to Columbus, of similar purport, was drawn out in form, and issued by the sovereigns in the city of Granada, on the thirtieth of the same month. In this, the dignities and prerogatives of viceroy and governor were made hereditary in his family; and he and his heirs were authorized to prefix the title of Don to their names; a distinction accorded in those days only to persons of rank and estate, though it has since lost all value, from being universally used in Spain.

All the royal documents issued on this occasion bore equally the signatures of Ferdinand and Isabella, but her separate crown of Castile defrayed all the expense; and, during her life, few persons, except Castilians, were permitted to establish themselves in the new territories.[1]

[1] Charlevoix, Hist. S. Domingo, lib. i. p. 79.

The port of Palos de Moguer was fixed upon as the place where the armament was to be fitted out, Columbus calculating, no doubt, on the co-operation of Martin Alonzo Pinzon, resident there, and on the assistance of his zealous friend the prior of the convent of La Rabida. Before going into the business details of this great enterprise, it is due to the character of the illustrious man who conceived and conducted it, most especially to notice the elevated, even though visionary spirit by which he was actuated. One of his principal objects was undoubtedly the propagation of the Christian faith. He expected to arrive at the extremity of Asia, and to open a direct and easy communication with the vast and magnificent empire of the Grand Khan. The conversion of that heathen potentate had, in former times, been a favorite aim of various pontiffs and pious sovereigns, and various missions had been sent to the remote regions of the East for that purpose. Columbus now considered himself about to effect this great work; to spread the light of revelation to the very ends of the earth, and thus to be the instrument of accomplishing one of the sublime predictions of Holy Writ. Ferdinand listened with complacency to these enthusiastic anticipations. With him, however, religion was subservient to interest; and he had found, in the recent conquest of Granada, that extending the sway of the church might be made a laudable means of extending his own dominions. According to the doctrines of the day, every nation that refused to acknowledge the truths of Christianity, was fair spoil for a Christian invader; and it is probable that Ferdinand was more stimulated by the accounts given of the wealth of Mangi, Cathay, and other provinces belonging to the Grand Khan, than by any anxiety for the conversion of him and his semi-barbarous subjects.

Isabella had nobler inducements; she was filled with a pious zeal at the idea of effecting such a great work of salvation. From different motives, therefore, both of the

sovereigns accorded with the views of Columbus in this
particular, and when he afterwards departed on his voyage,
letters were actually given him for the Grand Khan of
Tartary.

The ardent enthusiasm of Columbus did not stop here.
Anticipating boundless wealth from his discoveries, he
suggested that the treasures thus acquired should be consecrated to the pious purpose of rescuing the holy sepulchre
of Jerusalem from the power of the infidels.   The sovereigns
smiled at this sally of the imagination, but expressed themselves well pleased with it, and assured him that even without the funds he anticipated, they should be well disposed
to that holy undertaking.[1]   What the king and queen,
however, may have considered a mere sally of momentary
excitement, was a deep and cherished design of Columbus.
It is a curious and characteristic fact, which has never been
particularly noticed, that the recovery of the holy sepulchre
was one of the great objects of his ambition, meditated
throughout the remainder of his life, and solemnly provided for in his will.   In fact, he subsequently considered
it the main work for which he was chosen by Heaven as
an agent, and that his great discovery was but a prepara-
tory dispensation of Providence to furnish means for its
accomplishment.

A home-felt mark of favor, characteristic of the kind
and considerate heart of Isabella, was accorded to Columbus before his departure from the court.   An albala, or
letter-patent, was issued by the queen on the 8th of May,
appointing his son Diego page to Prince Juan, the heir
apparent, with an allowance for his support; an honor
granted only to the sons of persons of distinguished rank.[2]

Proteste a vuestras Altezas que toda la ganancia desta mi empresa
se gastase en la conquista de Jerusalem, y vuestras Altezas se rieron,
y dijeron que les placia, y que sin este tenian aquella gana.   Primer
Viage de Colon, Navarrete, tom. i. p. 117.
  [2] Navarrete, Colec. de Viages, tom. ii. doc. 11.

Thus gratified in his dearest wishes, after a course of delays and disappointments sufficient to have reduced any ordinary man to despair, Columbus took leave of the court on the 12th of May, and set out joyfully for Palos. Let those who are disposed to faint under difficulties, in the prosecution of any great and worthy undertaking, remember that eighteen years elapsed after the time that Columbus conceived his enterprise, before he was enabled to carry it into effect; that the greater part of that time was passed in almost hopeless solicitation, amidst poverty, neglect, and taunting ridicule; that the prime of his life had wasted away in the struggle, and that when his perseverance was finally crowned with success, he was about his fifty-sixth year. His example should encourage the enterprising never to despair.

CHAPTER VIII.

COLUMBUS AT THE PORT OF PALOS.—PREPARATIONS FOR THE VOYAGE OF DISCOVERY.

On arriving at Palos, Columbus repaired immediately to the neighboring convent of La Rabida, where he was received with open arms by the worthy prior, Fray Juan Perez, and again became his guest.[1] The port of Palos, for some misdemeanor, had been condemned by the royal council to serve the crown for one year with two armed caravels; and these were destined to form part of the armament of Columbus, who was furnished with the necessary papers and vouchers to enforce obedience in all matters necessary for his expedition.

On the following morning, the 23d of May, Columbus, accompanied by Fray Juan Perez, whose character and station gave him great importance in the neighborhood, proceeded to the church of St. George in Palos, where the

[1] Oviedo, Cronica de las Indias, lib. ii. cap. 5.

alcalde, the regidors, and many of the inhabitants of the
place had been notified to attend. Here, in presence of
them all, in the porch of the church, a royal order was
read by a notary public, commanding the authorities of
Palos to have two caravels ready for sea within ten days
after this notice, and to place them and their crews at the
disposal of Columbus. The latter was likewise empowered
to procure and fit out a third vessel. The crews of all
three were to receive the ordinary wages of seamen employed in armed vessels, and to be paid four months in
advance. They were to sail in such direction as Columbus,
under the royal authority, should command, and were to
obey him in all things, with merely one stipulation, that
neither he nor they were to go to St. George la Mina, on
the coast of Guinea, nor any other of the lately discovered
possessions of Portugal. A certificate of their good conduct, signed by Columbus, was to be the discharge of their
obligation to the crown.[1]

Orders were likewise read, addressed to the public
authorities, and the people of all ranks and conditions,
in the maritime borders of Andalusia, commanding them
to furnish supplies and assistance of all kinds, at reasonable
prices, for the fitting out of the vessels; and penalties were
denounced on such as should cause any impediment. No
duties were to be exacted for any articles furnished to the
vessels; and all criminal processes against the person or
property of any individual engaged in the expedition was
to be suspended during his absence, and for two months
after his return.[2]

With these orders the authorities promised implicit
compliance; but, when the nature of the intended expedition came to be known, astonishment and dismay fell upon
the little community. The ships and crews demanded for
such a desperate service were regarded in the light of
sacrifices. The owners of vessels refused to furnish them;

[1] Navarrete, Colec. de Viages, tom. ii. doc. 6.   [2] Idem, doc. 8, 9.

·the boldest seamen shrank from such a wild and chimerical cruise into the wilderness of the ocean. All kinds of ·frightful tales and fables were conjured up concerning the unknown regions of the deep ; and nothing can be a stronger ·evidence of the boldness of this undertaking than the extreme dread of it in a community composed of some of the most adventurous navigators of the age.

Weeks elapsed without a vessel being procured, or any ·thing else being done in fulfillment of the royal orders. Further mandates were therefore issued by the sovereigns, ·ordering the magistrates of the coast of Andalusia to press into the service any vessels they might think proper, belonging to Spanish subjects, and to oblige the masters and crews to sail with Columbus in whatever direction he should be sent by royal command. Juan de Peñalosa, an officer of the royal household, was sent to see that this order was properly complied with, receiving two hundred maravedis a day as long as he was occupied in the business, which sum, together with other penalties expressed in the mandate, was to be exacted from such as should be disobedient and delinquent. This letter was acted upon by Columbus in Palos and the neighboring town of Moguer, but apparently with as little success as the preceding. The communities of those places were thrown into complete confusion ; tumults took place ; but nothing of consequence was effected. At length Martin Alonzo Pinzon stepped forward, with his brother Vicente Yañez Pinzon ; both navigators of great courage and ability, owners of vessels, and having seamen in their employ. They were related, also, to many of the seafaring inhabitants of Palos and Moguer, and had great influence throughout the neighborhood. They engaged to sail on the expedition, and furnished one of the vessels required. Others, with their owners and crews, were pressed into the service by the magistrates, under the arbitrary mandate of the sovereigns ; and it is a striking instance of the despotic authority exercised over commerce in those times, that respectable individuals should thus be compelled to engage, with persons and ships, in what appeared to them a mad and desperate enterprise.

During the equipment of the vessels, troubles and difficulties arose among the seamen who had been compelled to embark. These were fomented and kept up by Gomez Rascon and Christoval Quintero, owners of the Pinta, one of the ships pressed into the service. All kinds of obstacles were thrown in the way, by these people and their friends, to retard or defeat the voyage. The calkers employed upon the vessels did their work in a careless and imperfect manner, and on being commanded to do it over again absconded.[1] Some of the seamen who had enlisted willingly repented of their hardihood, or were dissuaded by their relatives, and sought to retract; others deserted and concealed themselves. Every thing had to be effected by the most harsh and arbitrary measures, and in defiance of popular prejudice and opposition.

The influence and example of the Pinzons had a great effect in allaying this opposition, and inducing many of their friends and relatives to embark. It is supposed that they had furnished Columbus with funds to pay the eighth part of the expense which he was bound to advance. It is also said that Martin Alonzo Pinzon was to divide with him his share of the profits. As no immediate profit, however, resulted from this expedition, no claim of the kind was ever brought forward. It is certain, however, that the assistance of the Pinzons was all-important, if not indispensable, in fitting out and launching the expedition.[2]

After the great difficulties made by various courts in patronizing this enterprise, it is surprising how inconsider-

[1] Las Casas, Hist. Ind., lib. i. cap. 77, MS.
[2] These facts concerning the Pinzons are mostly taken from the testimony given, many years afterwards, in a suit between Don Diego, the son of Columbus, and the crown.

able an armament was required. It is evident that Columbus had reduced his requisitions to the narrowest limits, lest any great expense should cause impediment. Three small vessels were apparently all that he had requested. Two of them were light barks, called caravels, not superior to river and coasting craft of more modern days. Representations of this class of vessels exist in old prints and paintings.[1] They are delineated as open, and without deck in the centre, but built up high at the prow and stern, with forecastles and cabins for the accommodation of the crew. Peter Martyr, the learned contemporary of Columbus, says that only one of the three vessels was decked. The smallness of the vessels was considered an advantage by Columbus, in a voyage of discovery, enabling him to run close to the shores, and to enter shallow rivers and harbors. In his third voyage, when coasting the Gulf of Paria, he complained of the size of his ship, being nearly a hundred tons burthen. But that such long and perilous expeditions, into unknown seas, should be undertaken in vessels without decks, and that they should live through the violent tempests, by which they were frequently assailed, remain among the singular circumstances of these daring voyages.

At length, by the beginning of August, every difficulty was vanquished, and the vessels were ready for sea. The largest, which had been prepared expressly for the voyage, and was decked, was called the Santa Maria: on board of this ship Columbus hoisted his flag. The second, called the Pinta, was commanded by Martin Alonzo Pinzon, accompanied by his brother Francisco Martin, as pilot. The third, called the Niña, had latine sails, and was commanded by the third of the brothers, Vicente Yañez Pinzon. There were three other pilots, Sancho Ruiz, Pedro Alonzo Niño, and Bartolomeo Roldan. Roderigo Sanchez of Segovia was inspector-general of the armament, and Diego de Arana,

[1] See Illustrations, article "Ships of Columbus."

a native of Cordova, chief alguazil. Roderigo de Escobar went as royal notary, an officer always sent in the armaments of the crown, to take official notes of all transactions. There were also a physician and a surgeon, together with various private adventurers, several servants, and ninety mariners; making, in all, one hundred and twenty persons.[1]

The squadron being ready to put to sea, Columbus, impressed with the solemnity of his undertaking, confessed himself to the friar Juan Perez, and partook of the sacrament of the communion. His example was followed by his officers and crew, and they entered upon their enterprise full of awe, and with the most devout and affecting ceremonials, committing themselves to the especial guidance and protection of Heaven. A deep gloom was spread over the whole community of Palos at their departure, for almost every one had some relative or friend on board of the squadron. The spirits of the seamen, already depressed by their own fears, were still more cast down at the affliction of those they left behind, who took leave of them with tears and lamentations, and dismal forebodings, as of men they were never to behold again.

[1] Charlevoix, Hist. St. Domingo, lib. i.   Muñoz, Hist. Nuevo Mundo, lib. ii.

BOOK III.

CHAPTER I.

DEPARTURE OF COLUMBUS ON HIS FIRST VOYAGE.

[1492.]

WHEN Columbus set sail on this memorable voyage, he commenced a regular journal, intended for the inspection of the Spanish sovereigns. Like all his other transactions, it evinces how deeply he was impressed with the grandeur and solemnity of his enterprise. He proposed to keep it, as he afterwards observed, in the manner of the Commentaries of Cesar. It opened with a stately prologue, wherein, in the following words, were set forth the motives and views which led to his expedition.

In nomine D. N. Jesu Christi. Whereas most Christian, most high, most excellent and most powerful princes, king and queen of the Spains, and of the islands of the sea, our sovereigns, in the present year of 1492, after your highnesses had put an end to the war with the Moors who ruled in Europe, and had concluded that warfare in the great city of Granada, where, on the second of January, of this present year, I saw the royal banners of your highnesses placed by force of arms on the towers of the Alhambra, which is the fortress of that city, and beheld the Moorish king sally forth from the gates of the city, and kiss the royal hands of your highnesses and of my lord the prince; and immediately in that same month, in consequence of the information which I had given to your highnesses of the

lands of India, and of a prince who is called the Grand
Khan, which is to say in our language, king of kings; how
that many times he and his predecessors had sent to Rome
to entreat for doctors of our holy faith, to instruct him in
the same; and that the holy father had never provided him
with them, and thus so many people were lost, believing in
idolatries, and imbibing doctrines of perdition; therefore
your highnesses, as catholic Christians and princes, lovers
and promoters of the holy Christian faith, and enemies of
the sect of Mahomet, and of all idolatries and heresies, determined to send me, Christopher Columbus, to the said
parts of India, to see the said princes, and the people and
lands, and discover the nature and disposition of them all,
and the means to be taken for the conversion of them to
our holy faith; and ordered that I should not go by land
to the east, by which it is the custom to go, but by a voyage
to the west, by which course, unto the present time, we do
not know for certain that any one hath passed. Your highnesses, therefore, after having expelled all the Jews from
your kingdoms and territories, commanded me, in the same
month of January, to proceed with a sufficient armament to
the said parts of India; and for this purpose bestowed great
favors upon me, ennobling me, that thenceforward I might
style myself Don, appointing me high admiral of the Ocean
sea, and perpetual viceroy and governor of all the islands
and continents I should discover and gain, and which hence-
forward may be discovered and gained in the Ocean sea;
and that my eldest son should succeed me, and so on from
generation to generation for ever. I departed, therefore,
from the city of Granada, on Saturday, the 12th of May,
of the same year 1492, to Palos, a seaport, where I armed
three ships, well calculated for such service, and sailed from
that port, well furnished with provisions and with many
seamen, on Friday, the 3d of August, of the same year,
half an hour before sunrise, and took the route for the
Canary Islands of your highnesses, to steer my course

thence, and navigate until I should arrive at the Indies, and deliver the embassy of your highnesses to those princes, and accomplish that which you had commanded. For this purpose I intend to write during this voyage, very punctually from day to day, all that I may do, and see, and experience, as will hereafter be seen. Also, my sovereign princes, beside describing each night all that has occurred in the day, and in the day the. navigation of the night, I propose to make a chart, in which I will set down the waters and lands of the Ocean sea in their proper situations under their bearings; and further, to compose a book, and illustrate the whole in picture by latitude from the equinoctial, and longitude from the west; and upon the whole it will be essential that I should forget sleep and attend closely to the navigation to accomplish these things, which will be a great labor." [1]

Thus are formally and expressly stated by Columbus the objects of this extraordinary voyage. The material facts still extant of his journal will be found incorporated in the present work. [2]

It was on Friday, the 3d of August, 1492, early in the

[1] Navarrete, Colec. Viag., tom. i. p. 1.

[2] An abstract of this journal, made by Las Casas, has recently been discovered, and is published in the first volume of the collection of Señor Navarrete. Many passages of this abstract had been previously inserted by Las Casas in his History of the Indies, and the same journal had been copiously used by Fernando Columbus in the history of his father. In the present account of this voyage, the author has made use of the journal contained in the work of Señor Navarrete, the manuscript history of Las Casas, the History of the Indies by Herrera, the Life of the Admiral by his son, the Chronicle of the Indies by Oviedo, the manuscript history of Ferdinand and Isabella by Andres Bernaldes, curate of Los Palacios, and the Letters and Decades of the Ocean Sea, by Peter Martyr; all of whom, with the exception of Herrera, were contemporaries and acquaintances of Columbus. These are the principal authorities which have been consulted, though scattered lights have occasionally been obtained from other sources.

morning, that Columbus set sail from the bar of Saltes, a small island formed by the arms of the Odiel, in front of the town of Huelva, steering in a southwesterly direction for the Canary islands, whence it was his intention to strike due west. As a guide by which to sail, he had prepared a map or chart, improved upon that sent him by Paulo Toscanelli. Neither of those now exist, but the globe or planisphere finished by Martin Behem in this year of the admiral's first voyage is still extant, and furnishes an idea of what the chart of Columbus must have been. It exhibits the coasts of Europe and Africa from the south of Ireland to the end of Guinea, and opposite to them, on the other side of the Atlantic, the extremity of Asia, or, as it was termed, India. Between them is placed the island of Cipango, or Japan, which, according to Marco Polo, lay fifteen hundred miles distant from the Asiatic coast. In his computations Columbus advanced this island about a thousand leagues too much to the east, supposing it to be about the situation of Florida;[1] and at this island he hoped first to arrive.

The exultation of Columbus at finding himself, after so many years of baffled hope, fairly launched on his grand enterprise, was checked by his want of confidence in the resolution and perseverance of his crews. As long as he, remained within reach of Europe, there was no security that, in a moment of repentance and alarm, they might not renounce the prosecution of the voyage, and insist on a return. Symptoms soon appeared to warrant his apprehensions. On the third day, the Pinta made signal of distress; her rudder was discovered to be broken and unhung. This Columbus surmised to be done through the contrivance of the owners of the caravel, Gomez Rascon and Christoval Quintero, to disable their vessel, and cause her to be left behind. As has already been observed, they had been pressed into the service greatly against their will, and

[1] Malte-Brun, Geograph. Universelle, tom. ii. p. 283.

their caravel seized upon for the expedition, in conformity to the royal orders.

Columbus was much disturbed at this occurrence. It gave him a foretaste of further difficulties to be apprehended from crews partly enlisted on compulsion, and all full of doubt and foreboding.   Trivial obstacles might, in the present critical state of his voyage, spread panic and mutiny through his ships, and entirely defeat the expedition.

The wind was blowing strongly at the time, so that he could not render assistance without endangering his own vessel. Fortunately, Martin Alonzo Pinzon commanded the Pinta, and being an adroit and able seaman, succeeded in securing the rudder with cords, so as to bring the vessel into management. This, however, was but a temporary and inadequate expedient; the fastenings gave way again on the following day, and the other ships were obliged to shorten sail until the rudder could be secured.

This damaged state of the Pinta, as well as her being in a leaky condition, determined the admiral to touch at the Canary islands, and seek a vessel to replace her. He considered himself not far from those islands, though a different opinion was entertained by the pilots of the squadron. The event proved his superiority in taking observations and keeping reckonings, for they came in sight of the Canaries on the morning of the 9th.

They were detained upwards of three weeks among these islands, seeking in vain another vessel. They were obliged, therefore, to make a new rudder for the Pinta, and repair her for the voyage. The latine sails of the Niña were also altered into square sails, that she might work more steadily and securely, and be able to keep company with the other vessels.

While sailing among these islands, the crew were terrified at beholding the lofty peak of Teneriffe sending forth volumes of flame and smoke, being ready to take alarm at any extraordinary phenomenon, and to construe it into a dis-

astrous portent.   Columbus took great pains to dispel their
apprehensions, explaining the natural causes of those volcanic fires, and verifying his explanations by citing Mount
Etna, and other well-known volcanoes.

While taking in wood and water and provisions in the
island of Gomera, a vessel arrived from Ferro, which reported that three Portuguese caravels had been seen hovering off that island, with the intention, it was said, of capturing Columbus.   The admiral suspected some hostile
stratagem on the part of the king of Portugal, in revenge
for his having embarked in the service of Spain; he therefore lost no time in putting to sea, anxious to get far from
those islands, and out of the track of navigation, trembling
lest something might occur to defeat his expedition, commenced under such inauspicious circumstances.

CHAPTER II.

CONTINUATION OF THE VOYAGE.—FIRST NOTICE OF THE VARIATION OF THE NEEDLE.

[1492.]

EARLY in the morning of the 6th of September, Columbus set sail from the island of Gomera, and now might be
said first to strike into the region of discovery; taking
leave of these frontier islands of the old world, and steering
westward for the unknown parts of the Atlantic.   For three
days, however, a profound calm kept the vessels loitering
with flagging sails, within a short distance of the land.
This was a tantalizing delay to Columbus, who was impatient to find himself far out of sight of either land or sail;
which, in the pure atmospheres of these latitudes, may be
descried at an immense distance.   On the following Sunday, the 9th of September, at daybreak, he beheld Ferro,

the last of the Canary islands, about nine leagues distant. This was the island whence the Portuguese caravels had been seen; he was therefore in the very neighborhood of danger. Fortunately a breeze sprang up with the sun, their sails were once more filled, and in the course of the day the heights of Ferro gradually faded from the horizon.

On losing sight of this last trace of land, the hearts of the crews failed them. They seemed literally to have taken leave of the world. Behind them was every thing dear to the heart of man; country, family, friends, life itself; before them every thing was chaos, mystery, and peril. In the perturbation of the moment, they despaired of ever more seeing their homes. Many of the rugged seamen shed tears, and some broke into loud lamentations. The admiral tried in every way to soothe their distress, and to inspire them with his own glorious anticipations. He described to them the magnificent countries to which he was about to conduct them: the islands of the Indian seas teeming with gold and precious stones; the regions of Mangi and Cathay, with their cities of unrivaled wealth and splendor. He promised them land and riches, and every thing that could arouse their cupidity, or inflame their imaginations; nor were these promises made for purposes of mere deception; he certainly believed that he should realize them all.

He now issued orders to the commanders of the other vessels, that, in the event of separation by any accident, they should continue directly westward; but that after sailing seven hundred leagues, they should lay by from midnight until daylight, as at about that distance he confidently expected to find land. In the meantime, as he thought it possible he might not discover land within the distance thus assigned, and as he foresaw that the vague terrors already awakened among the seamen would increase with the space which intervened between them and their homes, he commenced a stratagem which he continued throughout the voyage. He kept two reckonings; one correct in which

the true way of the ship was noted, and which was retained
in secret for his own government; in the other, which was
open to general inspection, a number of leagues was daily
subtracted from the sailing of the ship, so that the crews
were kept in ignorance of the real distance they had advanced.[1]

On the 11th of September, when about one hundred and
fifty leagues west of Ferro, they fell in with part of a mast,
which from its size appeared to have belonged to a vessel
of about a hundred and twenty tons burthen, and which
had evidently been a long time in the water. The crews,
tremblingly alive to every thing that could excite their
hopes or fears, looked with rueful eye upon this wreck of
some unfortunate voyager, drifting ominously at the entrance of those unknown seas.

On the 13th of September, in the evening, being about
two hundred leagues from the island of Ferro, Columbus
for the first time noticed the variation of the needle; a
phenomenon which had never before been remarked. He
perceived about nightfall that the needle, instead of pointing to the north star, varied about half a point, or between
five and six degrees, to the northwest, and still more on
the following morning. Struck with this circumstance, he
observed it attentively for three days, and found that the
variation increased as he advanced. He at first made no
mention of this phenomenon, knowing how ready his people
were to take alarm, but it soon attracted the attention of
the pilots, and filled them with consternation. It seemed
as if the very laws of nature were changing as they ad-

[1] It has been erroneously stated that Columbus kept two journals.
It was merely in the reckoning, or log-book, that he deceived the
crew. His journal was entirely private, and intended for his own
use and the perusal of the sovereigns. In a letter written from
Granada, in 1503, to Pope Alexander VII, he says that he had kept
an account of his voyages, in the style of the Commentaries of Cesar,
which he intended to submit to his holiness.

vanced, and that they were entering another world, subject to unknown influences.[1] They apprehended that the compass was about to lose its mysterious virtues, and, without this guide, what was to become of them in a vast and trackless ocean?

Columbus tasked his science and ingenuity for reasons with which to allay their terror. He observed that the direction of the needle was not to the polar star, but to some fixed and invisible point. The variation, therefore, was not caused by any fallacy in the compass, but by the movement of the north star itself, which, like the other heavenly bodies, had its changes and revolutions, and every day described a circle round the pole. The high opinion which the pilots entertained of Columbus as a profound astronomer gave weight to this theory, and their alarm subsided. As yet the solar system of Copernicus was unknown: the explanation of Columbus, therefore, was highly plausible and ingenious, and it shows the vivacity of his mind, ever ready to meet the emergency of the moment. The theory may at first have been advanced merely to satisfy the minds of others, but Columbus appears subsequently to have remained satisfied with it himself. The phenomenon has now become familiar to us, but we still continue ignorant of its cause. It is one of those mysteries of nature, open to daily observation and experiment, and apparently simple from their familiarity, but which on investigation make the human mind conscious of its limits; baffling the experience of the practical, and humbling the pride of science.

[1] Las Casas, Hist. Ind., lib. i. cap. 6.

CHAPTER III.

CONTINUATION OF THE VOYAGE.—VARIOUS TERRORS OF
THE SEAMEN.

[1492.]

On the 14th of September, the voyagers were rejoiced
by the sight of what they considered harbingers of land.
A heron, and a tropical bird called the Rabo de Junco,[1]
neither of which are supposed to venture far to sea, hovered
about the ships. On the following night they were struck
with awe at beholding a meteor, or, as Columbus calls it in
his journal, a great flame of fire, which seemed to fall
from the sky into the sea, about four or five leagues distant.
These meteors, common in warm climates, and especially
under the tropics, are always seen in the serene azure sky
of those latitudes, falling as it were from the heavens; but
never beneath a cloud. In the transparent atmosphere of
one of those beautiful nights, where every star shines with
the purest lustre, they often leave a luminous train behind
them which lasts for twelve or fifteen seconds, and may
well be compared to a flame.

The wind had hitherto been favorable, with occasional
though transient clouds and showers. They had made
great progress each day, though Columbus, according to
his secret plan, contrived to suppress several leagues in
the daily reckoning left open to the crew.

They had now arrived within the influence of the trade
wind, which, following the sun, blows steadily from east to
west between the tropics, and sweeps over a few adjoining
degrees of ocean. With this propitious breeze directly aft,
they were wafted gently but speedily over a tranquil sea,
so that for many days they did not shift a sail. Columbus
perpetually recurs to the bland and temperate serenity of

---

[1] The water-wagtail.

the weather, which in this tract of the ocean is soft and refreshing without being cool. In his artless and expressive language he compares the pure and balmy mornings to those of April in Andalusia, and observes that they wanted but the song of the nightingale to complete the illusion. "He had reason to say so," observes the venerable Las Casas; "for it is marvelous the suavity which we experience when half way towards these Indies; and the more the ships approach the lands, so much more do they perceive the temperance and softness of the air, the clearness of the sky, and the amenity and fragrance sent forth from the groves and forests; much more certainly than in April in Andalusia."[1]

They now began to see large patches of herbs and weeds drifting from the west, and increasing in quantity as they advanced. Some of these weeds were such as grow about rocks, others such as are produced in rivers; some were yellow and withered, others so green as to have apparently been recently washed from land. On one of these patches was a live crab, which Columbus carefully preserved. They saw also a white tropical bird, of a kind which never sleeps upon the sea. Tunny fish also played about the ships, one of which was killed by the crew of the Niña. Columbus now called to mind the account given by Aristotle of certain ships of Cadiz, which, coasting the shores outside of the straits of Gibraltar, were driven westward by an impetuous east wind, until they reached a part of the ocean covered with vast fields of weeds, resembling sunken islands, among which they beheld many tunny fish. He supposed himself arrived in this weedy sea, as it had been called, from which the ancient mariners had turned back in dismay, but which he regarded with animated hope, as indicating the vicinity of land. Not that he had yet any idea of reaching the object of his search, the eastern end of Asia; for, according to his computation, he had come

[1] Las Casas, Hist. Ind., lib. i. cap. 36, MS.

but three hundred and sixty leagues [1] since leaving the Canary islands, and he placed the main land of India much farther on.

On the 18th of September the same weather continued; a soft steady breeze from the east filled every sail, while, to use the words of Columbus, the sea was as calm as the Guadalquiver at Seville. He fancied that the water of the sea grew fresher as he advanced, and noticed this as a proof of the superior sweetness and purity of the air. [2]

The crews were all in high spirits; each ship strove to get in the advance, and every seaman was eagerly on the look-out; for the sovereigns had promised a pension of ten thousand maravedis to him who should first discover land. Martin Alonzo Pinzon crowded all canvas, and, as the Pinta was a fast sailer, he generally kept the lead. In the afternoon he hailed the admiral and informed him, that, from the flight of a great number of birds, and from the appearance of the northern horizon, he thought there was land in that direction.

There was in fact a cloudiness in the north, such as often hangs over land; and at sunset it assumed such shapes and masses that many fancied they beheld islands. There was a universal wish, therefore, to steer for that quarter. Columbus, however, was persuaded that they were mere illusions. Every one who has made a sea voyage must have witnessed the deceptions caused by clouds resting upon the horizon, especially about sunset and sunrise; which the eye, assisted by the imagination and desire, easily converts into the wished-for land. This is particularly the case within the tropics, where the clouds at sunset assume the most singular appearances.

On the following day there were drizzling showers, unaccompanied by wind, which Columbus considered favor-

[1] Of twenty to the degree of latitude, the unity of distance used throughout this work.

[2] Las Casas Hist. Ind., lib. i. cap. 36.

able signs; two boobies also flew on board the ships, birds which, he observed, seldom fly twenty leagues from land. He sounded, therefore, with a line of two hundred fathoms, but found no bottom. He supposed he might be passing between islands, lying to the north and south; but was unwilling to waste the present favoring breeze by going in search of them; beside, he had confidently affirmed that land was to be found by keeping steadfastly to the west; his whole expedition had been founded on such a presumption; he should, therefore, risk all credit and authority with his people were he to appear to doubt and waver, and to go groping blindly from point to point of the compass. He resolved, therefore, to keep one bold course always westward, until he should reach the coast of India; and afterwards, if advisable, to seek these islands on his return.[1]

Notwithstanding his precaution to keep the people ignorant of the distance they had sailed, they were now growing extremely uneasy at the length of the voyage. They had advanced much farther west than ever man had sailed before, and though already beyond the reach of succor, still they continued daily leaving vast tracts of ocean behind them, and pressing onward and onward into that apparently boundless abyss. It is true they had been flattered by various indications of land, and still others were occurring; but all mocked them with vain hopes: after being hailed with a transient joy, they passed away, one after another, and the same interminable expanse of sea and sky continued to extend before them. Even the bland and gentle breeze, uniformly aft, was now conjured by their ingenious fears into a cause of alarm; for they began to imagine that the wind, in these seas, might always prevail from the east, and if so, would never permit their return to Spain.

[1] Hist. del Almirante, cap. 20. Extracts from Journal of Columb., Navarrete, T. i. p. 16.

Columbus endeavored to dispel these gloomy presages, sometimes by argument and expostulation, sometimes by awakening fresh hopes, and pointing out new signs of land. On the 20th of September the wind veered, with light breezes from the southwest. These, though adverse to their progress, had a cheering effect upon the people, as they proved that the wind did not always prevail from the east.[1] Several birds also visited the ships; three, of a small kind which keep about groves and orchards, came singing in the morning, and flew away again in the evening. Their song cheered the hearts of the dismayed mariners, who hailed it as the voice of land. The larger fowl, they observed, were strong of wing, and might venture far to sea; but such small birds were too feeble to fly far, and their singing showed that they were not exhausted by their flight.

On the following day there was either a profound calm, or light winds from the southwest. The sea, as far as the eye could reach, was covered with weeds; a phenomenon, often observed in this part of the ocean, which has sometimes the appearance of a vast inundated meadow. This has been attributed to immense quantities of submarine plants, which grow at the bottom of the sea until ripe, when they are detached by the motion of the waves and currents, and rise to the surface.[2] These fields of weeds were at first regarded with great satisfaction, but at length they became, in many places, so dense and matted, as in some degree to impede the sailing of the ships, which must have been under very little headway. The crews now called to mind some tale about the frozen ocean, where ships were said to be sometimes fixed immovable. They endeavored, therefore, to avoid as much as possible these floating masses, lest

[1] Mucho me fue necesario este viento contrario, porque mi gente andaban muy estimulados, que pensaban que no ventaban estos mares vientos para volver á España. Primer Viage de Colon. Navarrete, tom. i. p. 12.

[2] Humboldt, Personal Narrative, book i. cap. 1.

some disaster of the kind might happen to themselves.[1] Others considered these weeds as proof that the sea was growing shallower, and began to talk of lurking rocks, and shoals, and treacherous quicksands; and of the danger of running aground, as it were, in the midst of the ocean, where their vessels might rot and fall to pieces, far out of the track of human aid, and without any shore where the crews might take refuge. They had evidently some confused notion of the ancient story of the sunken island of Atalantis, and feared that they were arriving at that part of the ocean where navigation was said to be obstructed by drowned lands, and the ruins of an ingulfed country.

To dispel these fears, the admiral had frequent recourse to the lead; but though he sounded with a deep-sea line, he still found no bottom. The minds of the crews, however, had gradually become diseased. They were full of vague terrors and superstitious fancies: they construed every thing into a cause of alarm, and harassed their commander by incessant murmurs.

For three days there was a continuance of light summer airs from the southward and westward, and the sea was as smooth as a mirror. A whale was seen heaving up its huge form at a distance, which Columbus immediately pointed out as a favorable indication, affirming that these fish were generally in the neighborhood of land. The crews, however, became uneasy at the calmness of the weather. They observed that the contrary winds which they experienced were transient and unsteady, and so light as not to ruffle the surface of the sea, which maintained a sluggish calm like a lake of dead water. Every thing differed, they said, in these strange regions from the world to which they had been accustomed. The only winds which prevailed with any constancy and force, were from the east, and they had not power to disturb the torpid stillness of the ocean; there was a risk, therefore, either of perishing amidst stagnant

[1] Hist. del Almirante, cap. 18.

and shoreless waters, or of being prevented, by contrary winds, from ever returning to their native country.

Columbus continued with admirable patience to reason with these fancies; observing that the calmness of the sea must undoubtedly be caused by the vicinity of land in the quarter whence the wind blew, which, therefore, had not space sufficient to act upon the surface, and heave up large waves. Terror, however, multiplies and varies the forms of ideal danger, a thousand times faster than the most active wisdom can dispel them. The more Columbus argued, the more boisterous became the murmurs of his crew, until, on Sunday, the 25th of September, there came on a heavy swell of the sea, unaccompanied by wind. This phenomenon often occurs in the broad ocean; being either the expiring undulations of some past gale, or the movement given to the sea by some distant current of wind; it was, nevertheless, regarded with astonishment by the mariners, and dispelled the imaginary terrors occasioned by the calm.

Columbus, who as usual considered himself under the immediate eye and guardianship of Heaven in this solemn enterprise, intimates in his journal that this swelling of the sea seemed providentially ordered to allay the rising clamors of his crew; comparing it to that which so miraculously aided Moses when conducting the children of Israel out of the captivity of Egypt.[1]

[1] "Como la mar estuviese mansa y llana murmuraba la gente diciendo que, pues por alli no habia mar grande que nunca ventaria para volver á España; pero despues alzóse mucho la mar y sin viento, que los asombraba; por lo cual dice aqui el Almirante; *asi que muy necesario me fué la mar alta, que no pareció, salvo el tiempo de los Judios cuando salieron de Egipto contra Moyses que los sacaba de captiverio.*"—Journal of Columb., Navarrete, tom. i. p. 12.

CHAPTER IV.

CONTINUATION OF THE VOYAGE.—DISCOVERY OF LAND.

[1492.]

THE situation of Columbus was daily becoming more and more critical. In proportion as he approached the regions where he expected to find land, the impatience of his crews augmented. The favorable signs which increased his confidence, were derided by them as delusive; and there was danger of their rebelling, and obliging him to turn back; when on the point of realizing the object of all his labors. They beheld themselves with dismay still wafted onward, over the boundless wastes of what appeared to them a mere watery desert, surrounding the habitable world. What was to become of them should their provisions fail? Their ships were too weak and defective even for the great voyage they had already made, but if they were still to press forward, adding at every moment to the immense expanse behind them, how should they ever be able to return, having no intervening port where they might victual and refit?

In this way they fed each other's discontents, gathering together in little knots, and fomenting a spirit of mutinous opposition: and when we consider the natural fire of the Spanish temperament and its impatience of control; and that a great part of these men were sailing on compulsion; we cannot wonder that there was imminent danger of their breaking forth into open rebellion and compelling Columbus to turn back. In their secret conferences they exclaimed against him as a desperado, bent, in a mad phantasy, upon doing something extravagant to render himself notorious. What were their sufferings and dangers to one evidently content to sacrifice his own life for the chance of distinction? What obligations bound them to continue on with him; or when were the terms of their agreement to be considered as fulfilled? They had already penetrated unknown seas, untraversed by a sail, far beyond where man had ever before ventured. They had done enough to gain themselves a character for courage and hardihood in undertaking such an enterprise and persisting in it so far. How much further were they to go in quest of a merely conjectured land? Were they to sail on until they perished, or until all return became impossible? In such case they would be the authors of their own destruction.

On the other hand, should they consult their safety, and turn back before too late, who would blame them? Any complaints made by Columbus would be of no weight; he was a foreigner, without friends or influence; his schemes had been condemned by the learned, and discountenanced by people of all ranks. He had no party to uphold him, and a host of opponents whose pride of opinion would be gratified by his failure. Or, as an effectual means of preventing his complaints, they might throw him into the sea, and give out that he had fallen overboard while busy with his instruments contemplating the stars; a report which no one would have either the inclination or the means to controvert.[1]

Columbus was not ignorant of the mutinous disposition of his crew, but he still maintained a serene and steady countenance; soothing some with gentle words; endeavoring to stimulate the pride or avarice of others, and openly menacing the refractory with signal punishment, should they do any thing to impede the voyage.

On the 25th of September, the wind again became favorable, and they were able to resume their course directly to the west. The airs being light, and the sea calm, the vessels sailed near to each other, and Columbus had much conversation with Martin Alonzo Pinzon on the

[1] Hist. del Almirante, cap. 19. Herrera, Hist. Ind., decad. i. lib. i. cap. 10.

subject of a chart, which the former had sent three days before on board of the Pinta. Pinzon thought that, according to the indications of the map, they ought to be in the neighborhood of Cipango, and the other islands which the admiral had therein delineated. Columbus partly entertained the same idea, but thought it possible that the ships might have been borne out of their track by the prevalent currents, or that they had not come so far as the pilots had reckoned. He desired that the chart might be returned, and Pinzon, tying it to the end of a cord, flung it on board to him. While Columbus, his pilot, and several of his experienced mariners were studying the map, and endeavoring to make out from it their actual position, they heard a shout from the Pinta, and looking up, beheld Martin Alonzo Pinzon mounted on the stern of his vessel, crying, "Land! land! Señor, I claim my reward!" He pointed at the same time to the southwest, where there was indeed an appearance of land at about twenty-five leagues' distance. Upon this Columbus threw himself on his knees and returned thanks to God; and Martin Alonzo repeated the *Gloria in excelsis*, in which he was joined by his own crew and that of the admiral.[1]

The seamen now mounted to the mast-head or climbed about the rigging, straining their eyes in the direction pointed out. The conviction became so general of land in that quarter, and the joy of the people so ungovernable, that Columbus found it necessary to vary from his usual course, and stand all night to the southwest. The morning light, however, put an end to all their hopes, as to a dream. The fancied land proved to be nothing but an evening cloud, and had vanished in the night. With dejected hearts they once more resumed their western course, from which Columbus would never have varied, but in compliance with their clamorous wishes.

For several days they continued on with the same pro-

[1] Journal of Columb., Primer Viage, Navarrete, tom. i.

pitious breeze, tranquil sea, and mild, delightful weather. The water was so calm that the sailors amused themselves with swimming about the vessel. Dolphins began to abound, and flying fish, darting into the air, fell-upon the decks. The continued signs of land diverted the attention of the crews, and insensibly beguiled them onward.

On the 1st of October, according to the reckoning of the pilot of the admiral's ship, they had come five hundred and eighty leagues west since leaving the Canary islands. The reckoning which Columbus showed the crew was five hundred and eighty-four, but the reckoning which he kept privately was seven hundred and seven.[1] On the following day, the weeds floated from east to west; and on the third day no birds were to be seen.

The crews now began to fear that they had passed between islands, from one to the other of which the birds had been flying. Columbus had also some doubts of the kind, but refused to alter his westward course. The people again uttered murmurs and menaces; but on the following day they were visited by such flights of birds, and the various indications of land became so numerous, that from a state of despondency they passed to one of confident expectation.

Eager to obtain the promised pension, the seamen were continually giving the cry of land, on the least appearance of the kind. To put a stop to these false alarms, which produced continual disappointments, Columbus declared that should any one give such notice, and land not be discovered within three days afterwards, he should thenceforth forfeit all claim to the reward.

On the evening of the 6th of October, Martin Alonzo Pinzon began to lose confidence in their present course, and proposed that they should stand more to the southward. Columbus, however, still persisted in steering directly west.[2]

[1] Navarrete, tom. i. p. 16.
[2] Journ. of Columbus, Navarrete, tom. i. p. 17.

Observing this difference of opinion in a person so important in his squadron as Pinzon, and fearing that chance or design might scatter the ships, he ordered that, should either of the caravels be separated from him, it should stand to the west, and endeavor as soon as possible to join company again: he directed, also, that the vessels should keep near to him at sunrise and sunset, as at these times the state of the atmosphere is most favorable to the discovery of distant land.

On the morning of the 7th of October, at sunrise, several of the admiral's crew thought they beheld land in the west, but so indistinctly that no one ventured to proclaim it, lest he should be mistaken, and forfeit all chance of the reward: the Niña, however, being a good sailer, pressed forward to ascertain the fact. In a little while a flag was hoisted at her mast-head, and a gun discharged, being the preconcerted signals for land. New joy was awakened throughout the little squadron, and every eye was turned to the west. As they advanced, however, their cloud-built hopes faded away, and before evening the fancied land had again melted into air.[1]

The crews now sank into a degree of dejection proportioned to their recent excitement; but new circumstances occurred to arouse them. Columbus, having observed great flights of small field-birds going towards the southwest, concluded they must be secure of some neighboring land, where they would find food and a resting-place. He knew the importance which the Portuguese voyagers attached to the flight of birds, by following which they had discovered most of their islands. He had now come seven hundred and fifty leagues, the distance at which he had computed to find the island of Cipango; as there was no appearance of it, he might have missed it through some mistake in the latitude. He determined, therefore, on the

[1] Hist. del Almirante, cap. 20. Journ. of Columbus, Navarrete, tom. i.

evening of the 7th of October, to alter his course to the west-southwest, the direction in which the birds generally flew, and continue that direction for at least two days. After all, it was no great deviation from his main course, and would meet the wishes of the Pinzons, as well as be inspiriting to his followers generally.

For three days they stood in this direction, and the further they went the more frequent and encouraging were the signs of land. Flights of small birds of various colors, some of them such as sing in the fields, came flying about the ships, and then continued towards the southwest, and others were heard also flying by in the night. Tunny fish played about the smooth sea, and a heron, a pelican, and a duck were seen, all bound in the same direction. The herbage which floated by was fresh and green, as if recently from land, and the air, Columbus observes, was sweet and fragrant as April breezes in Seville

All these, however, were regarded by the crews as so many delusions beguiling them on to destruction; and when on the evening of the third day they beheld the sun go down upon a shoreless horizon, they broke forth into turbulent clamor. They exclaimed against this obstinacy in tempting fate by continuing on into a boundless sea. They insisted upon turning homeward, and abandoning the voyage as hopeless. Columbus endeavored to pacify them by gentle words and promises of large rewards; but finding that they only increased in clamor, he assumed a decided tone. He told them it was useless to murmur; the expedition had been sent by the sovereigns to seek the Indies, and, happen what might, he was determined to persevere, until, by the blessing of God, he should accomplish the enterprise.[1]

[1] Hist. del Almirante, cap. 20. Las Casas, lib. i. Journal of Columb., Navarrete, Colec., tom. i. p. 19.

It has been asserted by various historians, that Columbus, a day or two previous to coming in sight of the New World, capitulated with

Columbus was now at open defiance with his crew, and his situation became desperate. Fortunately the manifesta-

his mutinous crew, promising, if he did not discover land within three days, to abandon the voyage. There is no authority for such an assertion either in the history of his son Fernando or that of the Bishop Las Casas, each of whom had the admiral's papers before him. There is no mention of such a circumstance in the extracts made from the journal by Las Casas, which have recently been brought to light; nor is it asserted by either Peter Martyr or the Curate of Los Palacios, both contemporaries and acquaintances of Columbus, and who could scarcely have failed to mention so striking a fact, if true. It rests merely upon the authority of Oviedo, who is of inferior credit to either of the authors above cited, and was grossly misled as to many of the particulars of this voyage by a pilot of the name of Hernan Perez Matheo, who was hostile to Columbus. In the manuscript process of the memorable lawsuit between Don Diego, son of the admiral, and the fiscal of the crown, is the evidence of one Pedro de Bilbao, who testifies that he heard many times that some of the pilots and mariners wished to turn back, but that the admiral promised them presents, and entreated them to wait two or three days, before which time he should discover land. ("Pedro de Bilbao oyo muchas veces que algunos pilotos y marineros querian volverse sino fuera por el Almirante que les prometio donos, les rogó esperasen dos o tres dias i que antes del termino descubriera tierra.") This, if true, implies no capitulation to relinquish the enterprise.

On the other hand, it was asserted by some of the witnesses in the above-mentioned suit, that Columbus, after having proceeded some few hundred leagues without finding land, lost confidence and wished to turn back; but was persuaded and even piqued to continue by the Pinzons. This assertion carries falsehood on its very face. It is in total contradiction to that persevering constancy and undaunted resolution displayed by Columbus, not merely in the present voyage, but from first to last of his difficult and dangerous career. This testimony was given by some of the mutinous men, anxious to exaggerate the merits of the Pinzons, and to depreciate that of Columbus. Fortunately, the extracts from the journal of the latter, written from day to day with guileless simplicity, and all the air of truth, disprove these fables, and show that on the very day previous to his discovery, he expressed a peremptory determination to persevere, in defiance of all dangers and difficulties.

tions of the vicinity of land were such on the following day
as no longer to admit a doubt. Beside a quantity of fresh
weeds, such as grow in rivers, they saw a green fish of a
kind which keeps about rocks; then a branch of thorn
with berries on it, and recently separated from the tree,
floated by them; then they picked up a reed, a small
board, and, above all, a staff artificially carved. All
gloom and mutiny now gave way to sanguine expectation; and throughout the day each one was eagerly on the
watch, in hopes of being the first to discover the long-
sought-for land.

In the evening, when, according to invariable custom on
board of the admiral's ship, the mariners had sung the
salve regina, or vesper hymn to the Virgin, he made an impressive address to his crew. He pointed out the goodness
of God in thus conducting them by soft and favoring
breezes across a tranquil ocean, cheering their hopes continually with fresh signs, increasing as their fears augmented,
and thus leading and guiding them to a promised land.
He now reminded them of the orders he had given on leaving the Canaries, that, after sailing westward seven hundred
leagues, they should not make sail after midnight. Present
appearances authorized such a precaution. He thought it
probable they would make land that very night; he
ordered, therefore, a vigilant look-out to be kept from the
forecastle, promising to whomsoever should make the discovery a doublet of velvet, in addition to the pension to be
given by the sovereigns.[1]

The breeze had been fresh all day, with more sea than
usual, and they had made great progress. At sunset they
had stood again to the west, and were ploughing the waves
at a rapid rate, the Pinta keeping the lead, from her
superior sailing. The greatest animation prevailed throughout the ships; not an eye was closed that night. As the
evening darkened, Columbus took his station on the top of

[1] Hist del Almirante, cap. 21.

the castle or cabin on the high poop of his vessel, ranging his eye along the dusky horizon, and maintaining an intense and unremitting watch. About ten o'clock, he thought he beheld a light glimmering at a great distance. Fearing his eager hopes might deceive him, he called to Pedro Gutierrez, gentleman of the king's bed-chamber, and inquired whether he saw such a light; the latter replied in the affirmative. Doubtful whether it might not yet be some delusion of the fancy, Columbus called Rodrigo Sanchez of Segovia, and made the same inquiry. By the time the latter had ascended the round-house, the light had disappeared. They saw it once or twice afterwards in sudden and passing gleams; as if it were a torch in the bark of a fisherman, rising and sinking with the waves; or in the hand of some person on shore, borne up and down as he walked from house to house. So transient and uncertain were these gleams, that few attached any importance to them; Columbus, however, considered them as certain signs of land, and, moreover, that the land was inhabited.

They continued their course until two in the morning, when a gun from the Pinta gave the joyful signal of land. It was first descried by a mariner named Rodrigo de Triana; but the reward was afterwards adjudged to the admiral, for having previously perceived the light. The land was now clearly seen about two leagues distant, whereupon they took in sail, and laid to, waiting impatiently for the dawn.

The thoughts and feelings of Columbus in this little space of time must have been tumultuous and intense. At length, in spite of every difficulty and danger, he had accomplished his object. The great mystery of the ocean was revealed; his theory, which had been the scoff of sages, · was triumphantly established; he had secured to himself a glory durable as the world itself.

It is difficult to conceive the feelings of such a man, at such a moment; or the conjectures which must have

thronged upon his mind, as to the land before him, covered with darkness.   That it was fruitful, was evident from
the vegetables which floated from its shores.   He thought,
too, that he perceived the fragrance of aromatic groves.
The moving light he had beheld proved it the residence of
man.   But what were its inhabitants?   Were they like
those of the other parts of the globe; or were they some
strange and monstrous race, such as the imagination was
prone in those times to give to all remote and unknown
regions?   Had he come upon some wild island far in the
Indian sea; or was this the famed Cipango itself, the object
of his golden fancies?   A thousand speculations of the
kind must have swarmed upon him, as, with his anxious
crews, he waited for the night to pass away; wondering
whether the morning light would reveal a savage wilderness, or dawn upon spicy groves, and glittering fanes, and
gilded cities, and all the splendor of oriental civilization.

BOOK IV.

CHAPTER I.

FIRST LANDING OF COLUMBUS IN THE NEW WORLD.

IT was on Friday morning, the 12th of October, that Columbus first beheld the new world. As the day dawned he saw before him a level island, several leagues in extent, and covered with trees like a continual orchard. Though apparently uncultivated, it was populous, for the inhabitants were seen issuing from all parts of the woods and running to the shore. They were perfectly naked, and, as they stood gazing at the ships, appeared by their attitudes and gestures to be lost in astonishment. Columbus made signal for the ships to cast anchor, and the boats to be manned and armed. He entered his own boat, richly attired in scarlet, and holding the royal standard; whilst Martin Alonzo Pinzon, and Vincent Jañez, his brother, put off in company in their boats, each with a banner of the enterprise emblazoned with a green cross, having on either side the letters F. and Y., the initials of the Castilian monarchs Fernando and Ysabel, surmounted by crowns.

As he approached the shore, Columbus, who was disposed for all kinds of agreeable impressions, was delighted with the purity and suavity of the atmosphere, the crystal transparency of the sea, and the extraordinary beauty of the vegetation. He beheld, also, fruits of an unknown kind upon the trees which overhung the shores. On landing he threw himself on his knees, kissed the earth, and returned thanks to God with tears of joy. His ex-

ample was followed by the rest, whose hearts indeed overflowed with the same feelings of gratitude. Columbus then
rising drew his sword, displayed the royal standard, and
assembling round him the two captains, with Rodrigo de
Escobedo, notary of the armament, Rodrigo Sanchez, and
the rest who had landed, he took solemn possession in the
name of the Castilian sovereigns, giving the island the
name of San Salvador. Having complied with the requisite
forms and ceremonies, he called upon all present to take the
oath of obedience to him, as admiral and viceroy, representing the persons of the sovereigns.[1]

The feelings of the crew now burst forth in the most
extravagant transports. They had recently considered
themselves devoted men, hurrying forward to destruction ;
they now looked upon themselves as favorites of fortune,
and gave themselves up to the most unbounded joy. They
thronged around the admiral with overflowing zeal, some
embracing him, others kissing his hands. Those who had
been most mutinous and turbulent during the voyage, were
now most devoted and enthusiastic. Some begged favors
of him, as if he had already wealth and honors in his gift.
Many abject spirits, who had outraged him by their insolence, now crouched at his feet, begging pardon for all the
trouble they had caused him, and promising the blindest
obedience for the future.[2]

The natives of the island, when, at the dawn of day, they
had beheld the ships hovering on their coast, had supposed

---

[1] In the Tablas Chronologicas of Padre Claudio Clemente, is con-
served a form of prayer, said to have been used by Columbus on this
occasion, and which, by order of the Castilian sovereigns, was afterwards used by Balboa, Cortez, and Pizarro in their discoveries.
"Domine Deus æterne et omnipotens, sacro tuo verbo cœlum, et
terram, et mare creasti ; benedicatur el glorificetur nomen tuum,
laudetur tua majestas, quæ dignita est per humilem servum tuum, ut
ejus sacrum nomen agnoscatur, et prædicetur in hac altera mundi
parte." Tab. Chron. de los Descub., decad. i. Valencia, 1689.

[2] Oviedo, lib. i. cap. 6. Las Casas, Hist. Ind., lib. i. cap. 40.

them monsters which had issued from the deep during the night. They had crowded to the beach, and watched their movements with awful anxiety. Their veering about, apparently without effort, and the shifting and furling of their sails, resembling huge wings, filled them with astonishment. When they beheld their boats approach the shore, and a number of strange beings clad in glittering steel, or raiment of various colors, landing upon the beach, they fled in affright to the woods. Finding, however, that there was no attempt to pursue nor molest them, they gradually recovered from their terror, and approached the Spaniards with great awe; frequently prostrating themselves on the earth, and making signs of adoration. During the ceremonies of taking possession, they remained gazing in timid admiration at the complexion, the beards, the shining armor, and splendid dress of the Spaniards. The admiral particularly attracted their attention, from his commanding height, his air of authority, his dress of scarlet, and the deference which was paid him by his companions; all which pointed him out to be the commander.[1] When they had still further recovered from their fears, they approached the Spaniards, touched their beards, and examined their hands and faces, admiring their whiteness. Columbus was pleased with their gentleness and confiding simplicity, and suffered their scrutiny with perfect acquiescence, winning them by his benignity. They now supposed that the ships had sailed out of the crystal firmament which bounded their horizon, or had descended from above on their ample wings, and that these marvelous beings were inhabitants of the skies.[2]

[1] Las Casas, ubi sup.

[2] The idea that the white men came from heaven was universally entertained by the inhabitants of the New World. When in the course of subsequent voyages the Spaniards conversed with the cacique Nicaragua, he inquired how they came down from the skies, whether flying or whether they descended on clouds. Herrera, decad. iii. lib. iv. cap. 5.

The natives of the island were no less objects of curiosity to the Spaniards, differing, as they did, from any race of men they had ever seen. Their appearance gave no promise of either wealth or civilization, for they were entirely naked, and painted with a variety of colors. With some it was confined merely to a part of the face, the nose, or around the eyes; with others it extended to the whole body, and gave them a wild and fantastic appearance. Their complexion was of a tawny or copper hue, and they were entirely destitute of beards. Their hair was not crisped, like the recently-discovered tribes of the African coast, under the same latitude, but straight and coarse, partly cut short above the ears, but some locks were left long behind and falling upon their shoulders. Their features, though obscured and disfigured by paint, were agreeable; they had lofty foreheads and remarkably fine eyes. They were of moderate stature and well-shaped; most of them appeared to be under thirty years of age : there was but one female with them, quite young, naked like her companions, and beautifully formed.

As Columbus supposed himself to have landed on an island at the extremity of India, he called the natives by the general appellation of Indians, which was universally adopted before the true nature of his discovery was known, and has since been extended to all the aboriginals of the New World.

The islanders were friendly and gentle. Their only arms were lances, hardened at the end by fire, or pointed with a flint, or the teeth or bone of a fish. There was no iron to be seen, nor did they appear acquainted with its properties; for, when a drawn sword was presented to them, they unguardedly took it by the edge.

Columbus distributed among them colored caps, glass beads, hawks' bells, and other trifles, such as the Portuguese were accustomed to trade with among the nations of the gold coast of Africa. They received them eagerly, hung the beads round their necks, and were wonderfully pleased with their finery, and with the sound of the bells. The Spaniards remained all day on shore, refreshing themselves after their anxious voyage amidst the beautiful groves of the island; and returned on board late in the evening, delighted with all they had seen.

On the following morning, at break of day, the shore was thronged with the natives; some swam off to the ships, others came in light barks which they called canoes, formed of a single tree, hollowed, and capable of holding from one man to the number of forty or fifty. These they managed dextrously with paddles, and, if overturned, swam about in the water with perfect unconcern, as if in their natural element, righting their canoes with great facility, and baluing them with calabashes.[1]

They were eager to procure more toys and trinkets, not, apparently, from any idea of their intrinsic value, but because every thing from the hands of the strangers possessed a supernatural virtue in their eyes, as having been brought from heaven; they even picked up fragments of glass and earthenware as valuable prizes. They had but few objects to offer in return, except parrots, of which great numbers were domesticated among them, and cotton yarn, of which they had abundance, and would exchange large balls of five and twenty pounds' weight for the merest trifle. They brought also cakes of a kind of bread called cassava, which constituted a principal part of their food, and was afterwards an important article of provisions with the Spaniards. It was formed from a great root called yuca, which they cultivated in fields. This they cut into small morsels, which they grated or scraped, and strained in a press, making a broad thin cake, which was afterwards dried hard, and would keep for a long time, being steeped in water

---

[1] The calabashes of the Indians, which served the purposes of glass and earthenware, supplying them with all sorts of domestic utensils, were produced on stately trees of the size of elms.

when eaten. It was insipid, but nourishing, though the
water strained from it in the preparation was a deadly
poison. There was another kind of yuca destitute of this
poisonous quality, which was eaten in the root, either boiled
or roasted.[1]

The avarice of the discoverers was quickly excited by
the sight of small ornaments of gold, worn by some of the
natives in their noses. These the latter gladly exchanged
for glass beads and hawks' bells; and both parties exulted
in the bargain, no doubt admiring each others' simplicity.
As gold, however, was an object of royal monopoly in all
enterprises of discovery, Columbus forbade any traffic in it
without his express sanction; and he put the same prohi-
bition on the traffic for cotton, reserving to the crown all
trade for it, wherever it should be found in any quantity.

He inquired of the natives where this gold was procured.
They answered him by signs, pointing to the south, where, he
understood them, dwelt a king of such wealth that he was
served in vessels of wrought gold. He understood, also,
that there was land to the south, the southwest, and the northwest; and that the people from the last-mentioned quarter
frequently proceeded to the southwest in quest of gold and
precious stones, making in their way descents upon the
islands, and carrying off the inhabitants. Several of the
natives showed him scars of wounds received in battles
with these invaders. It is evident that a great part of this
fancied intelligence was self-delusion on the part of Columbus; for he was under a spell of the imagination, which
gave its own shapes and colors to every object. He was
persuaded that he had arrived among the islands described
by Marco Polo, as lying opposite Cathay, in the Chinese
sea, and he construed every thing to accord with the account
given of those opulent regions. Thus the enemies which
the natives spoke of as coming from the northwest, he concluded to be the people of the main-land of Asia, the sub-

[1] Acosta, Hist. Ind., lib. iv. cap. 17.

jects of the great Khan of Tartary, who were represented by the Venetian traveler as accustomed to make war upon the islands, and to enslave their inhabitants. The country to the south, abounding in gold, could be no other than the famous island of Cipango; and the king who was served out of vessels of gold, must be the monarch whose magnificent city and gorgeous palace, covered with plates of gold, had been extolled in such splendid terms by Marco Polo.

The island where Columbus had thus, for the first time, set his foot upon the New World, was called by the natives, Guanahanè. It still retains the name of San Salvador, which he gave to it, though called by the English, Cat Island.[1] The light which he had seen the evening previous to his making land, may have been on Watling's Island, which lies a few leagues to the east. San Salvador is one of the great cluster of the Lucayos, or Bahama Islands, which stretch southeast and northwest, from the coast of Florida to Hispaniola, covering the northern coast of Cuba.

On the morning of the 14th of October, the admiral set off at daybreak with the boats of the ships to reconnoitre the island, directing his course to the northeast. The coast was surrounded by a reef of rocks, within which there was depth of water and sufficient harbor to receive all the ships in Christendom. The entrance was very narrow; within there were several sand-banks, but the water was as still as in a pool.[2]

The island appeared throughout to be well wooded, with streams of water, and a large lake in the centre. As the boats proceeded, they passed two or three villages, the inhabitants of which, men as well as women, ran to the

[1] Some dispute having recently arisen as to the island on which Columbus first landed, the reader is referred for a discussion of this question to the Illustrations of this work, article "First Landing of Columbus."

[2] Primer Viage de Colon. Navarrete, tom. i.

shores, throwing themselves on the ground, lifting up their hands and eyes, either giving thanks to Heaven, or worshiping the Spaniards as supernatural beings. They ran along parallel to the boats, calling after the Spaniards, and inviting them by signs to land, offering them various fruits and vessels of water. Finding, however, that the boats continued on their course, many threw themselves into the sea and swam after them, and others followed in canoes. The admiral received them all with kindness, giving them glass beads and other trifles, which were received with transport as celestial presents, for the invariable idea of the savages was, that the white men had come from the skies.

In this way they pursued their course, until they came to a small peninsula, which with two or three days' labor might be separated from the main-land and surrounded with water, and was therefore specified by Columbus as an excellent situation for a fortress. On this were six Indian cabins, surrounded by groves and gardens as beautiful as those of Castile. The sailors being wearied with rowing, and the island not appearing to the admiral of sufficient importance to induce colonization, he returned to the ships, taking seven of the natives with him, that they might acquire the Spanish language and serve as interpreters.

Having taken in a supply of wood and water, they left the island of San Salvador the same evening, the admiral being impatient to arrive at the wealthy country to the south, which he flattered himself would prove the famous island of Cipango.

CHAPTER II.

CRUISE AMONG THE BAHAMA ISLANDS.

[1492.]

On leaving San Salvador, Columbus was at a loss which way to direct his course. A great number of islands, green and level and fertile, invited him in different directions. The Indians on board of his vessel intimated by signs that they were innumerable, well peopled, and at war with one another. They mentioned the names of above a hundred. Columbus now had no longer a doubt that he was among the islands described by Marco Polo as studding the vast sea of Chin, or China, and lying at a great distance from the main-land. These, according to the Venetian, amounted to between seven and eight thousand, and abounded with drugs and spices and odoriferous trees; together with gold and silver and many other precious objects of commerce.[1]

Animated by the idea of exploring this opulent archipelago, he selected the largest island in sight for his next visit; it appeared to be about five leagues' distance, and he understood from his Indians, that the natives were richer than those of San Salvador, wearing bracelets and anklets, and other ornaments of massive gold.

The night coming on, Columbus ordered that the ships should lie to, as the navigation was difficult and dangerous among these unknown islands, and he feared to venture upon a strange coast in the dark. In the morning they again made sail, but meeting with counter-currents, it was not until sunset that they anchored at the island. The next morning (16th) they went on shore, and Columbus took solemn possession, giving the island the name of Santa Maria de la Concepcion. The same scene occurred with the inhabitants as with those of San Salvador. They

[1] Marco Polo, book iii. chap. 4; Eng. translation by W. Marsden.

manifested the same astonishment and awe; the same
gentleness and simplicity, and the same nakedness and
absence of all wealth. Columbus looked in vain for
bracelets and anklets of gold, or for any other precious
articles: they had been either fictions of his Indian guides,
or his own misinterpretations.

Returning on board, he prepared to make sail, when one
of the Indians of San Salvador, who was on board of the
Niña, plunged into the sea, and swam to a large canoe
filled with natives. The boat of the caravel put off in
pursuit, but the Indians managed in their light bark with
too much velocity to be overtaken, and, reaching the land,
fled to the woods. The sailors took the canoe as a prize,
and returned on board the caravel. Shortly afterwards a
small canoe approached one of the ships, from a different
part of the island, with a single Indian on board, who came
to offer a ball of cotton in exchange for hawks' bells. As
he paused when close to the vessel, and feared to enter,
several sailors threw themselves into the sea and took him
prisoner.

Columbus, having seen all that passed from his station
on the high poop of the vessel, ordered the captive to be
brought to him; he came trembling with fear, and humbly
offered his ball of cotton as a gift. The admiral received
him with the utmost benignity, and declining his offering,
put a colored cap upon his head, strings of green beads
around his arms, and hawks' bells in his ears, then ordering
him and his ball of cotton to be replaced in the canoe, dismissed him, astonished and overjoyed. He ordered that
the canoe, also, which had been seized and was fastened to
the Niña, should be cast loose, to be regained by its pro-
prietors. When the Indian reached the shore, his countrymen thronged round him, examining and admiring his
finery, and listening to his account of the kind treatment
he experienced.

Such were the gentle and sage precautions continually

taken by Columbus to impress the natives favorably. Another instance of the kind occurred after leaving the island of Conception, when the caravels stood for the larger island, several leagues to the west. Midway between the two islands, they overtook a single Indian in a canoe. He had a mere morsel of cassava bread and a calabash of water for sea-stores, and a little red paint, like dragon's blood, for personal decoration when he should land. A string of glass beads, such as had been given to the natives of San Salvador, showed that he had come thence, and was probably passing from island to island, to give notice of the ships. Columbus admired the hardihood of this simple navigator, making such an extensive voyage in so frail a bark. As the island was still distant, he ordered that both the Indian and his canoe should be taken on board; where he treated him with the greatest kindness, giving him bread and honey to eat, and wine to drink. The weather being very calm, they did not reach the island until too dark to anchor, through fear of cutting their cables with rocks. The sea about these islands was so transparent, that in the daytime they could see the bottom and choose their ground; and so deep, that at two gun-shot distance there was no anchorage. Hoisting out the canoe of their Indian voyager, therefore, and restoring to him all his effects, they sent him joyfully ashore, to prepare the natives for their arrival, while the ships lay to until morning.

This kindness had the desired effect. The natives surrounded the ships in their canoes during the night, bringing fruits and roots, and the pure water of their springs. Columbus distributed trifling presents among them, and to those who came on board he gave sugar and honey.

Landing the next morning, he gave to this island the name of Fernandina, in honor of the king; it is the same at present called Exuma. The inhabitants were similar in every respect to those of the preceding islands, excepting that they appeared more ingenious and intelligent. Some

10

of the women wore mantles and aprons of cotton, but for
the most part they were entirely naked. Their habitations
were constructed in the form of a pavilion or high circular
tent, of branches of trees, of reeds and palm leaves. They
were kept very clean and neat, and sheltered under spreading trees. For beds they had nets of cotton extended from
two posts, which they called *hamacs*, a name since in universal use among seamen.

In endeavoring to circumnavigate the island, Columbus
found, within two leagues of the northwest cape, a noble
harbor, sufficient to hold a hundred ships, with two entrances
formed by an island which lay in the mouth of it. Here,
while the men landed with the casks in search of water, he
reposed under the shade of the groves, which he says were
more beautiful than any he had ever beheld; "the country
was as fresh and green as in the month of May in Andalusia; the trees, the fruits, the herbs, the flowers, the very
stones for the most part, as different from those of Spain
as night from day." [1] The inhabitants gave the same
proofs as the other islanders, of being totally unaccustomed
to the sight of civilized man. They regarded the Spaniards
with awe and admiration, approached them with propitia-
tory offerings of whatever their poverty, or rather their
simple and natural mode of life, afforded; the fruits of
their fields and groves, the cotton, which was their article
of greatest value, and their domesticated parrots. They
took those who were in search of water to the coolest
springs, the sweetest and freshest runs, filling their casks,
and rolling them to the boats; thus seeking in every way
to gratify their celestial visitors.

However pleasing this state of primeval poverty might
be to the imagination of a poet, it was a source of continual
disappointment to the Spaniards, whose avarice had been
whetted to the quick by scanty specimens of gold, and by

---

[1] Primer Viage de Colon. Navarrete lib. i.

the information of golden islands continually given by the Indians.

Leaving Fernandina, on the 19th of October, they steered to the southeast in quest of an island called Saometo, where Columbus understood, from the signs of the guides, there was a mine of gold, and a king, the sovereign of all the surrounding islands, who dwelt in a large city and possessed great treasures, wearing rich clothing and jewels of gold. They found the island, but neither the monarch nor the mine; either Columbus had misunderstood the natives, or they, measuring things by their own poverty, had exaggerated the paltry state and trivial ornaments of some savage chieftain. Delightful as the other islands had appeared, Columbus declared that this surpassed them all. Like those, it was covered with trees and shrubs and herbs of unknown kind. The climate had the same soft temperature; the air was delicate and balmy; the land was higher, with a fine verdant hill; the coast of a fine sand, gently laved by transparent billows.

At the southwest end of the island he found fine lakes of fresh water, overhung with groves, and surrounded by banks covered with herbage. Here he ordered all the casks of the ships to be filled. "Here are large lakes," says he, in his journal, "and the groves about them are marvelous, and here and in all the island every thing is green, as in April in Andalusia. The singing of the birds is such, that it seems as if one would never desire to depart hence. There are flocks of parrots which obscure the sun, and other birds, large and small, of so many kinds, all different from ours, that it is wonderful; and beside, there are trees of a thousand species, each having its particular fruit and all of marvelous flavor, so that I am in the greatest trouble in the world not to know them, for I am very certain that they are each of great value. I shall bring home some of them as specimens, and also some of the herbs." To this beautiful island he gave the name of his royal patroness,

Isabella, it is the same at present called Isla Larga and Exumeta. Columbus was intent on discovering the drugs and spices of the east, and on approaching this island, had fancied he perceived in the air the spicy odors said to be wafted from the islands of the Indian seas. "As I arrived at this cape," says he, "there came thence a fragrance so good and soft of the flowers or trees of the land, that it was the sweetest thing in the world. I believe there are here many herbs and trees which would be of great price in Spain for tinctures, medicines, and spices, but I know nothing of them, which gives me great concern." [1]

The fish, which abounded in these seas, partook of the novelty which characterized most of the objects in this new world. They rivaled the birds in tropical brilliancy of color, the scales of some of them glancing back the rays of light like precious stones; as they sported about the ships, they flashed gleams of gold and silver through the clear waves; and the dolphins, taken out of their element, delighted the eye with the changes of colors ascribed in fable to the chameleon.

No animals were seen in these islands, excepting a species of dog which never barked, a kind of coney or rabbit called "utia" by the natives, together with numerous lizards and guanas. The last were regarded with disgust and horror by the Spaniards, supposing them to be fierce and noxious serpents; but they were found afterwards to be perfectly harmless, and their flesh to be esteemed a great delicacy by the Indians.

For several days Columbus hovered about this island, seeking in vain to find its imaginary monarch, or to establish a communication with him, until, at length, he reluctantly became convinced of his error. No sooner, however, did one delusion fade away, than another succeeded. In reply to the continual inquiries made by the Spaniards, after the source whence they procured their gold, the

[1] Primer Viage de Colon. · Navarrete, cap. 1.

natives uniformly pointed to the south. Columbus now
began to hear of an island in that direction, called Cuba,
but all that he could collect concerning it from the signs of
the natives was colored by his imagination. He understood
it to be of great extent, abounding in gold, and pearls, and
spices, and carrying on an extensive commerce in those
precious articles; and that large merchant ships came to
trade with its inhabitants.

Comparing these misinterpreted accounts with the coast
of Asia as laid down on his map, after the descriptions of
Marco Polo, he concluded that this island must be Cipango,
and the merchant ships mentioned must be those of the
Grand Khan, who maintained an extensive commerce in
these seas. He formed his plan accordingly, determining
to sail immediately for this island, and make himself
acquainted with its ports, cities, and productions, for the
purpose of establishing relations of traffic. He would then
seek another great island called Bohio, of which the natives
gave likewise marvelous accounts. His sojourn in those
islands would depend upon the quantities of gold, spices,
precious stones, and other objects of oriental trade which
he should find there. After this he would proceed to the
main-land of India, which must be within ten days' sail,
seek the city Quinsai, which, according to Marco Polo, was
one of the most magnificent capitals in the world; he
would there deliver in person the letters of the Castilian
sovereigns to the Grand Khan, and, when he received his
reply, return triumphantly to Spain with this document, to
prove that he had accomplished the great object of his
voyage.[1] Such was the splendid scheme with which Columbus fed his imagination, when about to leave the Bahamas
in quest of the island of Cuba.

[1] Journal of Columbus. Navarrete, tom. i.

CHAPTER III.

DISCOVERY AND COASTING OF CUBA.

[1492.]

FOR several days the departure of Columbus was delayed by contrary winds and calms, attended by heavy showers, which last had prevailed, more or less, since his arrival among the islands. It was the season of the autumnal rains, which in those torrid climates succeed the parching heats of summer, commencing about the decrease of the August moon, and lasting until the month of November.

At length, at midnight, October 24th, he set sail from the island of Isabella, but was nearly becalmed until mid-day; a gentle wind then sprang up, and, as he observes, began to blow most amorously. Every sail was spread, and he stood towards the west-southwest, the direction in which he was told the land of Cuba lay from Isabella. After three days' navigation, in the course of which he touched at a group of seven or eight small islands, which he called Islas de Arena, supposed to be the present Mucaras islands, and having crossed the Bahama bank and channel, he arrived, on the morning of the 28th October, in sight of Cuba. The part which he first discovered, is supposed to be the coast to the west of Nuevitas del Principe.

As he approached this noble island, he was struck with its magnitude, and grandeur of its features; its high and airy mountains, which reminded him of those of Sicily; its fertile valleys, and long sweeping plains watered by noble rivers; its stately forests; its bold promontories, and stretching headlands, which melted away into the remotest distance. He anchored in a beautiful river, of transparent clearness, free from rocks and shoals, its banks overhung with trees. Here, landing, and taking possession of the

island, he gave it the name of Juana, in honor of Prince
Juan, and to the river the name of San Salvador.

On the arrival of the ships, two canoes put off from the
shore, but fled on seeing the boat approach to sound the
river for anchorage. The admiral visited two cabins, abandoned by their inhabitants. They contained but a few nets
made of the fibres of the palm-tree, hooks and harpoons of
bone, and some other fishing implements, and one of the
kind of dogs he had met with on the smaller islands, which
never bark. He ordered that nothing should be taken
away or deranged.

Returning to his boat, he proceeded for some distance up
the river, more and more enchanted with the beauty of the
country. The banks were covered with high and wide-
spreading trees; some bearing fruits, others flowers, while
in some both fruit and flower were mingled, bespeaking a
perpetual round of fertility : among them were many
palms, but different from those of Spain and Africa; with
the great leaves of these, the natives thatched their cabins.

The continual eulogies made by Columbus on the beauty
of the country were warranted by the kind of scenery he
was beholding. There is a wonderful splendor, variety, and
luxuriance in the vegetation of those quick and ardent
climates. The verdure of the groves, and the colors of
the flowers and blossoms, derive a vividness from the transparent purity of the air, and the deep serenity of the azure
heavens. The forests, too, are full of life, swarming with
birds of brilliant plumage. Painted varieties of parrots
and woodpeckers create a glitter amidst the verdure of the
grove, and humming-birds rove from flower to flower, resembling, as has well been said, animated particles of a
rainbow. The scarlet flamingoes, too, seen sometimes
through an opening of a forest in a distant savanna, have
the appearance of soldiers drawn up in battalion, with an
advanced scout on the alert, to give notice of approaching
danger. Nor is the least beautiful part of animated nature

the various tribes of insects peopling every plant, and displaying brilliant coats of mail, which sparkle like precious gems.[1]

Such is the splendor of animal and vegetable creation in these tropical climates, where an ardent sun imparts its own lustre to every object, and quickens nature into exuberant fecundity. The birds, in general, are not remarkable for their notes, for it has been observed that in the feathered race sweetness of song rarely accompanies brilliancy of plumage. Columbus remarks, however, that there were various kinds which sang sweetly among the trees, and he frequently deceived himself in fancying that he heard the voice of the nightingale, a bird unknown in these countries. He was, in fact, in a mood to see every thing through a favoring medium. His heart was full to overflowing, for he was enjoying the fulfillment of his hopes, and the hard-earned but glorious reward of his toils and perils. Every thing round him was beheld with the enamored and exulting eye of a discoverer, where triumph mingles with admiration; and it is difficult to conceive the rapturous state of his feelings, while thus exploring the charms of a virgin world, won by his enterprise and valor.

From his continual remarks on the beauty of scenery, and from his evident delight in rural sounds and objects, he appears to have been extremely open to those happy influences, exercised over some spirits, by the graces and wonders of nature. He gives utterance to these feelings with characteristic enthusiasm, and at the same time with the artlessness and simplicity of diction of a child. When speaking of some lovely scene among the groves, or along the flowery shores of these favored islands, he says, "one could live there for ever."—Cuba broke upon him like an elysium. "It is the most beautiful island," he says, "that

[1] The ladies of Havanna, on gala occasions, wear in their hair numbers of those insects, which have a brilliancy equal to rubies, sapphires, or diamonds.

eyes ever beheld, full of excellent ports and profound
rivers." The climate was more temperate here than in the
other islands, the nights being neither hot nor cold, while
the birds and crickets sang all night long. Indeed there is
a beauty in a tropical night, in the depth of the dark blue
sky, the lambent purity of the stars, and the resplendent
clearness of the moon, that spreads over the rich landscape
and the balmy groves, a charm more captivating than the
splendor of the day.

In the sweet smell of the woods, and the odor of the
flowers, Columbus fancied he perceived the fragrance of
oriental spices; and along the shores he found shells of the
kind of oyster which produces pearls. From the grass
growing to the very edge of the water, he inferred the
peacefulness of the ocean which bathes these islands, never
lashing the shores with angry surges. Ever since his arrival
among these Antilles, he had experienced nothing but soft
and gentle weather, and he concluded that a perpetual
serenity reigned over these happy seas. He was little suspicious of the occasional bursts of fury to which they are
liable. Charlevoix, speaking from actual observation, remarks, " The sea of those islands is commonly more tranquil than ours; but, like certain people who are excited
with difficulty, and whose transports of passion are as violent as they are rare, so when the sea becomes irritated, it
is terrible. It breaks all bounds, overflows the country,
sweeps away all things that oppose it, and leaves frightful
ravages behind, to mark the extent of its inundations. It
is after these tempests, known by the name of hurricanes,
that the shores are covered with marine shells, which greatly
surpass in lustre and beauty those of the European seas." [1]
It is a singular fact, however, that the hurricanes, which
almost annually devastate the Bahamas, and other islands
in the immediate vicinity of Cuba, have been seldom known
to extend their influence to this favored land. It would

[1] Charlevoix, Hist. St. Domingo, lib. i. p. 20. Paris, 1730.

seem as if the very elements were charmed into gentleness as they approached it.

In a kind of riot of the imagination, Columbus finds at every step something to corroborate the information he had received, or fancied he had received, from the natives. He had conclusive proofs, as he thought, that Cuba possessed mines of gold, and groves of spices, and that its shores abounded with pearls. He no longer doubted that it was the island of Cipango, and weighing anchor, coasted along westward, in which direction, according to the signs of his interpreters, the magnificent city of its king was situated. In the course of his voyage, he landed occasionally, and visited several villages; particularly one on the banks of a large river, to which he gave the name of Rio de los Mares.[1] The houses were neatly built of branches of palm-trees in the shape of pavilions, not laid out in regular streets, but scattered here and there, among the groves, and under the shade of broad spreading trees, like tents in a camp; as is still the case in many of the Spanish settlements, and in the villages in the interior of Cuba. The inhabitants fled to the mountains, or hid themselves in the woods. Columbus carefully noted the architecture and furniture of their dwellings. The houses were better built than those he had hitherto seen, and were kept extremely clean. He found in them rude statues, and wooden masks, carved with considerable ingenuity. All these were indications of more art and civilization than he had observed in the smaller islands, and he supposed they would go on increasing as he approached terra firma. Finding in all the cabins implements for fishing, he concluded that these coasts were inhabited merely by fishermen, who carried their fish to the cities in the interior. He thought also he had found the skulls of cows, which proved that there were cattle in the island; though these are supposed to have been skulls of the manati or sea-calf found on this coast.

[1] Now called Savandah la Mer.

After standing to the northwest for some distance, Columbus came in sight of a great headland, to which, from the groves with which it was covered, he gave the name of the Cape of Palms, and which forms the eastern entrance to what is now known as Laguna de Moron. Here three Indians, natives of the island of Guanahani, who were on board of the Pinta, informed the commander, Martin Alonzo Pinzon, that behind the cape there was a river, whence it was but four days' journey to Cubanacan, a place abounding in gold. By this they designated a province situated in the centre of Cuba; *nacan*, in their language, signifying the midst. Pinzon, however, had studied intently the map of Toscanelli, and had imbibed from Columbus all his ideas respecting the coast of Asia. He concluded, therefore, that the Indians were talking of Cublai Khan, the Tartar sovereign, and of certain parts of his dominions described by Marco Polo.[1] He understood from them that Cuba was not an island, but terra firma, extending a vast distance to the north, and that the king who reigned in this vicinity was at war with the Great Khan.

This tissue of errors and misconceptions he immediately communicated to Columbus. It put an end to the delusion in which the admiral had hitherto indulged, that this was the island of Cipango; but it substituted another no less agreeable. He concluded that he must have reached the mainland of Asia, or as he termed it, India, and if so, he could not be at any great distance from Mangi and Cathay, the ultimate destination of his voyage. The prince in question, who reigned over this neighboring country, must be some oriental potentate of consequence; he resolved, therefore, to seek the river beyond the Cape of Palms, and dispatch a present to the monarch, with one of the letters of recommendation from the Castilian sovereigns; and after visiting his dominions, he would proceed to the capital of Cathay, the residence of the Grand Khan.

[1] Las Casas, lib. i. cap. 44, MS.

Every attempt to reach the river in question, however, proved ineffectual. Cape stretched beyond cape; there was no good anchorage; the wind became contrary, and the appearance of the heavens threatening rough weather, he put back to the Rio de los Mares.

On the first of November, at sunrise, he sent the boats on shore to visit several houses, but the inhabitants fled to the woods. He supposed that they must mistake his armament for one of the scouring expeditions sent by the Grand Khan to make prisoners and slaves. He sent the boat on shore again in the afternoon, with an Indian interpreter, who was instructed to assure the people of the peaceable and beneficent intentions of the Spaniards, and that they had no connection with the Grand Khan. After the Indian had proclaimed this from the boat to the savages upon the beach, part of it, no doubt, to their great perplexity, he threw himself into the water and swam to shore. He was well received by the natives, and succeeded so effectually in calming their fears, that before evening there were more than sixteen canoes about the ships, bringing cotton yarn and other simple articles of traffic. Columbus forbade all trading for anything but gold, that the natives might be tempted to produce the real riches of their country. They had none to offer; all were destitute of ornaments of the precious metals, excepting one, who wore in his nose a piece of wrought silver. Columbus understood this man to say that the king lived about the distance of four days' journey in the interior; that many messengers had been dispatched to give him tidings of the arrival of the strangers upon the coast; and that in less than three days' time messengers might be expected from him in return, and many merchants from the interior, to trade with the ships. It is curious to observe how ingeniously the imagination of Columbus deceived him at every step, and how he wove every thing into a uniform web of false conclusions. Poring over the map of Toscanelli, referring to the reckonings of his voyage, and musing on the misinterpreted words of the Indians, he imagined that he must be on the borders of Cathay, and about one hundred leagues from the capital of the Grand Khan. Anxious to arrive there, and to delay as little as possible in the territories of an inferior prince, he determined not to await the arrival of messengers and merchants, but to dispatch two envoys to seek the neighboring monarch at his residence.

For this mission he chose two Spaniards, Rodrigo de Jerez and Luis de Torres; the latter a converted Jew, who knew Hebrew and Chaldaic, and even something of Arabic, one or other of which Columbus supposed might be known to this oriental prince. Two Indians were sent with them as guides, one a native of Guanahani, and the other an inhabitant of the hamlet on the bank of the river. The ambassadors were furnished with strings of beads and other trinkets for traveling expenses. Instructions were given them to inform the king that Columbus had been sent by the Castilian sovereigns, a bearer of letters and a present, which he was to deliver personally, for the purpose of establishing an amicable intercourse between the powers. They were likewise to inform themselves accurately about the situation and distances of certain provinces, ports, and rivers, which the admiral specified by name from the descriptions which he had of the coast of Asia. They were moreover provided with specimens of spices and drugs, for the purpose of ascertaining whether any articles of the kind abounded in the country. With these provisions and instructions the ambassadors departed, six days being allowed them to go and return. Many, at the present day, will smile at this embassy to a naked savage chieftain in the interior of Cuba, in mistake for an Asiatic monarch; but such was the singular nature of this voyage, a continual series of golden dreams, and all interpreted by the deluding volume of Marco Polo.

CHAPTER IV.

FURTHER COASTING OF CUBA.

WHILE awaiting the return of his ambassadors, the admiral ordered the ships to be careened and repaired; and employed himself in collecting information concerning the country. On the day after their departure, he ascended the river in boats for the distance of two leagues, until he came to fresh water. Here landing, he climbed a hill to obtain a view of the interior. His view, however, was shut in by thick and lofty forests, of wild but beautiful luxuriance. Among the trees were some which he considered linaloes; many were odoriferous, and he doubted not possessed valuable aromatic qualities. There was a general eagerness among the voyagers to find the precious articles of commerce which grow in the favored climes of the East; and their imaginations were continually deceived by their hopes.

For two or three days the admiral was excited by reports of cinnamon-trees, and nutmegs, and rhubarb; but, on examination, they all proved fallacious. He showed the natives specimens of those and various other spices and drugs, and understood from them that those articles abounded to the southeast. He showed them gold and pearls also, and several old Indians spoke of a country where the natives wore ornaments of them round their necks, arms, and ankles. They repeatedly mentioned the word Bohio, which Columbus supposed to be the name of the place in question, and that it was some rich district or island. They mingled, however, great extravagancies with their imperfect accounts, describing nations at a distance who had but one eye; others who had the heads of dogs. and who were cannibals—cutting the throats of their prisoners and sucking their blood.[1]

[1] Primer Viage de Colon. Navarrete, lxxi. p. 48.

All these reports of gold, and pearls, and spices, many of which were probably fabrications to please the admiral, tended to keep up the persuasion that he was among the valuable coasts and islands of the East. On making a fire to heat the tar for careening the ships, the seamen found that the wood they burnt sent forth a powerful odor, and, on examining it, declared that it was mastic. The wood abounded in the neighboring forests, insomuch that Columbus flattered himself a thousand quintals of this precious gum might be collected every year; and a more abundant supply procured than that furnished by Scios, and other islands of the Archipelago. In the course of their researches in the vegetable kingdom, in quest of the luxuries of commerce, they met with the potato, a humble root, little valued at the time, but a more precious acquisition to man than all the spices of the East.

On the 6th of November, the two ambassadors returned, and every one crowded to hear tidings of the interior of the country, and of the prince to whose capital they had been sent. After penetrating twelve leagues, they had come to a village of fifty houses, built similarly to those of the coast, but larger; the whole village containing at least a thousand inhabitants. The natives received them with great solemnity, conducted them to the best house, and placed them in what appeared to be intended for chairs of state, being wrought out of single pieces of wood, into the forms of quadrupeds. They then offered them fruits and vegetables. Having complied with the laws of savage courtesy and hospitality, they seated themselves on the ground around their visitors, and waited to hear what they had to communicate.

The Israelite, Luis de Torres, found his Hebrew, Chaldaic, and Arabic of no avail, and the Lucayen interpreter had to be the orator. He made a regular speech, after the Indian manner, in which he extolled the power, the wealth, and munificence of the white men. When he had finished, the Indians crowded round these wonderful beings, whom, as usual, they considered more than human. Some touched them, examining their skin and raiment, others kissed their hands and feet, in token of submission or adoration. In a little while the men withdrew, and were succeeded by the women, and the same ceremonies were repeated. Some of the women had a slight covering of netted cotton round the middle, but in general both sexes were entirely naked. There seemed to be ranks and orders of society among them, and a chieftain of some authority; whereas among all the natives they had previously met with, a complete equality seemed to prevail.

There was no appearance of gold, or other precious articles, and when they showed specimens of cinnamon, pepper, and other spices, the inhabitants told them they were not to be found in that neighborhood, but far off to the southwest.

The envoys determined, therefore, to return to the ships. The natives would fain have induced them to remain for several days; but seeing them bent on departing, a great number were anxious to accompany them, imagining they were about to return to the skies. They took with them, however, only one of the principal men, with his son, who were attended by a domestic.

On their way back, they for the first time witnessed the use of a weed, which the ingenious caprice of man has since converted into an universal luxury, in defiance of the opposition of the senses. They beheld several of the natives going about with firebrands in their hands, and certain dried herbs which they rolled up in a leaf, and lighting one end, put the other in their mouths, and continued exhaling and puffing out the smoke. A roll of this kind they called a tobacco, a name since transferred to the plant of which the rolls were made. The Spaniards, although prepared to meet with wonders, were struck with astonishment at this singular and apparently nauseous indulgence.[1]

[1] Primer Viage de Colon. Navarrete, tom. i. p. 51.

On their return to the ships, they gave favorable accounts of the beauty and fertility of the country. They had met with many hamlets of four or five houses, well peopled, embowered among trees, laden with unknown fruits of tempting hue and delightful flavor. Around them were fields, cultivated with the agi or sweet pepper, potatoes, maize or Indian corn, a species of lupin or pulse, and yuca, whereof they made their cassava bread. These, with the fruits of the groves, formed their principal food. There were vast quantities of cotton, some just sown, some in full growth. There was great store of it also in their houses, some wrought into yarn, or into nets, of which they made their hammocks. They had seen many birds of rare plumage, but unknown species; many ducks; several small partridges; and they heard the song of a bird which they had mistaken for the nightingale. All that they had seen, however, betokened a primitive and simple state of society. The wonder with which they had been regarded, showed clearly that the people were strangers to civilized man, nor could they hear of any inland city superior to the one they had visited.

The report of the envoys put an end to many splendid fancies of Columbus, about the barbaric prince and his capital. He was cruising, however, in a region of enchantment, in which pleasing chimeras started up at every step, exercising by turns a power over his imagination. During the absence of the emissaries, the Indians had informed him

"Hallaron por el camino mucha gente que atravesaban a sus pueb-los mugeres y hombres: siempre los hombres con un tison en las manos y ciertos yerbas para tomar sus sahumerios, que son unas yerbas secas metidas en una cierta hoja seca tambien à manera de mosquete hecho de papel de los que hacen los muchachos la Pascua del Espiritu Santo, y encondido por una parte de el, por la otra chupan ó sorban ó reciben con el resuello por adentro aquel humo; con el qual se adormecen las carnes y cuasi emborracho, y asi diz que no sienten el caasancio. Estos mosquetos, ó como los llamáremas, llamen ellos tabacos."—Las Casas, Hist. Gen. Ind., lib. i. cap. 46.

by signs, of a place to the eastward, where the people collected gold along the river banks by torchlight, and afterwards wrought it into bars with hammers. In speaking of
this place they again used the words Babeque and Bohio,
which he, as usual, supposed to be the proper names of
islands or countries. The true meaning of these words has
been variously explained. It is said that they were
applied by the Indians to the coast of terra firma, called
also by them Caritaba.[1] It is also said that Bohio means a
house, and was often used by the Indians to signify the
populousness of an island. Hence it was frequently applied to Hispaniola, as well as the more general name of
Hayti, which means highland, and occasionally Quisqueya
(*i. e.* the whole), on account of its extent.

The misapprehension of these, and other words, was a
source of perpetual error to Columbus. Sometimes he supposed Babeque and Bohio to signify the same island;
sometimes to be different places or islands; and Quisqueya
he supposed to mean Quisai or Quinsai (*i. e.* the celestial
city), mentioned by Marco Polo.

His great object was to arrive at some opulent and
civilized country of the East, with which he might establish
commercial relations, and whence he might carry home a·
quantity of oriental merchandise as a rich trophy of his
discovery. The season was advancing; the cool nights
gave hints of approaching winter; he resolved, therefore,
not to proceed further to the north, nor to linger about
uncivilized places, which, at present, he had not the means
of colonizing, but to return to the east-southeast, in quest of
Babeque, which he trusted might prove some rich and
civilized island on the coast of Asia.

Before leaving the river, to which he had given the
name of Rio de Mares, he took several of the natives to
carry with him to Spain, for the purpose of teaching them
the language, that, in future voyages, they might serve as

[1] Muñoz, Hist. N. Mundo, cap. 3.

interpreters. He took them of both sexes, having learned from the Portuguese discoverers, that the men were always more contented on the voyage, and serviceable on their return, when accompanied by females. With the religious feeling of the day, he anticipated great triumphs to the faith and glory to the crown, from the conversion of these savage nations, through the means of the natives thus instructed. He imagined that the Indians had no system of religion, but a disposition to receive its impressions ; as they regarded with great reverence and attention the religious ceremonies of the Spaniards, soon repeating by rote any prayer taught them, and making the sign of the cross with the most edifying devotion. They had an idea of a future state, but limited and confused. "They confess the soul to be immortal," says Peter Martyr, "and having put off the bodily clothing, they imagine it goes forth to the woods and the mountains, and that it liveth there perpetually in caves ; nor do they exempt it from eating and drinking, but that it should be fed there. The answering voices heard from caves and hollows, which the Latines call echoes, they suppose to be the souls of the departed, wandering through those places." [1]

From the natural tendency to devotion which Columbus thought he discovered among them, from their gentle natures, and their ignorance of all warlike arts, he pronounces it an easy matter to make them devout members of the church, and loyal subjects of the crown. He concludes his speculations upon the advantages to be derived from the colonization of these parts by anticipating a great trade for gold, which must abound in the interior ; for pearls and precious stones, of which, though he had seen none, he had received frequent accounts ; for gums and spices, of which he thought he had found indubitable traces ; and for the cotton, which grew wild in vast quantities. Many of these articles, he observes, would probably

[1] P. Martyr, decad. viii. cap. 9; M. Lock's translation, 1612.

find a nearer market than Spain, in the ports and cities of the Great Khan, at which he had no doubt of soon arriving.[1]

CHAPTER V.

SEARCH AFTER THE SUPPOSED ISLAND OF BABEQUE.— DESERTION OF THE PINTA.

[1492.]

ON the 12th of November, Columbus turned his course to the east-southeast, to follow back the direction of the coast. This may be considered another critical change in his voyage, which had a great effect upon his subsequent discoveries. He had proceeded far within what is called the old channel, between Cuba and the Bahamas. In two or three days more, he would have discovered his mistake in supposing Cuba a part of terra firma : an error in which he continued to the day of his death. He might have had intimation also of the vicinity of the continent, and have stood for the coast of Florida, or have been carried thither by the gulf stream, or, continuing along Cuba where it bends to the southwest, might have struck over to the opposite coast of Yucatan, and have realized his most sanguine anticipations in becoming the discoverer of Mexico. It was sufficient glory for Columbus, however, to have discovered a new world. Its more golden regions were reserved to give splendor to succeeding enterprises.

He now ran along the coast for two or three days without stopping to explore it, as no populous towns or cities were to be seen. Passing by a great cape, to which he gave the name of Cape Cuba, he struck eastward in search of Babeque, but on the 14th a head wind and boisterous sea obliged him to put back and anchor in a deep and secure harbor, to which he gave the name of Puerto del Principe.

[1] Primer Viage de Colon. Navarrete, tom. i.

Here he erected a cross on a neighboring height, in token of possession. A few days were passed in exploring with his boats an archipelago of small but beautiful islands in the vicinity, since known as *El jardin del Rey*, or the king's garden. The gulf, studded with these islands, he named the sea of Nuestra Señora; in modern days it has been a lurking-place for pirates, who have found secure shelter and concealment among the channels and solitary harbors of this archipelago. These islands were covered with noble trees, among which the Spaniards thought they discovered mastic and aloes.

On the 19th Columbus again put to sea, and for two days made ineffectual attempts, against head winds, to reach an island directly east, about sixty miles distant, which he supposed to be Babeque. The wind continuing obstinately adverse and the sea rough, he put his ship about towards evening of the 20th, making signals for the other vessels to follow him. His signals were unattended to by the Pinta, which was considerably to the eastward. Columbus repeated the signals, but they were still unattended to. Night coming on, he shortened sail and hoisted signal lights to the mast-head, thinking Pinzon would yet join him, which he could easily do, having the wind astern; but when the morning dawned, the Pinta was no longer to be seen.[1]

Columbus was disquieted by this circumstance. Pinzon was a veteran navigator, accustomed to hold a high rank among his nautical associates. The squadron had in a great measure been manned and fitted out through his influence and exertions; he could ill brook subordination therefore to Columbus, whom he perhaps did not consider his superior in skill and knowledge, and who had been benefited by his purse. Several misunderstandings and disputes had accordingly occurred between them in the

[1] Las Casas, Hist. Ind., tom. i. cap. 27. Hist. del Almirante, cap. 29. Journal of Columbus. Navarrete, tom. i.

course of the voyage, and when Columbus saw Pinzon thus
parting company, without any appointed rendezvous, he
suspected either that he intended to take upon himself a
separate command and prosecute the enterprise in his own
name; or hasten back to Spain and bear off the glory of
the discovery. To attempt to seek him, however, was
fruitless: he was far out of sight; his vessel was a superior
sailer, and it was impossible to say what course he had
steered. Columbus stood back, therefore, for Cuba, to
finish the exploring of its coast; but he no longer possessed his usual serenity of mind and unity of purpose,
and was embarrassed in the prosecution of his discoveries
by doubts of the designs of Pinzon.

On the 24th of November he regained Point Cuba, and
anchored in a fine harbor formed by the mouth of a river,
to which he gave the name of St. Catherine. It was bordered by rich meadows; the neighboring mountains were
well wooded, having pines tall enough to make masts for
the finest ships, and noble oaks. In the bed of the river
were found stones veined with gold.

Columbus continued for several days coasting the residue
of Cuba, extolling the magnificence, freshness, and verdure
of the scenery, the purity of the rivers, and the number
and commodiousness of the harbors. Speaking in his
letters to the sovereigns of one place, to which he gave the
name of Puerto Santo, he says, in his artless but enthusiastic language, "The amenity of this river, and the clearness of the water, through which the sand at the bottom
may be seen; the multitude of palm-trees of various forms,
the highest and most beautiful that I have met with, and
an infinity of other great and green trees; the birds in
rich plumage and the verdure of the fields, render this
country, most serene princes, of such marvelous beauty,
that it surpasses all others in charms and graces, as the day
doth the night in lustre. For which reason I often say to
my people, that, much as I endeavor to give a complete

account of it to your majesties, my tongue cannot express the whole truth, nor my pen describe it; and I have been so overwhelmed at the sight of so much beauty, that I have not known how to relate it." [1]

The transparency of the water, which Columbus attributed to the purity of the rivers, is the property of the ocean in these latitudes. So clear is the sea in the neighborhood of some of these islands, that in still weather the bottom may be seen, as in a crystal fountain; and the inhabitants dive down four or five fathoms in search of conchs, and other shell-fish, which are visible from the surface. The delicate air and pure waters of these islands are among their greatest charms.

As a proof of the gigantic vegetation, Columbus mentions the enormous size of the canoes formed from single trunks of trees. One that he saw was capable of containing one hundred and fifty persons. Among other articles found in the Indian dwellings was a cake of wax, which he took to present to the Castilian sovereigns, "for where there is wax," said he, "there must be a thousand other good things." [2] It is since supposed to have been brought from Yucatan, as the inhabitants of Cuba were not accustomed to gather wax.[3]

On the 5th of December he reached the eastern end of Cuba, which he supposed to be the eastern extremity of Asia; he gave it, therefore, the name of Alpha and Omega, the beginning and the end. He was now greatly perplexed what course to take. If he kept along the coast as it bent to the southwest, it might bring him to the more civilized and opulent parts of India; but if he took this course, he must abandon all hope of finding the island of Babeque, which the Indians now said lay to the northeast, and of which they still continued to give the most marvelous

[1] Hist. del Almirante, cap. 29.
[2] Journal of Columbus. Navarrete, tom. i.
[3] Herrera, Hist. Ind, decad. i.

accounts. It was a state of embarrassment characteristic of this extraordinary voyage, to have a new and unknown world thus spread out to the choice of the explorer, where wonders and beauties invited him on every side; but where, whichever way he turned, he might leave the true region of profit and delight behind.

CHAPTER VI.

DISCOVERY OF HISPANIOLA.

[1492.]

WHILE Columbus was steering at large beyond the eastern extremity of Cuba, undetermined what course to take, he descried land to the southeast, gradually increasing upon the view; its high mountains towering above the clear horizon, and giving evidence of an island of great extent. The Indians, on beholding it, exclaimed *Bohio*, the name by which Colnmbus understood them to designate some country which abounded in gold. When they saw him standing in that direction, they showed great signs of terror, imploring him not to visit it, assuring him, by signs, that the inhabitants were fierce and cruel, that they had but one eye, and were cannibals. The wind being unfavorable, and the nights long, during which they did not dare to make sail in these unknown seas, they were a great part of two days working up to the island.

In the transparent atmosphere of the tropics, objects are descried at a great distance, and the purity of the air and serenity of the deep blue sky give a magical effect to the scenery. Under these advantages, the beautiful island of Hayti revealed itself to the eye as they approached. Its mountains were higher and more rocky than those of the other islands; but the rocks rose from among rich forests. The mountains swept down into luxuriant plains and green savannas; while the appearance of cultivated fields, of numerous fires at night, and columns of smoke by day, showed it to be populous. It rose before them in all the splendor of tropical vegetation, one of the most beautiful islands in the world, and doomed to be one of the most unfortunate.

In the evening of the 6th of December, Columbus entered a harbor at the western end of the island, to which he gave the name of St. Nicholas, by which it is called at the present day. The harbor was spacious and deep, surrounded with large trees, many of them loaded with fruit; while a beautiful plain extended in front of the port, traversed by a fine stream of water. From the number of canoes seen in various parts, there were evidently large villages in the neighborhood, but the natives had fled with terror at sight of the ships.

Leaving the harbor of St. Nicholas on the 7th, they coasted along the northern side of the island. It was lofty and mountainous, but with green savannas and long sweeping plains. At one place they caught a view up a rich and smiling valley that ran far into the interior, between two mountains, and appeared to be in a high state of cultivation.

For several days they were detained in a harbor which they called Port Conception;[1] a small river emptied into it, after winding through a delightful country. The coast abounded with fish, some of which even leapt into their boats. They cast their nets, therefore, and caught great quantities, and among them several kinds similar to those of Spain,—the first fish they had met with resembling those

---

[1] Now known by the name of the Bay of Moustique.

NOTE.—The author has received very obliging and interesting letters, dated in 1847, from T. S. Heneken, Esq., many years a resident of St. Domingo, giving names, localities, and other particulars connected with the transactions of Columbus in that island. These will be thankfully made use of and duly cited in the course of the work.

of their own country. The notes of the bird which they
mistook for the nightingale, and of several others to which
they were accustomed, reminded them strongly of the
groves of their distant Andalusia.   They fancied the
features of the surrounding country resembled those of
the more beautiful provinces of Spain, and, in consequence, the admiral named the island Hispaniola.

Desirous of establishing some intercourse with the natives, who had abandoned the coast on his arrival, he dispatched six men, well armed, into the interior. They found
several cultivated fields, and traces of roads, and places
where fires had been made, but the inhabitants had fled
with terror to the mountains.

Though the whole country was solitary and deserted,
Columbus consoled himself with the idea, that there must
be populous towns in the interior, where the people had
taken refuge, and that the fires he had beheld had been
signal fires, like those lighted up on the mountains of
Spain, in the times of Moorish war, to give the alarm when
there was any invasion of the seaboard.

On the 12th of December, Columbus, with great solemnity, erected a cross on a commanding eminence, at the entrance of the harbor, in sign of having taken possession. As
three sailors were rambling about the vicinity, they beheld
a large number of the natives, who immediately took flight;
but the sailors pursued them, and captured a young female,
whom they brought to the ships. She was perfectly naked;
a bad omen as to the civilization of the island; but an
ornament of gold in the nose gave hope of the precious
metal. The admiral soon soothed her terror by his kindness, and by presents of beads, brass rings, hawks' bells,
and other trinkets, and, having had her clothed, sent her
on shore accompanied by several of the crew, and three of
the Indian interpreters. So well pleased was she with her
finery, and with the kind treatment she had experienced,
that she would gladly have remained with the Indian

women whom she found on board. The party sent with her returned on board late in the night, without venturing to her village, which was far inland. Confident of the favorable impression which the report given by the woman must produce, the admiral, on the following day, dispatched nine stout-hearted, well armed men, to seek the village, accompanied by a native of Cuba as an interpreter. They found it about four and a half leagues to the southeast, in a fine valley, on the banks of a beautiful river.[1] It contained one thousand houses, but the inhabitants fled as they approached. The interpreter overtook them, and assured them of the goodness of these strangers, who had descended from the skies, and went about the world making precious and beautiful presents. Thus assured, the natives ventured back to the number of two thousand. They approached the Spaniards with slow and trembling steps, often pausing and putting their hands upon their heads, in token of profound reverence and submission. They were a well-formed race, fairer and handsomer than the natives of the other islands.[2] While the Spaniards were conversing with them by means of their interpreter, another mutitude approached, headed by the husband of the female captive. They brought her in triumph on their shoulders, and the husband was profuse in his gratitude for the kindness with which she had been treated, and the magnificent presents which had been bestowed upon her.

The Indians now conducted the Spaniards to their houses, and set before them cassava bread, fish, roots, and fruits of various kinds. They brought also great numbers of domesticated parrots, and indeed offered freely whatever they possessed. The great river flowing through this valley was bordered with noble forests, among which were

[1] This village was formerly known by the name of Gros Morne, situated on the banks of the river of "Trois Rivieres," which empties itself half a mile west of Port de Paix. Navarrete, tom. i.
[2] Las Casas, lib. i. cap. 53, MS.

palms, bananas, and many trees covered with fruit and flowers. The air was mild as in April; the birds sang all day long, and some were even heard in the night. The Spaniards had not learned as yet to account for the difference of seasons in this opposite part of the globe; they were astonished to hear the voice of this supposed nightingale singing in the midst of December, and considered it a proof that there was no winter in this happy climate. They returned to the ships enraptured with the beauty of the country; surpassing, as they said, even the luxuriant plains of Cordova. All that they complained of was, that they saw no signs of riches among the natives. And here it is impossible to refrain from dwelling on the picture given by the first discoverers, of the state of manners in this eventful island before the arrival of the white men. According to their accounts, the people of Hayti existed in that state of primitive and savage simplicity, which some philosophers have fondly pictured as the most enviable on earth ; surrounded by natural blessings, without even a knowledge of artificial wants. The fertile earth produced the chief part of their food almost without culture; their rivers and sea-coast abounded with fish, and they caught the utia, the guana, and a variety of birds. This, to beings of their frugal and temperate habits, was great abundance, and what nature furnished thus spontaneously, they willingly shared with all the world. Hospitality, we are told, was with them a law of nature universally observed ; there was no need of being known to receive its succors; every house was as open to the stranger as his own.[1] Columbus, too, in a letter to Luis de St. Angel, observes, "True it is that after they felt confidence, and lost their fear of us, they were so liberal with what they possessed, that it would not be believed by those who had not seen it. If any thing was asked of them, they never said no, but rather gave it cheerfully, and showed as much amity as if

[1] Charlevoix. Hist. St. Doming., lib. i.

they gave their very hearts; and whether the thing were
of value, or of little price, they were content with whatever
was given in return. * * * In all these islands it appears
to me that the men are all content with one wife, but they
give twenty to their chieftain or king. The women seem
to work more than the men; and I have not been able to
understand whether they possess individual property; but
rather think that whatever one has all the rest share,
especially in all articles of provisions." [1]

One of the most pleasing descriptions of the inhabitants
of this island is given by old Peter Martyr, who gathered
it, as he says, from the conversations of the admiral himself.
" It is certain," says he, " that the land among these people
is as common as the sun and water; and that 'mine and
thine,' the seeds of all mischief, have no place with them.
They are content with so little, that in so large a country
they have rather superfluity than scarceness; so that they
seem to live in the golden world, without toil, living in open
gardens; not intrenched with dykes, divided with hedges,
or defended with walls. They deal truly one with another,
without laws, without books, and without judges. They
take him for an evil and mischievous man, who taketh
pleasure in doing hurt to another; and albeit they delight
not in superfluities, yet they make provision for the increase of such roots whereof they make their bread, contented with such simple diet, whereby health is preserved
and disease avoided." [2]

Much of this picture may be overcolored by the imagination, but it is generally confirmed by contemporary
historians. They all concur in representing the life of
these islanders as approaching to the golden state of
poetical felicity; living under the absolute but patriarchal
and easy rule of their caciques, free from pride, with few

[1] Letter of Columbus to Luis de St. Angel. Navarrete, tom. i. p.
167.

[2] P. Martyr, decad. i. lib. iii.; Transl. of Richard Eden, 1555.

wants, an abundant country, a happily-tempered climate, and a natural disposition to careless and indolent enjoyment.

CHAPTER VII.

COASTING OF HISPANIOLA.

[1492.]

WHEN the weather became favorable, Columbus made another attempt, on the 14th of December, to find the island of Babeque, but was again baffled by adverse winds. In the course of this attempt, he visited an island lying opposite to the harbor of Conception, to which, from its abounding in turtle, he gave the name of Tortugas.[1] The natives had fled to the rocks and forests, and alarm fires blazed along the heights. The country was so beautiful, that he gave to one of the valleys the name of Valle de Paraiso, or the Vale of Paradise, and called a fine stream the Guadalquiver, after that renowned river which flows through some of the fairest provinces of Spain.[2]

Setting sail on the 16th of December, at midnight, Columbus steered again for Hispaniola. When half-way across the gulf which separates the islands, he perceived a canoe navigated by a single Indian, and, as on a former occasion, was astonished at his hardihood in venturing so far from land in so frail a bark, and at his adroitness in keeping it above water, as the wind was fresh, and there was some sea running. He ordered both him and his canoe to be taken on board; and having anchored near a village on the coast of Hispaniola, at present known as Puerto de Paz, he sent him on shore well regaled and enriched with various presents.

[1] This island in after times became the headquarters of the famous Bucaniers.

[2] Journal of Columbus. Navarrete, Colec., tom. i. p. 91.

Galley coasting the island of Hispaniola, from an illustration of a letter written by Columbus to Don Raphael Xansis, treasurer of the King of Spain. An
extremely rare edition of the letter exists in the library of Milan. The original sketch is supposed to have been made with a pen by Columbus.

In the early intercourse with these people, kindness never seems to have failed in its effect. The favorable accounts given by this Indian, and by those with whom the Spaniards had communicated in their previous landings, dispelled the fears of the islanders. A friendly intercourse soon took place, and the ships were visited by a cacique of the neighborhood. From this chieftain and his counselors, Columbus had further information of the island of Babeque, which was described as lying at no great distance. No mention is afterwards made of this island, nor does it appear that he made any further attempt to seek it. No such island exists in the ancient charts, and it is probable that this was one of the numerous misinterpretations of Indian words, which led the first discoverers into so many fruitless researches. The people of Hispaniola appeared handsomer to Columbus than any he had yet met with, and of a gentle and peaceable disposition. Some of them had ornaments of gold, which they readily gave away or exchanged for any trifle. The country was finely diversified with lofty mountains and green valleys, which stretched away inland as far as the eye could reach. The mountains were of such easy ascent, that the highest of them might be ploughed with oxen, and the luxuriant growth of the forests manifested the fertility of the soil. The valleys were watered by numerous clear and beautiful streams; they appeared to be cultivated in many places, and to be fitted for grain, for orchards, and pasturage.

While detained at this harbor by contrary winds, Columbus was visited by a young cacique, who came borne by four men on a sort of litter, and attended by two hundred of his subjects. The admiral being at dinner when he arrived, the young chieftain ordered his followers to remain without, and entering the cabin, took his seat beside Columbus, not permitting him to rise or use any ceremony. Only two old men entered with him, who appeared to be his counselors, and who seated themselves at his feet. If any thing were

given him to eat or drink, he merely tasted it, and sent it
to his followers, maintaining an air of great gravity and
dignity. He spoke but little, his two counselors watching
his lips, and catching and communicating his ideas. After
dinner he presented the admiral with a belt curiously
wrought, and two pieces of gold. Columbus gave him a
piece of cloth, several amber beads, colored shoes, and a
flask of orange-flower water; he showed him a Spanish
coin, on which were the likenesses of the king and queen,
and endeavored to explain to him the power and grandeur
of those sovereigns; he displayed, also, the royal banners
and the standard of the cross; but it was all in vain to
attempt to convey any clear idea by these symbols; the
cacique could not be made to believe that there was a region
on the earth which produced these wonderful people and
wonderful things; he joined in the common idea that the
Spaniards were more than mortal, and that the country
and sovereigns they talked of must exist somewhere in the
skies.

In the evening the cacique was sent on shore in the boat
with great ceremony, and a salute fired in honor of him.
He departed in the state in which he had come, carried on
a litter, accompanied by a great concourse of his subjects;
not far behind him was his son, borne and escorted in like
manner, and his brother on foot, supported by two attendants. The presents which he had received from the admiral
were carried triumphantly before him.

They procured but little gold in this place, though whatever ornaments the natives possessed they readily gave
away. The region of promise lay still further on, and one
of the old counselors of the cacique told Columbus that he
would soon arrive at islands rich in the precious ore. Before leaving this place, the admiral caused a large cross to
be erected in the centre of the village, and from the readiness with which the Indians assisted, and their implicit imi-
tation of the Spaniards in their acts of devotion, he inferred

12

that it would be an easy matter to convert them all to Christianity.

On the 19th of December they made sail before daylight, but with an unfavorable wind, and on the evening of the 20th they anchored in a fine harbor, to which Columbus gave the name of St. Thomas, supposed to be what at present is called the Bay of Acùl. It was surrounded by a beautiful and well-peopled country. The inhabitants came off, some in canoes, some swimming, bringing fruits of various unknown kinds, of great fragrance and flavor. These they gave freely with whatever else they possessed, especially their golden ornaments, which they saw were particularly coveted by the strangers. There was a remarkable frankness and generosity about these people; they had no idea of traffic, but gave away every thing with spontaneous liberality. Columbus would not permit his people, however, to take advantage of this free disposition, but ordered that something should always be given in exchange. Several of the neighboring caciques visited the ships, bringing presents, and inviting the Spaniards to their villages, where, on going to land, they were most hospitably entertained.

On the 22d of December, a large canoe filled with natives came on a mission from a grand cacique named Guacanagari, who commanded all that part of the island. A principal servant of the chieftain came in the canoe, bringing the admiral a present of a broad belt, wrought ingeniously with colored beads and bones, and a wooden mask, the eyes, nose, and tongue of which were of gold. He delivered also a message from the cacique, begging that the ships might come opposite to his residence, which was on a part of the coast a little further to the eastward. The wind preventing an immediate compliance with this invitation, the admiral sent the notary of the squadron, with several of the crew, to visit the cacique. He resided in a town, situated on a river, at what they called Punta Santa, at present Grande Riviere. It was the largest and best built town they had yet seen. The cacique received them in a kind of public square, which had been swept and prepared for the occasion, and treated them with great honor, giving to each a dress of cotton. The inhabitants crowded round them, bringing provisions and refreshments of various kinds. The seamen were received into their houses as distinguished guests; they gave them garments of cotton, and whatever else appeared to have value in their eyes, asking nothing in return, but if any thing were given, appearing to treasure it up as a sacred relic.

The cacique would have detained them all night, but their orders obliged them to return. On parting with them, he gave them presents of parrots and pieces of gold for the admiral, and they were attended to their boats by a crowd of the natives, carrying the presents for them and vying with each other in rendering them service.

During their absence, the admiral had been visited by a great number of canoes and several inferior caciques: all assured him that the island abounded with wealth; they talked, especially, of Cibao, a region in the interior, further to the east, the cacique of which, as far as they could be understood, had banners of wrought gold. Columbus, deceiving himself as usual, fancied that this name Cibao must be a corruption of Cipango, and that this chieftain with golden banners must be identical with the magnificent prince of that island, mentioned by Marco Polo.[1]

[1] Journal of Columb. Navarrete, Colec., tom. i. Hist. del Almirante, cap. 32. Herrera, decad. i. lib. i. cap. 15, 16.

CHAPTER VIII.

SHIPWRECK.

[1492.]

ON the morning of the 24th of December, Columbus set sail from Port St. Thomas before sunrise, and steered to the eastward, with an intention of anchoring at the harbor of the cacique Guacanagari. The wind was from the land, but so light as scarcely to fill the sails, and the ships made but little progress. At eleven o'clock at night, being Christmas eve, they were within a league or a league and a half of the residence of the cacique; and Columbus, who had hitherto kept watch, finding the sea calm and smooth, and the ship almost motionless, retired to rest, not having slept the preceding night. He was, in general, extremely wakeful on his coasting voyages, passing whole nights upon deck in all weathers; never trusting to the watchfulness of others, where there was any difficulty or danger to be provided against. In the present instance he felt perfectly secure; not merely on account of the profound calm, but because the boats on the preceding day, in their visit to the cacique, had reconnoitred the coast, and had reported that there were neither rocks nor shoals in their course.

No sooner had he retired, than the steersman gave the helm in charge to one of the ship-boys, and went to sleep. This was in direct violation of an invariable order of the admiral, that the helm should never be intrusted to the boys. The rest of the mariners who had the watch took like advantage of the absence of Columbus, and in a little while the whole crew was buried in sleep. In the meantime the treacherous currents, which run swiftly along this coast, carried the vessel quietly, but with force, upon a sand-bank. The heedless boy had not noticed the breakers, although they made a roaring that might have been heard a league. No sooner, however, did he feel the rudder strike, and hear the tumult of the rushing sea, than he began to cry for aid. Columbus, whose careful thoughts never permitted him to sleep profoundly, was the first on deck. The master of the ship, whose duty it was to have been on watch, next made his appearance, followed by others of the crew, half awake. The admiral ordered them to take the boat and carry out an anchor astern, to warp the vessel off. The master and the sailors sprang into the boat; but, confused, as men are apt to be when suddenly awakened by an alarm, instead of obeying the commands of Columbus, they rowed off to the other caravel, about half a league to windward.

In the meantime the master had reached the caravel, and made known the perilous state in which he had left the vessel. He was reproached with his pusillanimous desertion; the commander of the caravel manned his boat and hastened to the relief of the admiral, followed by the recreant master covered with shame and confusion.

It was too late to save the ship, the current having set her more upon the bank. The admiral, seeing that his boat had deserted him, that the ship had swung across the stream, and that the water was continually gaining upon her, ordered the mast to be cut away, in the hope of lightening her sufficiently to float her off. Every effort was in vain. The keel was firmly bedded in the sand; the shock had opened several seams; while the swell of the breakers, striking her broadside, left her each moment more and more aground, until she fell over on one side. Fortunately the weather continued calm, otherwise the ship must have gone to pieces, and the whole crew might have perished amidst the currents and breakers.

The admiral and her men took refuge on board the caravel. Diego de Arana, chief judge of the armament, and Pedro Gutierrez, the king's butler, were immediately sent on shore as envoys to the cacique Guacanagari, to inform him of the intended visit of the admiral, and of his disastrous shipwreck. In the meantime, as a light wind had sprung up from shore, and the admiral was ignorant of his situation, and of the rocks and banks that might be lurking around him, he lay to until daylight.

The habitation of the cacique was about a league and a half from the wreck. When he heard of the misfortune of his guest, he manifested the utmost affliction, and even shed tears. He immediately sent all his people, with all the canoes, large and small, that could be mustered; and so active were they in their assistance, that in a little while the vessel was unloaded. The cacique himself, and his brothers and relatives, rendered all the aid in their power, both on sea and land; keeping vigilant guard that every thing should be conducted with order, and the property secured from injury or theft. From time to time he sent some one of his family, or some principal person of his attendants, to console and cheer the admiral, assuring him that every thing he possessed should be at his disposal.

Never, in a civilized country, were the vaunted rites of hospitality more scrupulously observed, than by this uncultivated savage. All the effects landed from the ships were deposited near his dwelling; and an armed guard surrounded them all night, until houses could be prepared in which to store them. There seemed, however, even among the common people, no disposition to take advantage of the misfortune of the stranger. Although they beheld what must in their eyes have been inestimable treasures, cast, as it were, upon their shores, and open to depredation, yet there was not the least attempt to pilfer, nor, in transporting the effects from the ships, had they appropriated the most trifling article. On the contrary, a general sympathy was visible in their countenances and actions; and to have witnessed their concern, one would have supposed the misfortune to have happened to themselves.[1]

"So loving, so tractable, so peaceable are these people," says Columbus in his journal, "that I swear to your Majesties, there is not in the world a better nation, nor a better land. They love their neighbors as themselves; and their discourse is ever sweet and gentle, and accompanied with a smile; and though it is true that they are naked, yet their manners are decorous and praiseworthy."

CHAPTER IX.

TRANSACTIONS WITH THE NATIVES.

[1492.]

On the 26th of December, Guacanagari came on board of the caravel Niña, to visit the admiral, and observing him to be very much dejected, was moved to tears. He repeated the message which he had sent, entreating Columbus not to be cast down by his misfortune, and offering every thing he possessed, that might render him aid or consolation. He had already given three houses to shelter the Spaniards, and to receive the effects landed from the wreck, and he offered to furnish more if necessary.

While they were conversing, a canoe arrived from another part of the island, bringing pieces of gold to be exchanged for hawks' bells. There was nothing upon which the natives set so much value as upon these toys. The Indians were extravagantly fond of the dance, which they performed to the cadence of certain songs, accompanied by the sound of a kind of drum, made from the trunk of a tree, and the rattling of hollow bits of wood; but when they hung the hawks' bells about their persons,

[1] Hist. del Almirante, cap. 32. Las Casas, lib. i. cap. 9.

and heard the clear musical sound responding to the movements of the dance, nothing could exceed their wild delight.

The sailors who came from the shore informed the admiral that considerable quantities of gold had been brought
to barter, and large pieces were eagerly given for the merest
trifle. This information had a cheering effect upon Columbus. The attentive cacique, perceiving the lighting up of
his countenance, asked what the sailors had communicated.
When he learnt its purport, and found that the admiral
was extremely desirous of procuring gold, he assured him
by signs, that there was a place not far off, among the
mountains, where it abounded to such a degree as to be
held in little value, and promised to procure him thence as
much as he desired. The place to which he alluded, and
which he called Cibao, was in fact a mountainous region
afterwards found to contain valuable mines; but Columbus
still confounded the name with that of Cipango.[1]

Guacanagari dined on board of the caravel with the
admiral, after which he invited him to visit his residence.
Here he had prepared a collation, as choice and abundant
as his simple means afforded, consisting of utias, or coneys,
fish, roots, and various fruits. He did every thing in his
power to honor his guest, and cheer him under his misfortune, showing a warmth of sympathy, yet delicacy of
attention, which could not have been expected from his
savage state. Indeed there was a degree of innate dignity and refinement displayed in his manners, that often
surprised the Spaniards. He was remarkably nice and
decorous in his mode of eating, which was slow and with
moderation, washing his hands when he had finished, and
rubbing them with sweet and odoriferous herbs, which
Columbus supposed was done to preserve their delicacy
and softness. He was served with great deference by his
subjects, and conducted himself towards them with a
gracious and prince-like majesty. His whole deportment,

[1] Primer Viage de Colon, Navarrete, tom. i. p. 114.

in the enthusiastic eyes of Columbus, betokened the inborn grace and dignity of lofty lineage.[1]

In fact, the sovereignty among the people of this island was hereditary, and they had a simple but sagacious mode of maintaining, in some degree, the verity of descent. On the death of a cacique without children, his authority passed to those of his sisters, in preference to those of his brothers, being considered most likely to be of his blood; for they observed, that a brother's reputed children may by accident have no consanguinity with their uncle; but those of his sister must certainly be the children of their mother. The form of government was completely despotic; the caciques had entire control over the lives, the property, and even the religion of their subjects. They had few laws, and ruled according to their judgment and their will; but they ruled mildly, and were implicitly and cheerfully obeyed. Throughout the course of the disastrous history of these islanders, after their discovery by the Europeans, there are continual proofs of their affectionate and devoted fidelity to their caciques.

After the collation, Guacanagari conducted Columbus to the beautiful groves which surrounded his residence. They were attended by upwards of a thousand of the natives, all perfectly naked, who performed several national games and dances, which Guacanagari had ordered, to amuse the melancholy of his guest.

When the Indians had finished their games, Columbus gave them an entertainment in return, calculated at the same time to impress them with a formidable idea of the military power of the Spaniards. He sent on board the caravel for a Moorish bow and a quiver of arrows, and a Castilian who had served in the wars of Granada, and was skillful in the use of them. When the cacique beheld the accuracy with which this man used his weapons, he was

[1] Las Casas, lib. i. cap. 70, MS. Primer Viage de Colon. Navarrete, tom. i. p. 114.

greatly surprised, being himself of an unwarlike character,
and little accustomed to the use of arms. He told the admiral that the Caribs, who often made descents upon his
territory, and carried off his subjects, were likewise armed
with bows and arrows. Columbus assured him of the protection of the Castilian monarchs, who would destroy the
Caribs, for he let him know that he had weapons far more
tremendous, against which there was no defence. In proof
of this, he ordered a lombard or heavy cannon, and an
arquebus, to be discharged.

On hearing the report the Indians fell to the ground, as
though they had been struck by a thunderbolt ; and when
they saw the effect of the ball, rending and shivering the
trees like a stroke of lightning, they were filled with dismay. Being told, however, that the Spaniards would defend
them with these arms against their dreaded enemies the
Caribs, their alarm was changed into exultation, considering themselves under the protection of the sons of heaven,
who had come from the skies armed with thunder and
lightning.

The cacique now presented Columbus with a mask carved
of wood, with the eyes, ears, and various other parts of gold ;
he hung plates of the same metal round his neck, and
placed a kind of golden coronet upon his head. He dispensed presents also among the followers of the admiral ;
acquitting himself in all things with a munificence that
would have done honor to an accomplished prince in civilized life.

Whatever trifles Columbus gave in return were regarded
with reverence as celestial gifts. The Indians, in admiring
the articles of European manufacture, continually repeated
the word *turey*, which in their language signifies heaven.
They pretended to distinguish the different qualities of gold
by the smell; in the same way, when any article of tin, of
silver, or other white metal was given them, to which they
were unaccustomed, they smelt it and declared it "turey,"

of excellent quality; giving in exchange pieces of the finest gold. Every thing, in fact, from the hands of the Spaniards, even a rusty piece of iron, an end of a strap, or a head of a nail, had an occult and supernatural value and smelt of turey. Hawks' bells, however, were sought by them with a mania only equaled by that of the Spaniards for gold. They could not contain their ecstasies at the sound, dancing and playing a thousand antics. On one occasion an Indian gave half a handful of gold dust in exchange for one of these toys, and no sooner was he in possession of it, than he bounded away to the woods, looking often behind him, fearing the Spaniards might repent of having parted so cheaply with such an inestimable jewel.[1]

The extreme kindness of the cacique, the gentleness of his people, the quantities of gold which were daily brought to be exchanged for the veriest trifles, and the information continually received of sources of wealth in the interior of this island, all contributed to console the admiral for his misfortune.

The shipwrecked crew, also, became fascinated with their easy and idle mode of life. Exempted by their simplicity from the cares and toils which civilized man inflicts upon himself by his many artificial wants, the existence of these islanders seemed to the Spaniards like a pleasant dream. They disquieted themselves about nothing. A few fields, cultivated almost without labor, furnished the roots and vegetables which formed a great part of their diet. Their rivers and coasts abounded with fish; their trees were laden with fruits of golden or blushing hue, and heightened by a tropical sun to delicious flavor and fragrance. Softened by the indulgence of nature, and by a voluptuous climate, a great part of their day was passed in indolent repose, and in the evenings they danced in their fragrant groves, to their national songs, or the sound of their sylvan drums.

Such was the indolent and holiday life of these simple

[1] Las Casas, lib. i. cap. 70, MS.

people; which, if it had not the great scope of enjoyment, nor the high-seasoned poignancy of pleasure which attend civilization, was certainly destitute of most of its artificial miseries. The venerable Las Casas, speaking of their perfect nakedness, observes, it seemed almost as if they were existing in the state of primeval innocence of our first parents, before their fall brought sin into the world. He might have added, that they seemed exempt likewise from the penalty inflicted on the children of Adam, that they should eat their bread by the sweat of their brow.

When the Spanish mariners looked back upon their own toilsome and painful life, and reflected on the cares and hardships that must still be their lot if they returned to Europe, it is no wonder that they regarded with a wistful eye the easy and idle existence of these Indians. Wherever they went they met with caressing hospitality. The men were simple, frank, and cordial; the women loving and compliant, and prompt to form those connections which anchor the most wandering heart. They saw gold glittering around them, to be had without labor, and every enjoyment to be procured without cost. Captivated by these advantages, many of the seamen represented to the admiral the difficulties and sufferings they must encounter on a return voyage, where so many would be crowded in a small caravel, and entreated permission to remain in the island.[1]

CHAPTER X.

BUILDING OF THE FORTRESS OF LA NAVIDAD.

[1492.]

THE solicitude expressed by many of his people to be left behind, added to the friendly and pacific character of the

[1] Primer Viage de Colon. Navarrete, tom. i. p. 116.

natives, now suggested to Columbus the idea of forming the
germ of a future colony. The wreck of the caravel would
afford materials to construct a fortress, which might be defended by her guns, and supplied with her ammunition;
and he could spare provisions enough to maintain a small
garrison for a year. The people who thus remained on the
island could explore it, and make themselves acquainted
with its mines, and other sources of wealth; they might, at
the same time, procure by traffic a large quantity of gold
from the natives; they could learn their language, and accustom themselves to their habits and manners, so as to be
of great use in future intercourse. In the meantime, the
admiral could return to Spain, report the success of his enterprise, and bring out reinforcements.

No sooner did this idea break upon the mind of Columbus, than he set about accomplishing it with his accustomed
promptness and celerity. The wreck was broken up and
brought piece-meal to shore; and a site chosen, and preparations made for the erection of a tower. When Guacanagari
was informed of the intention of the admiral to leave a
part of his men for the defence of the island from the
Caribs, while he returned to his country for more, he was
greatly overjoyed. His subjects manifested equal delight
at the idea of retaining these wonderful people among
them; and at the prospect of the future arrival of the
admiral, with ships freighted with hawks' bells, and other
precious articles. They eagerly lent their assistance in
building the fortress; little dreaming that they were assist-
ing to place on their necks the galling yoke of perpetual
and toilsome slavery.

The preparations for the fortress were scarcely commenced, when certain Indians, arriving at the harbor,
brought a report that a great vessel, like those of the
admiral, had anchored in a river at the eastern end of the
island. These tidings, for a time, dispelled a thousand uneasy conjectures which had harassed the mind of Columbus,

for of course this vessel could be no other than the Pinta. He immediately procured a canoe from Guacanagari, with several Indians to navigate it, and dispatched a Spaniard with a letter to Pinzon, couched in amicable terms, making no complaints of his desertion, but urging him to join company immediately.

After three days' absence the canoe returned. The Spaniard reported that he had pursued the coast for twenty leagues, but had neither seen nor heard any thing of the Pinta; he considered the report, therefore, as incorrect. Other rumors, however, were immediately afterwards circulated at the harbor, of this large vessel to the eastward; but, on investigation, they appeared to Columbus to be equally undeserving of credit. He relapsed, therefore, into his doubts and anxieties in respect to Pinzon. Since the shipwreck of his vessel, the desertion of that commander had become a matter of still more serious moment, and had obliged him to alter all his plans. Should the Pinta be lost, as was very possible in a voyage of such extent and exposed to so many uncommon perils, there would then be but one ship surviving, of the three which had set sail from Palos, and that one an indifferent sailer. On the precarious return of that crazy bark, across an immense expanse of ocean, would depend the ultimate success of the expedition. Should that one likewise perish, every record of this great discovery would be swallowed up with it; the name of Columbus would only be remembered as that of a mad adventurer, who, despising the opinions of the learned and the counsels of the wise, had departed into the wilds of the ocean never to return; the obscurity of his fate, and its imagined horrors, might deter all future enterprise, and thus the new world might remain as heretofore, unknown to civilized man. These considerations determined Columbus to abandon all further prosecution of his voyage; to leave unexplored the magnificent regions which were inviting him on every hand; to give up all hope for the present of

finding his way to the dominions of the Grand Khan, and
to lose no time in returning to Spain and reporting his discovery.

While the fortress was building, he continued to receive
every day new proofs of the amity and kindness of
Guacanagari. Whenever he went on shore to superintend
the works, he was entertained in the most hospitable manner by that chieftain. He had the largest house in the
place prepared for his reception, strewed or carpeted with
palm-leaves, and furnished with low stools of a black and
shining wood that looked like jet. When he received the
admiral, it was always in a style of princely generosity,
hanging around his neck some jewel of gold, or making him
some present of similar value.

On one occasion, he came to meet him on his landing,
attended by five tributary caciques, each carrying a coronet
of gold; they conducted him with great deference to the
house already mentioned, where, seating him in one of the
chairs, Guacanagari took off his own coronet of gold and
placed it upon his head : Columbus in return took from
his neck a collar of fine-colored beads, which he put round
that of the cacique; he invested him with his own mantle
of fine cloth, gave him a pair of colored boots, and put on
his finger a large silver ring, upon which metal the Indians
set a great value, it not being found in their island.

The cacique exerted himself to the utmost to procure a
great quantity of gold for the admiral before his departure
for Spain. The supplies thus furnished, and the vague
accounts collected through the medium of signs and imperfect interpretations, gave Columbus magnificent ideas
of the wealth in the interior of this island. The names of
caciques, mountains, and provinces were confused together
in his imagination, and supposed to mean various places
where great treasure was to be found; above all, the name
of Cibao continually occurred, the golden region among
the mountains, whence the natives procured most of the

ore for their ornaments. In the pimento or red pepper
which abounded in the island, he fancied he found a trace
of oriental spices, and he thought he had met with specimens of rhubarb.

Passing, with his usual excitability, from a state of doubt
and anxiety to one of sanguine anticipation, he now considered his shipwreck as a providential event mysteriously
ordained by heaven to work out the success of his enterprise. Without this seeming disaster, he should never
have remained to find out the secret wealth of the island,
but should merely have touched at various parts of the
coast, and passed on. As a proof that the particular hand
of Providence was exerted in it, he cites the circumstance
of his having been wrecked in a perfect calm, without wind
or wave ; and the desertion of the pilot and mariners, when
sent to carry out an anchor astern ; for, had they performed
his orders, the vessel would have been hauled off, they
would have pursued their voyage, and the treasures of the
island would have remained a secret. But now he looked
forward to glorious fruits to be reaped from this seeming
evil; "for he hoped," he said, "that when he returned
from Spain, he should find a ton of gold collected in traffic
by those whom he had left behind, and mines and spices
discovered in such quantities, that the sovereigns, before
three years, would be able to undertake a crusade for the
deliverance of the holy sepulchre ; " the grand object to
which he had proposed that they should dedicate the fruits
of this enterprise.

Such was the visionary, yet generous, enthusiasm of
Columbus, the moment that prospects of vast wealth broke
upon his mind. What in some spirits would have awakened a grasping and sordid avidity to accumulate, immediately filled his imagination with plans of magnificent
expenditure. But how vain are our attempts to interpret
the inscrutable decrees of Providence! The shipwreck,
which Columbus considered an act of divine favor, to

reveal to him the secrets of the land, shackled and limited
all his after discoveries. It linked his fortunes, for the
remainder of his life, to this island, which was doomed to
be to him a source of cares and troubles, to involve him
in a thousand perplexities, and to becloud his declining
years with humiliation and disappointment.

CHAPTER XI.

REGULATION OF THE FORTRESS OF LA NAVIDAD.—DEPART-
URE OF COLUMBUS FOR SPAIN.

So great was the activity of the Spaniards in the construction of their fortress, and so ample the assistance
rendered by the natives, that in ten days it was sufficiently
complete for service. A large vault had been made, over
which was erected a strong wooden tower, and the whole
was surrounded by a wide ditch. It was stored with all
the ammunition saved from the wreck, or that could be
spared from the caravel ; and, the guns being mounted, the
whole had a formidable aspect, sufficient to overawe and
repulse this naked and unwarlike people. Indeed Columbus
was of opinion that but little force was necessary to subju-
gate the whole island. He considered a fortress, and the
restrictions of a garrison, more requisite to keep the
Spaniards themselves in order, and prevent their wandering about, and committing acts of licentiousness among
the natives.

The fortress being finished, he gave it, as well as the
adjacent village and the harbor, the name of La Navidad,
or the Nativity, in memorial of their having escaped from
the shipwreck on Christmas day. Many volunteered to
remain on the island, from whom he selected thirty-nine of
the most able and exemplary, and among them a physician,
ship-carpenter, calker, cooper, tailor, and gunner, all expert
at their several callings. The command was given to Diego

13

de Arana, a native of Cordova, and notary and alguazil to
the armament, who was to retain all the powers vested in
him by the catholic sovereigns.   In case of his death,
Pedro Gutierrez was to command, and, he dying, Rodrigo
de Escobedo.   The boat of the wreck was left with them,
to be used in fishing; a variety of seeds to sow, and a
large quantity of articles for traffic, that they might procure as much gold as possible against the admiral's return.[1]

As the time drew nigh for his departure, Columbus
assembled those who were to remain in the island, and
made them an earnest address, charging them, in the name
of the sovereigns, to be obedient to the officer left in
command; to maintain the utmost respect and reverence
for the cacique Guacanagari and his chieftains, recollecting
how deeply they were indebted to his goodness, and how
important a continuance of it was to their welfare.   To
be circumspect in their intercourse with the natives, avoid-
ing disputes, and treating them always with gentleness and
justice; and, above all, being discreet in their conduct
towards the Indian women, misconduct in this respect
being the frequent source of troubles and disasters in the
intercourse with savage nations.   He warned them, moreover, not to scatter themselves asunder, but to keep together,
for mutual safety; and not to stray beyond the friendly
territory of Guacanagari.   He enjoined it upon Arana,
and the others in command, to acquire a knowledge of
the productions and mines of the island, to procure gold
and spices, and to seek along the coast a better situation
for a settlement, the present harbor being inconvenient and
dangerous, from the rocks and shoals which beset its
entrance.

On the 2d of January, 1493, Columbus landed to take a
farewell of the generous cacique and his chieftains, intending the next day to set sail.   He gave them a parting

[1] Primer Viage de Colon.   Navarrete, tom. i.   Hist. del Almirante,
cap. 33.

feast at the house devoted to his use, and commended to
their kindness the men who were to remain, especially
Diego de Arana, Pedro Gutierrez, and Rodrigo de Escobedo, his lieutenants, assuring the cacique that, when he returned from Castile, he would bring abundance of jewels
more precious than any he or his people had yet seen. The
worthy Guacanagari showed great concern at the idea of
his departure, and assured him that, as to those who remained, he should furnish them with provisions, and render
them every service in his power.

Once more to impress the Indians with an idea of the
warlike prowess of the white men, Columbus caused the
crews to perform skirmishes and mock-fights, with swords,
bucklers, lances, crossbows, arquebuses, and cannon. The
Indians were astonished at the keenness of the swords, and
at the deadly power of the cross-bows and arquebuses; but
they were struck with awe when the heavy Lombards were
discharged from the fortress, wrapping it in wreaths of
smoke, shaking the forests with their report, and shivering
the trees with the balls of stone used in artillery in those
times. As these tremendous powers, however, were all to
be employed for their protection, they rejoiced while they
trembled, since no Carib would now dare to invade their
island.[1]

The festivities of the day being over, Columbus embraced
the cacique and his principal chieftains, and took a final
leave of them. Guacanagari shed tears; for while he had
been awed by the dignified demeanor of the admiral, and
the idea of his superhuman nature, he had been completely
won by the benignity of his manners. Indeed, the parting
scene was sorrowful on all sides. The arrival of the ships
had been an event of wonder and excitement to the islanders, who had as yet known nothing but the good qualities
of their guests, and had been enriched by their celestial
gifts; while the rude seamen had been flattered by the

[1] Primer Viage de Colon. Navarrete, tom. i. p. 121.

blind deference paid them, and captivated by the kindness and unlimited indulgence with which they had been treated.

The sorest parting was between the Spaniards who embarked and those who remained behind, from the strong sympathy caused by companionship in perils and adventures. The little garrison, however, evinced a stout heart, looking forward to the return of the admiral from Spain with large reinforcements, when they promised to give him a good account of all things in the island. The caravel was detained a day longer by the absence of some of the Indians whom they were to take to Spain. At length the signal-gun was fired; the crew gave a parting cheer to the handful of comrades thus left in the wilderness of an unknown world, who echoed their cheering as they gazed wistfully after them from the beach, but who were destined never to welcome their return.

NOTE *about the localities in the preceding chapter, extracted from the letter of T. S. Heneken, Esq.*

Guacanagari's capital town was called Guarico. From the best information I can gather, it was situated a short distance from the beach, where the village of Petit Anse now stands; which is about two miles southeast of Cape Haytien.

Oviedo says that Columbus took in water for his homeward voyage from a small stream to the northwest of the anchorage; and presuming him to have been at anchor off Petit Anse, this stream presents itself falling from the Picolet mountain, crossing the present town of Cape Haytien, and emptying into the bay near the Arsenal.

The stream which supplied Columbus with water was dammed up at the foot of the mountain by the French when in possession of the country, and its water now feeds a number of public fountains.

Punta Santa could be no other than the present Point Picolet.

Beating up from St. Nicholas Mole along an almost precipitous and iron-bound coast, a prospect of unrivaled splendor breaks upon the view on turning this point; the spacious bay, the extensive plains, and the distant cordilleras of the Cibao mountains, impose upon the mind an impression of vastness, fertility, and beauty.

The fort of La Navidad must have been erected near Haut du Cap, as it could be approached in boats by rowing up the river, and there is no other river in the vicinity that admits a passage for boats.

The locality of the town of Guacanagari has always been known by the name of Guarico. The French first settled at Petit Anse; subsequently they removed to the opposite side of of the bay and founded the town of Cape Francois, now Cape Haytien; but the old Indian name Guarico continues in use among all the Spanish inhabitants of the vicinity.

BOOK V.

CHAPTER I.

COASTING TOWARDS THE EASTERN END OF HISPANIOLA.—
MEETING WITH PINZON.—AFFAIR WITH THE NATIVES
AT THE GULF OF SAMANA.

[1493.]

It was on the 4th of January that Columbus set sail
from La Navidad on his return to Spain. The wind being
light, it was necessary to tow the caravel out of the harbor,
and clear of the reefs. They then stood eastward, towards
a lofty promontory destitute of trees, but covered with
grass, and shaped like a tent, having at a distance the appearance of a towering island, being connected with Hispaniola by a low neck of land. To this promontory Columbus gave the name of Monte Christi, by which it is still
known. The country in the immediate neighborhood was
level, but further inland rose a high range of mountains,
well wooded, with broad, fruitful valleys between them,
watered by abundant streams. The wind being contrary,
they were detained for two days in a large bay to the west
of the promontory. On the 6th, they again made sail with
a land breeze, and, weathering the cape, advanced ten
leagues, when the wind again turned to blow freshly from
the east. At this time a sailor, stationed at the mast-head
to look out for rocks, cried out that he beheld the Pinta at
a distance. The certainty of the fact gladdened the heart
of the admiral, and had an animating effect throughout the
ship; for it was a joyful event to the mariners once more to

meet with their comrades, and to have a companion bark in their voyage through these lonely seas.

The Pinta came sweeping towards them, directly before the wind. The admiral was desirous of having a conversation with Martin Alonzo Pinzon, and seeing that all attempt was fruitless from the obstinacy of the adverse wind, and that there was no safe anchorage in the neighborhood, he put back to the bay a little west of Monte Christi, whither he was followed by the Pinta. On their first interview, Pinzon endeavored to excuse his desertion, alleging that he had been compelled to part company by stress of weather, and had ever since been seeking to rejoin the admiral. Columbus listened passively but dubiously to his apologies; and the suspicions he had conceived appeared to be warranted by subsequent information. He was told that Pinzon had been excited by accounts given him by one of the Indians on board of his vessel of a region to the eastward, abounding in gold. Taking advantage, therefore, of the superior sailing of his vessel, he had worked to windward, when the other ships had been obliged to put back, and had sought to be the first to discover and enjoy this golden region. After separating from his companions he had been entangled for several days among a cluster of small islands, supposed to have been the Caicos, but had at length been guided by the Indians to Hispaniola. Here he remained three weeks, trading with the natives in the river already mentioned, and collected a considerable quantity of gold, one half of which he retained as captain, the rest he divided among his men to secure their fidelity and secrecy.

Such were the particulars privately related to Columbus; who, however, repressed his indignation at this flagrant breach of duty, being unwilling to disturb the remainder of his voyage with any altercations with Pinzon, who had a powerful party of relatives and townsmen in the armament. To such a degree, however, was his confidence in his confederates impaired, that he determined to return forthwith to Spain, though under other circumstances he would have been tempted to explore the coast in hopes of freighting his ships with treasure.[1]

The boats were accordingly dispatched to a large river, in the neighborhood, to procure a supply of wood and water for the voyage. This river, called by the natives the Yaqui, flows from the mountains of the interior and throws itself into the bay; receiving, in its course, the contributions of various minor streams. Many particles of gold were perceived among the sands at its mouth, and others were found adhering to the hoops of the water casks.[2] Columbus gave it, therefore, the name of Rio del Oro, or the Golden River: it is at present called the Santiago.

In this neighborhood were turtles of great size. Columbus also mentions in his journal that he saw three mermaids which elevated themselves above the surface of the sea, and he observes that he had before seen such on the coasts of Africa. He adds that they were by no means the beautiful beings they had been represented, although they possessed some traces of the human countenance. It is supposed that these must have been manate or sea-calves, seen indistinctly and at a distance; and that the imagination of Columbus, disposed to give a wonderful character to every thing in this new world, had identified these misshapen animals with the sirens of ancient story.

On the evening of the 9th January they again made sail, and on the following day arrived at the river where Pinzon had been trading, to which Columbus gave the name of Rio de Gracia; but it took the appellation of its original discoverer, and long continued to be known as the river of

[1] Hist. del Almirante, cap. 34.
[2] Las Casas suggests that these may have been particles of marcasite, which abounds in this river, and in the other streams which fall from the mountains of Cibaó. Las Casas, Hist. Ind., lib. i. cap. 76.

Martin Alonzo.[1] The natives of this place complained that Pinzon, on his previous visit, had violently carried off four men and two girls. The admiral, finding they were retained on board of the Pinta to be carried to Spain and sold as slaves, ordered them to be immediately restored to their homes, with many presents, and well clothed, to atone for the wrong they had experienced. This restitution was made with great unwillingness, and many high words, on the part of Pinzon.

The wind being favorable, for in these regions the trade wind is often alternated during autumn and winter by northwesterly breezes, they continued coasting the island, until they came to a high and beautiful headland, to which they gave the name of Capo del Enamorado, or the Lovers' Cape, but which at present is known as Cape Cabron. A little beyond this, they anchored in a bay, or rather gulf, three leagues in breadth, and extending so far inland, that Columbus at first supposed it an arm of the sea, separating Hispaniola from some other land. On landing they found the natives quite different from the gentle and pacific people hitherto met with on this island. They were of a ferocious aspect, and hideously painted. Their hair was long, tied behind, and decorated with the feathers of parrots and other birds of gaudy plumage. Some were armed with war-clubs; others had bows of the length of those used by the English archers, with arrows of slender reeds, pointed with hard wood, or tipped with bone or the tooth of a fish. Their swords were of palm wood, as hard and heavy as iron; not sharp, but broad, nearly of the thickness of two fingers, and capable, with one blow, of cleaving through a helmet to the very brains.[2] Though thus prepared for combat, they made no attempt to molest the Spaniards; on the contrary, they sold them two of their bows and several

---

[1] It is now called Porto Caballo, but the surrounding plain is called the Savanna of Martin Alonzo.—T. S. HENEKEN.

[2] Las Casas, Hist. Ind., lib. i. cap. 77, MS.

of their arrows, and one of them was prevailed upon to go on board of the admiral's ship.

Columbus was persuaded, from the ferocious looks and hardy undaunted manner of this wild warrior, that he and his companions were of the nation of Caribs, so much dreaded throughout these seas, and that the gulf in which he was anchored must be a strait separating their island from Hispaniola. On inquiring of the Indian, however, he still pointed to the east, as the quarter where lay the Caribbean islands. He spoke also of an island, called Mantinino, which Columbus fancied him to say was peopled merely by women, who received the Caribs among them once a year, for the sake of continuing the population of their island. All the male progeny resulting from such visits were delivered to the fathers, the female remained with the mothers.

This Amazonian island is repeatedly mentioned in the course of the voyages of Columbus, and is another of his self-delusions, to be explained by the work of Marco Polo. That traveler described two islands near the coast of Asia, one inhabited solely by women, the other by men, between which a similar intercourse subsisted;[1] and Columbus, supposing himself in that vicinity, easily interpreted the signs of the Indians to coincide with the descriptions of the Venetian.

Having regaled the warrior, and made him various presents, the admiral sent him on shore, in hopes, through his mediation, of opening a trade for gold with his companions. As the boat approached the land, upwards of fifty savages, armed with bows and arrows, war-clubs, and javelins, were seen lurking among the trees. On a word from the Indian who was in the boat, they laid by their arms and came forth to meet the Spaniards. The latter, according to directions from the admiral, endeavored to purchase several of their weapons, to take as curiosities to

[1] Marco Polo, book iii. chap. 34; Eng. edit. of Marsden.

Spain. They parted with two of their bows; but, suddenly conceiving some distrust, or thinking to overpower this handful of strangers, they rushed to the place where they had left their weapons, snatched them up, and returned with cords, as if to bind the Spaniards. The latter immediately attacked them, wounded two, put the rest to flight, and would have pursued them, but were restrained by the pilot who commanded the boat. This was the first contest with the Indians, and the first time that native blood was shed by the white men in the new world. Columbus was grieved to see all his exertions to maintain an amicable intercourse vain: he consoled himself with the idea, however, that if these were Caribs, or frontier Indians of warlike character, they would be inspired with a dread of the force and weapons of the white men, and be deterred from molesting the little garrison of Fort Nativity. The fact was, that these were of a bold and hardy race, inhabiting a mountainous district called Ciguay, extending five and twenty leagues along the coast, and several leagues into the interior. They differed in language, look, and manners from the other natives of the island, and had the rude, but independent and vigorous character of mountaineers.

Their frank and bold spirit was evinced on the day after the skirmish, when a multitude appearing on the beach, the admiral sent a large party, well armed, on shore in the boat. The natives approached as freely and confidently as if nothing had happened; neither did they betray, throughout their subsequent intercourse, any signs of lurking fear or enmity. The cacique who ruled over the neighboring country was on the shore. He sent to the boat a string of beads formed of small stones, or rather of the hard part of shells, which the Spaniards understood to be a token and assurance of amity; but they were not yet aware of the full meaning of this symbol, the wampum belt, the pledge of peace, held sacred among the Indians.

The chieftain followed shortly after, and entering the boat with only three attendants, was conveyed on board of the caravel.

This frank and confiding conduct, so indicative of a brave and generous nature, was properly appreciated by Columbus; he received the cacique cordially, set before him a collation such as the caravel afforded, particularly biscuits and honey, which were great dainties with the Indians, and after showing him the wonders of the vessel, and making him and his attendants many presents, sent them to land highly gratified. The residence of the cacique was at such a distance that he could not repeat his visit; but, as a token of high regard, he sent to the admiral his coronet of gold. In speaking of these incidents, the historians of Columbus have made no mention of the name of this mountain chief; he was doubtless the same who, a few years afterwards, appears in the history of the island under the name of Mayonabex, cacique of the Ciguayans, and will be found acquitting himself with valor, frankness, and magnanimity, under the most trying circumstances.

Columbus remained a day or two longer in the bay, during which time the most friendly intercourse prevailed with the natives, who brought cotton, and various fruits and vegetables, but still maintained their warrior character, being always armed with bows and arrows. Four young Indians gave such interesting accounts of the islands situated to the east, that Columbus determined to touch there on his way to Spain, and prevailed on them to accompany him as guides. Taking advantage of a favorable wind, therefore, he sailed before daylight on the 16th of January from this bay, to which, in consequence of the skirmish with the natives, he gave the name of Golfo de las Flechas, or the Gulf of Arrows, but which is now known by the name of the Gulf of Samana.

On leaving the bay, Columbus at first steered to the

northeast, in which direction the young Indians assured
him he would find the island of the Caribs; and that of
Mantinino, the abode of the Amazons; it being his desire
to take several of the natives of each, to present to the
Spanish sovereigns. After sailing about sixteen leagues,
however, his Indian guides changed their opinion, and
pointed to the southeast. This would have brought him
to Porto Rico, which, in fact, was known among the Indians as the island of Carib. The admiral immediately
shifted sail, and stood in this direction. He had not proceeded two leagues, however, when a most favorable breeze
sprang up for the voyage to Spain. He observed a gloom
gathering on the countenances of the sailors, as they di-
verged from the homeward route. Reflecting upon the
little hold he had upon the feelings and affections of these
men, the insubordinate spirit they had repeatedly evinced,
the uncertainty of the good faith of Pinzon, and the leaky
condition of his ships, he was suddenly brought to a pause.
As long as he protracted his return, the whole fate of his
discovery was at the mercy of a thousand contingencies,
and an adverse accident might bury himself, his crazy
barks, and all the records of his voyage for ever in the
ocean. Repressing, therefore, the strong inclination to
seek further discoveries, and determined to place what he
had already made beyond the reach of accident, he once
more shifted sail, to the great joy of his crews, and resumed his course for Spain.[1]

[1] Journal of Columb. Navarrete, tom. i. Las Casas, Hist. Ind.,
lib. i. cap. 77. Hist. del Almirante, cap. 34, 35.

CHAPTER II.

RETURN VOYAGE.—VIOLENT STORMS.—ARRIVAL AT THE
AZORES.

[1493.]

THE trade winds which had been so propitious to Columbus on his outward voyage, were .equally adverse to
him on his return. The favorable breeze soon died away,
and throughout the remainder of January there was a
prevalence of light winds from the eastward, which prevented any great progress. He was frequently detained
also by the bad sailing of the Pinta, the foremast of which
was so defective that it could carry but little sail. The
weather continued mild and pleasant, and the sea so calm,
that the Indians whom they were taking to Spain would
frequently plunge into the water, and swim about the ships.
They saw many tunny fish, one of which they killed, as
likewise a large shark; these gave them a temporary supply of provisions, of which they soon began to stand in
need, their sea stock being reduced to bread and wine and
Agi peppers, which last they had learnt from the Indians
to use as an important article of food.

In the early part of February, having run to about the
thirty-eighth degree of north latitude, and got out of the
track swept by the trade-winds, they had more favorable
breezes, and were enabled to steer direct for Spain. From
the frequent changes of their course, the pilots became perplexed in their reckonings, differing widely among themselves, and still more widely from the truth. Columbus,
beside keeping a careful reckoning, was a vigilant observer
of those indications furnished by the sea, the air, and the
sky; the fate of himself and his ships, in the unknown
regions which he traversed, often depended upon these observations; and the sagacity at which he arrived, in

deciphering the signs of the elements, was looked upon by
the common seamen as something almost supernatural. In
the present instance, he noticed where the great bands of
floating weeds commenced, and where they finished; and
in emerging from among them, concluded himself to be in
about the same degree of longitude as when he encountered
them on his outward voyage; that is to say, about two hundred and sixty leagues west of Ferro. On the 10th of
February, Vicente Yañes Pinzon, and the pilots Ruiz and
Bartolomeo Roldan, who were on board of the admiral's
ship, examined the charts and compared their reckonings
to determine their situation, but could not come to any
agreement. They all supposed themselves at least one
hundred and fifty leagues nearer Spain than what Columbus believed to be the true reckoning, and in the latitude
of Madeira, whereas he knew them to be nearly in a direction for the Azores. He suffered them, however, to remain
in their error, and even added to their plerplexity, that they
might retain but a confused idea of the voyage, and he
alone possess a clear knowledge of the route to the newly-
discovered countries.[1]

On the 12th of February, as they were flattering themselves with soon coming in sight of land, the wind came on
to blow violently, with a heavy sea; they still kept their
course to the east, but with great labor and peril. On the
following day, after sunset, the wind and swell increased;
there were three flashes of lightning in the north-northeast,
considered by Columbus as signals of an approaching tempest. It soon burst upon them with frightful violence:
their small and crazy vessels, open and without decks, were
little fitted for the wild storms of the Atlantic; all night
they were obliged to scud under bare poles. As the morning dawned of the 14th, there was a transient pause, and
they made a little sail; but the wind rose again from the
south with redoubled vehemence, raging thoughout the day,

[1] Las Casas, Hist. Ind., lib. i. cap. 70.

and increasing in fury in the night; while the vessels labored terribly in a cross sea, the broken waves of which threatened at each moment to overwhelm them, or dash them to pieces. For three hours they lay to, with just sail enough to keep them above the waves; but the tempest still augmenting, they were obliged again to scud before the wind. The Pinta was soon lost sight of in the darkness of the night. The admiral kept as much as possible to the northeast, to approach the coast of Spain, and made signal lights at the mast-head for the Pinta to do the same, and to keep in company. The latter, however, from the weakness of her foremast, could not hold the wind, and was obliged to scud before it, directly north. For some time she replied to the signals of the admiral, but her lights gleamed more and more distant, until they ceased entirely, and nothing more was seen of her.

Columbus continued to scud all night, full of forebodings of the fate of his own vessel, and of fears for the safety of that of Pinzon. As the day dawned, the sea presented a frightful waste of wild broken waves, lashed into fury by the gale; he looked round anxiously for the Pinta, but she was nowhere to be seen. He now made a little sail, to keep his vessel ahead of the sea, lest its huge waves should break over her. As the sun rose, the wind and the waves rose with it, and thoughout a dreary day, the helpless bark was driven along by the fury of the tempest.

Seeing all human skill baffled and confounded, Columbus endeavored to propitiate heaven by solemn vows and acts of penance. By his orders, a number of beans, equal to the number of persons on board, were put into a cap, on one of which was cut the sign of the cross. Each of the crew made a vow, that, should he draw forth the marked bean, he would make a pilgrimage to the shrine of Santa Maria de Guadalupe, bearing a wax taper of five pounds' weight. The admiral was the first to put in his hand, and the lot fell upon him. From that moment he considered himself a

14

pilgrim, bound to perform the vow. Another lot was cast
in the same way, for a pilgrimage to the chapel of our Lady
of Loretto, which fell upon a seaman named Pedro de Villa,
and the admiral engaged to bear the expenses of his journey. A third lot was also cast for a pilgrimage to Santa
Clara de Moguer, to perform a solemn mass, and to watch
all night in the chapel, and this likewise fell upon Columbus.

The tempest still raging with unabated violence, the
admiral and all the mariners made a vow, that, if spared,
wherever they first landed, they would go in procession
barefooted and in their shirts, to offer up prayers and
thanksgivings in some church dedicated to the Holy Virgin.
Beside these general acts of propitiation, each one made his
private vow, binding himself to some pilgrimage, or vigil, or
other rite of penitence and thanksgiving at his favorite
shrine. The heavens, however, seemed deaf to their vows;
the storm grew still more wild and frightful, and each man
gave himself up for lost. The danger of the ship was
augmented by the want of ballast, the consumption of the
water and provisions having lightened her so much, that
she rolled and tossed about at the mercy of the waves.
To remedy this, and to render her more steady, the admiral
ordered that all the empty casks should be filled with sea-
water, which in some measure gave relief.

During this long and awful conflict of the elements, the
mind of Columbus was a prey to the most distressing
anxiety. He feared that the Pinta had foundered in the
storm. In such case the whole history of his discovery, the
secret of the New World, depended upon his own feeble
bark, and one surge of the ocean might bury it for ever in
oblivion. The tumult of his thoughts may be judged from
his own letter to the sovereigns. " I could have supported
this evil fortune with less grief," said he, " had my person
alone been in jeopardy, since I am a debtor for my life to
the supreme Creator, and have at other times been within a

step of death. But it was a cause of infinite sorrow and
trouble, to think that, after having been illuminated from
on high with faith and certainty to undertake this enterprise, after having victoriously achieved it, and when on the
point of convincing my opponents, and securing to your
highnesses great glory and vast increase of dominions, it
should please the divine Majesty to defeat all by my death.
It would have been more supportable also, had I not been
accompanied by others who had been drawn on by my per-
suasions, and who, in their distress, cursed not only the
hour of their coming, but the fear inspired by my words
which prevented their turning back, as they had at various
times determined. Above all, my grief was doubled when
I thought of my two sons, whom I had left at school in Cordova, destitute, in a strange land, without any testimony of
the services rendered by their father, which, if known,
might have inclined your highnesses to befriend them. And
although, on the one hand, I was comforted by faith that
the Deity would not permit a work of such great exaltation
to his church, wrought through so many troubles and contradictions, to remain imperfect; yet, on the other hand, I
reflected on my sins, as a punishment for which he might
intend that I should be deprived of the glory which would
redound to me in this world." [1]

In the midst of these gloomy apprehensions, an expedient suggested itself, by which, though he and his ships
should perish, the glory of his achievement might survive
to his name, and its advantages be secured to his sovereigns.
He wrote on parchment a brief account of his voyage and
discovery, and of his having taken possession of the newly-
found lands in the name of their Catholic majesties. This
he sealed and directed to the king and queen; superscribing
a promise of a thousand ducats to whomsoever should deliver
the packet unopened. He then wrapped it in a waxed cloth,
which he placed in the centre of a cake of wax, and inclos-

Hist. del Almirante, cap. 36.

ing the whole in a large barrel, threw it into the sea, giving
his men to suppose he was performing some religious vow.
Lest this memorial should never reach the land, he enclosed
a copy in a similar manner, and placed it upon the poop, so
that, should the caravel be swallowed up by the waves, the
barrel might float off and survive.

These precautions in some measure mitigated his anxiety,
and he was still more relieved when, after heavy showers,
there appeared at sunset a streak of clear sky in the west,
giving hopes that the wind was about to shift to that quarter. These hopes were confirmed; a favorable breeze succeeded, but the sea still ran so high and tumultuously, that
little sail could be carried during the night.

On the morning of the 15th, at daybreak, the cry of land
was given by Rui Garcia, a mariner in the main-top. The
transports of the crew, at once more gaining sight of the
Old World, were almost equal to those experienced on first
beholding the New. The land bore east-northeast, directly
over the prow of the caravel; and the usual diversity of
opinion concerning it arose among the pilots. One thought
it the island of Madeira; another the rock of Cintra near
Lisbon; the most part, deceived by their ardent wishes,
placed it near Spain. Columbus, however, from his private
reckonings and observations, concluded it to be one of the
Azores. A nearer approach proved it to be an island: it
was but five leagues distant, and the voyagers were congratulating themselves upon the assurance of speedily being in
port, when the wind veered again to the east-northeast,
blowing directly from the land, while a heavy sea kept
rolling from the west.

For two days they hovered in sight of the island, vainly
striving to reach it, or to arrive at another island of which
they caught glimpses occasionally through the mist and rack
of the tempest. On the evening of the 17th they approached
so near the first island as to cast anchor, but parting their
cable, had to put to sea again, where they remained beating

about until the following morning, when they anchored
under shelter of its northern side.   For several days,
Columbus had been in such a state of agitation and anxiety,
as scarcely to take food or repose.   Although suffering
greatly from a gouty affection to which he was subject,
yet he had maintained his watchful post on deck, exposed
to wintry cold, to the pelting of the storm, and the drenching surges of the sea.   It was not until the night of the 17th
that he got a little sleep, more from the exhaustion of nature
than from any tranquillity of mind.   Such were the difficulties and perils which attended his return to Europe: had
one-tenth part of them beset his outward voyage, his timid
and factious crew would have risen in arms against the
enterprise, and he never would have discovered the New
World.

CHAPTER III.

TRANSACTIONS AT THE ISLAND OF ST. MARY'S.

[1493.]

ON sending the boat to land, Columbus ascertained the
island to be St. Mary's, the most southern of the Azores,
and a possession of the crown of Portugal.   The inhabitants,
when they beheld the light caravel riding at anchor, were
astonished that it had been able to live through the gale
which had raged for fifteen days with unexampled fury;
but when they heard from the boat's crew that this tempest-tossed vessel brought tidings of a strange country
beyond the ocean, they were filled with wonder and curiosity.   To the inquiries about a place where the caravel
might anchor securely, they replied by pointing out a harbor in the vicinity; but prevailed on three of the mariners
to remain on shore, and gratify them with further particulars of this unparalleled voyage.

In the evening, three men of the island hailed the caravel,

and a boat being sent for them, they brought on board
fowls, bread, and various refreshments, from Juan de Castañeda, governor of the island, who claimed an acquaintance with Columbus, and sent him many compliments and
congratulations. He apologized for not coming in person,
owing to the lateness of the hour and the distance of his
residence, but promised to visit the caravel the next morning, bringing further refreshments, and the three men, whom
he still kept with him to satisfy his extreme curiosity respecting the voyage. As there were no houses on the
neighboring shore, the messengers remained on board all
night.

On the following morning, Columbus reminded his people
of their vow to perform a pious procession at the first place
where they should land. On the neighboring shore, at no
great distance from the sea, was a small hermitage or chapel
dedicated to the Virgin, and he made immediate arrangements for the performance of the rite. The three messengers, on returning to the village, sent a priest to perform
mass, and one-half of the crew landing, walked in procession, barefooted, and in their shirts, to the chapel ; while the
admiral awaited their return, to perform the same ceremony
with the remainder.

An ungenerous reception, however, awaited the poor
tempest-tossed mariners on their first return to the abode of
civilized men, far different from the sympathy and hospitality they had experienced among the savages of the New
World. Scarcely had they begun their prayers and
thanksgivings, when the rabble of the village, horse and
foot, headed by the governor, surrounded the hermitage and
took them all prisoners.

As an intervening point of land hid the hermitage from
the view of the caravel, the admiral remained in ignorance
of this transaction. When eleven o'clock arrived without
the return of the pilgrims, he began to fear that they were
detained by the Portuguese, or that the boat had been

shattered upon the surf-beaten rocks which bordered the
island. Weighing anchor, therefore, he stood in a direction to command a view of the chapel and the adjacent
shore; whence he beheld a number of armed horsemen,
who, dismounting, entered the boat and made for the
caravel. The admiral's ancient suspicions of Portuguese
hostility towards himself and his enterprises were immediately revived; and he ordered his men to arm themselves,
but to keep out of sight, ready either to defend the vessel or
surprise the boat. The latter, however, approached in a
pacific manner; the governor of the island was on board,
and, coming within hail, demanded assurance of personal
safety in case he should enter the caravel. This the
admiral readily gave, but the Portuguese still continued at
a wary distance. The indignation of Columbus now broke
forth; he reproached the governor with his perfidy, and
with the wrong he did, not merely to the Spanish monarchs,
but to his own sovereign, by such a dishonorable outrage.
He informed him of his own rank and dignity; displayed
his letters patent, sealed with the royal seal of Castile, and
threatened him with the vengeance of his government.
Castañeda replied in a vein of contempt and defiance, de-
declaring that all he had done was in conformity to the
commands of the king his sovereign.

After an unprofitable altercation, the boat returned to
shore, leaving Columbus much perplexed by this unexpected
hostility, and fearful that a war might have broken out between Spain and Portugal during his absence. The next
day the weather became so tempestuous that they were
driven from their anchorage, and obliged to stand to sea
toward the island of St. Michael. For two days the ship
continued beating about in great peril, half of her crew being detained on shore, and the greater part of those on
board being landsmen and Indians, almost equally useless
in difficult navigation. Fortunately, although the waves
ran high, there were none of those cross seas which had re-

cently prevailed, otherwise, being so feebly manned, the caravel could scarcely have lived through the storm.

On the evening of the 22d, the weather having moderated, Columbus returned to his anchorage at St. Mary's. Shortly after his arrival, a boat came off, bringing two priests and a notary. After a cautious parley and an assurance of safety, they came on board, and requested a sight of the papers of Columbus, on the part of Castañeda, assuring him that it was the disposition of the governor to render him every service in his power, provided he really sailed in service of the Spanish sovereigns. Columbus supposed it a manœuvre of Castañeda to cover a retreat from the hostile position he had assumed; restraining his indignation, however, and expressing his thanks for the friendly disposition of the governor, he showed his letters of commission, which satisfied the priests and the notary. On the following morning, the boat and mariners were liberated. The latter, during their detention, had collected information from the inhabitants which elucidated the conduct of Castañeda.

The king of Portugal, jealous lest the expedition of Columbus might interfere with his own discoveries, had sent orders to his commanders of islands and distant ports to seize and detain him wherever he should be met with.[1] In compliance with these orders, Castañeda had, in the first instance, hoped to surprise Columbus in the chapel, and, failing in that attempt, had intended to get him in his power by stratagem, but was deterred by finding him on his guard. Such was the first reception of the admiral on his return to the old world, an earnest of the crosses and troubles with which he was to be requited throughout life, for one of the greatest benefits that ever man conferred upon his fellow-beings.

[1] Hist. del Almirante, cap. 39.   Las Casas, Hist. Ind., lib. i. cap. 72.

CHAPTER IV.

ARRIVAL AT PORTUGAL.—VISIT TO THE COURT.

[1493.]

COLUMBUS remained two days longer at the island of St. Mary's, endeavoring to take in wood and ballast, but was prevented by the heavy surf which broke upon the shore. The wind veering to the south, and being dangerous for vessels at anchor off the island, but favorable for the voyage to Spain, he set sail on the 24th of February, and had pleasant weather until the 27th, when, being within one hundred and twenty-five leagues of Cape St. Vincent, he again encountered contrary gales and a boisterous sea. His fortitude was scarcely proof against these perils and delays, which appeared to increase, the nearer he approached his home; and he could not help uttering a complaint at thus being repulsed, as it were, "from the very door of the house." He contrasted the rude storms which raged about the coasts of the old world, with the genial airs, the tranquil seas, and balmy weather which he supposed perpetually to prevail about the countries he had discovered. "Well," says he, "may the sacred theologians and sage philosophers declare that the terrestrial paradise is in the uttermost extremity of the East, for it is the most temperate of regions."

After experiencing several days of stormy and adverse weather, about midnight on Saturday the 2d of March, the caravel was struck by a squall of wind, which rent all her sails, and, continuing to blow with resistless violence, obliged her to scud under bare poles, threatening her each moment with destruction. In this hour of darkness and peril, the crew again called upon the aid of Heaven. A lot was cast for the performance of a bare-footed pilgrimage to the shrine of Santa Maria de la Cueva in Huelva, and, as usual, the lot fell upon Columbus. There was something singular in the recurrence of this circumstance. Las Casas devoutly considers it as an intimation from the Deity to the admiral that these storms were all on his account, to humble his pride, and prevent his arrogating to himself the glory of a discovery which was the work of God, and for which he had merely been chosen as an instrument.[1]

Various signs appeared of the vicinity of land, which they supposed must be the coast of Portugal : the tempest, however, increased to such a degree, that they doubted whether any of them would survive to reach a port. The whole crew made a vow, in case their lives were spared, to fast upon bread and water the following Saturday. The turbulence of the elements was still greater in the course of the following night. The sea was broken, wild, and mountainous ; at one moment the light caravel was tossed high in the air, and the next moment seemed sinking in a yawning abyss. The rain at times fell in torrents,—and the lightning flashed and thunder pealed from various parts of the heavens.

In the first watch of this fearful night, the seamen gave the usually welcome cry of land, but it now only increased the general alarm. They knew not where they were, nor where to look for a harbor ; they dreaded being driven on shore, or dashed upon rocks ; and thus the very land they had so earnestly desired was a terror to them. Taking in sail, therefore, they kept to sea as much as possible, and waited anxiously for the morning light.

At daybreak on the 4th of March, they found themselves off the rock of Cintra, at the mouth of the Tagus. Though entertaining a strong distrust of the good-will of Portugal, the still prevailing tempest left Columbus no alternative but to run in for shelter ; he accordingly anchored about three o'clock, opposite to Rastallo, to the great joy of

[1] Las Casas, Hist. Ind., lib. i. cap. 73.

the crew, who returned thanks to God for their escape from
so many perils.

The inhabitants came off from various parts of the shore,
congratulating them upon what they considered a miracu-
lous preservation. They had been watching the vessel the
whole morning with great anxiety, and putting up prayers
for her safety. The oldest mariners of the place assured
Columbus they had never known so tempestuous a winter;
many vessels had remained for months in port, weatherbound, and there had been numerous shipwrecks.

Immediately on his arrival, Columbus dispatched a
courier to the king and queen of Spain, with tidings of his
discovery. He wrote also to the king of Portugal, then at
Valparaiso, requesting permission to go with his vessel to
Lisbon; for a report had gone abroad that his caravel was
laden with gold, and he felt insecure in the mouth of the
Tagus, in the neighborhood of a place like Rastello, scantily
peopled by needy and adventurous inhabitants. To prevent any misunderstanding as to the nature of his voyage,
he assured the king that he had not been on the coast of
Guinea, nor to any other of the Portuguese colonies, but
had come from Cipango and the extremity of India, which
he had discovered by sailing to the west.

On the following day, Don Alonzo de Acuña, the captain
of a large Portuguese man-of-war, stationed at Rastello,
summoned Columbus on board his ship, to give an account
of himself and his vessel. The latter asserted his rights
and dignities as admiral of the Castilian sovereigns, and
refused to leave his vessel, or to send any one in his place.
No sooner, however, did the commander learn his rank, and
the extraordinary nature of his voyage, than he came to
the caravel with great sound of drums, fifes, and trumpets,
manifesting the courtesy of a brave and generous spirit,
and making the fullest offer of his services.

When the tidings reached Lisbon of this wonderful bark,
anchored in the Tagus, freighted with the people and pro-

ductions of a newly-discovered world, the effect may be more easily conceived than described. Lisbon, for nearly a century, had derived its chief glory from its maritime discoveries, but here was an achievement that eclipsed them all. Curiosity could scarcely have been more excited had the vessel come freighted with the wonders of another planet. For several days the Tagus presented a gay and moving picture, covered with barges and boats of every kind, swarming round the caravel. From morning till night the vessel was thronged with visitors, among whom were cavaliers of high distinction, and various officers of the crown. All hung with rapt attention upon the accounts given by Columbus and his crew, of the events of their voyage, and of the New World they had discovered; and gazed with insatiable curiosity upon the specimens of unknown plants and animals, but, above all, upon the Indians, so different from any race of men hitherto known. Some were filled with generous enthusiasm at the idea of a discovery, so sublime and so beneficial to mankind; the avarice of others was inflamed by the description of wild, unappropriated regions, teeming with gold, with pearls and spices; while others repined at the incredulity of the king and his councilors, by which so immense an acquisition had been for ever lost to Portugal.

On the 8th of March, a cavalier, called Don Martin de Norofia, came with a letter from King John, congratulating Columbus on his arrival, and inviting him to the court, which was then at Valparaiso, about nine leagues from Lisbon. The king, with his usual magnificence, issued orders at the same time that every thing which the admiral required, for himself, his crew, or his vessel, should be furnished promptly and abundantly, without cost.

Columbus would gladly have declined the royal invitation, feeling distrust of the good faith of the king; but tempestuous weather had placed him in his power, and he thought it prudent to avoid all appearance of suspicion.

He set forth, therefore, that very evening for Valparaiso, accompanied by his pilot. The first night he slept at Sacamben, where preparations had been made for his honorable entertainment. The weather being rainy, he did not reach Valparaiso until the following night. On approaching the royal residence, the principal cavaliers of the king's household came forth to meet him, and attended him with great ceremony to the palace. His reception by the monarch was worthy of an enlightened prince. He ordered him to seat himself in his presence, an honor only granted to persons of royal dignity; and after many congratulations on the result of his enterprise, assured him that every thing in his kingdom that could be of service to his sovereigns or himself was at his command.

A long conversation ensued, in which Columbus gave an account of his voyage, and of the countries he had discovered. The king listened with much seeming pleasure, but with secret grief and mortification: reflecting that this splendid enterprise had once been offered to himself, and had been rejected. A casual observation showed what was passing in his thoughts. He expressed a doubt whether the discovery did not really appertain to the crown of Portugal, according to the capitulations of the treaty of 1479 with the Castilian sovereigns. Columbus replied that he had never seen those capitulations, nor knew anything of their nature: his orders had been not to go to La Mina, nor the coast of Guinea, which orders he had carefully observed. The king made a gracious reply, expressing himself satisfied that he had acted correctly, and persuaded that these matters would be readily adjusted between the two powers, without the need of umpires. On dismissing Columbus for the night, he gave him in charge, as guest, to the prior of Crato, the principal personage present, by whom he was honorably and hospitably entertained.

On the following day, the king made many minute inquiries as to the soil, productions, and people of the newly-discovered countries, and the route taken in the voyage; to all which Columbus gave the fullest replies, endeavoring to show in the clearest manner that these were regions heretofore undiscovered and unappropriated by any Christian power. Still the king was uneasy lest this vast and undefined discovery should in some way interfere with his own newly-acquired territories. He doubted whether Columbus had not found a short way to those very countries which were the object of his own expeditions, and which were comprehended in the papal bull, granting to the crown of Portugal all the lands which it should discover from Cape Non to the Indies.

On suggesting these doubts to his councilors, they eagerly confirmed them. Some of these were the very persons who had once derided this enterprise, and scoffed at Columbus as a dreamer. To them, its success was a source of confusion; and the return of Columbus, covered with glory, a deep humiliation. Incapable of conceiving the high and generous thoughts which elevated him at that moment above all mean considerations, they attributed to all his actions the most petty and ignoble motives. His rational exultation was construed into an insulting triumph, and they accused him of assuming a boastful and vainglorious tone, when talking with the king of his discovery; as if he would revenge himself upon the monarch for having rejected his propositions.[1] With the greatest eagerness, therefore, they sought to foster the doubts which had sprung up in the royal mind. Some who had seen the natives

[1] Vasconcelos, Vida de D. Juan II., lib. vi. The Portugese historians in general charge Columbus with having conducted himself loftily, and talked in vaunting terms of his discoveries, in his conversations with the king. It is evident their information must have been derived from prejudiced courtiers. Faria y Souza, in his *Europa Portuguesa* (Parte iii. cap. 4), goes so far as to say that Columbus entered into the port of Rastello merely to make Portugal sensible, by the sight of the trophies of his discovery, how much she had lost by not accepting his propositions.

brought in the caravel, declared that their color, hair, and manners, agreed with the descriptions of the people of that part of India which lay within the route of the Portuguese discoveries, and which had been included in the papal bull. Others observed that there was but little distance between the Tercera Islands, and those which Columbus had discovered, and that the latter, therefore, clearly appertained to Portugal. Seeing the king much perturbed in spirit, some even went so far as to propose, as a means of impeding the prosecution of these enterprises, that Columbus should be assassinated; declaring that he deserved death for attempting to deceive and embroil the two nations, by his pretended discoveries. It was suggested that his assassination might easily be accomplished without incurring any odium; advantage might be taken of his lofty deportment to pique his pride, provoke him into an altercation, and then dispatch him as if in casual and honorable encounter.

It is difficult to believe that such wicked and dastardly counsel could have been proposed to a monarch so upright as John II, but the fact is asserted by various historians, Portuguese as well as Spanish,[1] and it accords with the perfidious advice formerly given to the monarch in respect to Columbus. There is a spurious loyalty about courts, which is often prone to prove its zeal by its baseness; and it is the weakness of kings to tolerate the grossest faults when they appear to arise from personal devotion.

Happily, the king had too much magnanimity to adopt the iniquitous measure proposed He did justice to the great merit of Columbus, and honored him as a distinguished benefactor of mankind; and he felt it his duty, as a generous prince, to protect all strangers driven by adverse fortune to his ports. Others of his council suggested a more bold and martial line of policy. They advised that Colum-

---

[1] Vasconcelos, Vida del Rei Don Juan II., lib. vi. Garcia de Resende, vida do Dom Joam II. Las Casas, Hist. Ind., lib. i. cap. 74, MS.

bus should be permitted to return to Spain; but that, before
he could fit out a second expedition, a powerful armament
should be dispatched, under the guidance of two Portuguese
mariners who had sailed with the admiral, to take possession of the newly-discovered country; possession being after
all the best title, and an appeal to arms the clearest mode
of settling so doubtful a question.

This counsel, in which there was a mixture of courage
and craft, was more relished by the king, and he resolved
privately, but promptly, to put it in execution, fixing upon
Don Francisco de Almeida, one of the most distinguished
captains of the age, to command the expedition.[1]

In the meantime, Columbus, after being treated with distinguished attention, was escorted back to his ship by Don
Martin de Noroña, and a numerous train of cavaliers of the
court, a mule being provided for himself, and another for
his pilot, to whom the king made a present of twenty espa-
dinas, or ducats of gold.[2] On his way, Columbus stopped
at the monastery of San Antonio, at Villa Franca, to visit
the queen, who had expressed an earnest wish to see this
extraordinary and enterprising man, whose achievement
was the theme of every tongue. He found her attended by
a few of her favorite ladies, and experienced the most flattering reception. Her majesty made him relate the principal events of his voyage, and describe the countries he had
found; and she and her ladies hung with eager curiosity
upon his narration. That night he slept at Llandra, and
being on the point of departing in the morning, a servant
of the king arrived, to attend him to the frontier, if he preferred to return to Spain by land, and to provide horses,
lodgings, and every thing he might stand in need of, at the
royal expense. The weather, however, having moderated,

[1] Vasconcelos, lib. vi.

[2] Twenty-eight dollars in gold of the present day, and equivalent
to seventy-four dollars, considering the depreciation of the precious
metals.

he preferred returning in his caravel. Putting to sea, therefore, on the 13th of March, he arrived safely at the bar of Saltes on sunrise of the 15th, and at mid-day entered the harbor of Palos; whence he had sailed on the 3d of August in the preceding year, having taken not quite seven months and a half to accomplish this most momentous of all maritime enterprises.[1]

CHAPTER V.

RECEPTION OF COLUMBUS AT PALOS.

[1493.]

THE triumphant return of Columbus was a prodigious event in the history of the little port of Palos, where everybody was more or less interested in the fate of his expedition. The most important and wealthy sea-captains of the place had engaged in it, and scarcely a family but had some relative or friend among the navigators. The departure of the ships, upon what appeared a chimerical and desperate cruise, had spread gloom and dismay over the place; and the storms which had raged throughout the winter had heightened the public despondency. Many lamented their friends as lost, while imagination lent mysterious horrors to their fate, picturing them as driven about over wild and desert wastes of water without a shore, or as perishing amidst rocks and quicksands and whirlpools; or a prey to those monsters of the deep, with which credulity peopled every distant and unfrequented sea. There was something more awful in such a mysterious fate than in death itself, under any defined and ordinary form.[2]

[1] Works generally consulted in this chapter:—Las Casas, Hist. Ind., lib. i. cap. 17; Hist. del Almirante, cap. 39, 40, 41; Journal of Columb., Navarrete, tom. i.

[2] In the maps and charts of those times, and even in those of a much later date, the variety of formidable and hideous monsters

15

Great was the agitation of the inhabitants, therefore, when they beheld one of the ships standing up the river; but when they learnt that she returned in triumph from the discovery of a world, the whole community broke forth into transports of joy. The bells were rung, the shops shut, all business was suspended: for a time there was nothing but hurry and tumult. Some were anxious to know the fate of a relative, others of a friend, and all to learn the particulars of so wonderful a voyage. When Columbus landed, the multitude thronged to see and welcome him, and a grand procession was formed to the principal church, to return thanks to God for so signal a discovery made by the people of that place,—forgetting, in their exultation, the thousand difficulties they had thrown in the way of the enterprise. Wherever Columbus passed, he was hailed with shouts and acclamations. What a contrast to his departure a few months before, followed by murmurs and execrations; or, rather, what a contrast to his first arrival at Palos, a poor pedestrian, craving bread and water for his child at the gate of a convent!

Understanding that the court was at Barcelona, he felt disposed to proceed thither immediately in his caravel; reflecting, however, on the dangers and disasters he had already experienced on the seas, he resolved to proceed by land. He dispatched a letter to the king and queen, informing them of his arrival, and soon after departed for Seville to await their orders, taking with him six of the natives whom he had brought from the New World. One had died at sea, and three were left ill at Palos.

It is a singular coincidence, which appears to be well authenticated, that on the very evening of the arrival of

depicted in all remote parts of the ocean, evince the terrors and dangers with which the imagination clothed it. The same may also be said of distant and unknown lands; the remote parts of Asia and Africa have monsters depicted in them which it would be difficult to trace to any originals in natural history.

Columbus at Palos, and while the peals of triumph were still ringing from its towers, the Pinta, commanded by Martin Alonzo Pinzon, likewise entered the river. After her separation from the admiral in the storm, she had been driven before the gale into the Bay of Biscay, and had made the port of Bayonne. Doubting whether Columbus had survived the tempest, Pinzon had immediately written to the sovereigns, giving information of the discovery he had made, and had requested permission to come to court, and communicate the particulars in person. As soon as the weather permitted, he had again set sail, anticipating a triumphant reception in his native port of Palos. When, on entering the harbor, he beheld the vessel of the admiral riding at anchor, and learnt the enthusiasm with which he had been received, the heart of Pinzon died within him. It is said that he feared to meet Columbus in this hour of his triumph, lest he should put him under arrest for his desertion on the coast of Cuba; but he was a man of too much resolution to indulge in such a fear. It is more probable that a consciousness of his misconduct made him unwilling to appear before the public in the midst of their enthusiasm for Columbus, and perhaps he sickened at the honors heaped upon a man whose superiority he had been so unwilling to acknowledge. Getting into his boat, therefore, he landed privately, and kept out of sight until he heard of the admiral's departure. He then returned to his home, broken in health and deeply dejected, considering all the honors and eulogiums heaped upon Columbus as so many reproaches on himself. The reply of the sovereigns to his letter at length arrived. It was of a reproachful tenor, and forbade his appearance at court. This letter completed his humiliation; the anguish of his feelings gave virulence to his bodily malady, and in a few days he died, a victim to deep chagrin.[1]

[1] Muñoz, Hist. N. Mundo, lib. iv. § 14. Charlevoix, Hist. St. Domin., lib. ii.

Let no one, however, indulge in harsh censures over the grave of Pinzon! His merits and services are entitled to the highest praise; his errors should be regarded with indulgence. He was one of the foremost in Spain to appreciate the project of Columbus, animating him by his concurrence and aiding him with his purse, when poor and unknown at Palos. He afterwards enabled him to procure and fit out ships, when even the mandates of the sovereigns were ineffectual; and finally embarked in the expedition with his brothers and his friends, staking life, property, every thing upon the event. He thus entitled himself to participate largely in the glory of this immortal enterprise; but unfortunately, forgetting for a moment the grandeur of the cause, and the implicit obedience due to his commander, he yielded to the incitements of self-interest, and committed that act of insubordination which has cast a shade upon his name. In extenuation of his fault, however, may be alleged his habits of command, which rendered him impatient of control; his consciousness of having rendered great services to the expedition, and of possessing property in the ships. That he was a man of great professional merit is admitted by all his contemporaries; that he naturally possessed generous sentiments and an honorable ambition, is evident from the poignancy with which he felt the disgrace drawn on him by his misconduct. A mean man would not have fallen a victim to self-upbraiding for having been convicted of a mean action. His story shows how one lapse from duty may counterbalance the merits of a thousand services; how one moment of weakness may mar the beauty of a whole life of virtue; and how important it is for a man, under all circumstances, to be true, not merely to others, but to himself.[1]

[1] After a lapse of years, the descendants of the Pinzons made strenuous representations to the crown of the merits and services of their family, endeavoring to prove, among other things, that but for the aid and encouragement of Martin Alonzo and his brothers, Columbus

would never have made his discovery. Some of the testimony rendered on this and another occasion was rather extravagant and absurd, as will be shown in another part of this work.[1] The Emperor Charles V, however, taking into consideration the real services of the brothers in the first voyage, and the subsequent expeditions and discoveries of that able and intrepid navigator Vincent Yañez Pinzon, granted to the family the well-merited rank and privileges of *Hidalguia*, a degree of nobility which constituted them noble hidalgos, with the right of prefixing the title of Don to their names. A coat of arms was also given them, emblematical of their services as discoverers. These privileges and arms are carefully preserved by the family at the present day.

The Pinzons at present reside principally in the little city of Moguer, about a league from Palos, and possess vineyards and estates about the neighborhood. They are in easy, if not affluent circumstances, and inhabit the best houses in Moguer. Here they have continued, from generation to generation, since the time of the discovery, filling places of public trust and dignity, enjoying the good opinion and good will of their fellow-citizens, and flourishing in nearly the same state in which they were found by Columbus, on his first visit to Palos. It is rare indeed to find a family, in this fluctuating world, so little changed by the revolutions of nearly three centuries and a half.

Whatever Palos may have been in the time of Columbus, it is now a paltry village of about four hundred inhabitants, who subsist chiefly by laboring in the fields and vineyards. The convent of La Rabida still exists, but is inhabited merely by two friars, with a noviciate and a lay brother. It is situated on a hill, surrounded by a scattered forest of pine trees, and overlooks the low sandy country of the sea-coast, and the windings of the river by which Columbus sallied forth upon the ocean.

[1] Vide Illustrations, article "Martin Alonso Pinzon."

CHAPTER VI.

RECEPTION OF COLUMBUS BY THE SPANISH COURT AT BARCELONA.

THE letter of Columbus to the Spanish monarchs had produced the greatest sensation at court. The event he announced was considered the most extraordinary of their prosperous reign, and, following so close upon the conquest of Granada, was pronounced a signal mark of divine favor for that triumph achieved in the cause of the true faith. The sovereigns themselves were for a time dazzled by this sudden and easy acquisition of a new empire, of indefinite extent, and apparently boundless wealth; and their first idea was to secure it beyond the reach of dispute. Shortly after his arrival in Seville, Columbus received a letter from them expressing their great delight, and requesting him to repair immediately to court, to concert plans for a second and more extensive expedition. As the summer, the time favorable for a voyage, was approaching, they desired him to make any arrangements at Seville or elsewhere that might hasten the expedition, and to inform them, by the return of the courier, what was to be done on their part. This letter was addressed to him by the title of "Don Christopher Columbus, our admiral of the ocean sea, and viceroy and governor of the islands discovered in the Indies;" at the same time he was promised still further rewards. Columbus lost no time in complying with the commands of the sovereigns. He sent a memorandum of the ships, men, and munitions requisite, and having made such dispositions at Seville as circumstances permitted, set out for Barcelona, taking with him the six Indians, and the various curiosities and productions brought from the New World.

The fame of his discovery had resounded throughout the nation, and as his route lay through several of the finest

and most populous provinces of Spain, his journey appeared
like the progress of a sovereign. Wherever he passed, the
country poured forth its inhabitants, who lined the road
and thronged the villages. The streets, windows, and balconies of the towns were filled with eager spectators, who
rent the air with acclamations. His journey was continually impeded by the multitude pressing to gain a sight of
him and of the Indians, who were regarded with as much
astonishment as if they had been natives of another planet.
It was impossible to satisfy the craving curiosity which
assailed him and his attendants at every stage with innumerable questions; popular rumor, as usual, had exaggerated
the truth, and had filled the newly-found country with all
kinds of wonders.

About the middle of April Columbus arrived at Barcelona, where every preparation had been made to give him
a solemn and magnificent reception. The beauty and
serenity of the weather in that genial season and favored
climate, contributed to give splendor to this memorable
ceremony. As he drew near the place, many of the youthful courtiers and hidalgos, together with a vast concourse
of the populace, came forth to meet and welcome him. His
entrance into this noble city has been compared to one of
those triumphs which the Romans were accustomed to de-
cree to conquerors. First, were paraded the Indians, painted according to their savage fashion, and decorated with
their national ornaments of gold. After these were borne
various kinds of live parrots, together with stuffed birds
and animals of unknown species, and rare plants, supposed
to be of precious qualities; while great care was taken to
make a conspicuous display of Indian coronets, bracelets,
and other decorations of gold, which might give an idea of
the wealth of the newly-discovered regions. After this, followed Columbus on horseback, surrounded by a brilliant
cavalcade of Spanish chivalry. The streets were almost
impassable from the countless multitude; the windows and

balconies were crowded with the fair; the very roofs were
covered with spectators. It seemed as if the public eye
could not be sated with gazing on these trophies of an unknown world; or on the remarkable man by whom it
had been discovered. There was a sublimity in this event
that mingled a solemn feeling with the public joy. It was
looked upon as a vast and signal dispensation of Providence, in reward for the piety of the monarchs; and the
majestic and venerable appearance of the discoverer, so different from the youth and buoyancy generally expected
from roving enterprise, seemed in harmony with the grandeur and dignity of his achievement.

To receive him with suitable pomp and distinction, the
sovereigns had ordered their throne to be placed in public
under a rich canopy of brocade of gold, in a vast and
splendid saloon. Here the king and queen awaited his
arrival, seated in state, with the prince Juan beside them,
and attended by the dignitaries of their court, and the
principal nobility of Castile, Valentia, Catalonia, and Arragon, all impatient to behold the man who had conferred
so incalculable a benefit upon the nation. At length Columbus entered the hall, surrounded by a brilliant crowd
of cavaliers, among whom, says Las Casas, he was conspicuous for his stately and commanding person, which with
his countenance, rendered venerable by his gray hairs, gave
him the august appearance of a senator of Rome: a modest
smile lighted up his features, showing that he enjoyed the
state and glory in which he came;[1] and certainly nothing
could be more deeply moving to a mind inflamed by noble
ambition, and conscious of having greatly deserved, than
these testimonials of the admiration and gratitude of a nation, or rather of a world. As Columbus approached, the
sovereigns rose, as if receiving a person of the highest rank.
Bending his knees, he offered to kiss their hands; but there
was some hesitation on their part to permit this act of

[1] Las Casas, Hist. Ind., lib. i. cap. 78, MS.

homage. Raising him in the most gracious manner, they ordered him to seat himself in their presence; a rare honor in this proud and punctilious court.[1]

At their request, he now gave an account of the most striking events of his voyage, and a description of the islands discovered. He displayed specimens of unknown birds, and other animals; of rare plants of medicinal and aromatic virtues; of native gold in dust, in crude masses, or labored into barbaric ornaments; and, above all, the natives of these countries, who were objects of intense and inexhaustible interest. All these he pronounced mere harbingers of greater discoveries yet to be made, which would add realms of incalculable wealth to the dominions of their majesties, and whole nations of proselytes to the true faith.

When he had finished, the sovereigns sank on their knees, and raising their clasped hands to heaven, their eyes filled with tears of joy and gratitude, poured forth thanks and praises to God for so great a providence: all present followed their example; a deep and solemn enthusiasm pervaded that splendid assembly, and prevented all common acclamations of triumph. The anthem *Te Deum laudamus*, chanted by the choir of the royal chapel, with the accompaniment of instruments, rose in a full body of sacred harmony; bearing up, as it were, the feelings and thoughts of the auditors to heaven, "so that," says the venerable Las Casas, "it seemed as if in that hour they communicated with celestial delights." Such was the solemn and pious manner in which the brilliant court of Spain celebrated this sublime event; offering up a grateful tribute of melody and praise, and giving glory to God for the discovery of another world.

When Columbus retired from the royal presence, he was attended to his residence by all the court, and followed by

[1] Las Casas, Hist. Ind., lib. i. cap. 78. Hist. del Almirante, cap. 81.

the shouting populace. For many days he was the object
of universal curiosity, and wherever he appeared, was surrounded by an admiring multitude.

While his mind was teeming with glorious anticipations,
his pious scheme for the deliverance of the holy sepulchre
was not forgotten. It has been shown that he suggested it
to the Spanish sovereigns at the time of first making his
propositions, holding it forth as the great object to be
effected by the profits of his discoveries. Flushed with the
idea of the vast wealth now to accrue to himself, he made
a vow to furnish within seven years an army, consisting of
four thousand horse, and fifty thousand foot, for the rescue
of 'the holy sepulchre, and a similar force within the five
following years. This vow was recorded in one of his
letters to the sovereigns, to which he refers, but which is
no longer extant; nor is it certain whether it was made at
the end of his first voyage, or at a subsequent date, when
the magnitude and wealthy result of his discoveries became
more fully manifest. He often alludes to it vaguely in his
writings, and he refers to it expressly in a letter to Pope
Alexander VI, written in 1502, in which he accounts also
for its non-fufillment. It is essential to a full comprehen-
sion of the character and motives of Columbus, that this
visionary project should be borne in recollection. It will
be found to have entwined itself in his mind with his enterprise of discovery, and that a holy crusade was to be the
consummation of those divine purposes, for which he considered himself selected by Heaven as an agent. It shows
how much his mind was elevated above selfish and mercenary views—how it was filled with those devout and heroic
schemes, which in the time of the crusades had inflamed
the thoughts and directed the enterprises of the bravest
warriors and most illustrious princes.

CHAPTER VII.

SOJOURN OF COLUMBUS AT BARCELONA.—ATTENTIONS
PAID HIM BY THE SOVEREIGNS AND COURTIERS.

THE joy occasioned by the great discovery of Columbus
was not confined to Spain; the tidings were spread far and
wide by the communications of ambassadors, the correspondence of the learned, the negotiations of merchants,
and the reports of travelers, and the whole civilized world
was filled with wonder and delight. How gratifying would
it have been, had the press at that time, as at present,
poured forth its daily tide of speculation on every passing
occurrence! With what eagerness should we seek to know
the first ideas and emotions of the public, on an event so
unlooked for and sublime! Even the first announcements
of it by contemporary writers, though brief and incidental,
derive interest from being written at the time; and from
showing the casual way in which such great tidings were
conveyed about the world. Allegretto Allegretti, in his
annals of Sienna for 1493, mentions it as just made known
there by the letters of their merchants who were in Spain,
and by the mouths of various travelers.[1] The news was
brought to Genoa by the return of her ambassadors Francisco Marchesi and Giovanni Antonio Grimaldi, and was
recorded among the triumphant events of the year:[2] for
the republic, though she may have slighted the opportunity
of making herself mistress of the discovery, has ever since
been tenacious of the glory of having given birth to the
discoverer. The tidings were soon carried to England,
which as yet was but a maritime power of inferior importance. They caused, however, much wonder in London,
and great talk and admiration in the court of Henry VII,

[1] Diarj Senesi de Alleg. Allegretti. Muratori; Ital. Script., tom.
xxiii.

[2] Foglieta, Istoria de Genova, lib. ii.

where the discovery was pronounced "a thing more divine than human." We have this on the authority of Sebastian Cabot himself, the future discoverer of the northern continent of America, who was in London at the time, and was inspired by the event with a generous spirit of emulation.[1]

Every member of civilized society, in fact, rejoiced in the occurrence, as one in which he was more or less interested. To some it opened a new and unbounded field of inquiry; to others, of enterprise; and every one awaited with intense eagerness the further development of this unknown world, still covered with mystery, the partial glimpses of which were so full of wonder. We have a brief testimony of the emotions of the learned in a letter, written at the time, by Peter Martyr to his friend Pomponius Laetus. "You tell me, my amiable Pomponius," he writes, "that you leaped for joy, and that your delight was mingled with tears, when you read my epistle, certifying to you the hitherto hidden world of the antipodes. You have felt and acted as became a man eminent for learning, for I can conceive no aliment more delicious than such tidings to a cultivated and ingenuous mind. I feel a wonderful exultation of spirits when I converse with intelligent men who have returned from these regions. It is like an accession of wealth to a miser. Our minds, soiled and debased by the common concerns of life and the vices of society, become elevated and ameliorated by contemplating such glorious events."[2]

Notwithstanding this universal enthusiasm, however, no one was aware of the real importance of the discovery. No one had an idea that this was a totally distinct portion of the globe, separated by oceans from the ancient world. The opinion of Columbus was universally adopted, that Cuba was the end of the Asiatic continent, and that the adjacent islands were in the Indian seas. This agreed with

[1] Hackluyt, Collect. Voyages, vol. iii. p. 7.
[2] Letters of P. Martyr, let. 153.

the opinions of the ancients, heretofore cited, about the moderate distance from Spain to the extremity of India, sailing westwardly. The parrots were also thought to resemble those described by Pliny, as abounding in the remote parts of Asia. The lands, therefore, which Columbus had visited were called the West Indies; and as he seemed to have entered upon a vast region of unexplored countries, existing in a state of nature, the whole received the comprehensive appellation of "The New World."

During the whole of his sojourn at Barcelona, the sovereigns took every occasion to bestow on Columbus personal marks of their high consideration. He was admitted at all times to the royal presence, and the queen delighted to converse with him on the subject of his enterprises. The king, too, appeared occasionally on horseback, with Prince Juan on one side, and Columbus on the other. To perpetuate in his family the glory of his achievement, a coat of arms was assigned him, in which the royal arms, the castle and lion, were quartered with his proper bearings, which were a group of islands surrounded by waves. To these arms was afterwards annexed the motto:

> A Castilla y á Leon,
> Nuevo mundo dio Colon.

> (To Castile and Leon
> Columbus gave a new world.)

The pension which had been decreed by the sovereigns to him who in the first voyage should discover land, was adjudged to Columbus, for having first seen the light on the shore. It is said that the seaman who first descried the land, was so incensed at being disappointed of what he conceived his merited reward, that he renounced his country and his faith, and going into Africa turned Mussulman; an anecdote which rests merely on the authority of Oviedo,[1]

[1] Oviedo, Cronico de las Indias, lib. ii. cap. 2.

who is extremely incorrect in his narration of this voyage, and inserts many falsehoods told him by the enemies of the admiral.

· It may, at first sight, appear but little accordant with the acknowledged magnanimity of Columbus, to have borne away the prize from this poor sailor, but this was a subject in which his whole ambition was involved, and he was doubtless proud of the honor of being personally the discoverer of the land as well as projector of the enterprise.

Next to the countenance shown him by the king and queen, may be mentioned that of Pedro Gonzalez de Mendoza, the grand cardinal of Spain, and first subject of the realm; a man whose elevated character for piety, learning, and high prince-like qualities, gave signal value to his favors. He invited Columbus to a banquet, where he assigned him the most honorable place at table, and had him served with the ceremonials which in those punctilious times were observed towards sovereigns. At this repast is said to have occurred the well-known anecdote of the egg. A shallow courtier present, impatient of the honors paid to Columbus, and meanly jealous of him as a foreigner, abruptly asked him whether he thought that, in case he had not discovered the Indies, there were not other men in Spain, who would have been capable of the enterprise? To this Columbus made no immediate reply, but, taking an egg, invited the company to make it stand on one end. Every one attempted it, but in vain; whereupon he struck it upon the table so as to break the end, and left it standing on the broken part; illustrating in this simple manner, that when he had once shown the way to the New World, nothing was easier than to follow it.[1]

[1] This anecdote rests on the authority of the Italian historian Benzoni (lib. i. p. 12, ed. Venetia, 1572). It has been condemned as trivial, but the simplicity of the reproof constitutes its severity, and was characteristic of the practical sagacity of Columbus. The universal popularity of the anecdote is a proof of its merit.

The favor shown Columbus by the sovereigns, insured him for a time the caresses of the nobility; for in a court every one vies with his neighbor in lavishing attentions upon the man "whom the king delighteth to honor." Columbus bore all these caresses and distinctions with becoming modesty, though he must have felt a proud satisfaction in the idea that they had been wrested, as it were, from the nation by his courage and perseverance. One can hardly recognize in the individual thus made the companion of princes, and the theme of general wonder and admiration, the same obscure stranger who but a short time before had been a common scoff and jest in this very court, derided by some as an adventurer, and pointed at by others as a madman. Those who had treated him with contumely during his long course of solicitation, now sought to efface the remembrance of it by adulations. Every one who had given him a little cold countenance, or a few courtly smiles, now arrogated to himself the credit of having been a patron and of having promoted the discovery of the New World. Scarce a great man about the court, but has been enrolled by his historian or biographer among the benefactors of Columbus; though, had one-tenth part of this boasted patronage been really exerted, he would never have had to linger seven years soliciting for an armament of three caravels. Columbus knew well the weakness of the patronage that had been given him. The only friends mentioned by him with gratitude, in his after letters, as having been really zealous and effective, were those two worthy friars, Diego de Deza, afterwards bishop of Palencia and Seville, and Juan Perez, the prior of the convent of La Rabida.

Thus honored by the sovereigns, courted by the great, idolized by the people, Columbus, for a time, drank the honeyed draught of popularity, before enmity and detraction had time to drug it with bitterness. His discovery burst with such sudden splendor upon the world, as to dazzle

envy itself, and to call forth the general acclamations of
mankind. Well would it be for the honor of human
nature, could history, like romance, close with the consummation of the hero's wishes; we should then leave Columbus
in the full fruition of great and well-merited prosperity.
But his history is destined to furnish another proof, if
proof be wanting, of the inconstancy of public favor, even
when won by distinguished services. No greatness was
ever acquired by more incontestable, unalloyed, and exalted
benefits rendered to mankind, yet none ever drew on
its possessor more unremitting jealousy and defamation; or
involved him in more unmerited distress and difficulty.
Thus it is with illustrious merit: its very effulgence draws
forth the rancorous passions of low and groveling minds,
which too often have a temporary influence in obscur-
ing it to the world; as the sun emerging with full splendor
into the heavens, calls up, by the very fervor of its rays,
the rank and noxious vapors, which, for a time, becloud its
glory.

CHAPTER VIII.

PAPAL BULL OF PARTITION.—PREPARATIONS FOR A SECOND VOYAGE OF COLUMBUS.

[1493.]

In the midst of their rejoicings, the Spanish sovereigns
lost no time in taking every measure necessary to secure
their new acquisitions. Although it was supposed that the
countries just discovered were part of the territories of the
Grand Khan, and of other oriental princes, considerably
advanced in civilization, yet there does not appear to have
been the least doubt of the right of their catholic majesties
to take possession of them. During the crusades, a doctrine
had been established among Christian princes extremely

favorable to their ambitious designs. According to this,
they had the right to invade, ravage, and seize upon the
territories of all infidel nations, under the plea of defeating
the enemies of Christ, and extending the sway of his church
on earth. In conformity to the same doctrine, the pope,
from his supreme authority over all temporal things, was
considered as empowered to dispose of all heathen lands
to such potentates as would engage to reduce them to the
dominion of the church, and to propagate the true faith
among their benighted inhabitants. It was in virtue of
this power, that Pope Martin V and his successors had
conceded to the crown of Portugal all the lands it might
discover from Cape Bojador to the Indies; and the catholic
sovereigns, in a treaty concluded in 1479 with the Portuguese monarch, had engaged themselves to respect the
territorial rights thus acquired. It was to this treaty
that John II alluded, in his conversation with Columbus,
wherein he suggested his title to the newly-discovered
countries.

On the first intelligence received from the admiral of his
success, therefore, the Spanish sovereigns took the immediate
precaution to secure the sanction of the pope. Alexander
VI had recently been elevated to the holy chair; a pontiff
whom some historians have stigmatized with every vice and
crime that could disgrace humanity, but whom all have
represented as eminently able and politic. He was a native
of Valencia, and being born a subject of the crown of
Arragon, it might be inferred, was favorably disposed to
Ferdinand; but in certain questions which had come before
him, he had already shown a disposition not the most
cordial towards the catholic monarch. At all events,
Ferdinand was well aware of his worldly and perfidious
character, and endeavored to manage him accordingly.
He dispatched ambassadors, therefore, to the court of
Rome, announcing the new discovery as an extraordinary
triumph of the faith; and setting forth the great glory and

16

gain which must redound to the church from the dissemi-
nation of Christianity throughout these vast and heathen
lands. Care was also taken to state, that the present discovery did not in the least interfere with the possessions
ceded by the holy chair to Portugal, all which had been
sedulously avoided. Ferdinand, who was at least as politic
as he was pious, insinuated a hint at the same time, by
which the pope might perceive that he was determined, at
all events, to maintain his important acquisitions. His
ambassadors were instructed to state that, in the opinion of
many learned men, these newly-discovered lands having
been taken possession of by the catholic sovereigns, their
title to the same did not require the papal sanction ; still,
as pious princes, obedient to the holy chair, they supplicated
his holiness to issue a bull, making a concession of them,
and of such others as might be discovered, to the crown of
Castile.

The tidings of the discovery were received, in fact, with
great astonishment and no less exultation by the court of
Rome. The Spanish sovereigns had already elevated themselves to high consequence in the eyes of the church, by
their war against the Moors of Spain, which had been considered in the light of a pious crusade ; and though richly
repaid by the acquisition of the kingdom of Granada, it
was thought to entitle them to the gratitude of all Christendom. The present discovery was a still greater achievement ; it was the fulfillment of one of the sublime promises
to the church ; it was giving to it " the heathen for an
inheritance, and the uttermost parts of the earth for a
possession." No difficulty, therefore, was made in granting what was considered but a modest request for so important a service ; though it is probable that the acquiescence
of the worldly-minded pontiff was quickened by the insinu-
ations of the politic monarch.

A bull was accordingly issued, dated May 2d, 1493, ced-
ing to the Spanish sovereigns the same rights, privileges, and

indulgènces, in respect to the newly-discovered regions, as
had been accorded to the Portuguese with regard to their
African discoveries, under the same condition of planting
and propagating the catholic faith. To prevent any con-
flicting claims, however, between the two powers in the
wide range of their discoveries, another bull was issued
on the following day, containing the famous line of demar-
cation, by which their territories were thought to be clearly
and permanently defined. This was an ideal line drawn
from the north to the south pole, a hundred leagues to the
west of the Azores and the Cape de Verd islands. All
land discovered by the Spanish navigators to the west of
this line, and which had not been taken possession of by
any Christian power before the preceding Christmas, was to
belong to the Spanish crown; all land discovered in the
contrary direction, was to belong to Portugal. It seems
never to have occurred to the pontiff, that, by pushing their
opposite careers of discovery, they might some day or other
come again in collision, and renew the question of territorial
right at the antipodes.

In the meantime, without waiting for the sanction of the
court of Rome, the utmost exertions were made by the
sovereigns to fit out a second expedition. To insure regu-
larity and dispatch in the affairs relative to the New
World, they were placed under the superintendence of
Juan Rodriguez de Fonseca, archdeacon of Seville, who
was successively promoted to the seas of Bajadoz, Palencia,
and Burgos, and finally appointed patriarch of the Indies.
He was a man of family and influence; his brothers Alonzo
and Antonio were seniors, or lords, of Coca and Alaejos,
and the latter was comptroller-general of Castile. Juan
Rodriguez de Fonseca is represented by Las Casas as a
worldly man, more calculated for temporal than spiritual
concerns, and well adapted to the bustling occupation of
fitting out and manning armadas. Notwithstanding the
high ecclesiastical dignities to which he rose, his worldly

employments seem never to have been considered incompatible with his sacred functions. Enjoying the perpetual, though unmerited favor of the sovereigns, he maintained the control of Indian affairs for about thirty years. He must undoubtedly have possessed talents for business, to insure him such a perpetuity of office: but he was malignant and vindictive; and in the gratification of his private resentments, not only heaped wrongs and sorrows upon the most illustrious of the early discoverers, but frequently impeded the progress of their enterprises, to the great detriment of the crown. This he was enabled to do privately and securely by his official situation. His perfidious conduct is repeatedly alluded to, but in guarded terms, by contemporary writers of weight and credit, such as the curate of Los Palacios, and the bishop Las Casas; but they evidently were fearful of expressing the fullness of their feelings. Subsequent Spanish historians, always more or less controlled by ecclesiastical supervision, have likewise dealt too favorably with this base-minded man. He deserves to be held up as a warning example of those perfidious beings in office, who too often lie like worms at the root of honorable enterprise, blighting, by their unseen influence, the fruits of glorious action, and disappointing the hopes of nations.

To assist Fonseca in his duties, Francisco Pinelo was associated with him as treasurer, and Juan de Soria as contador, or comptroller. Their office, for the transaction of Indian affairs, was fixed at Seville; extending its vigilance at the same time to the port of Cadiz, where a custom-house was established for this new branch of navigation. Such was the germ of the Royal India House, which afterwards rose to such great power and importance. A correspondent office was ordered to be instituted in Hispaniola, under the direction of the admiral. These offices were to interchange registers of the cargoes, crews, and munition of each ship, by accountants who sailed with it.

All persons thus employed were dependants upon the two comptrollers-general, superior ministers of the royal revenue; since the crown was to be at all the expenses of the colony, and to receive all the emoluments.

The most minute and rigorous account was to be exacted of all expenses and proceeds; and the most vigilant caution observed as to the persons employed in the concerns of the newly-discovered lands. No one was permitted to go there either to trade or to form an establishment, without express license from the sovereigns, from Columbus, or from Fonseca, under the heaviest penalties. The ignorance of the age as to enlarged principles of commerce, and the example of the Portuguese in respect to their African possessions, have been cited in excuse of the narrow and jealous spirit here manifested; but it always more or less influenced the policy of Spain in her colonial regulations.

Another instance of the despotic sway maintained by the crown over commerce, is manifested in a royal order, that all ships in the ports of Andalusia, with their captains, pilots, and crews, should be held in readiness to serve in this expedition. Columbus and Fonseca were authorized to freight or purchase any of those vessels they might think proper, and to take them by force, if refused, even though they had been freighted by other persons, paying what they should conceive a reasonable price. They were furthermore authorized to take the requisite provisions, arms, and ammunition, from any place or vessel in which they might be found, paying a fair price to the owners; and they might compel, not merely mariners, but any officer holding any rank or station whatever, whom they should deem necessary to the service, to embark in the fleet on a reasonable pay and salary. The civil authorities, and all persons of rank and standing, were called upon to render all requisite aid in expediting the armament, and warned against creating any impediment, under penalty of privation of office and confiscation of estate.

To provide for the expenses of the expedition, the royal revenue arising from two-thirds of the church-tithes was placed at the disposition of Pinelo ; and other funds were drawn from a disgraceful source, from the jewels and other valuables, the sequestrated property of the unfortunate Jews, banished from the kingdom, according to a bigoted edict of the preceding year. As these resources were still inadequate, Pinelo was authorized to supply the deficiency by a loan. Requisitions were likewise made for provisions of all kinds, as well as for artillery, powder, muskets, lances, corselets, and cross-bows. This latter weapon, notwithstanding the introduction of firearms, was still preferred by many to the arquebus, and considered more formidable and destructive; the other having to be used with a match-lock, and being so heavy as to require an iron rest. The military stores which had accumulated during the war with the Moors of Granada, furnished a great part of these supplies. Almost all the preceding orders were issued by the 23d of May, while Columbus was yet at Barcelona. Rarely has there been witnessed such a scene of activity in the dilatory offices of Spain.

As the conversion of the heathens was professed to be the grand object of these discoveries, twelve zealous and able ecclesiastics were chosen for the purpose, to accompany the expedition. Among these was Bernardo Buyl or Boyle, a Benedictine monk, of talent and reputed sanctity, but one of those subtle politicians of the cloister, who in those days glided into all temporal concerns. He had acquitted himself with success in recent negotiations with France, relative to the restitution of Rousillon. Before the sailing of the fleet, he was appointed by the pope his apostolical vicar for the New World, and placed as superior over his ecclesiastical brethren. This pious mission was provided with all things necessary for the dignified performance of its functions; the queen supplying from her own chapel the ornaments and vestments to be used in all solemn cere-

.monies. Isabella, from the first, took the most warm and compassionate interest in the welfare of the Indians. Won by the accounts given by Columbus of their gentleness and simplicity, and looking upon them as committed by Heaven to her especial care, her heart was filled with concern at their destitute and ignorant condition. She ordered that great care should be taken of their religious instruction; that they should be treated with the utmost kindness; and enjoined Columbus to inflict signal punishment on all Spaniards who should be guilty of outrage or injustice towards them.

By way, it was said, of offering to Heaven the first-fruits of these pagan nations, the six Indians whom Columbus had brought to Barcelona were baptized with great state and ceremony; the king, the queen, and Prince Juan officiating as sponsors. Great hopes were entertained that, on their return to their native country, they would facilitate the introduction of Christianity among their countrymen. One of them, at the request of Prince Juan, remained in his household, but died not long afterwards: a Spanish historian remarked that, according to what ought to be our pious belief, he was the first of his nation that entered heaven.[1]

Before the departure of Columbus from Barcelona, the provisional agreement made at Santa Fé was confirmed, granting him the titles, emoluments, and prerogatives of admiral, viceroy, and governor of all the countries he had discovered, or might discover. He was intrusted also with the royal seal, with authority to use the name of their majesties in granting letters patent and commissions within the bounds of his jurisdiction; with the right also, in case of absence, to appoint a person in his place, and to invest him, for the time, with the same powers.

It had been premised in the agreement, that for all vacant offices in the government of the islands and main-

[1] Herrera, Hist. Ind., decad. i. lib. ii. cap. 5.

land, he should nominate three candidates, out of which number the sovereign should make a choice; but now, to save time, and to show their confidence in Columbus, they empowered him to appoint at once such persons as he thought proper, who were to hold their offices during the royal pleasure. He had likewise the title and command of captain-general of the armament about to sail, with unqualified powers as to the government of the crews, the establishments to be formed in the New World, and the ulterior discoveries to be undertaken.

This was the honey-moon of royal favor, during which Columbus enjoyed the unbounded and well-merited confidence of his sovereigns, before envious minds had dared to insinuate a doubt of his integrity. After receiving every mark of public honor and private regard, he took leave of the sovereigns on the 28th of May. The whole court accompanied him from the palace to his dwelling, and attended, also, to pay him farewell honors on his departure from Barcelona for Seville.

CHAPTER IX.

DIPLOMATIC NEGOTIATIONS BETWEEN THE COURTS OF SPAIN AND PORTUGAL WITH RESPECT TO THE NEW DISCOVERIES.

[1493.]

THE anxiety of the Spanish monarchy for the speedy departure of the expedition was heightened by the proceedings of the court of Portugal. John II had unfortunately among his councilors certain politicians of that short-sighted class, who mistake craft for wisdom. By adopting their perfidious policy, he had lost the New World when it was an object of honorable enterprise; in compliance with their advice, he now sought to retrieve it by stratagem. He had accordingly prepared a large armament, the avowed object of which was an expedition to

Africa, but its real destination to seize upon the newly-discovered countries. To lull suspicion, Don Ruy de Sande was sent ambassador to the Spanish court, requesting permission to procure certain prohibited articles from Spain for this African voyage. He required, also, that the Spanish sovereigns should forbid their subjects to fish beyond Cape Bojador, until the possessions of the two nations should be properly defined. The discovery of Columbus, the real object of solicitude, was treated as an incidental affair. The manner of his arrival and reception in Portugal was mentioned; the congratulations of King John on the happy result of his voyage; his satisfaction at finding that the admiral had been instructed to steer westward from the Canary Islands, and his hope that the Castilian sovereigns would continue to enjoin a similar track on their navigators,—all to the south of those islands being granted by papal bull to the crown of Portugal. He concluded by intimating the entire confidence of King John, that should any of the newly-discovered islands appertain by right to Portugal, the matter would be adjusted in that spirit of amity which existed between the two crowns.

Ferdinand was too wary a politician to be easily deceived. He had received early intelligence of the real designs of King John, and before the arrival of his ambassador had himself dispatched Don Lope de Herrera to the Portuguese court, furnished with double instructions, and with two letters of widely opposite tenor. The first was couched in affectionate terms, acknowledging the hospitality and kindness shown to Columbus, and communicating the nature of his discoveries; requesting at the same time that the Portuguese navigators might be prohibited from visiting those newly-discovered lands, in the same manner that the Spanish sovereigns had prohibited their subjects from interfering with the African possessions of Portugal.

In case, however, the ambassador should find that King
John had either sent, or was about to send, vessels to the
New World, he was to withhold the amicable letter, and
present the other, couched in stern and peremptory terms,
and forbidding any enterprise of the kind.[1]   A keen
diplomatic game ensued between the two sovereigns, perplexing to any spectator not acquainted with the secret of
their play.   Resende, in his history of King John II,
informs us, that the Portuguese monarch, by large presents,
or rather bribes, held certain of the confidential members
of the Castilian cabinet in his interest, who informed him
of the most secret councils of their court.   The roads were
thronged with couriers; scarce was an intention expressed
by Ferdinand to his ministers, but it was conveyed to his
rival monarch.   The result was, that the Spanish sovereigns
seemed as if under the influence of some enchantment.
King John anticipated all their movements, and appeared
to dive into their very thoughts.   Their ambassadors were
crossed on the road by Portuguese ambassadors, empowered
to settle the very points about which they were going to
make remonstrances.   Frequently, when Ferdinand proposed a sudden and perplexing question to the envoys at
his court, which apparently would require fresh instructions
from the sovereigns, he would be astonished by a prompt
and positive reply; most of the questions which were likely
to occur having, through secret information, been foreseen
and provided for.   As a surmise of treachery in the cabinet
might naturally arise, King John, while he rewarded his
agents in secret, endeavored to divert suspicions from them
upon others, making rich presents of jewels to the Duke de
Infantado and other Spanish grandees of incorruptible
integrity.[2]

[1] Herrera, Hist. Ind., decad. i. lib. ii.   Zurita, Anales de Aragon,
lib. i. cap. 25.

[2] Resende, Vida del Rey Dom Joam II, cap. 157.   Faria y Souza,
Europa Portuguesa, tom. ii. cap. 4, p. 3.

Such is the intriguing diplomatic craft which too often passes for refined policy, and is extolled as the wisdom of the cabinet; but all corrupt and disingenuous measures are unworthy of an enlightened politician and a magnanimous prince. The grand principles of right and wrong operate in the same way between nations as between individuals; fair and open conduct, and inviolable faith, however they may appear adverse to present purposes, are the only kind of policy that will insure ultimate and honorable success.

King John, having received intelligence, in the furtive manner that has been mentioned, of the double instructions furnished to Don Lope de Herrera, received him in such a manner as to prevent any resort to his peremptory letter. He had already dispatched an extra envoy to the Spanish court to keep it in good humor, and he now appointed Doctor Pero Diaz and Don Ruy de Pena ambassadors to the Spanish sovereigns, to adjust all questions relative to the new discoveries, and promised that no vessel should be permitted to sail on a voyage of discovery within sixty days after their arrival at Barcelona.

These ambassadors were instructed to propose, as a mode of effectually settling all claims, that a line should be drawn from the Canaries due west: all lands and seas north of it to appertain to the Castilian court; all south to the crown of Portugal, excepting any islands already in possession of either powers.[1]

Ferdinand had now the vantage-ground; his object was to gain time for the preparation and departure of Columbus, by entangling King John in long diplomatic negotiations.[2] In reply to his proposals, he dispatched Don Pedro de Ayala and Don Garcia Lopez de Caravajal on a solemn embassy to Portugal, in which there was great outward pomp and parade, and many professions of amity, but the whole purport of which was to propose to submit the ter-

---

[1] Zurita, lib. i. cap. 25. Herrera, decad. i. lib. ii. cap. 5.
[2] Vasconcelos, Don Juan II, lib. vi.

ritorial questions which had risen between them to arbitra-
tion, or to the court of Rome. This stately embassy moved
with becoming slowness, but a special envoy was sent in
advance to apprise the king of Portugal of its approach,
in order to keep him waiting for its communications.

King John understood the whole nature and object of
the embassy, and felt that Ferdinand was foiling him. The
ambassadors at length arrived, and delivered their creden-
tials with great form and ceremony. As they retired from
his presence, he looked after them contemptuously : " This
embassy from our cousin," said he, " wants both head and
feet." He alluded to the character both of the mission
and the envoys. Don Garcia de Caravajal was vain
and frivolous, and Don Pedro de Ayala was lame of one
leg.[1]

In the height of his vexation, King John is even said to
have held out some vague show of hostile intentions, taking
occasion to let the ambassadors discover him reviewing his
cavalry and dropping ambiguous words in their hearing,
which might be construed into something of menacing im-
port.[2] The embassy returned to Castile, leaving him in a
state of perplexity and irritation ; but whatever might be
his chagrin, his discretion prevented him from coming to an
open rupture. He had some hopes of interference on the
part of the pope, to whom he had sent an embassy, complain-
ing of the pretended discoveries of the Spaniards, as infring-
ing the territories granted to Portugal by papal bull, and
earnestly imploring redress. Here, as has been shown, his
wary antagonist had been beforehand with him, and he was
doomed again to be foiled. The only reply his ambassador
received, was a reference to the line of partition from pole
to pole, so sagely devised by his holiness.[3] Such was this
royal game of diplomacy, where the parties were playing

[1] Vasconcelos, lib. vi. Barros, Asia, d. i. lib. iii. cap. 2.
[2] Vasconcelos, lib. vi.
[3] Herrera, decad. i. lib. ii. cap. 5.

for a newly-discovered world. John II was able and intelligent, and had crafty councilors to advise him in all his moves; but whenever deep and subtle policy was required, Ferdinand was master of the game.

CHAPTER X.

FURTHER PREPARATIONS FOR THE SECOND VOYAGE.—CHARACTER OF ALONSO DE OJEDA.—DIFFERENCE OF CO-LUMBUS WITH SORIA AND FONSECA.

[1493.]

DISTRUSTFUL of some attempt on the part of Portugal to interfere with their discoveries, the Spanish sovereigns, in the course of their negotiations, wrote repeatedly to Columbus, urging him to hasten his departure. His zeal, however, needed no incitement; immediately on arriving at Seville, in the beginning of June, he proceeded with all diligence to fit out the armament, making use of the powers given him to put in requisition the ships and crews which were in the harbors of Andalusia. He was joined soon after by Fonseca and Soria, who had remained for a time at Barcelona; and with their united exertions, a fleet of seventeen vessels, large and small, was soon in a state of preparation. The best pilots were chosen for the service, and the crews were mustered in presence of Soria the comptroller. A number of skillful husbandmen, miners, carpenters, and other mechanics, were engaged for the projected colony. Horses, both for military purposes and for stocking the country, cattle, and domestic animals of all kinds, were likewise provided. Grain, seeds of various plants, vines, sugar-canes, grafts, and saplings, were embarked, together with a great quantity of merchandise, consisting of trinkets, beads, hawks' bells, looking-glasses, and other showy trifles, calculated for trafficking with . the natives. Nor was there wanting an abundant supply of provisions of all sorts, munitions of war, and medicines and refreshments for the sick.

An extraordinary degree of excitement prevailed respecting this expedition. The most extravagant fancies were entertained with respect to the New World. The accounts given by the voyagers who had visited it were full of exaggeration; for in fact they had nothing but vague and confused notions concerning it, like the recollection of a dream, and it has been shown that Columbus himself had beheld every thing through the most delusive medium. The vivacity of his descriptions, and the sanguine anticipations of his ardent spirit, while they roused the public to a wonderful degree of enthusiasm, prepared the way for bitter disappointment. The cupidity of the avaricious was inflamed with the idea of regions of unappropriated wealth, where the rivers rolled over golden sands, and the mountains teemed with gems and precious metals; where the groves produced sprices and perfumes, and the shores of the ocean were sown with pearl. Others had conceived visions of a loftier kind. It was a romantic and stirring age, and the wars with the Moors being over, and hostilities with the French suspended, the bold and restless spirits of the nation, impatient of the monotony of peaceful life, were eager for employment. To these, the New World presented a vast field for wild enterprise and extraordinary adventure, so congenial to the Spanish character in that period of its meridian fervor and brilliancy. Many hidalgos of high rank, officers of the royal household, and Andalusian cavaliers, schooled in arms, and inspired with a passion for hardy achievements by the romantic wars of Granada, pressed into the expedition, some in the royal service, others at their own cost. To them it was the commencement of a new series of crusades, surpassing in extent and splendor the chivalrous enterprises to the Holy Land. They pictured to themselves vast and beautiful islands of the ocean to be overrun and subdued; their internal wonders to be explored, and the banner of the cross to be planted on the walls of the cities they were supposed to contain. Thence they were to make their way to the shores of India, or rather Asia, penetrate into Mangi and Cathay, convert, or, what was the same thing, conquer, the Grand Khan, and thus open a glorious career of arms among the splendid countries and semi-barbarous nations of the East. Thus, no one had any definite idea of the object or nature of the service on which he was embarking, or the situation and character of the region to which he was bound. Indeed, during this fever of the imagination, had sober facts and cold realities been presented, they would have been rejected with disdain; for there is nothing of which the public is more impatient than of being disturbed in the indulgence of any of its golden dreams.

Among the noted personages who engaged in the expedition, was a young cavalier of the name of Don Alonso de Ojeda, celebrated for his extraordinary personal endowments and his daring spirit; and who distinguished himself among the early discoverers by many perilous expeditions and singular exploits. He was of a good family, cousin-german to the venerable Father Alonso de Ojeda, Inquisitor of Spain; had been brought up under the patronage of the Duke of Medina Celi, and had served in the wars against the Moors. He was of small stature, but vigorous make, well proportioned; dark complexioned, of handsome, animated countenance, and incredible strength and agility. Expert at all kinds of weapons, accomplished in all manly and warlike exercises, an admirable horseman, and a partisan soldier of the highest order; bold of heart, free of spirit, open of hand; fierce in fight, quick in brawl, but ready to forgive and prone to forget an injury; he was for a long time the idol of the rash and roving youth who engaged in the early expeditions to the New World, and has been made the hero of many wonderful tales. On

introducing him to historical notice, Las Casas gives an
anecdote of one of his exploits, which would be unworthy
of record, but that it exhibits the singular character of the
man.

Queen Isabella being in the tower of the cathedral of
Seville, better known as the Giralda, Ojeda, to entertain
her majesty, and to give proofs of his courage and agility,
mounted on a great beam which projected in the air, twenty
feet from the tower, at such an immense height from the
ground, that the people below looked like dwarfs, and it
was enough to make Ojeda himself shudder to look down.
Along this beam he walked briskly, and with as much
confidence as though he had been pacing his chamber.
When arrived at the end, he stood on one leg, lifting the
other in the air; then turning nimbly round, he returned
in the same way to the tower, unaffected by the giddy
height, whence the least false step would have precipitated
him and dashed him to pieces. He afterwards stood with
one foot on the beam, and placing the other against the
wall of the building, threw an orange to the summit of
the tower, a proof, says Las Casas, of immense muscular
strength. Such was Alonso de Ojeda, who soon became
conspicuous among the followers of Columbus, and was
always foremost in every enterprise of an adventurous nature; who courted peril as if for the very love of danger,
and seemed to fight more for the pleasure of fighting than
for the sake of distinction.[1]

The number of persons permitted to embark in the expedition had been limited to one thousand; but such was the
urgent application of volunteers to be allowed to enlist
without pay, that the number had increased to twelve hundred. Many more were refused for want of room in the
ships for their accommodation, but some contrived to get
admitted by stealth, so that eventually about fifteen hun-

[1] Las Casas, lib. i., MS. Pizarro, Varones Ilustres. Herrera,
Hist. Ind., decad i. lib. ii. cap. 5.

dred set sail in the fleet. As Columbus, in his laudable zeal for the welfare of the enterprise, provided every thing that might be necessary in various possible emergencies, the expenses of the outfit exceeded what had been anticipated. This gave rise to occasional demurs on the part of the comptroller Juan de Soria, who sometimes refused to sign the accounts of the admiral, and in the course of their transactions seemed to have forgotten the deference due both to his character and station. For this he received repeated and severe reprimands from the sovereigns, who emphatically commanded that Columbus should be treated with the greatest respect, and every thing done to facilitate his plans and yield him satisfaction. From similar injunctions inserted in the royal letters to Fonseca, the archdeacon of Seville, it is probable that he also had occasionally indulged in the captious exercise of his official powers. He appears to have demurred to various requisitions of Columbus, particularly one for footmen and other domestics for his immediate service, to form his household and retinue as admiral and viceroy; a demand which was considered superfluous by the prelate, as all who embarked in the expedition were at his command. In reply, the sovereigns ordered that he should be allowed ten *escuderos de à pie*, or footmen, and twenty persons in other domestic capacities, and reminded Fonseca of their charge that, both in the nature and mode of his transactions with the admiral, he should study to give him content; observing that, as the whole armament was intrusted to his command, it was but reasonable that his wishes should be consulted, and no one embarrass him with punctilios and difficulties.[1]

These trivial differences are worthy of particular notice, from the effect they appear to have had on the mind of Fonseca, for from them we must date the rise of that singular hostility which he ever afterwards manifested towards Columbus; which every year increased in rancor, and

[1] Navarrete, Colec., tom. ii. Documentos, Nos. 62-66.

17

which he gratified in the most invidious manner, by secretly
multiplying impediments and vexations in his path.

While the expedition was yet lingering in port, intelligence was received that a Portuguese caravel had set sail
from Madeira and steered for the west. Suspicions were
immediately awakened that she was bound for the lately-
discovered lands. Columbus wrote an account of it to the
sovereigns, and proposed to dispatch a part of his fleet in
pursuit of her. His proposition was approved, but not
carried into effect. On remonstrances being made to the
court of Lisbon, King John declared that the vessel had
sailed without his permission, and that he would send three
caravels to bring her back. This only served to increase
the jealousy of the Spanish monarchs, who considered the
whole a deep-laid stratagem, and that it was intended the
vessels should join their forces, and pursue their course
together to the New World. Columbus was urged, therefore, to depart without an hour's delay, and instructed to
steer wide of Cape St. Vincent, and entirely avoid the
Portuguese coasts and islands, for fear of molestation. If
he met with any vessels in the seas he had explored, he was
to seize them, and inflict rigorous punishment on the crews.
Fonseca was also ordered to be on the alert, and in case
any expedition sailed from Portugal to send double the
force after it. These precautions, however, proved unnecessary. Whether such caravels actually did sail, and
whether they were sent with sinister motives by Portugal,
does not appear; nothing was either seen or heard of them
by Columbus in the course of his voyage.

It may be as well, for the sake of distinctness, to anticipate, in this place, the regular course of history, and mention the manner in which this territorial question was
finally settled between the rival sovereigns. It was impossible for King John to repress his disquiet at the indefinite
enterprises of the Spanish monarchs; he did not know how
far they might extend, and whether they might not fore-

stall him in all his anticipated discoveries in India. Finding, however, all attempts fruitless to gain by stratagem an advantage over his wary and skillful antagonist, and despairing of any further assistance from the court of Rome, he had recourse, at last, to fair and amicable negotiations, and found, as is generally the case with those who turn aside into the inviting but crooked paths of craft, that had he kept to the line of frank and open policy, he would have saved himself a world of perplexity, and have arrived sooner at his object. He offered to leave to the Spanish sovereigns the free prosecution of their western discovery, and to conform to the plan of partition by a meridian line: but he represented that this line had not been drawn far enough to the west; that while it left the wide ocean free to the range of Spanish enterprise, his navigators could not venture more than a hundred leagues west of his possessions, and had no scope or sea-room for their southern voyages.

After much difficulty and discussion, this momentous dispute was adjusted by deputies from the two crowns, who met at Tordesillas in Old Castile, in the following year, and on the 7th of June, 1494, signed a treaty, by which the papal line of partition was moved to three hundred and seventy leagues west of the Cape de Verd Islands. It was agreed that within six months an equal number of caravels and mariners, on the part of the two nations, should rendezvous at the island of the Grand Canary, provided with men learned in astronomy and navigation. They were to proceed thence to the Cape de Verd Islands, and thence westward three hundred and seventy leagues, and determine the proposed line from pole to pole, dividing the ocean between the two nations.[1] Each of the two powers engaged solemnly to observe the bounds thus prescribed, and to prosecute no enterprise beyond its proper limits;

[1] Zurita, Hist del Rey Fernand., lib. i. cap. 29. Vasconcelos, lib. vi.

though it was agreed that the Spanish navigators might traverse freely the eastern parts of the ocean in prosecuting their rightful voyages. Various circumstances impeded the proposed expedition to determine the line, but the treaty remained in force, and prevented all further discussions.

Thus, says Vasconcelos, this great question, the greatest ever agitated between the two crowns, for it was the partition of a new world, was amicably settled by the prudence and address of two of the most politic monarchs that ever swayed the sceptre. It was arranged to the satisfaction of both parties, each holding himself entitled to the vast countries that might be discovered within his boundary, without any regard to the rights of the native inhabitants.

BOOK VI.

CHAPTER I.

[1493.]

THE departure of Columbus on his second voyage of discovery presented a brilliant contrast to his gloomy embarkation at Palos. On the 25th of September, at the dawn of day, the bay of Cadiz was whitened by his fleet. There were three large ships of heavy burden,[1] and fourteen caravels, loitering with flapping sails, and awaiting the signal to get under way. The harbor resounded with the well-known note of the sailor, hoisting sail, or weighing anchor; a motley crowd were hurrying on board, and taking leave of their friends in the confidence of a prosperous voyage and triumphant return. There was the high-spirited cavalier, bound on romantic enterprise; the hardy navigator, ambitious of acquiring laurels in these unknown seas; the roving adventurer, seeking novelty and excitement; the keen, calculating speculator, eager to profit by the ignorance of savage tribes; and the pale missionary from the cloister, anxious to extend the dominion of the church, or devoutly zealous for the propagation of

---

[1] Peter Martyr says they were carracks (a large species of merchant vessel, principally used in coasting trade), of one hundred tons burden, and that two of the caravels were much larger than the rest, and more capable of bearing decks from the size of their masts.—Decad. i. lib. i.

the faith. All were full of animation and lively hope.
Instead of being regarded by the populace as devoted men,
bound upon a dark and desperate enterprise, they were contemplated with envy, as favored mortals, bound to golden
regions and happy climes, where nothing but wealth, and
wonder, and delights awaited them. Columbus, conspicuous
for his height and his commanding appearance, was attended by his two sons Diego and Fernando, the eldest but
a stripling, who had come to witness his departure,[1] both
proud of the glory of their father. Wherever he passed,
every eye followed him with admiration, and every tongue
praised and blessed him. Before sunrise the whole fleet
was under way; the weather was serene and propitious,
and as the populace watched their parting sails bright-
ening in the morning beams, they looked forward to their
joyful return laden with the treasures of the New World.

According to the instructions of the sovereigns, Columbus steered wide of the coasts of Portugal and of its islands,
standing to the southwest of the Canaries, where he arrived
on the 1st of October. After touching at the Grand
Canary, he anchored on the 5th at Gomera, to take in a
supply of wood and water. Here also he purchased calves,
goats, and sheep, to stock the island of Hispaniola; and
eight hogs, from which, according to Las Casas, the infinite
number of swine was propagated, with which the Spanish
settlements in the New World subsequently abounded. A
number of domestic fowls were likewise purchased, which
were the origin of the species in the New World; and the
same might be said of the seeds of oranges, lemons, ber-
gamots, melons, and various orchard fruits,[2] which were
thus first introduced into the islands of the west, from the
Hesperides or Fortunate Islands of the Old World.[3]

[1] Hist. del Almirante, cap. 44.

[2] Las Casas, Hist. Ind., lib. i. cap. 83.

[3] Humboldt is of opinion that there were wild oranges, small and
bitter, as well as wild lemons, in the New World, prior to the dis-

On the 7th, when about to sail, Columbus gave to the commander of each vessel a sealed letter of instructions, in which was specified his route to the harbor of Nativity, the residence of the cacique Guacanagari. This was only to be opened in case of being separated by accident, as he wished to make a mystery, as long as possible, of the exact route to the newly-discovered country, lest adventurers of other nations, and particularly the Portuguese, should follow in his track, and interfere with his enterprises.[1]

After making sail from Gomera, they were becalmed for a few days among the Canaries, until, on the 13th of October, a fair breeze sprang up from the east, which soon carried them out of sight of the island of Ferro. Columbus held his course to the southwest, intending to keep considerably more to the southward than in his first voyage, in hopes of falling in with the islands of the Caribs, of which he had received such vague and wonderful accounts from the Indians.[2] Being in the region of the trade-winds, the breeze continued fair and steady, with a quiet sea and pleasant weather, and by the 24th they had made four hundred and fifty leagues west of Gomera, without seeing any of those fields of sea-weeds encountered within a much less distance on their first voyage. At that time their appearance was important, and almost providential, inspiring continual hope, and enticing them forward in their dubious enterprise. Now they needed no such signals, being full of confidence and lively anticipation, and on seeing a swallow circling about the ships, and being visited occasionally by sudden showers, they began to look out cheerily for land.

Towards the latter part of October they had in the night a gust of heavy rain, accompanied by the severe thunder

covery. Caldcleugh also mentions that the Brazilians consider the small bitter wild orange of native origin.—Humboldt, Essai Politique sur l'Isle de Cuba, tom. i. p. 68.

[1] Las Casas, M. Sup.   [2] Letter of Dr. Chanca.

and lightning of the tropics.   It lasted for four hours, and
they considered themselves in much peril, until they beheld
several of those lambent flames playing about the tops of
the masts, and gliding along the rigging, which have always
been objects of superstitious fancies among sailors.   Fernando Columbus makes remarks on them strongly characteristic of the age in which he lived.   "On the same
Saturday, in the night, was seen St. Elmo, with seven
lighted tapers, at the topmast: there was much rain and
great thunder; I mean to say, that those lights were seen,
which mariners affirm to be the body of St. Elmo, on beholding which they chant litanies and orisons, holding it
for certain, that in the tempest in which he appears, no
one is in danger.   Be that as it may, I leave the matter to
them; but if we may believe Pliny, similar lights have
sometimes appeared to the Roman mariners during tempests
at sea, which they said were Castor and Pollux, of which
likewise Seneca makes mention." [1]

On the evening of Saturday, the 2d of November, Columbus was convinced from the color of the sea, the nature of the waves, and the variable winds and frequent
showers, that they must be near to land; he gave orders,
therefore, to take in sail, and to maintain a vigilant watch
throughout the night.   He had judged with his usual sagacity.   In the morning a lofty island was descried to the
west, at the sight of which there were shouts of joy throughout the fleet.   Columbus gave to the island the name of
Dominica, from having discovered it on Sunday.   As the

[1] Hist. del Almirante, cap. 45.   A similar mention is made of this
nautical superstition in the voyage of Magellan.   "During these
great storms, they said that St. Elmo appeared at the topmast with
a lighted candle, and sometimes with two, upon which the people
shed tears of joy, receiving great consolation, and saluted him
according to the custom of mariners.   He remained visible for a
quarter of an hour, and then disappeared, with a great flash of
lightning, which blinded the people."—Herrera, decad. ii. lib. iv.
cap. 10.

ships moved gently onward, other islands rose to sight, covered with forests, while flights of parrots, and other tropical birds, passed from one to the other.

The crews were now assembled on the decks of the several ships, to return thanks to God for their prosperous voyage, and their happy discovery of land, chanting the *Salve Regina* and other anthems. Such was the solemn manner in which Columbus celebrated all his discoveries, and which, in fact, was generally observed by the Spanish and Portuguese voyagers.

CHAPTER II.

TRANSACTIONS AT THE ISLAND OF GUADALOUPE.

[1493.]

THE islands among which Columbus had arrived were a part of that beautiful cluster called by some the Antilles, which sweep almost in a semicircle from the eastern end of Porto Rico to the coast of Paria on the southern continent, forming a kind of barrier between the main ocean and the Caribbean sea.

During the first day that he entered this archipelago, Columbus saw no less than six islands of different magnitude. They were clothed in tropical vegetation, and the breezes from them were sweetened by the fragrance of their forests.

After seeking in vain for good anchorage at Dominica, he stood for another of the group, to which he gave the name of his ship, Marigalante. Here he landed, displayed the royal banner, and took possession of the archipelago in the name of his sovereigns. The island appeared to be uninhabited; a rich and dense forest overspread it; some of the trees were in blossom, others laden with unknown fruits, others possessing spicy odors—among which was one with the leaf of the laurel and the fragrance of the clove.

Hence they made sail for an island of larger size, with a remarkable mountain; one peak, which proved afterwards to be the crater of a volcano, rose to a great height, with streams of water gushing from it. As they approached within three leagues, they beheld a cataract of such height, that, to use the words of the narrator, it seemed to be falling from the sky. As it broke into foam in its descent, many at first believed it to be merely a stratum of white rock.[1] To this island, which was called by the Indians Turuqueira,[2] the admiral gave the name of Guadaloupe, having promised the monks of our Lady of Guadaloupe in Estremadura to call some newly-discovered place after their convent.

Landing here on the 4th, they visited a village near the shore, the inhabitants of which fled, some even leaving their children behind in their terror and confusion. These the Spaniards soothed with caresses, binding hawks' bells and other trinkets round their arms. This village, like most of those of the island, consisted of twenty or thirty houses, built round a public place or square. The houses were constructed of trunks of trees interwoven with reeds and branches, and thatched with palm-leaves. They were square, not circular like those of the other islands,[3] and each had its portico or shelter from the sun. One of the porticos was decorated with images of serpents tolerably carved in wood. For furniture they had hammocks of cotton net, and utensils formed of calabashes or earthenware, equal to the best of those of Hispaniola. There were large quantities of cotton; some in the wool, some in yarn, and some wrought into cloth of very tolerable text-

[1] Letter of Dr. Chanca.

[2] Letter of Dr. Chanca. Peter Martyr calls it Carucueira, or Queraquiera, decad. i. lib. ii.

[3] Hist. del Almirante, cap. 62.

ure; and many bows and arrows, the latter tipped with sharp bones. Provisions seemed to abound. There were many domesticated geese like those of Europe, and parrots as large as household fowls, with blue, green, white, and scarlet plumage, being the splendid species called guaca-mayos. Here also the Spaniards first met with the anana, or pine-apple, the flavor and fragrance of which astonished and delighted them. In one of the houses they were surprised to find a pan or other utensil of iron, not having ever met with that metal in the New World. Fernando Colon supposes that it was formed of a certain kind of heavy stone found among those islands, which, when burnt, has the appearance of shining iron; or it might have been some utensil brought by the Indians from Hispaniola. Certain it is, that no native iron was ever found among the people of these islands.

In another house was the stern-post of a vessel. How had it reached these shores, which appeared never to have been visited by the ships of civilized man? Was it the wreck of some vessel from the more enlightened countries of Asia, which they supposed to lie somewhere in this direction? Or a part of the caravel which Columbus had lost at the island of Hispaniola during his first voyage? Or a fragment of some European ship which had drifted across the Atlantic? The latter was most probably the case. The constant current which sets over from the coast of Africa, produced by the steady prevalence of the trade-winds, must occasionally bring wrecks from the Old World to the New; and long before the discovery of Columbus, the savages of the islands and the coasts may have gazed with wonder at fragments of European barks which have floated to their shores.

What struck the Spaniards with horror was the sight of human bones, vestiges, as they supposed, of unnatural repasts; and skulls, apparently used as vases and other household utensils. These dismal objects convinced them that they were now in the abodes of the Cannibals, or Caribs, whose predatory expeditions and ruthless character rendered them the terror of these seas.

The boat having returned on board, Columbus proceeded upwards of two leagues, until he anchored, late in the evening, in a convenient port. The island on this side extended for the distance of five and twenty leagues, diversified with lofty mountains and broad plains. Along the coast were small villages and hamlets, the inhabitants of which fled in affright. On the following day the boats landed, and succeeded in taking and bringing off a boy and several women. The information gathered from them confirmed Columbus in his idea that this was one of the islands of the Caribs. He learnt that the inhabitants were in league with two neighboring islands, but made war upon all the rest. They even went on predatory enterprises, in canoes made from the hollow trunks of trees, to the distance of one hundred and fifty leagues. Their arms were bows and arrows pointed with the bones of fishes, or shells of tortoises, and poisoned with the juice of a certain herb. They made descents upon the islands, ravaged the villages, carried off the youngest and handsomest of the women, whom they retained as servants or companions, and made prisoners of the men, to be killed and eaten.

After hearing such accounts of the natives of this island, Columbus was extremely uneasy at finding, in the evening, that Diego Marque, a captain of one of the caravels, and eight men, were missing. They had landed early in the morning without leave, and straying into the woods, had not since been seen or heard of. The night passed away without their return. On the following day parties were sent in various directions in quest of them, each with a trumpeter to sound calls and signals. Guns were fired from the ships, and arquebuses on shore, but all to no purpose, and the parties returned in the evening, wearied with a fruitless search. In several hamlets, they had met with proofs of the cannibal propensities of the natives. Human limbs were suspended to the beams of the houses, as if curing for provisions; the head of a young man recently killed, was yet bleeding; some parts of his body were roasting before the fire, others boiling with the flesh of geese and parrots.[1]

Several of the natives, in the course of the day, had been seen on the shore, gazing with wonder at the ships, but when the boats approached, they fled to the woods and mountains. Several women came off to the Spaniards for refuge, being captives from other islands. Columbus ordered that they should be decorated with hawks' bells, and strings of beads and bugles, and sent on shore, in hopes of enticing off some of the men. They soon returned to the boats stripped of their ornaments, and imploring to be taken on board the ships. The admiral learnt from them that most of the men of the island were absent, the king having sailed some time before with ten canoes and three hundred warriors, on a cruise in quest of prisoners and booty. When the men went forth on these expeditions, the women remained to defend their shores from invasion. They were expert archers, partaking of the warrior spirit of their husbands, and almost equaling them in force and intrepidity.[2]

The continued absence of the wanderers perplexed Columbus extremely. He was impatient to arrive at Hispaniola, but unwilling to sail while there was a possibility of their being alive and being recovered. In this emergency Alonzo de Ojeda, the same young cavalier whose exploit on the tower of the cathedral at Seville has been mentioned, volunteered to scour the island with forty men in quest of them. He departed accordingly, and during his absence the ships took in wood and water, and part of the crews were permitted to land, wash their clothes, and recreate themselves.

[1] P. Martyr, Letter 147, to Pomponio Læto. Idem, decad. i. lib. ii.
[2] Peter Martyr, decad. iii. lib. ix.

Ojeda and his followers pushed far into the interior; firing off arquebuses and sounding trumpets in the valleys and from the summits of cliffs and precipices, but were only answered by their own echoes. The tropical luxuriance and density of the forests rendered them almost impenetrable; and it was necessary to wade a great many rivers, or probably the windings and doublings of the same stream. The island appeared to be naturally fertile in the extreme. The forests abounded with aromatic trees and shrubs, among which Ojeda fancied he perceived the odor of precious gums and spices. There was honey in hollow trees and in the clefts of rocks: abundance of fruit also; for, according to Peter Martyr, the Caribs, in their predatory cruisings, were accustomed to bring home the seeds and roots of all kinds of plants from the distant islands and countries which they overran.

Ojeda returned without any tidings of the stragglers. Several days had now elapsed since their disappearance. They were given up for lost, and the fleet was about sailing, when, to the universal joy, a signal was made by them from the shore. When they came on board, their haggard and exhausted looks bespoke what they had suffered. For several days they had been perplexed in trackless forests, so dense as almost to exclude the light of day. They had clambered rocks, waded rivers, and struggled through briers and thickets. Some who were experienced seamen climbed the trees, to get a sight of the stars, by which to govern their course; but the spreading branches and thick foliage shut out all view of the heavens. They were harassed with the fear, that the admiral, thinking them dead, might set sail and leave them in this wilderness, cut off for ever from their homes and the abodes of civilized man. At length, when almost reduced to despair, they had arrived at the sea-shore, and following it for some time, beheld, to their great joy, the fleet riding quietly at anchor. They brought with them several Indian women and boys; but in all their wanderings they had not met with any man; the greater part of the warriors, as has been said, being fortunately absent on an expedition.

Notwithstanding the hardships they had endured, and his joy at their return, Columbus put the captain under arrest, and stopped part of the rations of the men, for having strayed away without permission, for in a service of such a critical nature it was necessary to punish every breach of discipline.[1]

CHAPTER III.

CRUISE AMONG THE CARIBBEE ISLANDS.

[1493.]

WEIGHING anchor on the 10th of November, Columbus steered toward the northwest, along this beautiful archipelago; giving names to the islands as they rose to view; such as Montserrat, Santa Maria la Redonda, Santa Maria la Antigua, and San Martin. Various other islands lofty and well wooded appeared to the north, southwest, and southeast; but he forbore to visit them. The weather proving boisterous, he anchored on the 14th at an island called Ayay by the Indians, but to which he gave the name of Santa Cruz. A boat well manned was sent on shore to get water and procure information. They found a village, deserted by the men; but secured a few women and boys, most of them captives from other islands. They soon had an instance of Carib courage and ferocity. While at the village they beheld a canoe from a distant part of the island come round a point of land and arrive in view of the ships. The Indians in the canoe, two of whom were females, remained gazing in mute amazement at the ships,

[1] Dr. Chanca's Letter. Hist. del Almirante, cap. 46.

and were so entranced that the boat stole close upon them before they perceived it. Seizing their paddles, they attempted to escape, but the boat being between them and the land, cut off their retreat. They now caught up their bows and arrows and plied them with amazing vigor and rapidity. The Spaniards covered themselves with their bucklers, but two of them were quickly wounded. The women fought as fiercely as the men, and one of them sent an arrow with such force that it passed through and through a buckler.

The Spaniards now ran their boat against the canoe and overturned it; some of the savages got upon sunken rocks, others discharged their arrows while swimming, as dextrously as though they had been upon firm land. It was with the utmost difficulty they could be overcome and taken: one of them who had been transfixed with a lance died soon after being brought aboard the ships. One of the women, from the obedience and deference paid to her, appeared to be their queen. She was accompanied by her son, a young man strongly made, with a frowning brow and lion's face. He had been wounded in the conflict. The hair of these savages was long and coarse, their eyes were encircled with paint, so as to give them a hideous expression; and bands of cotton were bound firmly above and below the muscular parts of the arms and legs, so as to cause them to swell to a disproportioned size; a custom prevalent among various tribes of the New World. Though captives in chains, and in the power of their enemies, they still retained a frowning brow and an air of defiance. Peter Martyr, who often went to see them in Spain, declares from his own experience, and that of others who accompanied him, that it was impossible to look at them without a sensation of horror; so menacing and terrible was their aspect. The sensation was doubtless caused in a great measure by the idea of their being cannibals. In this skirmish, according to the same writer, the Indians used poisoned arrows; and one of the Spaniards died within a few days, of a wound received from one of the females.[1]

Pursuing his voyage, Columbus soon came in sight of a great cluster of islands, some verdant and covered with forests, but the greater part naked and sterile, rising into craggy mountains; with rocks of a bright azure color, and some of a glistering white. These, with his usual vivacity of imagination, he supposed to contain mines of rich metals and precious stones. The islands lying close together, with the sea beating roughly in the narrow channels which divided them, rendered it dangerous to enter among them with the large ships. Columbus sent in a small caravel with lateen sails, to reconnoitre, which returned with the report that there were upwards of fifty islands, apparently inhabited. To the largest of this group he gave the name of Santa Ursula, and called the others the Eleven Thousand Virgins.[2]

Continuing his course, he arrived one evening in sight of a great island covered with beautiful forests, and indented with fine havens. It was called by the natives Boriquen, but he gave it the name of San Juan Bautista; it is the same since known by the name of Porto Rico. This was the native island of most of the captives who had fled to the ships for refuge from the Caribs. According to their accounts, it was fertile and populous, and under the dominion of a single cacique. Its inhabitants were not given to rove, and possessed but few canoes. They were subject to frequent invasions from the Caribs, who were their implacable enemies. They had become warriors, therefore, in their own defence, using the bow and arrow and the war club; and in their contests with their cannibal foes, they retorted upon them their own atrocities, devouring their prisoners in revenge.

[1] P. Martyr, decad. i. lib. ii. Hist. del Almirante, cap. 47. Las Casas, Hist. Ind., cap. 85. MS. Lett. of Dr. Chanca.

[2] P. Martyr, decad. i. lib. ii. Letter of Dr. Chanca.

18

After running for a whole day along the beautiful coast of this island, they anchored in a bay at the west end, abounding in fish. On landing, they found an Indian village, constructed as usual round a common square, like a market-place, with one large and well-built house. A spacious road led thence to the sea-side, having fences on each side, of interwoven reeds, inclosing fruitful gardens. At the end of the road was a kind of terrace, or look-out, constructed of reeds, and overhanging the water. The whole place had an air of neatness and ingenuity, superior to the ordinary residences of the natives, and appeared to be the abode of some important chieftain. All, however, was silent and deserted. Not a human being was to be seen, during the time they remained at the place. The natives had concealed themselves at the sight of the squadron. After remaining here two days, Columbus made sail, and stood for the island of Hispaniola. Thus ended his cruise among the Caribbee islands, the account of whose fierce and savage people was received with eager curiosity by the learned of Europe, and considered as settling one dark and doubtful question to the disadvantage of human nature. Peter Martyr, in his letter to Pomponius Lætus, announces the fact with fearful solemnity. "The stories of the Lestrigonians and of Polyphemus, who fed on human flesh, are no longer doubtful! Attend, but beware, lest thy hair bristle with horror!"

That many of the pictures given us of this extraordinary race of people have been colored by the fears of the Indians, and the prejudices of the Spaniards, is highly probable. They were constantly the terror of the former, and the brave and obstinate opponents of the latter. The evidences adduced of their cannibal propensities must be received with large allowances for the careless and inaccurate observations of seafaring men, and the preconceived belief of the fact, which existed in the minds of the Spaniards. It was a custom among the natives of many of the islands, and of other parts of the New World, to preserve the remains of their deceased relatives and friends; sometimes the entire body; sometimes only the head, or some of the limbs, dried at the fire; sometimes the mere bones. These, when found in the dwellings of the natives of Hispaniola, against whom no prejudice of the kind existed, were correctly regarded as relics of the deceased, preserved through affection or reverence; but any remains of the kind found among the Caribs, were looked upon with horror as proofs of cannibalism.

The warlike and unyielding character of these people, so different from that of the pusillanimous nations around them, and the wide scope of their enterprises and wanderings, like those of the nomade tribes of the Old World, entitle them to distinguished attention. They were trained to war from their infancy. As soon as they could walk, their intrepid mothers put in their hands the bow and arrow, and prepared them to take an early part in the hardy enterprises of their fathers. Their distant roamings by sea made them observant and intelligent. The natives of the other islands only knew how to divide time by day and night, by the sun and moon; whereas these had acquired some knowledge of the stars, by which to calculate the times and seasons.[1]

The traditional accounts of their origin, though of course extremely vague, are yet capable of being verified to a great degree by geographical facts, and open one of the rich veins of curious inquiry and speculation which abound in the New World. They are said to have migrated from the remote valleys embosomed in the Apalachian mountains. The earliest accounts we have of them represent them with weapons in their hands, continually engaged in wars, winning their way and shifting their abode, until, in the course of time, they found themselves at the extremity of Florida. Here, abandoning the northern continent, they passed over

[1] Hist. del Almirante, cap. 62.

to the Lucayos, and thence gradually, in the process of
years, from island to island of that vast and verdant chain,
which links, as it were, the end of Florida to the coast of
Paria, on the southern continent.   The archipelago extending from Porto Rico to Tobago was their strong-hold, and
the island of Guadaloupe in a manner their citadel. Hence
they made their expeditions, and spread the terror of their
name through all the surrounding countries. Swarms of
them landed upon the southern continent, and overran some
parts of terra firma.   Traces of them have been discovered
far in the interior of that vast country through which flows
the Oroonoko.   The Dutch found colonies of them on the
banks of the Ikouteka, which empties into the Surinam;
along the Esquibi, the Maroni, and other rivers of Guayana;
and in the country watered by the windings of the Cayenne;
and it would appear that they extended their wanderings to
the shores of the southern ocean, where, among the aboriginals of Brazil, were some who called themselves Caribs,.
distinguished from the surrounding Indians by their superior
hardihood, subtlety, and enterprise.[1]

To trace the footsteps of this roving tribe throughout its
wide migrations. from the Apalachian mountains of the
northern continent, along the clusters of islands which stud
the Gulf of Mexico and the Carribbean Sea to the shores of
Paria, and so across the vast regions of Guayana and Ama-
zonia to the remote coast of Brazil, would be one of the
most curious researches in aboriginal history, and throw
much light upon the mysterious question of the population
of the New World.

[1] Rochefort, Hist. Nat. des Iles Antilles; Rotterdam, 1665.

CHAPTER IV.

ARRIVAL AT THE HARBOR OF LA NAVIDAD.—DISASTER OF THE FORTRESS.

[1493.]

On the 22d of November, the fleet arrived off what was soon ascertained to be the eastern extremity of Hayti, or, as the admiral had named it, Hispaniola. The greatest excitement prevailed throughout the armada, at the thoughts of soon arriving at the end of their voyage. Those who had been here in the preceding voyage, remembered the pleasant days they had passed among the groves of Hayti; and the rest looked forward with eagerness to scenes painted to them with the captivating illusions of the golden age.

As the fleet swept with easy sail along the green shore, a boat was sent to land to bury a Biscayan sailor, who had died of the wound of an arrow received in the late skirmish. Two light caravels hovered near the shore to guard the boat's crew, while the funeral ceremony was performed on the beach, under the trees. Several natives came off to the ship, with a message to the admiral from the cacique of the neighborhood, inviting him to land, and promising great quantities of gold; anxious, however, to arrive at La Navidad, Columbus dismissed them with presents and continued his course. Arriving at the gulf of Las Flechas, or, as it is now called, the gulf of Semana, the place where, in his preceding voyage, a skirmish had occurred with the natives, he set on shore one of the young Indians of the place, who had accompanied him to Spain, and had been converted to Christianity. He dismissed him finely appareled and loaded with trinkets, anticipating favorable effects from his accounts to his countrymen of the wonders he had seen, and the kind treatment he had experienced. The young Indian made many fair promises, but either for-

got them all, on regaining his liberty and his native
mountains, or fell a victim to envy caused by his wealth and
finery. Nothing was seen or heard of him more.[1] Only
one Indian of those who had been to Spain now remained
in the fleet; a young Lucayan, native of the island of
Guanahani, who had been baptized at Barcelona, and
had been named after the admiral's brother, Diego Colon.
He continued always faithful and devoted to the Spaniards.

On the 25th, Columbus anchored in the harbor of Monte
Christi; anxious to fix upon a place for a settlement in the
neighborhood of the stream to which, in his first voyage, he
had given the name of the Rio del Oro, or the Golden
River. As several of the mariners were ranging the coast,
they found, on the green and moist banks of a rivulet, the
bodies of a man and boy; the former with a cord of
Spanish grass about his neck, and his arms extended and
tied by the wrists to a stake in the form of a cross. The
bodies were in such a state of decay, that it was impossible
to ascertain whether they were Indians or Europeans.
Sinister doubts, however, were entertained, which were confirmed on the following day; for on revisiting the shore,
they found, at some distance from the former, two other
bodies, one of which, having a beard, was evidently the
corpse of a white man.

The pleasant anticipations of Columbus on his approach
to La Navidad were now overcast with gloomy forebodings.
The experience recently had of the ferocity of some of the
inhabitants of these islands, made him doubtful of the
amity of others, and he began to fear that some misfortune
might have befallen Arana and his garrison.

The frank and fearless manner, however, in which a
number of the natives came off to the ships, and their unembarrassed demeanor, in some measure allayed his suspicions; for it did not appear probable that they would venture thus confidently among the white men, with the con-

[1] Herrera, Hist. Ind., decad. i. lib. ii. cap. 9.

sciousness of having recently shed the blood of their companions.

On the evening of the 27th, he arrived opposite the harbor of La Navidad, and cast anchor about a league from the land, not daring to enter in the dark, on account of the dangerous reefs. It was too late to distinguish objects. Impatient to satisfy his doubts, therefore, he ordered two cannon to be fired. The report echoed along the shore, but there was no reply from the fort. Every eye was now directed to catch the gleam of some signal light; every ear listened to hear some friendly shout; but there was neither light nor shout, nor any other sign of life: all was darkness and deathlike silence.[1]

Several hours were passed in dismal suspense, and every one longed for the morning light, to put an end to his uncertainty. About midnight a canoe approached the fleet; when within a certain distance, it paused, and the Indians who were in it, hailing one of the vessels, asked for the admiral. When directed to his ship they drew near, but would not venture on board until they saw Columbus. He showed himself at the side of his vessel, and a light being held up, his countenance and commanding person were not to be mistaken. They now entered the ship without hesitation. One of them was a cousin of the cacique Guacanagari, and brought a present from him of two masks ornamented with gold. Columbus inquired about the Spaniards who had remained on the island. The information which the native gave was somewhat confused, or perhaps was imperfectly understood, as the only Indian interpreter on board was the young Lucayan, Diego Colon, whose native language was different from that of Hayti. He told Columbus that several of the Spaniards had died of sickness; others had fallen in a quarrel among themselves, and others had removed to a different part of the island, where they had taken to themselves Indian wives. That Guacanagari

[1] Letter of Dr. Chanca. Navarrete, Colec. de Viage, tom. i.

had been assailed by Caonabo, the fierce cacique of the golden mountains of Cibao, who had wounded him in battle, and burnt his village; and that he remained ill of his wound in a neighboring hamlet, or he would have hastened in person to welcome the admiral.[1]

Melancholy as were these tidings, they relieved Columbus from a dark and dismal surmise. Whatever disasters had overwhelmed his garrison, it had not fallen a sacrifice to the perfidy of the natives: his good opinion of the gentleness and kindness of these people had not been misplaced; nor had their cacique forfeited the admiration inspired by his benevolent hospitality. Thus the most corroding care was dismissed from his mind; for, to a generous spirit, there is nothing so disheartening, as to discover treachery where it has reposed confidence and friendship. It would seem also that some of the garrison were yet alive, though scattered about the island; they would doubtless soon hear of his arrival, and would hasten to rejoin him, well qualified to give information of the interior.

Satisfied of the friendly disposition of the natives, the cheerfulness of the crews was in a great measure restored. The Indians who had come on board were well entertained, and departed in the night gratified with various presents, promising to return in the morning with the cacique Guacanagari. The mariners now awaited the dawn of day with reassured spirits, expecting that the cordial intercourse and pleasant scenes of the first voyage would be renewed.

The morning dawned and passed away, and the day advanced and began to decline, without the promised visit from the cacique. Some apprehensions were now entertained that the Indians who had visited them the preceding night might be drowned, as they had partaken freely of wine, and their small canoe was easy to be overset. There was a silence and an air of desertion about the whole

[1] Dr. Chanca's Letter, Hist. del Almirante, cap. 48. Herrera, Hist. Ind., decad. i. lib. i. cap. 9.

neighborhood extremely suspicious. On their preceding visit the harbor had been a scene of continual animation ; canoes gliding over the clear waters, Indians in groups on the shores, or under the trees, or swimming off to the caravel. Now, not a canoe was to be seen, not an Indian hailed them from the land ; nor was there any smoke rising from among the groves, to give a sign of habitation.

After waiting for a long time in vain, Columbus sent a boat to the shore to reconnoitre. On landing, the crew hastened and sought the fortress. It was a ruin ; the palisadoes were beaten down, and the whole presented the appearance of having been sacked, burnt, and destroyed. Here and there were broken chests, spoiled provisions, and the ragged remains of European garments. Not an Indian approached them. They caught sight of two or three lurking at a distance among the trees, and apparently watching them ; but they vanished into the woods on finding themselves observed. Meeting no one to explain the melancholy scene before them, they returned with dejected hearts to the ships, and related to the admiral what they had seen.

Columbus was greatly troubled in mind at this intelligence, and the fleet having now anchored in the harbor, he went himself to shore on the following morning. Repairing to the ruins of the fortress, he found everything as had been described, and searched in vain for the remains of dead bodies. No traces of the garrison were to be seen, but broken utensils, and torn vestments, scattered here and there among the grass. There were many surmises and conjectures. If the fortress had been sacked, some of the garrison might yet survive, and might either have fled from the neighborhood, or been carried into captivity. Cannon and arquebuses were discharged, in hopes, if any of the survivors were hid among rocks and thickets, they might hear them and come forth ; but no one made his appearance. A mournful and lifeless silence reigned over the place. The suspicion of treachery on the part of

Guacanagari was again revived, but Columbus was unwilling to indulge it. On looking further, the village of that cacique was found a mere heap of burnt ruins, which showed that he had been involved in the disaster of the garrison.

Columbus had left orders with Arana and the other officers to bury all the treasure they might procure, or, in case of sudden danger, to throw it into the well of the fortress. He ordered excavations to be made, therefore, among the ruins, and the well to be cleared out. While this search was making, he proceeded with the boats to explore the neighborhood, partly in hopes of gaining intelligence of any scattered survivors of the garrison, and partly to look out for a better situation for a fortress. After proceeding about a league he came to a hamlet, the inhabitants of which had fled, taking whatever they could with them, and hiding the rest in the grass. In the houses were European articles, which evidently had not been procured by barter, such as stockings, pieces of cloth, an anchor of the caravel which had been wrecked, and a beautiful Moorish robe, folded in the form in which it had been brought from Spain.[1]

Having passed some time in contemplating these scattered documents of a disastrous story, Columbus returned to the ruins of the fortress. The excavations and search in the well had proved fruitless; no treasure was to be found. Not far from the fort, however, they had discovered the bodies of eleven men, buried in different places, and which were known, by their clothing, to be Europeans. They had evidently been for some time in the ground, the grass having grown upon their graves.

In the course of the day a number of the Indians made their appearance, hovering timidly at a distance. Their apprehensions were gradually dispelled until they became perfectly communicative. Some of them could speak a few

[1] Letter of Dr. Chanca. Cura de los Palacios, cap. 120.

words of Spanish, and knew the names of all the men who had remained with Arana. By this means, and by the aid of the interpreter, the story of the garrison was in some measure ascertained.

· It is curious to note this first foot-print of civilization in the New World. Those whom Columbus had left behind, says Oviedo, with the exception of the commander, Don Diego Arana, and one or two others, were but little calculated to follow the precepts of so prudent a person, or to discharge the critical duties enjoined upon them. They were principally men of the lowest order, or mariners who knew not how to conduct themselves with restraint or sobriety on shore.[1] No sooner had the admiral departed, than all his counsels and commands died away from their minds. Though a mere handful of men, surrounded by savage tribes and dependent upon their own prudence and good conduct, and upon the good will of the natives, for very existence, yet they soon began to indulge in the most wanton abuses. Some were prompted by rapacious avarice, and sought to possess themselves, by all kinds of wrongful means, of the golden ornaments and other valuable property of the natives. Others were grossly sensual, and, not content with two or three wives allowed to each by Guacanagari, seduced the wives and daughters of the Indians.

Fierce brawls ensued among them about their ill-gotten spoils and the favors of the Indian women ; and the natives beheld with astonishment the beings whom they had worshipped, as descended from the skies, abandoned to the grossest of earthly passions, and raging against each other with worse than brutal ferocity.

Still these dissensions might not have been very dangerous, had they observed one of the injunctions of Columbus, and kept together in the fortress, maintaining military vigilance, but all precaution of the kind was soon forgotten. In vain

[1] Oviedo, Hist. Ind., lib. ii. cap. 12.

did Don Diego de Arana interpose his authority; in vain
did every inducement present itself which could bind man
and man together in a foreign land. All order, all subordination, all unanimity, was at an end. Many abandoned
the fortress, and lived carelessly and at random about the
neighborhood; every one was for himself, or associated with
some little knot of confederates to injure and despoil the
rest. Thus factions broke out among them, until ambition
arose to complete the destruction of their mimic empire.
Pedro Gutierrez and Rodrigo de Escobedo, whom Columbus
had left as lieutenants to the commander, to succeed to him
in case of accident, took advantage of these disorders, and
aspired to an equal share in the authority, if not to the
supreme control.[1] Violent affrays succeeded, in which a
Spaniard named Jacomo was killed. Having failed in
their object, Gutierrez and Escobedo withdrew from the
fortress with nine of their adherents, and a number of their
women; and turned their thoughts on distant enterprise.
Having heard marvelous accounts of the mines of Cibao,
and the golden sands of its mountain rivers, they set off for
that district, flushed with the thoughts of amassing immense treasure. Thus they disregarded another strong
injunction of Columbus, which was to keep within the
friendly territories of Guacanagari. The region to which
they repaired was in the interior of the island, within the
province of Maguana, ruled by the famous Caonabo, called
by the Spaniards the Lord of the Golden House. This renowned chieftain was a Carib by birth, and possessed the
fierceness and enterprise of his nation. He had come an
adventurer to Hispaniola, and by his courage and address,
and his warlike exploits, had made himself the most potent
of its caciques. The inhabitants universally stood in awe
of him from his Carib origin, and he was the hero of the
island, when the ships of the white men suddenly appeared
upon its shores. The wonderful accounts of their power

[1] Oviedo, Hist. Ind.,lib. ii. cap. 12.

and prowess had reached him among his mountains, and he had the shrewdness to perceive that his consequence must decline before such formidable intruders. The departure of Columbus gave him hopes that their intrusion would be but temporary. The discords and excesses of those who remained, while they moved his detestation, inspired him with increasing confidence. No sooner did Gutierrez and Escobedo, with their companions, take refuge in his dominions, than he put them to death. He then formed a league with the cacique of Marien, whose territories adjoined those of Guacanagari on the west, and concerted a sudden attack upon the fortress. Emerging with his warriors from among the mountains, and traversing great tracts of forest with profound secrecy, he arrived in the vicinity of the village without being discovered. The Spaniards, confiding in the gentle and pacific nature of the Indians, had neglected all military precautions. But ten men remained in the fortress with Arana, and these do not appear to have maintained any guard. The rest were quartered in houses in the neighborhood. In the dead of the night, when all were wrapped in sleep, Caonabo and his warriors burst upon the place with frightful yells, got possession of the fortress before their inmates could put themselves upon their defence, and surrounded and set fire to the houses in which the rest of the white men were sleeping. Eight of the Spaniards fled to the sea-side pursued by the savages, and, rushing into the waves, were drowned; the rest were massacred. Guacanagari and his subjects fought faithfully in defence of their guests, but not being of a warlike character, were easily routed; the cacique was wounded by the hand of Caonabo, and his village was burnt to the ground.[1]

Such was the history of the first European establishment

---

[1] Herrera, Hist. Ind., decad. i. lib. ii. cap. 9. Letter of Dr. Chanca. Peter Martyr, decad. i. lib. ii. Hist. del Almirante, cap. 49. Cura de los Palacios, cap. 120, MS. Muñoz, Hist. N. Mundo, lib. iv.

in the New World. It presents in a diminutive compass an epitome of the gross vices which degrade civilization, and the grand political errors which sometimes subvert the mightiest empires. All law and order being relaxed by corruption and licentiousness, public good was sacrificed to private interest and passion, the community was convulsed by divers factions and dissensions, until the whole was shaken asunder by two aspiring demagogues, ambitious of the command of a petty fortress in a wilderness, and the supreme control of eight-and-thirty men.

CHAPTER V.

TRANSACTIONS WITH THE NATIVES.—SUSPICIOUS CONDUCT OF GUACANAGARI.

[1493.]

THE tragical story of the fortress, as gathered from the Indians at the harbor, received confirmation from another quarter. One of the captains, Melchor Maldonado, coasting to the east with his caravel in search of some more favorable situation for a settlement, was boarded by a canoe in which were two Indians. One of them was the brother of Guacanagari, and entreated him, in the name of the cacique, to visit him at the village where he lay ill of his wound. Maldonado immediately went on shore with two or three of his companions. They found Guacanagari confined by lameness to his hammock, surrounded by seven of his wives. The cacique expressed great regret at not being able to visit the admiral. He related various particulars concerning the disasters of the garrison, and the part which he and his subjects had taken in its defence, showing his wounded leg bound up. His story agreed with that already related. After treating the Spaniards with his accustomed hospitality, he presented to each of them at parting a golden ornament.

On the following morning, Columbus repaired in person to visit the cacique. To impress him with an idea of his present power and importance, he appeared with a numerous train of officers, all richly dressed or in glittering armor. They found Guacanagari reclining in a hammock of cotton net. He exhibited great emotion on beholding the admiral, and immediately adverted to the death of the Spaniards. As he related the disasters of the garrison he shed many tears, but dwelt particularly on the part he had taken in the defense of his guests, pointing out several of his subjects present who had received wounds in the battle. It was evident from the scars that the wounds had been received from Indian weapons.

Columbus was readily satisfied of the good faith of Guacanagari. When he reflected on the many proofs of an open and generous nature, which he had given at the time of his shipwreck, he could not believe him capable of so dark an act of perfidy. An exchange of presents now took place. The cacique gave him eight hundred beads of a certain stone called ciba, which they considered highly precious, and one hundred of gold, a golden coronet, and three small calabashes filled with gold dust, and thought himself outdone in munificence when presented with a number of glass beads, hawks' bells, knives, pins, needles, small mirrors, and ornaments of copper, which metal he seemed to prefer to gold.[1]

Guacanagari's leg had been violently bruised by a stone. At the request of Columbus, he permitted it to be examined by a surgeon who was present. On removing the bandage no signs of a wound were to be seen, although he shrunk with pain whenever the limb was handled.[2] As some time had elapsed since the battle, the external bruise might

---

[1] Letter of Dr. Chanca. Navarrete, Colec., tom. i.
[2] Letter of Dr. Chanca. Cura de los Palacios, cap. 120.

have disappeared, while a tenderness remained in the part.
Several present, however, who had not been in the first
voyage, and had witnessed nothing of the generous conduct
of the cacique, looked upon his lameness as feigned, and
the whole story of the battle a fabrication, to conceal his
real perfidy. Father Boyle especially, who was of a vindictive spirit, advised the admiral to make an immediate
example of the chieftain. Columbus, however, viewed the
matter in a different light. Whatever prepossessions he
might have were in favor of the cacique; his heart refused
to believe in his criminality. Though conscious of innocence, Guacanagari might have feared the suspicions of the
white men, and have exaggerated the effects of his wound;
but the wounds of his subjects made by Indian weapons,
and the destruction of his village, were strong proofs to
Columbus of the truth of his story. To satisfy his more
suspicious followers, and to pacify the friar, without gratifying his love for persecution, he observed that true policy
dictated amicable conduct towards Guacanagari, at least
until his guilt was fully ascertained. They had too great
a force at present to apprehend any thing from his hostility,
but violent measures in this early stage of their intercourse
with the natives might spread a general panic, and impede
all their operations on the island. Most of his officers
concurred in this opinion; so it was determined, notwithstanding the inquisitorial suggestions of the friar, to take
the story of the Indians for current truth, and to continue
to treat them with friendship.

At the invitation of Columbus, the cacique, though still
apparently in pain from his wound,[1] accompanied him to
the ships that very evening. He had wondered at the
power and grandeur of the white men when they first visited his shores with two small caravels; his wonder was infinitely increased on beholding a fleet riding at anchor in
the harbor, and on going on board of the admiral's ship,

[1] Hist. del Almirante, cap. 89.

which was a vessel of heavy burden. Here he beheld the
Carib prisoners. So great was the dread of them among
the timid inhabitants of Hayti, that they contemplated
them with fear and shuddering, even though in chains.[1]
That the admiral had dared to invade these terrible beings
in their very island, and had dragged them as it were from
their strong-holds, was, perhaps, one of the greatest proofs
to the Indians of the irresistible prowess of the white men.

Columbus took the cacique through the ship. The various
works of art; the plants and fruits of the Old World;
domestic fowls of different kinds, cattle, sheep, swine, and
other animals, brought to stock the island, all were wonders
to him; but what most struck him with amazement, was
the horses. He had never seen any but the most diminutive quadrupeds, and was astonished at their size, their
great strength, terrific appearance, yet perfect docility.[2]
He looked upon all these extraordinary objects as so many
wonders brought from heaven, which he still believed to be
the native home of the white men.

On board of the ship were ten of the women delivered
from Carib captivity. They were chiefly natives of the
island of Boriquen, or Porto Rico. These soon attracted
the notice of the cacique, who is represented to have been
of an amorous complexion. He entered into conversation
with them; for though the islanders spoke different languages, or, rather, as is more probable, different dialects of
the same language, they were able, in general, to understand each other. Among these women was one distinguished above her companions by a certain loftiness of air
and manner; she had been much noticed and admired by
the Spaniards, who had given her the name of Catalina.
The cacique spoke to her repeatedly with great gentleness
of tone and manner, pity in all probability being mingled
with his admiration; for though rescued from the hands of

[1] Peter Martyr, letter 153 to Pomponius Lætus.
[2] Hist. del Almirante, ubi sup. Letter of Dr. Chanca.

19 .

the Caribs, she and her companions were in a manner captives on board of the ship.

A collation was now spread before the chieftain, and Columbus endeavored in every way to revive their former cordial intercourse. He treated his guest with every manifestation of perfect confidence, and talked of coming to live with him in his present residence, and of building houses in the vicinity. The cacique expressed much satisfaction at the idea, but observed that the situation of the place was unhealthy, which was indeed the case. Notwithstanding every demonstration of friendship, however, the cacique was evidently ill at ease. The charm of mutual confidence was broken. It was evident that the gross licentiousness of the garrison had greatly impaired the veneration of the Indians for their heaven-born visitors. Even the reverence for the symbols of the Christian faith, which Columbus endeavored to inculcate, was frustrated by the profligacy of its votaries. Though fond of ornaments, it was with the greatest difficulty the cacique could be prevailed upon by the admiral to suspend an image of the Virgin about his neck, when he understood it to be an object of Christian adoration.[1]

The suspicions of the chieftain's guilt gained ground with many of the Spaniards. Father Boyle, in particular, regarded him with an evil eye, and privately advised the admiral, now that he had him on board, to detain him prisoner; but Columbus rejected the counsel of the crafty friar, as contrary to sound policy and honorable faith. It is difficult, however, to conceal lurking ill-will. The cacique, accustomed, in his former intercourse with the Spaniards, to meet with faces beaming with gratitude and friendship, could not but perceive their altered looks. Notwithstanding the frank and cordial hospitality of the admiral, therefore, he soon begged permission to return to land.[2]

[1] Hist. del Almirante, cap. 49.
[2] Peter Martyr, decad. i. lib. ii.

The next morning there was a mysterious movement among the natives on shore. A messenger from the cacique inquired of the admiral how long he intended to remain at the harbor, and was informed that he should sail on the following day. In the evening the brother of Guacanagari came on board, under pretext of bartering a quantity of gold; he was observed to converse in private with the Indian women, and particularly with Catalina, the one whose distinguished appearance had attracted the attention of Guacanagari. After remaining some time on board, he returned to the shore. It would seem, from subsequent events, that the cacique had been touched by the situation of this Indian beauty, or captivated by her charms; and had undertaken to deliver her from bondage.

At midnight, when the crew were buried in their first sleep, Catalina awakened her companions. The ship was anchored full three miles from the shore, and the sea was rough; but they let themselves down from the side of the vessel, and swam bravely for the shore. With all their precautions, they were overheard by the watch, and the alarm was given. The boats were hastily manned, and gave chase in the direction of a light blazing on the shore, an evident beacon for the fugitives. Such was the vigor of these sea-nymphs, that they reached the land in safety; four were retaken on the beach; but the heroic Catalina with the rest of her companions made good their escape into the forest.

When the day dawned, Columbus sent to Guacanagari to demand the fugitives; or if they were not in his possession, that he would have search made for them. The residence of the cacique, however, was silent and deserted; not an Indian was to be seen. Either conscious of the suspicions of the Spaniards, and apprehensive of their hostility, or desirous to enjoy his prize unmolested, the cacique had removed with all his effects, his household, and his followers, and had taken refuge with his island

beauty in the interior. This sudden and mysterious desertion gave redoubled force to the doubts heretofore entertained, and Guacanagari was generally stigmatized as a
traitor to the white men, and the perfidious destroyer of the
garrison.[1]

CHAPTER VI.

FOUNDING OF THE CITY OF ISABELLA.—MALADIES OF THE
SPANIARDS.

[1493.]

THE misfortunes of the Spaniards both by sea and land,
in the vicinity of this harbor, threw a gloom round the
neighborhood. The ruins of the fortress, and the graves
of their murdered countrymen, were continually before
their eyes, and the forests no longer looked beautiful while
there was an idea that treachery might be lurking in their
shades. The silence and dreariness, also, caused by the desertion of the natives, gave a sinister appearance to the
place. It began to be considered by the credulous mariners, as under some baneful influence or malignant star.
These were sufficient objections to discourage the founding
of a settlement, but there were others of a more solid nature. The land in the vicinity was low, moist, and unhealthy, and there was no stone for building; Columbus
determined, therefore, to abandon the place altogether, and
found his projected colony in some more favorable situation. No time was to be lost; the animals on board the
ships were suffering from long confinement; and the multitude of persons, unaccustomed to the sea, and pent up in
the fleet, languished for the refreshment of the land. The
lighter caravels, therefore, scoured the coast in each direction, entering the rivers and harbors, in search of an ad-

[1] Peter Martyr, decad. i. lib. ii. Letter of Dr. Chanca. Cura de
los Palacios, cap. 120, MS.

vantageous site. They were instructed also to make inquiries after Guacanagari, of whom Columbus, notwithstanding every suspicious appearance, still retained a favorable opinion. The expeditions returned after ranging a considerable extent of coast without success. There were fine rivers and secure ports, but the coast was low and marshy, and deficient in stone. The country was generally deserted, or if any natives were seen, they fled immediately to the woods. Melchor Maldonado had proceeded to the eastward, until he came to the dominions of a cacique, who at first issued forth at the head of his warriors, with menacing aspect, but was readily conciliated. From him he learnt that Guacanagari had retired to the mountains. Another party discovered an Indian concealed near a hamlet, having been disabled by a wound received from a lance when fighting against Caonabo. His account of the destruction of the fortress agreed with that of the Indians at the harbor, and concurred to vindicate the cacique from the charge of treachery. Thus the Spaniards continued uncertain as to the real perpetrators of this dark and dismal tragedy.

Being convinced that there was no place in this part of the island favorable for a settlement, Columbus weighed anchor on the 7th of December, with the intention of seeking the port of La Plata. In consequence of adverse weather, however, he was obliged to put into a harbor about ten leagues east of Monte Christi; and on considering the place, was struck with its advantages.

The harbor was spacious, and commanded by a point of land, protected on one side by a natural rampart of rocks, and on another by an impervious forest, presenting a strong position for a fortress. There were two rivers, one large and the other small, watering a green and beautiful plain, and offering advantageous situations for mills. About a bow-shot from the sea, on the banks of one of the rivers, was an Indian village. The soil appeared to be fertile, the waters to abound in excellent fish, and the climate to be temperate and genial; for the trees were in leaf, the shrubs in flower, and the birds in song, though it was the middle of December. They had not yet become familiarized with the temperature of this favored island, where the rigors of winter are unknown, where there is a perpetual succession, and even intermixture, of fruit and flower, and where smiling verdure reigns throughout the year.

Another grand inducement to form their settlement in this place was the information received from the Indians of the adjacent village, that the mountains of Cibao, where the gold mines were situated, lay at no great distance, and almost parallel to the harbor. It was determined, therefore, that there could not be a situation more favorable for their colony.

An animated scene now commenced. The troops and various persons belonging to the land-service, and the various laborers and artificers to be employed in building, were disembarked. The provisions, articles of traffic, guns and ammunition for defence, and implements of every kind, were brought to shore, as were also the cattle and live stock, which had suffered excessively from long restraint, especially the horses. There was a general joy at escaping from the irksome confinement of the ships, and once more treading the firm earth, and breathing the sweetness of the fields. An encampment was formed on the margin of the plain, around a basin or sheet of water, and in a little while the whole place was in activity. Thus was founded the first Christian city of the New World, to which Columbus gave the name of Isabella, in honor of his royal patroness.

A plan was formed, and streets and squares projected. The greatest diligence was then exerted in erecting a church, a public storehouse, and a residence for the admiral. These were built of stone, the private houses were constructed of wood, plaster, reeds, or such materials as the exigency of the case permitted, and for a short time every one exerted himself with the utmost zeal.

Maladies, however, soon broke out. Many, unaccustomed to the sea, had suffered greatly from confinement and sea-sickness, and from subsisting for a length of time on salt provisions much damaged, and mouldy biscuit. They suffered great exposure on the land also, before houses could be built for their reception; for the exhalations of a hot and moist climate, and a new, rank soil, the humid vapors from rivers, and the stagnant air of close forests, render the wilderness a place of severe trial to constitutions accustomed to old and highly-cultivated countries. The labor also of building houses, clearing fields, setting out orchards, and planting gardens, having all to be done with great haste, bore hard upon men, who, after tossing so long upon the ocean, stood in need of relaxation and repose.

The maladies of the mind mingled with those of the body. Many, as has been shown, had embarked in the expedition with visionary and romantic expectations. Some had anticipated the golden regions of Cipango and Cathay, where they were to amass wealth without toil or trouble; others a region of Asiatic luxury, abounding with delights; and others a splendid and open career for gallant adventures and chivalrous enterprises. What then was their disappointment to find themselves confined to the margin of an island; surrounded by impracticable forests; doomed to struggle with the rudeness of a wilderness; to toil painfully for mere subsistence, and to attain every comfort by the severest exertion. As to gold, it was brought to them from various quarters, but in small quantities, and it was evidently to be procured only by patient and persevering labor. All these disappointments sank deep into their hearts; their spirits flagged as their golden dreams melted away, and the gloom of despondency aided the ravages of disease.

Columbus himself did not escape the prevalent maladies.

The arduous nature of his enterprise, the responsibility
under which he found himself, not merely to his followers
and his sovereigns, but to the world at large, had kept his
mind in continual agitation. The cares of so large a
squadron; the incessant vigilance required, not only
against the lurking dangers of these unknown seas, but
against the passions and follies of his followers; the distress
he had suffered from the fate of his murdered garrison, and
his uncertainty as to the conduct of the barbarous tribes by
which he was surrounded; all these had harassed his mind
and broken his rest while on board the ship: since landing,
new cares and toils had crowded upon him, which, added
to the exposures incident to his situation in this new
climate, completely overpowered his strength. Still, though
confined for several weeks to his bed by severe illness, his
energetic mind rose superior to the sufferings of the body,
and he continued to give directions about the building of
the city, and to superintend the general concerns of the
expedition.[1]

CHAPTER VII.

EXPEDITION OF ALONSO DE OJEDA TO EXPLORE THE IN-
TERIOR OF THE ISLAND.—DISPATCH OF THE SHIPS TO
SPAIN.

[1493.]

THE ships having discharged their cargoes, it was
necessary to send the greater part of them back to Spain.
Here new anxieties pressed upon the mind of Columbus.
He had hoped to find treasures of gold and precious
merchandise accumulated by the men left behind on the

[1] Hist. del Almirante, cap. 50. Herrera, Hist. Ind., decad. i. lib.
ii. cap. 10. Peter Martyr, decad. i. lib. ii. Letter of Dr. Chanca,
etc.

first voyage; or at least the sources of wealthy traffic ascertained, by which speedily to freight his vessels. The destruction of the garrison had defeated all those hopes. He was aware of the extravagant expectations entertained by the sovereigns and the nation. What would be their disappointment when the returning ships brought nothing but a tale of disaster! Something must be done, before the vessels sailed, to keep up the fame of his discoveries, and justify his own magnificent representations.

As yet he knew nothing of the interior of the island. If it were really the island of Cipango, it must contain populous cities, existing probably in some more cultivated region, beyond the lofty mountains with which it was intersected. All the Indians concurred in mentioning Cibao as the tract of country whence they derived their gold. The very name of its cacique, Caonabo, signifying "The Lord of the Golden House," seemed to indicate the wealth of his dominions. The tracts where the mines were said to abound, lay at a distance of but three or four days journey, directly in the interior; Columbus determined, therefore, to send an expedition to explore it, previous to the sailing of the ships. If the result should confirm his hopes, he would then be able to send home the fleet with confidence, bearing tidings of the discovery of the golden mountains of Cibao.[1]

The person he chose for this enterprise was Alonso de Ojeda, the same cavalier who has been already noticed for his daring spirit and great bodily force and agility. Delighting in all service of a hazardous and adventurous nature, Ojeda was the more stimulated to this expedition from the formidable character of the mountain cacique, Caonabo, whose dominions he was to penetrate. He set out from the harbor, early in January, 1494, accompanied by a small force of well-armed and determined men, several of them young and spirited cavaliers like himself. He struck

[1] Herrera, Hist. Ind., dec. i. lib. ii. cap. 10.

directly southward into the interior. For the two first days, the march was toilsome and difficult, through a country abandoned by its inhabitants; for terror of the Spaniards extended along the sea-coast. On the second evening they came to a lofty range of mountains, which they ascended by an Indian path, winding up a steep and narrow defile, and they slept for the night at the summit. Hence, the next morning, they beheld the sun rise with great glory over a vast and delicious plain, covered with noble forests, studded with villages and hamlets, and enlivened by the shining waters of the Yagui.

Descending into this plain, Ojeda and his companions boldly entered the Indian villages. The inhabitants, far from being hostile, overwhelmed them with hospitality, and, in fact, impeded their journey by their kindness. They had also to ford many rivers in traversing this plain, so that they were five or six days in reaching the chain of mountains which locked up, as it were, the golden region of Cibao. They penetrated into this district, without meeting with any other obstacles than those presented by the rude nature of the country. Caonabo, so redoubtable for his courage and ferocity, must have been in some distant part of his dominions, for he never appeared to dispute their progress. The natives received them with kindness; they were naked and uncivilized, like the other inhabitants of the island, nor were there any traces of the important cities which their imaginations had once pictured forth. They saw, however, ample signs of natural wealth. The sands of the mountain-streams glittered with particles of gold; these the natives would skillfully separate, and give to the Spaniards, without expecting a recompense. In some places they picked up large specimens of virgin ore from the beds of the torrents, and stones streaked and richly impregnated with it. Peter Martyr affirms that he saw a mass of rude gold weighing nine ounces, which Ojeda himself had found in one of the brooks.[1]

[1] Peter Martyr, decad. i. lib. ii.

All these were considered as mere superficial washings of the soil, betraying the hidden treasures lurking in the deep veins and rocky bosoms of the mountains, and only requir- ing the hand of labor to bring them to light. As the object of his expedition was merely to ascertain the nature of the country, Ojeda led back his little band to the harbor, full of enthusiastic accounts of the golden promise of these mountains. A young cavalier of the name of Gorvalan, who had been dispatched at the same time on a similar ex- pedition, and who had explored a different tract of country, returned with similar reports. These flattering accounts served for a time to reanimate the drooping and desponding colonists, and induced Columbus to believe that it was only necessary to explore the mines of Cibao, to open inexhausti- ble sources of riches. He determined, as soon as his health would permit, to repair in person to the mountains, and seek a favorable site for a mining establishment.[1]

The season was now propitious for the return of the fleet, and Columbus lost no time in dispatching twelve of the ships under the command of Antonio de Torres, retaining only five for the service of the colony.

By this opportunity he sent home specimens of the gold found among the mountains and rivers of Cibao, and all such fruits and plants as were curious, or appeared to be valuable. He wrote in the most sanguine terms of the ex- peditions of Ojeda and Gorvalan, the last of whom returned to Spain in the fleet. He repeated his confident anticipa- tions of soon being able to make abundant shipments of gold, of precious drugs, and spices; the search for them being delayed for the present by the sickness of himself and people, and the cares and labors required in building the infant city. He described the beauty and fertility of the island; its range of noble mountains; its wide, abun- dant plains, watered by beautiful rivers; the quick fecun- dity of the soil, evinced in the luxuriant growth of the

[1] Hist. del Almirante, cap. 50.

sugar cane, and of various grains and vegetables brought
from Europe.

As it would take some time, however, to obtain provisions
from their fields and gardens, and the produce of their live
stock, adequate to the subsistence of the colony, which consisted of about a thousand souls; and as they could not
accustom themselves to the food of the natives, Columbus
requested present supplies from Spain. Their provisions
were already growing scanty. Much of their wine had
been lost, from the badness of the casks; and the colonists,
in their infirm state of health, suffered greatly from the
want of their accustomed diet. There was an immediate
necessity of medicines, clothing, and arms. Horses were
required, likewise, for the public works, and for military
service; being found of great effect in awing the natives,
who had the utmost dread of those animals. He requested
also an additional number of workmen and mechanics, and
men skilled in mining and in smelting and purifying ore.
He recommended various persons to the notice and favor
of the sovereigns, among whom was Pedro Margerite, an
Arragonian cavalier of the order of St. Jago, who had a
wife and children to be provided for, and who, for his good
services, Columbus begged might be appointed to a command in the order to which he belonged. In like manner he
entreated patronage for Juan Aguado, who was about to
return in the fleet, making particular mention of his merits.
From both of these men he was destined to experience the
most signal ingratitude.

In these ships he sent also the men, women, and children
taken in the Caribbee Islands, recommending that they
should be carefully instructed in the Spanish language and
the Christian faith. From the roving and adventurous nature of these people, and their general acquaintance with
the various languages of this great archipelago, he thought
that, when the precepts of religion and the usages of civ-

ilization had reformed their savage manners and cannibal propensities, they might be rendered eminently serviceable as interpreters, and as means of propagating the doctrines of Christianity.

Among the many sound and salutary suggestions in this letter, there is one of a most pernicious tendency, written in that mistaken view of natural rights prevalent at the day, but fruitful of much wrong and misery in the world. Considering that the greater the number of these cannibal pagans transferred to the catholic soil of Spain, the greater would be the number of souls put in the way of salvation, he proposed to establish an exchange of them as slaves, against live stock, to be furnished by merchants to the colony. The ships to bring such stock were to land nowhere but at the island of Isabella, where the Carib captives would be ready for delivery. A duty was to be levied on each slave for the benefit of the royal revenue. In this way the colony would be furnished with all kinds of live stock free of expense; the peaceful islanders would be freed from warlike and inhuman neighbors; the royal treasury would be greatly enriched; and a vast number of souls would be snatched from perdition, and carried, as it were, by main force to heaven. Such is the strange sophistry by which upright men may sometimes deceive themselves. Columbus feared the disappointment of the sovereigns in respect to the product of his enterprises, and was anxious to devise some mode of lightening their expenses until he could open some ample source of profit. The conversion of infidels, by fair means or foul, by persuasion or force, was one of the popular tenets of the day; and in recommending the enslaving of the Caribs, Columbus thought that he was obeying the dictates of his conscience, when he was in reality listening to the incitements of his interest. It is but just to add, that the sovereigns did not accord with his ideas, but ordered that the Caribs should be converted like the rest of the islanders; a command which emanated from the merciful heart of Isabella, who ever showed herself the benign protectress of the Indians.

The fleet put to sea on the 2d of February, 1494. Though it brought back no wealth to Spain, yet expectation was kept alive by the sanguine letter of Columbus, and the specimens of gold which he transmitted : his favorable accounts were corroborated by letters from Friar Boyle, Doctor Chanca, and other persons of credibility, and by the personal reports of Gorvalan. The sordid calculations of petty spirits were as yet overruled by the enthusiasm of generous minds, captivated by the lofty nature of these enterprises. There was something wonderfully grand in the idea of thus introducing new races of animals and plants, of building cities, extending colonies, and sowing the seeds of civilization and of enlightened empire in this beautiful but savage world. It struck the minds of learned and classical men with admiration, filling them with pleasant dreams and reveries, and seeming to realize the poetical pictures of the olden time. " Columbus," says old Peter Martyr, " has begun to build a city, as he has lately written to me, and to sow our seeds and propagate our animals! Who of us shall now speak with wonder of Saturn, Ceres, and Triptolemus, traveling about the earth to spread new inventions among mankind? Or of the Phœnicians who built Tyre or Sidon? Or of the Tyrians themselves, whose roving desires led them to migrate into foreign lands, to build new cities, and establish new communities?"[1]

Such were the comments of enlightened and benevolent men, who hailed with enthusiasm the discovery of the New World, not for the wealth it would bring to Europe, but for the field it would open for glorious and benevolent enterprise, and the blessings and improvements of civilized life, which it would widely dispense through barbarous and uncultivated regions.

[1] Letter 153, to Pomponius Lætus.

NOTE.

Isabella at the present day is quite overgrown with forest, in the midst of which are still to be seen partly standing, the pillars of the church, some remains of the king's storehouses, and part of the residence of Columbus, all built of hewn stone. The small fortress is also a prominent ruin; and a little north of it is a circular pillar about ten feet high and as much in diameter, of solid masonry, nearly entire; which appears to have had a wooden gallery or battlement round the top for the convenience of room, and in the centre of which was planted the flag-staff. Having discovered the remains of an iron clamp imbedded in the stone, which served to secure the flag-staff itself, I tore it out, and now consign to you this curious relic of the first foothold of civilization in the New World, after it has been exposed to the elements nearly three hundred and fifty years.—*From the letter of T. S. Heneken, Esq.*

CHAPTER VIII.

DISCONTENTS AT ISABELLA.—MUTINY OF BERNAL DIAZ DE PISA.

[1494.]

THE embryo city of Isabella was rapidly assuming a form. A dry stone wall surrounded it, to protect it from any sudden attack of the natives; although the most friendly disposition was evinced by the Indians of the vicinity, who brought supplies of their simple articles of food, and gave them in exchange for European trifles. On the day of the Epiphany, the 6th of February, the church being sufficiently completed, high mass was celebrated with great pomp and ceremony, by Friar Boyle and the twelve ecclesiastics. The affairs of the settlement being thus apparently in a regular train, Columbus, though still confined by indisposition, began to make arrangements for his contemplated expedition to the mountains of Cibao, when an unexpected disturbance in his little community for a time engrossed his attention.

The sailing of the fleet for Spain had been a melancholy
sight to many whose terms of enlistment compelled them
to remain on the island.   Disappointed in their expectations
of immediate wealth, disgusted with the labors imposed on
them, and appalled by the maladies prevalent throughout
the community, they began to look with horror upon the
surrounding wilderness, as destined to be the grave of their
hopes and of themselves.   When the last sail disappeared,
they felt as if completely severed from their country ; and
the tender recollections of home, which had been checked
for a time by the novelty and bustle around them, rushed
with sudden force upon their minds.   To return to Spain
became their ruling idea, and the same want of reflection
which had hurried them into the enterprise, without inquiring into its real nature, now prompted them to extricate
themselves from it, by any means however desperate.

Where popular discontents prevail, there is seldom wanting some daring spirit to give them a dangerous direction.
One Bernal Diaz de Pisa, a man of some importance, who
had held a civil office about the court, had come out with
the expedition as comptroller : he seems to have presumed
upon his official powers, and to have had early differences
with the admiral.   Disgusted with his employment in the
colony, he soon made a faction among the discontented, and
proposed that they should take advantage of the indisposition of Columbus, to seize upon some or all of the five
ships in the harbor, and return in them to Spain.   It would
be easy to justify their clandestine return, by preferring a
complaint against the admiral, representing the fallacy of
his enterprises, and accusing him of gross deceptions and
exaggerations in his accounts of the countries he had discovered.   It is probable that some of these people really
considered him culpable of the charges thus fabricated
against him ; for, in the disappointment of their avaricious
hopes, they overlooked the real value of those fertile islands,
which were to enrich nations by the produce of their soil.

Every country was sterile and unprofitable in their eyes, that did not immediately teem with gold. Though they had continual proofs in the specimens brought by the natives to the settlement, or furnished to Ojeda and Gorvalan, that the rivers and mountains in the interior abounded with ore, yet even these daily proofs were falsified in their eyes. One Fermin Cedo, a wrong-headed and obstinate man, who had come out as assayer and purifier of metals, had imbibed the same prejudice against the expedition with Bernal Diaz. He pertinaciously insisted that there was no gold in the island; or at least that it was found in such inconsiderable quantities as not to repay the search. He declared that the large grains of virgin ore brought by the natives had been melted; that they had been the slow accumulation of many years, having remained a long time in the families of the Indians, and handed down from generation to generation; which in many instances was probably the case. Other specimens, of a large size, he pronounced of a very inferior quality, and debased with brass by the natives. The words of this man outweighed the evidence of facts, and many joined him in the belief that the island was really destitute of gold. It was not until some time afterwards that the real character of Fermin Cedo was ascertained, and the discovery made, that his ignorance was at least equal to his obstinacy and presumption; qualities apt to enter largely into the compound of a meddlesome and mischievous man.[1]

Encouraged by such substantial co-operation, a number of turbulent spirits concerted to take immediate possession of the ships and make sail for Europe. The influence of Bernal Diaz de Pisa at court would obtain for them a favorable hearing, and they trusted to their unanimous representations, to prejudice Columbus in the opinion of the public, ever fickle in its smiles, and most ready to turn

[1] Cura de los Palacios, cap. 120, 122, MS.

20

suddenly and capriciously from the favorite it has most idolized.

Fortunately this mutiny was discovered before it proceeded to action. Columbus immediately ordered the ringleaders to be arrested. On making investigations, a memorial or information against himself, full of slanders and misrepresentations, was found concealed in the buoy of one of the ships. It was in the handwriting of Bernal Diaz. The admiral conducted himself with great moderation. Out of respect to the rank and station of Diaz, he forbore to inflict any punishment; but confined him on board one of the ships, to be sent to Spain for trial, together with the process or investigation of his offence, and the seditious memorial which had been discovered. Several of the inferior mutineers were punished according to the degree of their culpability, but not with the severity which their offence deserved. To guard against any recurrence of a similar attempt, Columbus ordered that all the guns and naval munitions should be taken out of four of the vessels, and put into the principal ship, which was given in charge to persons in whom he could place implicit confidence.[1]

This was the first time Columbus exercised the right of punishing delinquents in his new government, and it immediately awakened the most violent animadversions. His measures, though necessary for the general safety; and characterized by the greatest lenity, were censured as arbitrary and vindictive. Already the disadvantage of being a foreigner among the people he was to govern was clearly manifested. He had national prejudices to encounter, of all others the most general and illiberal. He had no natural friends to rally round him; whereas the mutineers had connections in Spain, friends in the colony, and met with sympathy in every discontented mind. An early hostility was thus engendered against Columbus, which continued to in-

[1] Herrera, Hist. Ind., decad. i. lib. ii. cap. 11. Hist. del Almirante, cap. 50.

crease throughout his life, and the seeds were sown of a series of factions and mutinies which afterwards distracted the island.

CHAPTER IX.

EXPEDITION OF COLUMBUS TO THE MOUNTAINS OF CIBAO.

[1494.]

HAVING at length recovered from his long illness, and the mutiny at the settlement being effectually checked, Columbus prepared for his immediate departure for Cibao. He intrusted the command of the city and the ships, during his absence, to his brother Don Diego, appointing able persons to counsel and assist him. Don Diego is represented by Las Casas, who knew him personally, as a man of great merit and discretion, of a gentle and pacific disposition, and more characterized by simplicity than shrewdness. He was sober in his attire, wearing almost the dress of an ecclesiastic, and Las Casas thinks he had secret hopes of preferment in the church;[1] indeed Columbus intimates as much when he mentions him in his will.

As the admiral intended to build a fortress in the mountains, and to form an establishment for working the mines, he took with him the necessary artificers, workmen, miners, munitions, and implements. He was also about to enter the territories of the redoubtable Caonabo: it was important, therefore, to take with him a force that should not only secure him against any warlike opposition, but should spread through the country a formidable idea of the power of the white men, and deter the Indians from any future violence, either towards communities or wandering individuals. Every healthy person, therefore, who could be spared from the settlement, was put in requisition, together with

[1] Las Casas, Hist. Ind., lib. i. cap. 82, MS.

all the cavalry that could be mustered; and every arrangement was made to strike the savages with the display of military splendor.

On the 12th of March, Columbus set out at the head of about four hundred men well armed and equipped, with shining helmets and corslets; with arquebuses, lances, swords, and cross-bows, and followed by a multitude of the neighboring Indians. They sallied from the city in martial array, with banners flying, and sound of drum and trumpet. Their march for the first day was across the plain between the sea and the mountains, fording two rivers, and passing through a fair and verdant country. They encamped in the evening, in the midst of pleasant fields, at the foot of a wild and rocky pass of the mountains.

The ascent of this rugged defile presented formidable difficulties to the little army, encumbered as it was with various implements and munitions. There was nothing but an Indian foot-path, winding among rocks and precipices, or through brakes and thickets, entangled by the rich vegetation of a tropical forest. A number of high-spirited young cavaliers volunteered to open a route for the army. They had probably learnt this kind of service in the Moorish wars, where it was often necessary on a sudden to open roads for the march of troops, and the conveyance of artillery across the mountains of Granada. Throwing themselves in advance with laborers and pioneers, whom they stimulated by their example, as well as by promises of liberal reward, they soon constructed the first road formed in the New World; and which was called El Puerto de los Hidalgos, or the Gentlemen's Pass, in honor of the gallant cavaliers who effected it.[1]

On the following day, the army toiled up this steep defile, and arrived where the gore of the mountain opened into

---

[1] Hist. del Almirante, cap. 50. Hidalgo, i. e., Hijo de Algo, literally, "a son of somebody," in contradistinction to an obscure and low-born man, a son of nobody.

the interior.   Here a land of promise suddenly burst upon their view.   It was the same glorious prospect which had delighted Ojeda and his companions.   Below lay a vast and delicious plain, painted and enameled, as it were, with all the rich variety of tropical vegetation.   The magnificent forests presented that mingled beauty and majesty of vegetable forms known only to these generous climates.   Palms of prodigious height, and spreading mahogany trees, towered from amid a wilderness of variegated foliage.   Freshness and verdure were maintained by numerous streams, which meandered gleaming through the deep bosom of the woodland; while various villages and hamlets, peeping from among the trees, and the smoke of others rising out of the midst of the forests, gave signs of a numerous population. The luxuriant landscape extended as far as the eye could reach, until it appeared to melt away and mingle with the horizon.   The Spaniards gazed with rapture upon this soft voluptuous country, which seemed to realize their ideas of a terrestrial paradise; and Columbus, struck with its vast extent, gave it the name of the Vega Real, or Royal Plain.[1]

[1] Las Casas, Hist. Ind., lib. i. cap. 90, MS.

Extract of a Letter from T. S. Heneken, Esq., dated Santiago (St. Domingo), 20th September, 1847.—The route over which Columbus traced his course from Isabella to the mountains of Cibao exists in all its primitive rudeness. The Puerto de los Hidalgos is still the narrow rugged footpath winding among rocks and precipices, leading through the only practicable defile which traverses the Monte Christi range of mountains in this vicinity, at present called the Pass of Marney; and it is somewhat surprising that, of this first and remarkable footprint of the white man in the New World, there does not at the present day exist the least tradition of its former name or importance.

The spring of cool and delightful water met with in the gorge, in a deep dark glen overshadowed by palm and mahogany trees, near the outlet where the magnificent Vega breaks upon the view, still continues to quench the thirst of the weary traveler.   When I drank from this lonely little fountain, I could hardly realize the fact that Columbus must likewise have partaken of its sparkling waters,

Having descended the rugged pass, the army issued upon the plain, in martial style, with great clangor of warlike instruments. When the Indians beheld this shining band of warriors, glittering in steel, emerging from the mountains with prancing steeds and flaunting banners, and heard, for the first time, their rocks and forests echoing to the din of drum and trumpet, they might well have taken such a wonderful pageant for a supernatural vision.

In this way Columbus disposed of his forces whenever he approached a populous village, placing the cavalry in front, for the horses inspired a mingled terror and admiration among the natives. Las Casas observes, that at first they supposed the rider and his horse to be one animal, and nothing could exceed their astonishment at seeing the horsemen dismount; a circumstance which shows that the alleged origin of the ancient fable of the Centaurs is at least founded in nature. On the approach of the army the Indians generally fled with terror, and took refuge in their houses. Such was their simplicity, that they merely put up a slight barrier of reeds at the portal, and seemed to consider themselves perfectly secure. Columbus, pleased to meet with such artlessness, ordered that these frail barriers should be scrupulously respected, and the inhabitants allowed to remain in their fancied security.[1] By degrees

when at the height of his glory, surrounded by cavaliers attired in the gorgeous costumes of the age, and warriors recently from the Moorish wars.

Judging by the distance stated to have been traveled over the plain, Columbus must have crossed the Yaqui near or at Ponton; which very likely received its name from the rafts or pontoons employed to cross the river. Abundance of reeds grow along its banks, and the remains of an Indian village are still very distinctly to be traced in the vicinity. By this route he avoided two large rivers, the Amina and the Mar, which discharged their waters into the Yaqui opposite Esperanza.

The road from Ponton to the river Hanique passes through the defiles of La Cuesta and Nicayagua.

[1] Las Casas, lib. sup. li. cap. 90.

their fears were allayed through the mediation of interpreters, and the distribution of trifling presents. Their kindness and gratitude could not then be exceeded, and the
march of the army was continually retarded by the hospitality of the numerous villages through which it passed.
Such was the frank communion among these people, that
the Indians who accompanied the army entered without
ceremony into the houses, helping themselves to any thing
of which they stood in need, without exciting surprise or
anger in the inhabitants: the latter offered to do the same
with respect to the Spaniards, and seemed astonished when
they met a repulse. This, it is probable, was the case
merely with respect to articles of food ; for we are told that
the Indians were not careless in their notions of property,
and the crime of theft was one of the few which were punished among them with great severity. Food, however, is
generally open to free participation in savage life, and is
rarely made an object of barter, until habits of trade have
been introduced by the white men. The untutored savage,
in almost every part of the world, scorns to make a traffic
of hospitality.

After a march of five leagues across the plain, they arrived at the banks of a large and beautiful stream, called
by the natives Yagui, but to which the admiral gave the
name of the River of Reeds. He was not aware that it
was the same stream, which, after winding through the
Vega, falls into the sea near Monte Christi, and which, in
his first voyage, he had named the River of Gold. On its
green banks the army encamped for the night, animated
and delighted with the beautiful scenes through which they
had passed. They bathed and sported in the waters of the
Yagui, enjoying the amenity of the surrounding landscape,
and the delightful breezes which prevail in that genial
season. " For though there is but little difference," observes
Las Casas, " from one month to another in all the year in
this island, and in most parts of these Indias, yet in the

period from September to May, it is like living in paradise." [1]

On the following morning they crossed this stream by the aid of canoes and rafts, swimming the horses over. For two days they continued their march through the same kind of rich level country, diversified by noble forests, and watered by abundant streams, several of which descended from the mountains of Cibao, and were said to bring down gold dust mingled with their sands. To one of these, the limpid waters of which ran over a bed of smooth round pebbles, Columbus gave the name of Rio Verde, or Green River, from the verdure and freshness of its banks. Its Indian name was Nicayagua, which it still retains. [2] In the course of this march they passed through numerous villages, where they experienced generally the same reception. The inhabitants fled at their approach, putting up their slight barricadoes of reeds, but, as before, they were easily won to familiarity, and tasked their limited means to entertain the strangers.

Thus penetrating into the midst of this great island, where every scene presented the wild luxuriance of beautiful but uncivilized nature, they arrived on the evening of the second day at a chain of lofty and rugged mountains, forming a kind of barrier to the Vega. These Columbus was told were the golden mountains of Cibao, whose region commenced at their rocky summits. The country now beginning to grow rough and difficult, and the people being way-worn, they encamped for the night at the foot of a steep defile, which led up into the mountains, and pioneers were sent in advance to open a road for the army. From this place they sent back mules for a supply of bread and wine, their provisions beginning to grow scanty, for they

---

[1] Las Casas, Hist. Ind., lib. i. cap. 90, MS.

[2] The name of Rio Verde was afterwards given to a small stream which crosses the road from Santiago to La Vega, a branch of the river Yuna.

had not as yet accustomed themselves to the food of the natives, which was afterwards found to be of that light digestible kind suitable to the climate.

On the next morning they resumed their march up a narrow and steep glen, winding among craggy rocks, where they were obliged to lead the horses. Arrived at the summit, they once more enjoyed a prospect of the delicious Vega, which here presented a still grander appearance, stretching far and wide on either hand, like a vast verdant lake. This noble plain, according to Las Casas, is eighty leagues in length, and from twenty to thirty in breadth, and of incomparable beauty.

They now entered Cibao, the famous region of gold, which, as if nature delighted in contrarieties, displayed a miser-like poverty of exterior, in proportion to its hidden treasures. Instead of the soft luxuriant landscape of the Vega, they beheld chains of rocky and sterile mountains, scantily clothed with lofty pines. The trees in the valleys also, instead of possessing the rich tufted foliage common to other parts of the island, were meagre and dwarfish, excepting such as grew on the banks of streams. The very name of the country bespoke the nature of the soil,— Cibao, in the language of the natives, signifying a stone. Still, however, there were deep glens and shady ravines among the mountains, watered by limpid rivulets, where the green herbage, and strips of woodland, were the more delightful to the eye from the neighboring sterility. But what consoled the Spaniards for the asperity of the soil, was to observe among the sands of those crystal streams glittering particles of gold, which, though scanty in quantity, were regarded as earnests of the wealth locked up within the mountains.

The natives having been previously visited by the exploring party under Ojeda, came forth to meet them with great alacrity, bringing food, and, above all, grains and particles of gold collected in the brooks and torrents.

From the quantities of gold dust in every stream, Columbus was convinced there must be several mines in the vicinity. He had met with specimens of amber and lapis lazuli, though in very small quantities, and thought that he had discovered a mine of copper. He was now about eighteen leagues from the settlement; the rugged nature of the mountains made a communication, even from this distance, laborious. He gave up the idea, therefore, of penetrating further into the country, and determined to establish a fortified post in this neighborhood, with a large number of men, as well to work the mines as to explore the rest of the province. He accordingly selected a pleasant situation on an eminence almost entirely surrounded by a small river called the Yanique, the waters of which were as pure as if distilled, and the sound of its current musical to the ear. In its bed were found curious stones of various colors, large masses of beautiful marble, and pieces of pure jasper. From the foot of the height extended one of those graceful and verdant plains, called savannas, which was freshened and fertilized by the river.[1]

On this eminence Columbus ordered a strong fortress of wood to be erected, capable of defence against any attack of the natives, and protected by a deep ditch on the side which the river did not secure. To this fortress he gave the name of St. Thomas, intended as a pleasant, though pious, reproof of the incredulity of Firmin Cedo and his doubting adherents, who obstinately refused to believe that the island produced gold, until they beheld it with their eyes and touched it with their hands.[2]

[1] Las Casas, Hist. Ind., lib. i. cap. 90, MS.

[2] Ibid.—*From the Letter of T. S. Heneken, Esq., 1847.*—Traces of the old fortress of St. Thomas still exist, though, as has happened to the Puerta de los Hidalgos, all tradition concerning it has long been lost.

Having visited a small Spanish village known by the name of Hanique, situated on the banks of that stream, I heard by accident the name of a farm at no great distance, called La Fortaleza. This

The natives, having heard of the arrival of the Spaniards in their vicinity, came flocking from various parts, anxious to obtain European trinkets. The admiral signified to them that any thing would be given in exchange for gold; upon hearing this some of them ran to a neighboring river, and gathering and sifting its sands, returned in a little while with considerable quantities of gold dust. One old man brought two pieces of virgin ore, weighing an ounce, and thought himself richly repaid when he received a hawk's bell. On remarking that the admiral was struck

excited my curiosity, and I proceeded to the spot, a short distance up the river; yet nothing could be learnt from the inhabitants; it was only by ranging the river's banks through a dense and luxuriant forest, that I by accident stumbled upon the site of the fortress.

The remarkable turn in the river; the ditch, still very perfect; the entrance and the covert ways on each side for descending to the river, with a fine esplanade of beautiful short grass in front, complete the picture described by Las Casas.

The square occupied by the fort is now completely covered with forest trees, undistinguishable from those of the surrounding country; which corresponds to this day exactly with the description given above, three centuries since, by Columbus, Ojeda, and Juan de Luxan.

The only change to notice is, that the neat little Indian villages, swarming with an innocent and happy population, have totally disappeared; there being at present only a few scattered huts of indigent Spaniards to be met with, buried in the gloom of the mountains.

The traces of those villages are rarely to be discovered at the present day. The situation of one near Ponton was well chosen for defence, being built on a high bank between deep and precipitous ravines. A large square occupied the centre; in the rear of each dwelling were thrown the sweepings of the apartments and the ashes from the fires, which form a line of mounds, mixed up with broken Indian utensils. As it lays in the direct road from Isabella, Cibao, and La Vega, and commands the best fording place in the neighborhood for crossing the river Yaqui in dry seasons, it must, no doubt, have been a place of considerable resort at the time of the discovery —most likely a pontoon or large canoe was stationed here for tho facility of communication between St. Thomas and Isabella, whence it derived its name.

with the size of these specimens, he affected to treat them
with contempt, as insignificant, intimating by signs, that in
his country, which lay within half a day's journey, they
found pieces of gold as big as an orange. Other Indians
brought grains of gold weighing ten and twelve drachms,
and declared that in the country whence they got them,
there were masses of ore as large as the head of a child.[1]
As usual, however, these golden tracts were always in some
remote valley, or along some rugged and sequestered
stream ; and the wealthiest spot was sure to be at the
greatest distance,—for the land of promise is ever beyond
the mountain.

CHAPTER X.

EXCURSION OF JUAN DE LUXAN AMONG THE MOUNTAINS.—
CUSTOMS AND CHARACTERISTICS OF THE NATIVES.—CO-
LUMBUS RETURNS TO ISABELLA.

[1494.]

WHILE the admiral remained among the mountains,
superintending the building of the fortress, he dispatched
a young cavalier of Madrid, named Juan de Luxan, with
a small band of armed men, to range about the country,
and explore the whole of the province, which, from the
reports of the Indians, appeared to be equal in extent to
the kingdom of Portugal. Luxan returned, after a few
days' absence, with the most satisfactory accounts. He
had traversed a great part of Cibao, which he found more
capable of cultivation than had at first been imagined. It
was generally mountainous, and the soil covered with large
round pebbles of a blue color, yet there was good pasturage
in many of the valleys. The mountains, also, being
watered by frequent showers, produced grass of surpris-

[1] Peter Martyr, decad. i. lib. iii.

ingly quick and luxuriant growth, often reaching to the
saddles of the horses. The forests seemed to Luxan to be
full of valuable spices; he being deceived by the odors
emitted by those aromatic plants and herbs which abound
in the woodlands of the tropics. There were great vines
also, climbing to the very summits of the trees, and bearing
clusters of grapes entirely ripe, full of juice, and of a
pleasant flavor. Every valley and glen possessed its
stream, large or small, according to the size of the neighboring mountain, and all yielding more or less gold, in
small particles. Luxan was supposed, likewise, to have
learned from the Indians many of the secrets of their
mountains; to have been shown the parts where the greatest quantity of ore was found, and to have been taken to
the richest streams. On all these points, however, he
observed a discreet mystery, communicating the particulars to no one but the admiral.[1]

The fortress of St. Thomas being nearly completed, Columbus gave it in command to Pedro Margarite, the same
cavalier whom he had recommended to the favor of the
sovereigns; and he left with him a garrison of fifty-six men.
He then set out on his return to Isabella. On arriving at
the banks of the Rio Verde, or Nicayagua, in the Royal
Vega, he found a number of Spaniards on their way to the
fortress with supplies. He remained, therefore, a few days
in the neighborhood, searching for the best fording place of
the river, and establishing a route between the fortress and
the harbor. During this time, he resided in the Indian villages, endeavoring to accustom his people to the food of the
natives, as well as to inspire the latter with a mingled feeling of good will and reverence for the white men.

From the report of Luxan, Columbus had derived some
information concerning the character and customs of the
natives, and he acquired still more from his own observations, in the course of his sojourn among the tribes of the

[1] Peter Martyr, decad. i. lib. iii.

mountains and the plains. And here a brief notice of a few of the characteristics and customs of these people may be interesting. They are given, not merely as observed by the admiral and his officers during this expedition, but as recorded some time afterwards, in a crude dissertation, by a friar of the name of Roman; a poor hermit, as he styled himself, of the order of the Ieronimites, who was one of the colleagues of Father Boyle, and resided for some time in the Vega as a missionary.

Columbus had already discovered the error of one of his opinions concerning these islanders, formed during his first voyage. They were not so entirely pacific, nor so ignorant of warlike arts, as he had imagined. He had been deceived by the enthusiasm of his own feelings, and by the gentleness of Guacanagari and his subjects. The casual descents of the Caribs had compelled the inhabitants of the sea-shore to acquaint themselves with the use of arms. Some of the mountain tribes near the coast, particularly those on the side which looked towards the Caribbee islands, were of a more hardy and warlike character than those of the plains. Caonabo, also, the Carib chieftain, had introduced something of his own warrior spirit into the centre of the island. Yet, generally speaking, the habits of the people were mild and gentle. If wars sometimes occurred among them, they were of short duration, and unaccompanied by any great effusion of blood; and, in general, they mingled amicably and hospitably with each other.

Columbus had also at first indulged in the error that the natives of Hayti were destitute of all notions of religion, and he had consequently flattered himself that it would be the easier to introduce into their minds the doctrines of Christianity; not aware that it is more difficult to light up the fire of devotion in the cold heart of an atheist, than to direct the flame to a new object, when it is already enkindled.. There are few beings, however, so destitute of reflection, as not to be impressed with the conviction of an overruling deity. A nation of atheists never existed. It was soon discovered that these islanders had their creed, though of a vague and simple nature. They believed in one supreme being, inhabiting the sky, who was immortal, omnipotent, and invisible; to whom they ascribed an origin, who had a mother, but no father.[1] They never addressed their worship directly to him, but employed inferior deities, called Zemes, as messengers and mediators. Each cacique had his tutelar deity of this order, whom he invoked and pretended to consult in all his public undertakings, and who was reverenced by his people. He had a house apart, as a temple to this deity, in which was an image of his Zemi, carved of wood or stone, or shaped of clay or cotton, and generally of some monstrous and hideous form. Each family and each individual had likewise a particular Zemi, or protecting genius, like the Lares and Penates of the ancients. They were placed in every part of their houses, or carved on their furniture; some had them of a small size, and bound them about their foreheads when they went to battle. They believed their Zemes to be transferable, with all their powers, and often stole them from each other. When the Spaniards came among them, they often hid their idols, lest they should be taken away. They believed that these Zemes presided over every object in nature, each having a particular charge or government. They influenced the seasons and the elements, causing sterile or abundant years; exciting hurricanes and whirlwinds, and tempests of rain and thunder, or sending sweet and temperate breezes and fruitful showers. They governed the seas and forests, the springs and fountains; like the Nereids, the Dryads, and Satyrs of antiquity. They gave success in hunting and fishing; they guided the waters of the mountains into safe channels, and led them down to wander through the plains, in gentle brooks and peaceful rivers; or, if incensed, they caused them to burst forth into rushing torrents and

[1] Escritura de Fr. Roman. Hist. del Almirante.

overwhelming floods, inundating and laying waste the valleys.

The natives had their Butios, or priests, who pretended to hold communion with these Zemes. They practised rigorous fasts and ablutions, and inhaled the powder or drank the infusion of a certain herb, which produced a temporary intoxication or delirium. In the course of this process, they professed to have trances and visions, and that the Zemes revealed to them future events, or instructed them in the treatment of maladies. They were, in general, great herbalists, and well acquainted with the medicinal properties of trees and vegetables. They cured diseases through their knowledge of simples, but always with many mysterious rites and ceremonies, and supposed charms; chanting, and burning a light in the chamber of the patient, and pretending to exorcise the malady, to expel it from the mansion, and to send it to the sea or to the mountain.[1]

Their bodies were painted or tattooed with figures of the Zemes, which were regarded with horror by the Spaniards, as so many representations of the devil; and the Butios, esteemed as saints by the natives, were abhorred by the former as necromancers. These Butios often assisted the caciques in practising deceptions upon their subjects, speaking oracularly through the Zemes, by means of hollow tubes; inspiriting the Indians to battle by predicting success, or dealing forth such promises or menaces as might suit the purposes of the chieftain.

There is but one of their solemn religious ceremonies of which any record exists. The cacique proclaimed a day when a kind of festival was to be held in honor of his Zemes. His subjects assembled from all parts, and formed a solemn procession; the married men and women decorated with their most precious ornaments, the young females entirely naked. The cacique, or the principal

[1] Oviedo, Cronic., lib. v. cap. 1.

personage, marched at their head, beating a kind of drum. In this way they proceeded to the consecrated house or temple, in which were set up the images of the Zemes. Arrived at the door, the cacique seated himself on the outside, continuing to beat his drum while the procession entered, the females carrying baskets of cakes ornamented with flowers, and singing as they advanced. These offerings were received by the Butios with loud cries, or rather howlings. They broke the cakes, after they had been offered to the Zemes, and distributed the portions to the heads of families, who preserved them carefully throughout the year, as preventive of all adverse accidents. This done, the females danced, at a given signal, singing songs in honor of the Zemes, or in praise of the heroic actions of their ancient caciques. The whole ceremony finished by invoking the Zemes to watch over and protect the nation.[1]

Besides the Zemes, each cacique had three idols or talismans, which were mere stones, but which were held in great reverence by themselves and their subjects. One they supposed had the power to produce abundant harvests, another to remove all pain from women in travail, and the third to call forth rain or sunshine. Three of these were sent home by Columbus to the sovereigns.[2]

The ideas of the natives with respect to the creation were vague and undefined. They gave their own island of Hayti priority of existence over all others, and believed that the sun and moon originally issued out of a cavern in the island to give light to the world. This cavern still exists, about seven or eight leagues from Cape François, now Cape Haytien, and is known by the name of La Voute à Minguet. It is about one hundred and fifty feet in depth, and nearly the same in height, but very narrow. It receives no light but from the entrance, and from a round

---

[1] Charlevoix, Hist. St. Domingo, lib. i. p. 56.
[2] Hist. del Almirante, cap. 61.

21

hole in the roof, whence it was said the sun and moon issued forth to take their places in the sky. The vault was so fair and regular, that it appeared a work of art rather than of nature. In the time of Charlevoix the figures of various Zemes were still to be seen cut in the rocks, and there were the remains of niches, as if to receive statues. This cavern was held in great veneration. It was painted, and adorned with green branches, and other simple decorations. There were in it two images or Zemes. When there was a want of rain, the natives made pilgrimages and processions to it, with songs and dances, bearing offerings of fruits and flowers.[1]

They believed that mankind issued from another cavern, the large men from a great aperture, the small men from a little cranny. They were for a long time destitute of women, but, wandering on one occasion near a small lake, they saw certain animals among the branches of the trees, which proved to be women. On attempting to catch them, however, they were found to be as slippery as eels, so that it was impossible to hold them. At length they employed certain men, whose hands were rendered rough by a kind of leprosy. These succeeded in securing four of these slippery females, from whom the world was peopled.

While the men inhabited this cavern, they dared only venture forth at night, for the sight of the sun was fatal to them, turning them into trees and stones. A cacique, named Vagoniona, sent one of his men forth from the cave to fish, who, lingering at his sport until the sun had risen, was turned into a bird of melodious note, the same which Columbus mistook for the nightingale. They added, that yearly about the time he had suffered this transformation, he came in the night, with a mournful song, bewailing his misfortune; which was the cause why that bird always sang in the night season.[2]

[1] Charlevoix, Hist. de St. Domingo, lib. i. p. 60.
[2] Fray Roman. Hist. del Almirante. P. Martyr, decad. i. lib. ix.

Like most savage nations, they had a tradition concerning the universal deluge, equally fanciful with most of the preceding; for it is singular how the human mind, in its natural state, is apt to account, by trivial and familiar causes, for great events. They said that there once lived in the island a mighty cacique, who slew his only son for conspiring against him. He afterwards collected and picked his bones, and preserved them in a gourd, as was the custom of the natives with the relics of their friends. On a subsequent day, the cacique and his wife opened the gourd to contemplate the bones of their son, when, to their astonishment, several fish, great and small, leaped out. Upon this the cacique closed the gourd, and placed it on the top of his house, boasting that he had the sea shut up within it, and could have fish whenever he pleased. Four brothers, however, who had been born at the same birth, and were curious intermeddlers, hearing of this gourd, came during the absence of the cacique to peep into it. In their carelessness they suffered it to fall upon the ground, where it was dashed to pieces; when lo! to their astonishment and dismay, there issued forth a mighty flood, with dolphins, and sharks, and tumbling porpoises, and great spouting whales; and the water spread, until it overflowed the earth, and formed the ocean, leaving only the tops of the mountains uncovered, which are the present islands.[1]

They had singular modes of treating the dying and the dead. When the life of a cacique was despaired of, they strangled him out of a principle of respect, rather than suffer him to die like the vulgar. Common people were extended in their hammocks, bread and water placed at their head, and they were then abandoned to die in solitude. Sometimes they were carried to the cacique, and if he permitted them the distinction, they were strangled. After death the body of a cacique was opened, dried at a fire, and preserved; of others the head only was treasured

[1] Escritura de Fray Roman, pobre Heremito.

up as a memorial, or occasionally a limb. Sometimes the
whole body was interred in a cave, with a calabash of water,
and a loaf of bread; sometimes it was consumed with fire
in the house of the deceased.

They had confused and uncertain notions of the existence
of the soul when separated from the body. They believed
in the apparitions of the departed at night, or by daylight
in solitary places, to lonely individuals; sometimes advancing as if to attack them, but upon the traveler's striking
at them they vanished, and he struck merely against trees
or rocks. Sometimes they mingled among the living, and
were only to be known by having no navels. The Indians,
fearful of meeting with these apparitions, disliked to go
about alone, and in the dark.

They had an idea of a place of reward, to which the
spirits of good men repaired after death, where they were
reunited to the spirits of those they had most loved during
life, and to all their ancestors. Here they enjoyed uninter-
ruptedly, and in perfection, those pleasures which constituted their felicity on earth. They lived in shady and
blooming bowers, with beautiful women, and banqueted on
delicious fruits. The paradise of these happy spirits was
variously placed, almost every tribe assigning some favorite
spot in their native province. Many, however, concurred
in describing this region as being near a lake in the western part of the island, in the beautiful province of Xaragua.
Here there were delightful valleys, covered with a delicate
fruit called the mamey, about the size of an apricot. They
imagined that the souls of the deceased remained concealed
among the airy and inaccessible cliffs of the mountains during the day, but descended at night into these happy valleys,
to regale on this consecrated fruit. The living were sparing,
therefore, in eating it, lest the souls of their friends should
suffer from want of their favorite nourishment.[1]

[1] Hist. del Almirante, cap. 61. Peter Martyr, decad. i. lib. ix.
Charlevoix, Hist. St. Domingo, lib. i.

The dances to which the natives seemed so immoderately addicted, and which had been at first considered by the Spaniards mere idle pastimes, were found to be often ceremonials of a serious and mystic character. They form indeed a singular and important feature throughout the customs of the aboriginals of the New World. In these are typified, by signs well understood by the initiated, and, as it were, by hieroglyphic action, their historical events, their projected enterprises, their hunting, their ambuscades, and their battles, resembling in some respects the Pyrrhic dances of the ancients. Speaking of the prevalence of these dances among the natives of Hayti, Peter Martyr observes that they performed them to the chant of certain metres and ballads, handed down from generation to generation, in which were rehearsed the deeds of their ancestors. "These rhymes or ballads," he adds, "they call areytos ; and as our minstrels are accustomed to sing to the harp and lute, so do they in like manner sing these songs, and dance to the same, playing on timbrels made of shells of certain fishes. These timbrels they call maguey. They have also songs and ballads of love, and others of lamentation or mourning ; some also to encourage them to the wars, all sung to tunes agreeable to the matter." It was for these dances, as has been already observed, that they were so eager to procure hawks' bells, suspending them about their persons, and keeping time with their sound to the cadence of the singers. This mode of dancing to a ballad has been compared to the dances of the peasants in Flanders during the summer, and to those prevalent throughout Spain to the sound of the castanets, and the wild popular chants said to be derived from the Moors ; but which, in fact, existed before their invasion, among the Goths who overran the peninsula.[1]

The earliest history of almost all nations has generally been preserved by rude heroic rhymes and ballads, and by

[1] Mariana, Hist. Esp., lib. v. cap. 1.

the lays of the minstrels; and such was the case with the
areytos of the Indians. "When a cacique died," says
Oviedo, "they sang in dirges his life and actions, and all
the good that he had done was recollected. Thus they
formed the ballads or areytos which constituted their history."[1] Some of these ballads were of a sacred character,
containing their traditional notions of theology, and the
superstitions and fables which comprised their religious
creeds. None were permitted to sing these but the sons
of caciques, who were instructed in them by their Butios.
They were chanted before the people on solemn festivals,
like those already described, accompanied by the sound of
a kind of drum, made from a hollow tree.[2]

Such are a few of the characteristics remaining on record
of these simple people, who perished from the face of the
earth before their customs and creeds were thought of
sufficient importance to be investigated. The present
work does not profess to enter into detailed accounts of
the countries and people discovered by Columbus, otherwise
than as they may be useful for the illustration of his
history; and perhaps the foregoing are carried to an unnecessary length, but they may serve to give greater interest
to the subsequent transactions of the island.

Many of these particulars, as has been observed, were collected by the admiral and his officers, during their excursion among the mountains and their sojourn in the plain.
The natives appeared to them a singularly idle and improvident race, indifferent to most of the objects of human
anxiety and toil. They were impatient of all kinds of
labor, scarcely giving themselves the trouble to cultivate
the yuca root, the maize, and the potato, which formed the
main articles of subsistence. For the rest, their streams

---

[1] Oviedo, Cron. de las Indias, lib. v. cap. 3,
[2] Fray Roman. Hist. del Almirante, cap. 61. P. Martyr, decad.
i. lib. ix. Herrera, Hist. Ind., decad. i. lib. iii. cap. 4. Oviedo, lib.
v. cap. 1.

abounded with fish; they caught the utia or coney, the
guana, and various birds; and they had a perpetual banquet from the fruits spontaneously produced by their
groves. Though the air was sometimes cold among the
mountains, yet they preferred submitting to a little temporary suffering, rather than take the trouble to weave garments from the gossampine cotton which abounded in their
forests. Thus they loitered away existence in vacant in-
activity, under the shade of their trees, or amusing themselves occasionally with various games and dances.

In fact, they were destitute of powerful motives to toil,
being free from most of those wants which doom mankind
in civilized life, or in less genial climes, to incessant labor.
They had no sterile winter to provide against, particularly
in the valleys and the plains, where, according to Peter
Martyr, "the island enjoyed perpetual spring-time, and
was blessed with continual summer and harvest. The trees
preserved their leaves throughout the year, and the
meadows continued always green." "There is no province,
nor any region," he again observes, "which is not remarkable for the majesty of its mountains, the fruitfulness of its
vales, the pleasantness of its hills, and delightful plains, with
abundance of fair rivers running through them. There
never was any noisome animal found in it, nor yet any
ravening four-footed beast; no lion, nor bear; no fierce
tigers, nor crafty foxes, nor devouring wolves, but all things
blessed and fortunate." [1]

In the soft region of the Vega, the circling seasons
brought each its store of fruits; and while some were
gathered in full maturity, others were ripening on the
boughs, and buds and blossoms gave promise of still future
abundance. What need was there of garnering up and
anxiously providing for coming days, to men who lived in
a perpetual harvest? What need, too, of toilfully spinning

[1] Peter Martyr, decad. iii. lib. ix., translated by R. Eden. London, 1555.

or laboring at the loom, where a genial temperature prevailed throughout the year, and neither nature nor custom prescribed the necessity of clothing?

The hospitality which characterizes men in such a simple easy mode of existence, was evinced towards Columbus and his followers during their sojourn in the Vega. Wherever they went it was a continual scene of festivity and rejoicing. The natives hastened from all parts, bearing presents, and laying the treasures of their groves, and streams, and mountains, at the feet of beings whom they still considered as descended from the skies to bring blessings to their island.

Having accomplished the purposes of his residence in the Vega, Columbus, at the end of a few days, took leave of its hospitable inhabitants, and resumed his march for the harbor, returning with his little army through the lofty and rugged gorge of the mountains called the Pass of the Hidalgos. As we accompany him in imagination over the rocky height, whence the Vega first broke upon the eye of the Europeans, we cannot help pausing to cast back a look of mingled pity and admiration over this beautiful but devoted region. The dream of natural liberty, of ignorant content, and loitering idleness, was as yet unbroken, but the fiat had gone forth; the white man had penetrated into the land; avarice, and pride, and ambition, and pining care, and sordid labor, and withering poverty, were soon to follow, and the indolent paradise of the Indian was about to disappear for ever.

CHAPTER XI.

ARRIVAL OF COLUMBUS AT ISABELLA.—SICKNESS OF THE COLONY.

[1494.]

ON the 29th of March, Columbus arrived at Isabella, highly satisfied with his expedition into the interior. The appearance of every thing in the vicinity of the harbor was calculated to increase his anticipations of prosperity. The plants and fruits of the Old World, which he was endeavoring to introduce into the island, gave promise of rapid increase. The orchards, fields, and gardens, were in a great state of forwardness. The seeds of various fruits had produced young plants; the sugar-cane had prospered exceedingly; a native vine, trimmed and dressed with care, had yielded grapes of tolerable flavor, and cuttings from European vines already began to form their clusters. On the 30th of March a husbandman brought to Columbus ears of wheat which had been sown in the latter part of January. The smaller kind of garden herbs came to maturity in sixteen days, and the larger kind, such as melons, gourds, pompions, and cucumbers, were fit for the table within a month after the seed had been put into the ground. The soil, moistened by brooks and rivers and frequent showers, and stimulated by an ardent sun, possessed those principles of quick and prodigal fecundity which surprise the stranger, accustomed to less vigorous climates.

The admiral had scarcely returned to Isabella, when a messenger arrived from Pedro Margarite, the commander at fort St. Thomas, informing him that the Indians of the vicinity had manifested unfriendly feelings, abandoning their villages and shunning all intercourse with the white men; and that Caonabo was assembling his warriors, and preparing to attack the fortress. The fact was, that the moment the admiral had departed, the Spaniards, no longer awed by his presence, had, as usual, listened only to their passions, and exasperated the natives by wresting from them their gold, and wronging them with respect to their women. Caonabo also had seen with impatience these detested intruders, planting their standard in the very midst of his mountains, and he knew that he had nothing to expect from them but vengeance.

The tidings from Margarite, however, caused but little solicitude in the mind of Columbus. From what he had seen of the Indians in the interior, he had no apprehensions from their hostility. He knew their weakness and their awe of white men, and, above all, he confided in their terror of the horses, which they regarded as ferocious beasts of prey, obedient to the Spaniards, but ready to devour their enemies. He contented himself, therefore, with sending Margarite a reinforcement of twenty men, with a supply of provisions and ammunition, and detaching thirty men to open a road between the fortress and the port.

What gave Columbus real and deep anxiety, was the sickness, the discontent, and dejection which continued to increase in the settlement. The same principles of heat and humidity which gave such fecundity to the fields, were fatal to the people. The exhalations from undrained marshes, and a vast continuity of forest, and the action of a burning sun upon a reeking vegetable soil, produced intermittent fevers, and various other of the maladies so trying to European constitutions in the uncultivated countries of the tropics. Many of the Spaniards suffered also under the torments of a disease hitherto unknown to them, the scourge, as was supposed, of their licentious intercourse with the Indian females; but the origin of which, whether American or European, has been a subject of great dispute. Thus the greater part of the colonists were either confined by positive illness, or reduced to great debility. The stock of medicines was soon exhausted; there was a lack of medical aid, and of the watchful attendance which is even more important than medicine to the sick. Every one who was well, was either engrossed by the public labors, or by his own wants or cares; having to perform all menial offices for himself, even to the cooking of his provisions. The public works, therefore, languished, and it was impossible to cultivate the soil in a sufficient degree to produce a supply of the fruits of the earth. Provisions began to fail, much of the stores brought from Europe had been wasted on board ship, or suffered to spoil through carelessness, and much had perished on shore from the warmth and humidity of the climate. It seemed impossible for the colonists to accommodate themselves to the food of the natives; and their infirm condition required the aliments to which they had been accustomed. To avert an absolute famine, therefore, it was necessary to put the people on a short allowance even of the damaged and unhealthy provisions which remained. This immediately caused loud and factious murmurs, in which many of those in office, who ought to have supported Columbus in his measures for the common safety, took a leading part: among those was Father Boyle, a priest as turbulent as he was crafty. He had been irritated, it is said, by the rigid impartiality of Columbus, who, in enforcing his salutary measures, made no distinction of rank or persons, and put the friar and his household on a short allowance as well as the rest of the community.

In the midst of this general discontent, the bread began to grow scarce. The stock of flour was exhausted, and there was no mode of grinding corn but by the tedious and toilsome process of the hand-mill. It became necessary, therefore, to erect a mill immediately, and other works were required equally important to the welfare of the settlement. Many of the workmen, however, were ill, some feigning greater sickness than they really suffered; for there was a general disinclination to all kind of labor which was not to produce immediate wealth. In this emergency, Columbus put every healthy person in requisition; and as the cavaliers and gentlemen of rank required food as well as the lower orders, they were called upon to take their share in the common labor. This was considered a cruel degradation by many youthful hidalgos of high blood and haughty spirit, and they refused to obey the summons. Columbus, however, was a strict disciplinarian, and felt the importance of making his authority respected. He resorted, therefore, to strong and compulsory measures, and enforced their obedience. This was another cause of the deep and lasting hostilities that sprang up against him. It aroused the immediate indignation of every person of birth and rank in the colony, and drew upon him the resentment of several of the proud families of Spain. He was inveighed against as an arrogant and upstart foreigner, who, inflated with a sudden acquisition of power, and consulting only his own wealth and aggrandizement, was trampling upon the rights and dignities of Spanish gentlemen, and insulting the honor of the nation.

Columbus may have been too strict and indiscriminate in his regulations. There are cases in which even justice may become oppressive, and where the severity of the law should be tempered with indulgence. What was mere toilsome labor to a common man, became humiliation and disgrace when forced upon a Spanish cavalier. Many of these young men had come out, not in the pursuit of wealth, but with romantic dreams inspired by his own representations; hoping, no doubt, to distinguish themselves by heroic achievements and chivalrous adventure, and to continue in the Indies the career of arms which they had commenced in the recent wars of Granada. Others had been brought up in soft, luxurious indulgence, in the midst of opulent families, and were little calculated for the rude perils of the seas, the fatigues of the land, and the hardships, the exposures, and deprivations which attend a new settlement in the wilderness. When they fell ill, their case soon became incurable. The ailments of the body were increased by sickness of the heart. They suffered under the irritation of wounded pride, and the morbid melancholy of disappointed hope; their sick-bed was destitute of all the tender care and soothing attention to which they had been accustomed; and they sank into the grave in all the sullenness of despair, cursing the day of their departure from their country.

The venerable Las Casas, and Herrera after him, record, with much solemnity, a popular belief current in the island at the time of his residence there, and connected with the untimely fate of these cavaliers.

In after years, when the seat of the colony was removed from Isabella on account of its unhealthy situation, the city fell to ruin, and was abandoned. Like all decayed and deserted places, it soon became an object of awe and superstition to the common people, and no one ventured to enter its gates. Those who passed near it, or hunted the wild swine which abounded in the neighborhood, declared they heard appalling voices issue from within its walls by night and day. The laborers became fearful, therefore, of cultivating the adjacent fields. The story went, adds Las Casas, that two Spaniards happened one day to wander among the ruined edifices of the place. On entering one of the solitary streets, they beheld two rows of men, evidently, from their stately demeanor, hidalgos of noble blood, and cavaliers of the court. They were richly attired in the old Castilian mode, with rapiers by their sides, and broad traveling hats, such as were worn at the time. The two men were astonished to behold persons of their rank and appearance apparently inhabiting that desolate place, unknown to the people of the island. They saluted them, and inquired whence they came and when they had arrived. The cavaliers maintained a gloomy

silence, but courteously returned the salutation by raising
their hands to their sombreros or hats, in taking off which
their heads came off also, and their bodies stood decapitated.
The whole phantom assemblage then vanished. So great
was the astonishment and horror of the beholders, that they
had nearly fallen dead, and remained stupefied for several
days.[1]

.. The foregoing legend is curious, as illustrating the superstitious character of the age, and especially of the people
with whom Columbus had to act. It shows, also, the deep
and gloomy impression made upon the minds of the common people by the death of these cavaliers, which operated
materially to increase the unpopularity of Columbus; as it
was mischievously represented, that they had been seduced
from their homes by his delusive promises, and sacrificed to
his private interests.

CHAPTER XII.

DISTRIBUTION OF THE SPANISH FORCES IN THE INTE-
RIOR.—PREPARATIONS FOR A VOYAGE TO CUBA.

[1494.]

.. The increasing discontents of the motley population of
Isabella and the rapid consumption of the scanty stores
which remained were causes of great anxiety to Columbus.
He was desirous of proceeding on another voyage of discovery, but it was indispensable, before sailing, to place the
affairs of the island in such a state as to secure tranquillity.
He determined, therefore, to send all the men that could be
spared from Isabella, into the interior; with orders to visit
the territories of the different caciques, and explore the
island. By this means they would be roused and ani-

[1] Las Casas, Hist. Ind., lib. i. cap. 92, MS. Herrera, Hist. Ind.,
decad. i. lib. ii. cap. 12.

mated; they would become accustomed to the climate and to the diet of the natives; and such a force would be displayed as to overawe the machinations of Caonabo or any other hostile cacique. In pursuance of this plan, every healthy person, not absolutely necessary to the concerns of the city or the care of the sick, was put under arms, and a little army mustered, consisting of two hundred and fifty cross-bow men, one hundred and ten arquebusiers, sixteen horsemen, and twenty officers. The general command of the forces was intrusted to Pedro Margarite, in whom Columbus had great confidence as a noble Catalonian, and a knight of the order of Santiago. Alonso de Ojeda was to conduct the army to the fortress of St. Thomas, where he was to succeed Margarite in the command; and the latter was to proceed with the main body of the troops on a military tour, in which he was particularly to explore the province of Cibao, and subsequently the other parts of the island.

Columbus wrote a long and earnest letter of instructions to Margarite, by which to govern himself in a service requiring such great circumspection. He charged him above all things to observe the greatest justice and discretion in respect to the Indians, protecting them from all wrong and insult, and treating them in such a manner as to secure their confidence and friendship. At the same time they were to be made to respect the property of the white men, and all thefts were to be severely punished. Whatever provisions were required from them for the subsistence of the army, were to be fairly purchased by persons whom the admiral appointed for that purpose; the purchases were to be made in the presence of the agent of the comptroller. If the Indians refused to sell the necessary provisions, then Margarite was to interfere and compel them to do so, acting, however, with all possible gentleness, and soothing them by kindness and caresses. No traffic was to be allowed between individuals and the natives, it being displeasing to the sov-

ereigns and injurious to the service; and it was always to
be kept in mind that their majesties were more desirous
of the conversion of the natives than of any riches to be
derived from them.

A strict discipline was to be maintained in the army, all
breach of orders to be severely punished, the men to be
kept together, and not suffered to wander from the main
body either singly or in small parties, lest they should be
cut off by the natives; for though these people were pusillanimous, there were no people so apt to be perfidious and
cruel as cowards.[1]

These judicious instructions, which, if followed, might
have preserved an amicable intercourse with the natives,
are more especially deserving of notice, because Margarite
disregarded them all, and by his disobedience brought
trouble on the colony, obloquy on the nation, destruction
on the Indians, and unmerited censure on Columbus.

In addition to the foregoing orders, there were particular
directions for the surprising and securing of the persons of
Caonabo and his brothers. The warlike character of that
chieftain, his artful policy, extensive power, and implacable
hostility, rendered him a dangerous enemy. The measures
proposed were not the most open and chivalrous, but Columbus thought himself justified in opposing stratagem to
stratagem with a subtle and sanguinary foe.

The 9th of April, Alonso de Ojeda sallied forth from
Isabella at the head of the forces, amounting to nearly four
hundred men. On arriving at the Rio del Oro in the
Royal Vega, he learnt that three Spaniards coming from
the fortress of St. Thomas had been robbed of their effects
by five indians, whom a neighboring cacique had sent to
assist them in fording the river; and that the cacique, instead of punishing the thieves, had countenanced them and
shared their booty. Ojeda was a quick, impetuous soldier,

[1] Letter of Columbus. Navarrete, Colec., tom. ii. Document No.
72.

whose ideas of legislation were all of a military kind. Having caught one of the thieves, he caused his ears to be cut off in the public square of the village: he then seized the cacique, his son, and nephew, and sent them in chains to the admiral, after which he pursued his march to the fortress.

In the mean time the prisoners arrived at Isabella in deep dejection. They were accompanied by a neighboring cacique, who, relying upon the merit of various acts of kindness which he had shown to the Spaniards, came to plead for their forgiveness. His intercessions appeared to be of no avail. Columbus felt the importance of striking awe into the minds of the natives with respect to the property of the white men. He ordered, therefore, that the prisoners should be taken to the public square with their hands tied behind them, their crime and punishment proclaimed by the crier, and their heads struck off. Nor was this a punishment disproportioned to their own ideas of justice, for we are told that the crime of theft was held in such abhorrence among them, that, though not otherwise sanguinary in their laws, they punished it with impalement.[1] It is not probable, however, that Columbus really meant to carry the sentence into effect. At the place of execution the prayers and tears of the friendly cacique were redoubled, pledging himself that there should be no repetition of the offence. The admiral at length made a merit of yielding to his entreaties, and released the prisoners. Just at this juncture a horseman arrived from the fortress, who, in passing by the village of the captive cacique, had found five Spaniards in the power of the Indians. The sight of his horse had put the multitude to flight, though upwards of four hundred in number. He had pursued the fugitives, wounding several with his lance, and had brought off his countrymen in triumph.

Convinced by this circumstance that nothing was to be

[1] Oviedo, Hist. Ind., lib. v. cap. 3.

apprehended from the hostilities of these timid people as long as his orders were obeyed, and confiding in the distribution he had made of his forces, both for the tranquillity of the colony and the island, Columbus prepared to depart on the prosecution of his discoveries. To direct the affairs of the island during his absence, he formed a junta, of which his brother Don Diego was president, and Father Boyle, Pedro Fernandez Coronel, Alonzo Sanchez Caravajal, and Juan de Luxan were councilors. He left his two largest ships in the harbor, being of too great a size and draft of water to explore unknown coasts and rivers, and he took with him three caravels, the Niña or Santa Clara, the San Juan, and the Cordera.

BOOK VII.

CHAPTER I.

VOYAGE TO THE EAST END OF CUBA.

[1494.]

THE expedition of Columbus, which we are now about to record, may appear of minor importance at the present day, leading as it did to no grand discovery, and merely extending along the coasts of islands with which the reader is sufficiently familiar. Some may feel impatient at the development of opinions and conjectures which have long since been proved to be fallacious, and the detail of exploring enterprises, undertaken in error, and which they know must end in disappointment. But to feel these voyages properly, we must, in a manner, divest ourselves occasionally of the information we possess, relative to the countries visited; we must transport ourselves to the time, and identify ourselves with Columbus, thus fearlessly launching into seas, where as yet a civilized sail had never been unfurled. We must accompany him, step by step, in his cautious, but bold, advances along the bays and channels of an unknown coast, ignorant of the dangers which might lurk around or which might await him in the interminable region of mystery that still kept breaking upon his view. We must, as it were, consult with him as to each new reach of shadowy land, and long line of promontory, that we see faintly emerging from the ocean and stretching along the distant horizon. We must watch with him each light canoe that comes skimming the billows, to gather from the looks, the ornaments, and the imperfect communications of its wandering crew, whether those unknown lands are also savage and uncultivated, whether they are islands in the ocean, untrodden as yet by civilized man, or tracts of the old continent of Asia, and wild frontiers of its populous and splendid empires. We must enter into his very thoughts and fancies, find out the data that assisted his judgment and the hints that excited his conjectures, and, for a time, clothe the regions through which we are accompanying him, with the gorgeous coloring of his own imagination. In this way we may delude ourselves into participation of the delight of exploring unknown and magnificent lands, where new wonders and beauties break upon us at every step, and we may ultimately be able, as it were from our own familiar acquaintance, to form an opinion of the character of this extraordinary man, and of the nature of his enterprises.

The plan of the present expedition of Columbus was to revisit the coast of Cuba at the point where he had abandoned it on his first voyage, and thence to explore it on the southern side. As has already been observed, he supposed it to be a continent, and the extreme end of Asia, and if so, by following its shores in the proposed direction, he must eventually arrive at Cathay and those other rich and commercial, though semi-barbarous, countries described by Mandeville and Marco Polo.[1]

He set sail with his little squadron from the harbor of Isabella on the 24th of April, and steered to the westward. After touching at Monte Christi, he anchored on the same day at the disastrous harbor of La Navidad. His object in revisiting this melancholy scene was to obtain an interview with Guacanagari, who, he understood, had returned to his former residence. He could not be persuaded of the perfidy of that cacique, so deep was the impression made upon his

[1] Cura de los Palacios, cap. 123, MS.

heart by past kindness; he trusted, therefore, that a frank explanation would remove all painful doubts, and restore a friendly intercourse, which would be highly advantageous to the Spaniards, in their present time of scarcity and suffering. Guacanagari, however, still maintained his equivocal conduct, absconding at the sight of the ships; and though several of his subjects assured Columbus that the cacique would soon make him a visit, he did not think it advisable to delay his voyage on such an uncertainty.

Pursuing his course, impeded occasionally by contrary winds, he arrived on the 29th at the port of St. Nicholas, whence he beheld the extreme point of Cuba, to which in his preceding voyage he had given the name of Alpha and Omega, but which was called by the natives Bayatiquiri, and is now known as Point Maysi. Having crossed the channel, which is about eighteen leagues wide, he sailed along the southern coast of Cuba for the distance of twenty leagues, when he anchored in a harbor, to which, from its size, he gave the name of Puerto Grande, at present called Guantanamo. The entrance was narrow and winding, though deep; the harbor expanded within like a beautiful lake, in the bosom of a wild and mountainous country, covered with trees, some of them in blossom, others bearing fruit. Not far from the shore were two cottages built of reeds, and several fires blazing in various parts of the beach gave signs of inhabitants. Columbus landed therefore, attended by several men well armed, and by the young Indian interpreter Diego Colyn, the native of the island of Guanahani who had been baptized in Spain. On arriving at the cottages, he found them deserted; the fires also were abandoned, and there was not a human being to be seen. The Indians had all fled to the woods and mountains. The sudden arrival of the ships had spread a panic throughout the neighborhood, and apparently interrupted the preparations for a rude but plentiful banquet. There were great quantities of fish, utias, and guanas; some suspended to the

branches of the trees, others roasting on wooden spits before
the fires.

The Spaniards, accustomed of late to slender fare, fell
without ceremony on this bounteous feast, thus spread for
them, as it were, in the wilderness. They abstained, however, from the guanas, which they still regarded with disgust as a species of serpent, though they were considered so
delicate a food by the savages, that, according to Peter
Martyr, it was no more lawful for the common people to
eat of them, than of peacocks and pheasants in Spain.[1]

After their repast, as the Spaniards were roving about the
vicinity, they beheld about seventy of the natives collected
on the top of a lofty rock, and looking down upon them
with great awe and amazement. On attempting to approach them, they instantly disappeared among the woods
and clefts of the mountain. One, however, more bold or
more curious than the rest, lingered on the brow of the
precipice, gazing with timid wonder at the Spaniards,
partly encouraged by their friendly signs, but ready in
an instant to bound away after his companions.

By order of Columbus, the young Lucayan interpreter
advanced and accosted him. The expressions of friendship,
in his own language, soon dispelled his apprehensions. He
came to meet the interpreter, and being informed by him
of the good intentions of the Spaniards, hastened to communicate the intelligence to his comrades. In a little while
they were seen descending from their rocks, and issuing
from their forests, approaching the strangers with great
gentleness and veneration. Through the means of the interpreter, Columbus learnt that they had been sent to the
coast by their cacique, to procure fish for a solemn banquet,
which he was about to give to a neighboring chieftain, and
that they roasted the fish to prevent it from spoiling in the
transportation. They seemed to be of the same gentle and
pacific character with the natives of Hayti. The ravages

[1] P. Martyr, decad. i. lib. iii.

that had been made among their provisions by the hungry Spaniards gave them no concern, for they observed that one night's fishing would replace all the loss. Columbus, however, in his usual spirit of justice, ordered that ample compensation should be made them, and, shaking hands, they parted mutually well pleased.[1]

Leaving this harbor on the 1st of May, the admiral continued to the westward, along a mountainous coast, adorned by beautiful rivers, and indented by those commodious harbors for which this island is so remarkable. As he advanced, the country grew more fertile and populous. The natives crowded to the shores, man, woman, and child, gazing with astonishment at the ships, which glided gently along at no great distance. They held up fruits and provisions, inviting the Spaniards to land; others came off in canoes, bringing cassava bread, fish, and calabashes of water, not for sale, but as offerings to the strangers, whom, as usual, they considered celestial beings descended from the skies. Columbus distributed the customary presents among them, which were received with transports of joy and gratitude. After continuing some distance along the coast, he came to another gulf or deep bay, narrow at the entrance and expanding within, surrounded by a rich and beautiful country. There were lofty mountains sweeping up from the sea, but the shores were enlivened by numerous villages, and cultivated to such a degree as to resemble gardens and orchards. In this harbor, which it is probable was the same at present called St. Jago de Cuba, Columbus anchored and passed a night, overwhelmed, as usual, with the simple hospitality of the natives.[2]

On inquiring of the people of this coast after gold, they uniformly pointed to the south, and, as far as they could be understood, intimated that it abounded in a great island which lay in that direction. The admiral, in the course of

[1] Peter Martyr, ubi sup.
[2] Cura de los Palacios, cap. 124, MS.

his first voyage, had received information of such an island, which some of his followers had thought might be Babeque, the object of so much anxious search and chimerical expectation. He had felt a strong inclination to diverge from his course and go in quest of it, and this desire increased with every new report. On the following day, therefore (the 3d of May), after standing westward to a high cape, he turned his prow directly south, and, abandoning for a time the coast of Cuba, steered off into the broad sea, in quest of this reported island.

CHAPTER II.

DISCOVERY OF JAMAICA.

[1494.]

COLUMBUS had not sailed many leagues before the blue summits of a vast and lofty island at a great distance began to rise like clouds above the horizon. It was two days and nights, however, before he reached its shores, filled with admiration, as he gradually drew near, at the beauty of its mountains, the majesty of its forests, the fertility of its valleys, and the great number of villages with which the whole face of the country was animated.

On approaching the land, at least seventy canoes, filled with savages gayly painted and decorated with feathers, sallied forth more than a league from the shore. They advanced in warlike array, uttering loud yells, and brandishing lances of pointed wood. The mediation of the interpreter. and a few presents to the crew of one of the canoes, which ventured nearer than the rest, soothed this angry armada, and the squadron pursued its course unmolested. Columbus anchored in a harbor about the centre

of the island, to which, from the great beauty of the surrounding country, he gave the name of Santa Gloria.[1]

On the following morning, he weighed anchor at daybreak, and coasted westward in search of a sheltered
harbor, where his ship could be careened and calked, as it
leaked considerably. After proceeding a few leagues, he
found one apparently suitable for the purpose. On sending
a boat to sound the entrance, two large canoes, filled with
Indians, issued forth, hurling their lances, but from such
distance as to fall short of the Spaniards. Wishing to
avoid any act of hostility that might prevent future intercourse, Columbus ordered the boat to return on board,
and finding there was sufficient depth of water for his ship,
entered and anchored in the harbor. Immediately the
whole beach was covered with Indians painted with a
variety of colors, but chiefly black, some partly clothed
with palm leaves, and all wearing tufts and coronets of
feathers. Unlike the hospitable islanders of Cuba and
Hayti, they appeared to partake of the warlike character
of the Caribs, hurling their javelins at the ships, and
making the shores resound with their yells and war-
whoops.

The admiral reflected that further forbearance might be
mistaken for cowardice. It was necessary to careen his
ship, and to send men on shore for a supply of water, but
previously it was advisable to strike an awe into the
savages, that might prevent any molestation from them.
As the caravels could not approach sufficiently near to the
beach where the Indians were collected, he dispatched the
boats well manned and armed. These, rowing close to the
shore, let fly a volley of arrows from their cross-bows, by
which several Indians were wounded, and the rest thrown
into confusion. The Spaniards then sprang on shore, and
put the whole multitude to flight; giving another discharge
with their cross-bows, and letting loose upon them a dog,

[1] Cura de los Palacios, cap. 125.

who pursued them with sanguinary fury.[1] This is the first
instance of the use of dogs against the natives, which were
afterwards employed with such cruel effect by the Spaniards
in their Indian wars. Columbus now landed and took
formal possession of the island, to which he gave the name
of Santiago; but it has retained its original Indian name
of Jamaica. The harbor, from its commodiousness, he
called Puerto Bueno: it was in the form of a horse-shoe,
and a river entered the sea in its vicinity.[2]

During the rest of the day, the neighborhood remained
silent and deserted. On the following morning, however,
before sunrise, six Indians were seen on the shore, making
signs of amity. They proved to be envoys sent by the
caciques with proffers of peace and friendship. These
were cordially returned by the admiral; presents of trinkets were sent to the chieftains; and in a little while the
harbor again swarmed with the naked and painted multitude, bringing abundance of provisions, similar in kind,
but superior in quality, to those of the other islands.

During three days that the ships remained in this harbor,
the most amicable intercourse was kept up with the natives. They appeared to be more ingenious, as well as more
warlike, than their neighbors of Cuba and Hayti. Their
canoes were better constructed, being ornamented with
carving and painting at the bow and stern. Many were of
great size, though formed of the trunks of single trees,
often from a species of the mahogany. Columbus measured
one, which was ninety-six feet long, and eight broad,[3] hollowed out of one of those magnificent trees which rise like
verdant towers amidst the rich forests of the tropics.
Every cacique prided himself on possessing a large canoe
of the kind, which he seemed to regard as his ship of state.
It is curious to remark the apparently innate difference be-

---

[1] Cura de los Palacios, cap. 125.
[2] Hist. del Almirante, ubi sup.
[3] Cura de los Palacios, cap. 124.

tween these island tribes. The natives of Porto Rico,
though surrounded by adjacent islands, and subject to frequent incursions of the Caribs, were of a pacific character,
and possessed very few canoes; while Jamaica, separated
by distance from intercourse with other islands, protected
in the same way from the dangers of invasion, and embosomed, as it were, in a peaceful mediterranean sea, was
inhabited by a warlike race, and surpassed all the other
islands in its maritime armaments.

His ship being repaired, and a supply of water taken in,
Columbus made sail, and continued along the coast to the
westward, so close to the shore, that the little squadron was
continually surrounded by the canoes of the natives, who
came off from every bay, and river, and headland, no
longer manifesting hostility, but anxious to exchange any
thing they possessed for European trifles. After proceeding about twenty-four leagues, they approached the western
extremity of the island, where, the coast bending to the
south, the wind became unfavorable for their further progress along the shore. Being disappointed in his hopes of
finding gold in Jamaica, and the breeze being fair for Cuba,
Columbus determined to return thither, and not to leave it
until he had explored its coast to a sufficient distance to
determine the question, whether it were terra firma or an
island.[1] To the last place at which he touched in Jamaica,
he gave the name of the Gulf of Buentiempo (or Fair
Weather), on account of the propitious wind which blew
for Cuba. Just as he was about to sail, a young Indian
came off to the ship, and begged the Spaniards would take
him to their country. He was followed by his relatives
and friends, who endeavored by the most affecting supplications to dissuade him from his purpose. For some time
he was distracted between concern for the distress of his
family, and an ardent desire to see the home of these wonderful strangers. Curiosity, and the youthful propensity

[1] Hist. del Almirante, cap. 54.

to rove, prevailed; he tore himself from the embraces of his friends, and, that he might not behold the tears of his sisters, hid himself in a secret part of the ship. Touched by this scene of natural affection, and pleased with the enterprising and confiding spirit of the youth, Columbus gave orders that he should be treated with especial kindness.[1]

It would have been interesting to have known something more of the fortunes of this curious savage, and of the impressions made upon so lively a mind by a first sight of the wonders of civilization,—whether the land of the white men equaled his hopes; whether, as is usual with savages, he pined amidst the splendors of cities for his native forests, and whether he ever returned to the arms of his family. The early Spanish historians seem never to have interested themselves in the feelings or fortunes of these first visitors from the New to the Old World. No further mention is made of this youthful adventurer.

CHAPTER III.

RETURN TO CUBA.—NAVIGATION AMONG THE ISLANDS CALLED THE QUEEN'S GARDENS.

[1494.]

SETTING sail from the gulf of Buentiempo, the squadron once more steered for the island of Cuba, and on the 18th of May arrived at a great cape, to which Columbus gave the name of Cabo de la Cruz, which it still retains. Here, landing at a large village, he was well received and entertained by the cacique and his subjects, who had long since heard of him and his ships. In fact, Columbus found, from the report of this chieftain, that the numerous Indians who had visited his ships during his cruise along the northern coast in his first voyage, had spread the story far and near

—————————
[1] Hist. del Almirante, cap. 54.

of these wonderful visitors who had descended from the sky, and had filled the whole island with rumors and astonishment.[1] The admiral endeavored to ascertain from this cacique and his people, whether Cuba was an island or a continent. They all replied that it was an island, but of infinite extent; for they declared that no one had ever seen the end of it. This reply, while it manifested their ignorance of the nature of a continent, left the question still in doubt and obscurity. The Indian name of this province of Cuba was Macaca.

Resuming his course to the west on the following day, Columbus came to where the coast suddenly swept away to the northeast for many leagues, and then curved around again to the west, forming an immense bay, or rather gulf. Here he was assailed by a violent storm, accompanied by awful thunder and lightning, which in these latitudes seem to rend the very heavens. Fortunately the storm was not of long duration, or his situation would have been perilous in the extreme; for he found the navigation rendered difficult by numerous keys[2] and sand-banks. These increased as he advanced, until the mariner stationed at the mast-head beheld the sea, as far as the eye could reach, completely studded with small islands; some were low, naked, and sandy, others covered with verdure, and others tufted with lofty and beautiful forests. They were of various sizes, from one to four leagues, and were generally the more fertile and elevated, the nearer they were to Cuba. Finding them to increase in number, so as to render it impossible to give names to each, the admiral gave the whole labyrinth of islands, which in a manner enameled the face of the ocean with variegated verdure, the name of the Queen's Gardens. He thought at first of leaving this archipelago on his right, and standing farther out to sea; but he called

[1] Cura de los Palacios, cap. 126.

[2] Keys, from Cayos, rocks which occasionally form small islands on the coast of America.

to mind that Sir John Mandeville and Marco Polo had
mentioned that the coast of Asia was fringed with islands
to the amount of several thousand. He persuaded himself
that he was among that cluster, and resolved not to lose
sight of the mainland, by following which, if it were
really Asia, he must soon arrive at the dominions of the
Grand Khan.

. Entering among these islands, therefore, Columbus soon
became entangled in the most perplexed navigation, in
which he was exposed to continual perils and difficulties
from sand-banks, counter currents, and sunken rocks. The
ships were compelled, in a manner, to grope their way, with
men stationed at the mast-head, and the lead continually
going. Sometimes they were obliged to shift their course,
within the hour, to all points of the compass; sometimes
they were straitened in a narrow channel, where it was
necessary to lower all sail, and tow the vessels out, lest they
should run aground; notwithstanding all which precautions, they frequently touched upon sand-banks, and were
extricated with great difficulty. The variableness of the
weather added to the embarrassment of the navigation;
though after a little while it began to assume some method
in its very caprices. In the morning the wind rose in the
east with the sun, and following his course through the
day, died away at sunset in the west. Heavy clouds gathered with the approach of evening, sending forth sheets of
lightning, and distant peals of thunder, and menacing a
furious tempest; but as the moon rose, the whole mass
broke away, part melting in a shower, and part dispersing
by a breeze which sprang up from the land.

There was much in the character of the surrounding
scenery to favor the idea of Columbus, that he was in the
Asiatic archipelago. As the ships glided along the smooth
and glassy canals which separated these verdant islands, the
magnificence of their vegetation, the soft odors wafted from
flowers, and blossoms, and aromatic shrubs, and the splen-

did plumage of the scarlet cranes, or rather flamingoes, which abounded in the meadows, and of other tropical birds which fluttered among the groves, resembled what is described of Oriental climes.

These islands were generally uninhabited. They found a considerable village, however, on one of the largest, where they landed on the 22d of May. The houses were abandoned by their inhabitants, who appeared to depend principally on the sea for their subsistence. Large quantities of fish were found in their dwellings, and the adjacent shore was covered with the shells of tortoises. There were also domesticated parrots, and scarlet cranes, and a number of dumb dogs, which it was afterwards found they fattened as an article of food. To this island the admiral gave the name of Santa Marta.

In the course of his voyage among these islands, Columbus beheld one day a number of the natives in a canoe on the still surface of one of the channels, occupied in fishing, and was struck with the singular means they employed. They had a small fish, the flat head of which was furnished with numerous suckers, by which it attached itself so firmly to any object, as to be torn in pieces rather than abandon its hold. Tying a line of great length to the tail of this fish, the Indians permitted it to swim at large; it generally kept near the surface of the water until it perceived its prey, when, darting down swiftly, it attached itself by the suckers-to the throat of a fish or to the under shell of a tortoise, nor did it relinquish its prey, until both were drawn up by the fisherman and taken out of the water. In this way the Spaniards witnessed the taking of a tortoise of immense size, and Fernando Columbus affirms that he himself saw a shark caught in the same manner on the coast of Veragua. The fact has been corroborated by the accounts of various navigators; and the same mode of fishing is said to be employed on the eastern coast of Africa, at Mozambique and at Madagascar. "Thus," it

has been observed, "savage people, who probably have
never held communication with each other, offer the most
striking analogies in their modes of exercising empire over
animals." [1] These fishermen came on board of the ships
in a fearless manner. They furnished the Spaniards with
a supply of fish, and would cheerfully have given them
every thing they possessed. To the admiral's inquiries
concerning those parts, they said that the sea was full of
islands to the south and to the west, but as to Cuba, it continued running to the westward without any termination.

Having extricated himself from this archipelago, Columbus steered for a mountainous part of the island of Cuba
about fourteen leagues distant, where he landed at a large
village on the 3d of June. Here he was received with that
kindness and amity which distinguished the inhabitants of
Cuba, whom he extolled above all the other islanders for
their mild and pacific character. Their very animals, he
said, were tamer, as well as larger and better, than those
of the other islands. Among the various articles of food
which the natives brought with joyful alacrity from all
parts, were stockdoves of uncommon size and flavor; perceiving something peculiar in their taste, Columbus ordered
the crops of several newly killed to be opened, in which
were found sweet spices.

While the crews of the boats were procuring water and
provisions, Columbus sought to gather information from
the venerable cacique, and several of the old men of the
village. They told him that the name of their province
was Ornofay; that further to the westward the sea was
again covered with innumerable islands, and had but little
depth. As to Cuba, none of them had ever heard that it
had an end to the westward; forty moons would not suffice
to reach to its extremity; in fact, they considered it interminable. They observed, however, that the admiral would
receive more ample information from the inhabitants of

---

[1] Humboldt, Essai Politique sur l'Ile de Cuba, tom. i. p. 364.

Mangon, an adjacent province, which lay towards the west. The quick apprehension of Columbus was struck with the sound of this name; it resembled that of Mangi, the richest province of the Grand Khan, bordering on the Ocean. He made further inquiries concerning the region of Mangon, and understood the Indians to say, that it was inhabited by people who had tails like animals, and wore garments to conceal them. He recollected that Sir John Mandeville, in his account of the remote parts of the East, had recorded a story of the same kind as current among certain naked tribes of Asia, and told by them in ridicule of the garments of their civilized neighbors, which they could only conceive useful as concealing some bodily defect.[1] He became, therefore, more confident than ever, that, by keeping along the coast to the westward, he should eventually arrive at the civilized realms of Asia. He flattered himself with the hopes of finding this region of Mangon to be the rich province of Mangi, and its people with tails and garments, the long-robed inhabitants of the empire of Tartary.

CHAPTER IV.

COASTING OF THE SOUTHERN SIDE OF CUBA.

[1494.]

ANIMATED by one of the pleasing illusions of his ardent imagination, Columbus pursued his voyage, with a prosperous breeze, along the supposed continent of Asia. He was now opposite that part of the southern side of Cuba, where, for nearly thirty-five leagues, the navigation is unembarrassed by banks and islands. To his left was the broad and open sea, the dark blue color of which gave token of ample depth; to his right extended the richly-

------

[1] Cura de los Palacios, cap. 127.

wooded province of Ornofay, gradually sweeping up into a range of interior mountains; the verdant coast watered by innumerable streams, and studded with Indian villages. The appearance of the ships spread wonder and joy along the sea-coast. The natives hailed with acclamations the arrival of these wonderful beings whose fame had circulated more or less throughout the island, and who brought with them the blessings of heaven. They came off swimming, or in their canoes, to offer the fruits and productions of the land, and regarded the white men almost with adoration. After the usual evening shower, when the breeze blew from the shore and brought off the sweetness of the land, it bore with it also the distant songs of the natives and the sound of their rude music, as they were probably celebrating, with their national chants and dances, the arrival of the white men. So delightful were these spicy odors and cheerful sounds to Columbus, who was at present open to all pleasurable influences, that he declared the night passed away as a single hour.[1]

It is impossible to resist noticing the striking contrasts which are sometimes presented by the lapse of time. The coast here described, so populous and animated, rejoicing in the visit of the discoverers, is the same that extends westward of the city of Trinidad, along the gulf of Xagua. All is now silent and deserted: civilization, which has covered some parts of Cuba with glittering cities, has rendered this a solitude. The whole race of Indians has long since passed away, pining and perishing beneath the domination of the strangers whom they welcomed so joyfully to their shores. Before me lies the account of a night recently passed on this very coast, by a celebrated traveler; but with what different feelings from those of Columbus! "I past," says he, "a great part of the night upon the deck. What deserted coasts! not a light to announce the cabin of a fisherman. From Batabano to Trinidad, a distance

[1] Cura de los Palacios.

of fifty leagues, there does not exist a village. Yet in the time of Columbus this land was inhabited even along the margin of the sea. When pits are digged in the soil, or the torrents plough open the surface of the earth, there are often found hatchets of stone and vessels of copper, relics of the ancient inhabitants of the island."[1]

For the greater part of two days the ships swept along this open part of the coast, traversing the wide gulf of Xagua. At length they came to where the sea became suddenly as white as milk, and perfectly turbid, as though flour had been mingled with it. This is caused by fine sand, or calcareous particles, raised from the bottom at certain depths by the agitation of the waves and currents. It spread great alarm through the ships, which was heightened by their soon finding themselves surrounded by banks and keys, and in shallow water. The further they proceeded, the more perilous became their situation. They were in a narrow channel, where they had no room to turn, and to beat out; where there was no hold for their anchors, and where they were violently tossed about by the winds, and in danger of being stranded. At length they came to a small island, where they found tolerable anchorage. Here they remained for the night in great anxiety; many were for abandoning all further prosecution of the enterprise, thinking that they might esteem themselves fortunate should they be able to return from whence they came. Columbus, however, could not consent to relinquish his voyage, now that he thought himself in the route for a brilliant discovery. The next morning he dispatched the smallest caravel to explore this new labyrinth of islands, and to penetrate to the mainland in quest of fresh water, of which the ships were in great need. The caravel returned with a report that the canals and keys of this group were as numerous and intricate as those of the Gardens of the Queen; that the mainland was bordered by deep marshes and a muddy

[1] Humboldt, Essai Pol. sur Cuba, tom. ii, p. 25.

coast, where the mangrove trees grew within the water, and
so close together, that they formed, as it were, an impenetrable wall: that within, the land appeared fertile and
mountainous; and columns of smoke, rising from various
parts, gave signs of numerous inhabitants.[1]   Under the
guidance of this caravel, Columbus now ventured to penetrate this little archipelago; working his way with great
caution, toil, and peril, among the narrow channels which
separated the sand-banks and islands, and frequently getting
aground.   At length he reached a low point of Cuba, to
which he gave the name of Point Serafin; within which
the coast swept off to the east, forming so deep a bay, that
he could not see the land at the bottom.   To the north,
however, there were mountains afar off, and the intermediate space was clear and open; the islands in sight lying
to the south and west; a description which agrees with that
of the great bay of Batabano.   Columbus now steered for
these mountains, with a fair wind and three fathoms of
water, and on the following day anchored on the coast near
a beautiful grove of palm-trees.

Here, a party was sent on shore for wood and water; and
they found two living springs in the midst of the grove.
While they were employed in cutting wood and filling their
water-casks, an archer strayed into the forest with his cross-
bow in search of game, but soon returned, flying with great
terror, and calling loudly upon his companions for aid.
He declared that he had not proceeded far, when he suddenly espied, through an opening glade, a man in a long
white dress, so like a friar of the order of St. Mary of
Mercy, that at first sight he took him for the chaplain of
the admiral.   Two others followed, in white tunics reaching
to their knees, and the three were of as fair complexions as
Europeans.   Behind these appeared many more to the
number of thirty, armed with clubs and lances.   They
made no signs of hostility, but remained quiet, the man in

[1] Cura de los Palacios, cap. 128.

the long white dress alone advancing to accost him; but he was so alarmed at their number, that he had fled instantly to seek the aid of his companions. The latter, however, were so daunted by the reported number of armed natives, that they had not courage to seek them nor to wait their coming, but hurried, with all speed, to the ships.

When Columbus heard this story he was greatly rejoiced, for he concluded that these must be the clothed inhabitants of Mangon, of whom he had recently heard, and that he had at length arrived at the confines of a civilized country, if not within the very borders of the rich province of Mangi. On the following day he dispatched a party of armed men in quest of these people clad in white, with orders to penetrate, if necessary, forty miles into the interior, until they met with some of the inhabitants; for he thought the populous and cultivated parts might be distant from the sea, and that there might be towns and cities beyond the woods and mountains of the coast. The party penetrated through a belt of thick forests which girdled the shore, and then entered upon a great plain or savanna, covered with rank grass and herbage as tall as ripe corn, and destitute of any road or footpath. Here they were so entangled and fettered, as it were, by matted grass and creeping vegetation, that it was with the utmost difficulty they could penetrate the distance of a mile, when they had to abandon the attempt, and return weary and exhausted to the ships.

Another party was sent on the succeeding day to penetrate in a different direction. They had not proceeded far from the coast, when they beheld the foot-prints of some large animal with claws, which some supposed the tracks of a lion, others of a griffon,[1] but which were probably made by

[1] Cardinal Pierre de Aliaco, a favorite author with Columbus, speaks repeatedly, in his Imago Mundi, of the existence of griffons in India; and Glanville, whose work, De Proprietatibus Rerum, was familiar to Columbus, describes them as having the body and claws

the alligators which abound in that vicinity. Dismayed at
the sight, they hastened back towards the sea-side. In their
way they passed through a forest, with lawns and meadows
opening in various parts of it, in which were flocks of cranes,
twice the size of those of Europe. Many of the trees and
shrubs sent forth those aromatic odors which were continually deceiving them with the hope of finding oriental
spices. They saw also abundance of grape-vines, that beautiful feature in the vegetation of the New World. Many
of these crept to the summits of the highest trees, overwhelming them with foliage, twisting themselves from
branch to branch, and bearing ponderous clusters of juicy
grapes. The party returned to the ships equally unsuccessful with their predecessors, and pronounced the country
wild and impenetrable, though exceedingly fertile. As a
proof of its abundance, they brought great clusters of the
wild grapes, which Columbus afterwards transmitted to the
sovereigns, together with a specimen of the water of the
White Sea through which he had passed.

As no tribe of Indians was ever discovered in Cuba wearing clothing, it is probable that the story of the men in
white originated in some error of the archer, who, full of
the idea of the mysterious inhabitants of Mangon, may
have been startled in the course of his lonely wandering in
the forest, by one of those flocks of cranes which it seems
abounded in the neighborhood. These birds, like the flamingoes, feed in company, with one stationed at a distance
as sentinel. When seen through the openings of the woodlands, standing in rows along a smooth savanna, or in a
glassy pool of water, their height and erectness give them,
at the first glance, the semblance of human figures.
Whether the story originated in error or in falsehood, it

of a lion, and the head and wings of an eagle, and as infesting the
mountains which abounded with gold and precious stones, so as to render the access to them extremely perilous.—*De Proprietat. Rerum,* lib.
xviii. cap. 150.

made a deep impression on the mind of Columbus, who was predisposed to be deceived, and to believe every thing that favored the illusion of his being in the vicinity of a civilized country.

After he had explored the deep bay to the east, and ascertained that it was not an arm of the sea, he continued westward, and, proceeding about nine leagues, came to an inhabited shore, where he had communications with several of the natives. They were naked as usual; but that he attributed to their being mere fishermen inhabiting a savage coast; he presumed the civilized regions to lie in the interior. As his Lucayan interpreter did not understand the language, or rather dialect, of this part of Cuba, all the information which he could obtain from the natives was necessarily received through the erroneous medium of signs and gesticulations. Deluded by his own favorite hypothesis, he understood from them that, among certain mountains which he saw far off to the west, there was a powerful king, who reigned in great state over many populous provinces; that he wore a white garment which swept the ground; that he was called a saint;[1] that he never spoke, but communicated his orders to his subjects by signs, which were implicitly obeyed.[2] In all this we see the busy imagination of the admiral interpreting every thing into unison with his preconceived ideas. Las Casas assures us that there was no cacique ever known in the island who wore garments, or answered in other respects to this description. This king, with a saintly title, was probably nothing more than a reflected image haunting the mind of Columbus, of that mysterious potentate, Prester John, who had long figured in the narrations of all eastern travelers, sometimes as a monarch, sometimes as a priest, the situation of whose empire and court was always a matter of doubt

[1] Que le Llamaban santo e que traia tunica blanca que le arastra por el suelo.—*Cura de los Palacios*, cap. 128.
[2] Herrera, Hist. Ind., dec. i. lib. ii. cap. 14.

and contradiction, and had recently become again an object of curious inquiry.

The information derived from these people concerning the coast to the westward was entirely vague. They said that it continued for at least twenty days' journey, but whether it terminated there they did not know. They appeared but little informed of any thing out of their immediate neighborhood. Taking an Indian from this place as a guide, Columbus steered for the distant mountains, said to be inhabited by this cacique in white raiment, hoping they might prove the confines of a more civilized country. He had not gone far before he was involved in the usual perplexities of keys, shelves, and sand-banks. The vessels frequently stirred up the sand and slime from the bottom of the sea; at other times they were almost imbedded in narrow channels, where there was no room to tack, and it was necessary to haul them forward by means of the capstan, to their great injury. At one time they came to where the sea was almost covered with tortoises; at another time flights of cormorants and wood-pigeons darkened the sun, and one day the whole air was filled with clouds of gaudy butterflies, until dispelled by the evening shower.

When they approached the mountainous regions, they found the coast bordered by drowned lands or morasses, and beset by such thick forests, that it was impossible to penetrate to the interior. They were several days seeking fresh water, of which they were in great want. At length they found a spring in a grove of palm-trees, and near it shells of the pearl oyster, from which Columbus thought there might be a valuable pearl-fishery in the neighborhood.

While thus cut off from all intercourse with the interior by a belt of swamp and forests, the country appeared to be well peopled. Columns of smoke ascended from various parts, which grew more frequent as the vessels advanced, until they rose from every rock and woody height. The

Spaniards were at a loss to determine whether these arose
from villages and towns, or whether from signal fires, to
give notice of the approach of the ships, and to alarm the
country ; such as were usual on European sea-shores, when
an enemy was descried hovering in the vicinity.

For several days Columbus continued exploring this
perplexed and lonely coast, whose intricate channels are
seldom visited, even at the present day, excepting by the
solitary and lurking bark of the smuggler. As he proceeded, however, he found that the coast took a general
bend to the southwest. This accorded precisely with the
descriptions given by Marco Polo of the remote coast of
Asia. He now became fully assured that he was on that
part of the Asiatic continent which is beyond the boundaries of the Old World as laid down by Ptolemy. Let
him but continue his coast, he thought, and he must surely
arrive to the point where this range of coast terminated
in the Aurea Chersonesus of the ancients.[1]

The ardent imagination of Columbus was always sallying
in the advance, and suggesting some splendid track of
enterprise. Combining his present conjectures as to his
situation with the imperfect lights of geography, he conceived a triumphant route for his return to Spain. Doubling the Aurea Chersonesus, he should emerge into the
seas frequented by the ancients, and bordered by the luxurious nations of the East. Stretching across the gulf of
the Ganges, he might pass by Taprobana, and, continuing
on to the straits of Babelmandel, arrive on the shores of
the Red Sea. Thence he might make his way by land to
Jerusalem, take shipping at Joppa, and traverse the Mediterranean to Spain. Or should the route from Ethiopia to
Jerusalem be deemed too perilous from savage and warlike
tribes, or should he not choose to separate from his vessels,
he might sail round the whole coast of Africa, pass triumphantly by the Portuguese, in their midway groping

[1] The present peninsula of Malacca.

along the shores of Guinea, and after having thus circumnavigated the globe, furl his adventurous sails at the Pillars of Hercules, the *ne plus ultra* of the ancient world! Such was the soaring meditation of Columbus, as recorded by one of his intimate associates;[1] nor is there any thing surprising in his ignorance of the real magnitude of our globe. The mechanical admeasurement of a known part of its circle has rendered its circumference a familiar fact in our day; but in his time it still remained a problem with the most profound philosophers.

CHAPTER V.

RETURN OF COLUMBUS ALONG THE SOUTHERN COAST OF CUBA.

[1494.]

THE opinion of Columbus, that he was coasting the continent of Asia, and approaching the confines of eastern civilization, was shared by all his fellow-voyagers, among whom were several able and experienced navigators. They were far, however, from sharing his enthusiasm. They were to derive no glory from the success of the enterprise, and they shrunk from its increasing difficulties and perils. The ships were strained and crazed by the various injuries they had received, in running frequently aground. Their cables and rigging were worn, their provisions were growing scanty, a great part of the biscuit was spoiled by the sea-water, which oozed in through innumerable leaks. The crews were worn out by incessant labor, and disheartened at the appearance of the sea before them, which continued to exhibit a mere wilderness of islands. They remonstrated, therefore, against persisting any longer in this voyage. They had already followed the coast far enough to satisfy

[1] Cura de los Palacios, cap. 123, MS.

their minds that it was a continent, and though they doubted not that civilized regions lay in the route they were pursuing, yet their provisions might be exhausted, and their vessels disabled, before they could arrive at them.

Columbus, as his imagination cooled, was himself aware of the inadequacy of his vessels to the contemplated voyage; but felt it of importance to his fame and to the popularity of his enterprises, to furnish satisfactory proofs that the land he had discovered was a continent. He therefore persisted four days longer in exploring the coast, as it bent to the southwest, until every one declared there could no longer be a doubt on the subject, for it was impossible so vast a continuity of land should belong to a mere island. The admiral was determined, however, that the fact should not rest on his own assertion merely, having had recent proofs of a disposition to gainsay his statements, and depreciate his discoveries. He sent round, therefore, a public notary, Fernand Perez de Luna, to each of the vessels, accompanied by four witnesses, who demanded formally of every person on board, from the captain to the shipboy, whether he had any doubt that the land before him was a continent, the beginning and end of the Indies, by which any one might return overland to Spain, and by pursuing the coast of which, they could soon arrive among civilized people. If any one entertained a doubt, he was called upon to express it, that it might be removed. On board of the vessels, as has been observed, were several experienced navigators and men well versed in the geographical knowledge of the times. They examined their maps and charts, and the reckonings and journals of the voyage, and after deliberating maturely, declared, under oath, that they had no doubt upon the subject. They grounded their belief principally upon their having coasted for three hundred and thirty-five leagues,[1] an extent un-

[1] This calculation evidently includes all the courses of the ships, in their various tacks along the coast. Columbus could hardly have

heard of as appertaining to an island, while the land continued to stretch forward interminably, bending towards the south, conformably to the description of the remote coasts of India.

Lest they should subsequently, out of malice or caprice, contradict the opinion thus solemnly avowed, it was proclaimed by the notary, that whoever should offend in such manner, if an officer, should pay a penalty of ten thousand maravedies; if a ship-boy, or person of like rank, he should receive a hundred lashes, and have his tongue cut out. A formal statement was afterwards drawn up by the notary, including the depositions and names of every individual; which document still exists.[1] This singular process took place near that deep bay called by some the bay of Philipina, by others of Cortes. At this very time, as has been remarked, a ship-boy from the mast-head might have overlooked the group of islands to the south, and beheld the open sea beyond.[2] Two or three days further sail would have carried Columbus round the extremity of Cuba; would have dispelled his illusion, and might have given an entirely different course to his subsequent discoveries. In his present conviction he lived and died; believing, to his last hour, that Cuba was the extremity of the Asiatic continent.

Relinquishing all further investigation of the coast, he stood to the southeast on the 13th of June, and soon came in sight of a large island with mountains rising majestically among this labyrinth of little keys. To this he gave the name of Evangelista. It is at present known as the island of Pines, and is celebrated for its excellent mahogany.

Here he anchored, and took in a supply of wood and

made such an error as to have given this extent to the southern side of the island, even including the inflections of the coast.

[1] Navarrete, Colec, tom. ii.

[2] Muñoz, Hist. N. Mundo, lib. v. p. 217.

water. He then stood to the south, along the shores of the island, hoping by turning its southern extremity to find an open route eastward for Hispaniola, and intending, on his way, to run along the southern side of Jamaica. He had not proceeded far before he came to what he supopsed to be a channel, opening to the southeast between Evangelista and some opposite island. After entering for some distance, however, he found himself inclosed in a deep bay, being the Lagoon of Siguanca, which penetrates far into the island.

Observing dismay painted on the faces of his crew at finding themselves thus land-locked and almost destitute of provisions, Columbus cheered them with encouraging words, and resolved to extricate himself from this perplexing maze by retracing his course along Cuba. Leaving the Lagoon, therefore, he returned to his last anchoring place, and set sail thence on the 25th of June, navigating back through the groups of islands between Evangelista and Cuba, and across a tract of the White Sea, which had so much appalled his people. Here he experienced a repetition of the anxieties, perils, and toils which had beset him in his advance along the coast. The crews were alarmed by the frequent changes in the color of the water, sometimes green, sometimes almost black, at other times as white as milk; at one time they fancied themselves surrounded by rocks, at another the sea appeared to be a vast sand-bank. On the 30th of June, the admiral's ship ran aground with such violence as to sustain great injury. Every effort to extricate her by sending out anchors astern was ineffectual, and it was necessary to drag her over the shoal by the prow. At length they emerged from the clusters of islands called the Jardins and Jardinelles, and came to the open part of the coast of Cuba. Here they once more sailed along the beautiful and fertile province of Ornofay, and were again delighted with fragrant and honeyed airs wafted from the land. Among the mingled odors, the admiral fancied he could perceive that of storax proceeding from the smoke of fires blazing on the shores.[1]

Here, Columbus sought some convenient harbor where he might procure wood and water, and allow his crews to enjoy repose and the recreations of the land; for they were exceedingly enfeebled and emaciated by the toils and privations of the voyage. For nearly two months they had been struggling with perpetual difficulties and dangers, and suffering from a scarcity of provisions. Among these uninhabited keys and drowned shores, their supplies from the natives had been precarious and at wide intervals; nor could the fresh provisions thus furnished last above a day, from the heat and humidity of the climate. It was the same case with any fish they might chance to catch, so that they had to depend almost entirely upon their daily allowance of ships' provisions, which was reduced to a pound of mouldy bread, and a small portion of wine. With joy, therefore, they anchored on the 7th of July in the mouth of a fine river, in this genial and abundant region. The cacique of the neighborhood, who reigned over an extensive territory, received the admiral with demonstrations of mingled joy and reverence, and his subjects came laden with whatever their country offorded, utias, birds of various kinds, particularly large pigeons, cassava bread, and fruits of a rich and aromatic flavor.

It was a custom with Columbus in all remarkable places which he visited, to erect crosses in conspicuous situations, to denote the discovery of the country, and its subjugation to the true faith. He ordered a large cross of wood, therefore, to be elevated on the bank of this river. This was done on a Sunday morning with great ceremony, and the celebration of a solemn mass. When he disembarked for this purpose, he was met upon the shore by the cacique,

---

[1] Humboldt (in his Essai Polit., tom. ii. p. 24) speaks of the fragrance of flowers and honey which exhales from this same coast, and which is perceptible to a considerable distance at sea.

and his principal favorite, a venerable Indian, fourscore years of age, of grave and dignified deportment. The old man brought a string of beads, of a kind to which the Indians attached a mystic value, and a calabash of a delicate kind of fruit; these he presented to the admiral in token of amity. He and the cacique then each took him by the hand and proceeded with him to the grove, where preparations had been made for the celebration of the mass: a multitude of the natives followed. While mass was performing in this natural temple, the Indians looked on with awe and reverence, perceiving from the tones and gesticulations of the priest, the lighted tapers, the smoking incense, and the devotion of the Spaniards, that it must be a ceremony of a sacred and mysterious nature. When the service was ended, the old man of fourscore, who had contemplated it with profound attention, approached Columbus, and made him an oration in the Indian manner.

"This which thou hast been doing," said he, " is well, for it appears to be thy manner of giving thanks to God. I am told that thou hast lately come to these lands with a mighty force, and subdued many countries, spreading great fear among the people; but be not, therefore, vainglorious. Know that, according to our belief, the souls of men have two journeys to perform after they have departed from the body. One to a place, dismal, and foul, and covered with darkness, prepared for those who have been unjust and cruel to their fellow-men; the other pleasant and full of delight, for such as have promoted peace on earth. If, then, thou art mortal and dost expect to die, and dost believe that each one shall be rewarded according to his deeds, beware that thou wrongfully hurt no man, nor do harm to those who have done no harm to thee."[1] The admiral, to whom this speech was explained by his Lucayan interpreter, Diego Colon, was greatly moved by

[1] Herrera, decad. i. lib. xi. cap. 14. Hist. del Almirante, cap. 57. Peter Martyr, decad. i. lib. iii. Cura de los Palacios, cap. 130.

the simple eloquence of this untutored savage. He told him in reply that he rejoiced to hear his doctrine respecting the future state of the soul, having supposed that no belief of the kind existed among the inhabitants of these countries. That he had been sent among them by his sovereigns, to teach them the true religion; to protect them from harm and injury; and especially to subdue and punish their enemies and persecutors, the Cannibals. That, therefore, all innocent and peaceable men might look up to him with confidence, as an assured friend and protector.

The old man was overjoyed at these words, but was equally astonished to learn that the admiral, whom he considered so great and powerful, was yet but a subject. His wonder increased when the interpreter told him of the riches, and splendor, and power of the Spanish monarchs, and of the wonderful things he had beheld on his visit to Spain. Finding himself listened to with eager curiosity by the multitude, the interpreter went on to describe the objects which had most struck his mind in the country of the white men. The splendid cities, the vast churches, the troops of horsemen, the great animals of various kinds, the pompous festivals and tournaments of the court, the glittering armies, and, above all, the bull-fights. The Indians all listened in mute amazement, but the old man was particularly excited. He was of a curious and wandering disposition, and had been a great voyager, having, according to his account, visited Jamaica, and Hispaniola, and the remote parts of Cuba.[1] A sudden desire now seized him to behold the glorious country thus described, and, old as he was, he offered to embark with the admiral. His wife and children, however, beset him with such lamentations and remonstrances, that he was obliged to abandon the intention, though he did it with great reluctance, asking repeatedly if the land they spoke of were not heaven, for it seemed to him impossible that earth could produce such wonderful beings.[2]

[1] Hist. del Almirante, cap. 57.   [2] Peter Martyr, decad. i. lib. iii.

CHAPTER VI.

COASTING VOYAGE ALONG THE SOUTH SIDE OF JAMAICA.

[1494.]

COLUMBUS remained for several days at anchor in the river; to which, from the Mass performed on its banks, he gave the name of Rio de la Misa. At length, on the 16th of July, he took leave of the friendly cacique and his ancient counselor, who beheld his departure with sorrowful countenances. He took a young Indian with him from this place, whom he afterwards sent to the Spanish sovereigns. Leaving to the left the Queen's Gardens, he steered south for the broad open sea and deep blue water, until having a free navigation he could stand eastward for Hispaniola. He had scarcely got clear of the islands, however, when he was assailed by furious gusts of wind and rain, which for two days pelted his crazy vessels, and harassed his enfeebled crews. At length, as he approached Cape Cruz, a violent squall struck the ships, and nearly threw them on their beam ends. Fortunately they were able to take in sail immediately, and, letting go their largest anchors, rode out the transient gale. The admiral's ship was so strained by the injuries received among the islands, that she leaked at every seam, and the utmost exertions of the weary crew could not prevent the water from gaining on her. At length they were enabled to reach Cape Cruz, where they anchored on the 18th July, and remained three days, receiving the same hospitable succor from the natives that they had experienced on their former visit. The wind continuing contrary for the return to Hispaniola, Columbus, on the 22d July, stood across for Jamaica, to complete the circumnavigation of that island. For nearly a month he continued beating to the eastward along its southern coast, experiencing just such variable winds and evening showers as

24

had prevailed along the shores of Cuba. Every evening
he was obliged to anchor under the land, often at nearly
the same place whence he had sailed in the morning. The
natives no longer manifested hostility, but followed the
ships in their canoes, bringing supplies of provisions. Columbus was so much delighted with the verdure, freshness,
and fertility of this noble island, that, had the state of his
vessels and crews permitted, he would gladly have remained to explore the interior. He spoke with admiration
of its frequent and excellent harbors, but was particularly
pleased with a great bay, containing seven islands, and surrounded by numerous villages.[1] Anchoring here one
evening, he was visited by a cacique who resided in a large
village, situated on an eminence of the loftiest and most
fertile of the islands. He came attended by a numerous
train, bearing refreshments, and manifested great curiosity
in his inquiries concerning the Spaniards, their ships, and
the region whence they came. The admiral made his
customary reply, setting forth the great power and the benign intentions of the Spanish sovereigns. The Lucayan
interpreter again enlarged upon the wonders he had beheld
in Spain, the prowess of the Spaniards, the countries they
had visited and subjugated, and, above all, their having
made descents on the islands of the Caribs, routed their
formidable inhabitants, and carried several of them into
captivity. To these accounts the cacique and his followers
remained listening in profound attention until the night
was advanced.

The next morning the ships were under way and standing along the coast with a light wind and easy sail, when
they beheld three canoes issuing from among the islands of
the bay. They approached in regular order; one, which
was very large and handsomely carved and painted, was in
the centre, a little in advance of the two others, which

[1] From the description, this must be the great bay east of Portland
Point, at the bottom of which is Old Harbor.

appeared to attend and guard it. In this was seated the
cacique and his family, consisting of his wife, two daughters,
two sons, and five brothers. One of the daughters was
eighteen years of age, beautiful in form and countenance;
her sister was somewhat younger; both were naked, according to the custom of these islands, but were of modest
demeanor. In the prow of the canoe stood the standard-
bearer of the cacique, clad in a mantle of variegated
feathers, with a tuft of gay plumes on his head, and bearing
in his hand a fluttering white banner. Two Indians with
caps or helmets of feathers of uniform shape and color, and
their faces painted in a similar manner, beat upon tabors;
two others, with hats curiously wrought of green feathers,
held trumpets of a fine black wood, ingeniously carved;
there were six others, in large hats of white feathers, who
appeared to be guards to the cacique.

Having arrived along side of the admiral's ship, the
cacique entered on board with all his train. He appeared
in full regalia. Around his head was a band of small
stones of various colors, but principally green, symmetri-
cally arranged, with large white stones at intervals, and
connected in front by a large jewel of gold. Two plates of
gold were suspended to his ears by rings of very small
green stones. To a necklace of white beads, of a kind
deemed precious by them, was suspended a large plate, in
the form of a fleur-de-lys, of guanin, an inferior species of
gold; and a girdle of variegated stones, similar to those
round his head, completed his regal decorations. His wife
was adorned in a similar manner, having also a very small
apron of cotton, and bands of the same round her arms
and legs. The daughters were without ornaments, excepting the eldest and handsomest, who had a girdle of small
stones, from which was suspended a tablet, the size of an
ivy leaf, composed of various colored stones embroidered
on network of cotton.

When the cacique entered on board the ship, he dis-

tributed presents of the productions of his island among
the officers and men. The admiral was at this time in his
cabin, engaged in his morning devotions. When he appeared on deck, the chieftain hastened to meet him with an
animated countenance. "My friend," said he, "I have
determined to leave my country, and to accompany thee.
I have heard from these Indians who are with thee, of the
irresistible power of thy sovereigns, and of the many nations thou hast subdued in their name. Whoever refuses
obedience to thee is sure to suffer. Thou hast destroyed
the canoes and dwellings of the Caribs, slaying their warriors, and carrying into captivity their wives and children.
All the islands are in dread of thee; for who can withstand
thee now that thou knowest the secrets of the land, and the
weakness of the people? Rather, therefore, than thou
shouldst take away my dominions, I will embark with all
my household in thy ships, and will go to do homage to thy
king and queen, and to behold their country, of which thy
Indians relate such wonders." When this speech was explained to Columbus, and he beheld the wife, the sons, and
daughters of the cacique, and thought upon the snares to
which their ignorance and simplicity would be exposed,
he was touched with compassion, and determined not
to take them from their native land. He replied to the
cacique, therefore, that he received him under his protection as a vassal of his sovereigns, but having many lands
yet to visit before he returned to his country, he would at
some future time fulfill his desire. Then taking leave with
many expressions of amity, the cacique, with his wife and
daughters, and all his retinue, re-embarked in the canoes,
returning reluctantly to their island, and the ships continued on their course.[1]

[1] Hitherto, in narrating the voyage of Columbus along the coast
of Cuba, I have been guided principally by the manuscript history
of the curate de los Palacios. His account is the most clear and satisfactory as to names, dates, and routes, and contains many charac-

CHAPTER VII.

VOYAGE ALONG THE SOUTH SIDE OF HISPANIOLA, AND
RETURN TO ISABELLA.

[1494.]

ON the 19th of August, Columbus lost sight of the
eastern extremity of Jamaica, to which he gave the name
of Cape Farol, at present called Point Morant. Steering
eastward, he beheld, on the following day, that long peninsula of Hispaniola, known by the name of Cape Tiburon,
but to which he gave the name of Cape San Miguel. He
was not aware that it was a part of the island of Hayti,
until, coasting along its southern side, a cacique came off
on the 23d of August, and called him by his title, address-
ing him with several words of Castilian. The sound of
these words spread joy through the ship, and the weary
seamen heard with delight that they were on the southern
coast of Hispaniola. They had still, however, many toilsome days before them. The weather was boisterous, the
wind contrary and capricious, and the ships were separated
from each other. About the end of August, Columbus
anchored at a small island, or rather rock, which rises
singly out of the sea opposite to a long cape, stretching
southward from the centre of the island, to which he gave
the name of Cape Beata. The rock at which he anchored

teristic particulars not inserted in any other history. His sources
of information were of the highest kind. Columbus was his guest
after his return to Spain in 1496, and left with him manuscripts,
journals, and memorandums; from these he made extracts, collating
them with the letters of Doctor Chanca, and other persons of note
who had accompanied the admiral.

I have examined two copies of the MS. of the curate de los Palacios, both in the possession of O. Rich, Esq. One, written in an ancient handwriting, in the early part of the sixteenth century, varies
from the other, but only in a few trivial particulars.

had the appearance, at a distance, of a tall ship under sail, from which circumstance the admiral called it " Alto Velo." Several seamen were ordered to climb to the top of the island, which commanded a great extent of ocean, and to look out for the other ships. Nothing of them was to be seen. On their return, the sailors killed eight sea-wolves, which were sleeping on the sands; they also knocked down many pigeons and other birds with sticks, and took others with the hand; for in this unfrequented island, the animals seemed to have none of that wildness and timidity produced by the hostility of man.

Being rejoined by the two caravels, he continued along the coast, passing the beautiful country watered by the branches of the Neyva, where a fertile plain, covered with villages and groves, extended into the interior. After proceeding some distance farther to the east, the admiral learnt from the natives who came off to the ships, that several Spaniards from the settlement had penetrated to their province. From all that he could learn from these people, every thing appeared to be going on well in the island. Encouraged by the tranquillity of the interior, he landed nine men here, with orders to traverse the island, and give tidings of his safe arrival on the coast.

Continuing to the eastward, he sent a boat on shore for water near a large village in a plain. The inhabitants issued forth with bows and arrows to give battle, while others were provided with cords to bind prisoners. These were the natives of Higuey, the eastern province of Hispaniola. They were the most warlike people of the island, having been inured to arms from the frequent descent of the Caribs. They were said also to make use of poisoned arrows. In the present instance, their hostility was but in appearance. When the crew landed, they threw by their weapons, and brought various articles of food, and asked for the admiral, whose fame had spread throughout the island, and in whose justice and magnanimity all appeared to repose confidence. After leaving this place, the weather, which had been so long variable and adverse, assumed a threatening appearance. A huge fish, as large as a moderate-sized whale, raised itself out of the water one day, having a shell on its neck like that of a tortoise, two great fins like wings, and a tail like that of a tunny fish. At sight of this fish, and at the indications of the. clouds and sky, Columbus anticipated an approaching storm, and sought for some secure harbor.[1] He found a channel opening between Hispaniola and a small island, called by the Indians Adamaney, but to which he gave the name of Saona: here he took refuge, anchoring beside a key or islet in the middle of the channel. On the night of his arrival there was an eclipse of the moon, and taking an observation, he found the difference of longitude between Saona and Cadiz to be five hours and twenty-three minutes.[2] This is upwards of eighteen degrees more than the true longitude; an error which must have resulted from the incorrectness of his table of eclipses.[3]

For eight days the admiral's ship remained weatherbound in this channel, during which time he suffered great anxiety for the fate of the other vessels, which remained at sea, exposed to the violence of the storm. They escaped, however, uninjured, and once more rejoined him when the weather had moderated.

Leaving the channel of Saona, they reached, on the 24th of September, the eastern extremity of Hispaniola, to which Columbus gave the name of Cape San Rafael, at present known as Cape Engaño. Hence they stood to the southeast, touching at the island of Mona, or, as the Indians called it, Amona, situated between Porto Rico and

[1] Herrera, Hist. Ind., decad. i. lib. ii. cap. 15. Hist. del Almirante, cap. 59.

[2] Herrera, ubi sup. Hist. Almirante, ubi sup.

[3] Five hours, twenty-five minutes, are equal to 80° 45′; whereas the true longitude of Saona is 62° 20′ west of Cadiz.

Hispaniola. It was the intention of Columbus, notwithstanding the condition of the ships, to continue farther
eastward, and to complete the discovery of the Caribbee
Islands, but his physical strength did not correspond to the
efforts of his lofty spirit.[1] The extraordinary fatigues both
of mind and body, during an anxious and harassing voyage
of five months, had preyed upon his frame. He had
shared in all the hardships and privations of the com-
monest seaman. He had put himself upon the same scanty
allowance, and exposed himself to the same buffetings of
wind and weather. But he had other cares and trials
from which his people were exempt. When the sailor,
worn out with the labors of his watch, slept soundly
amidst the howling of the storm, the anxious commander
maintained his painful vigil, through long sleepless nights,
amidst the pelting of the tempest, and the drenching surges
of the sea. The safety of his ships depended upon his
watchfulness; but, above all, he felt that a jealous nation,
and an expecting world, were anxiously awaiting the result of his enterprise. During a great part of the present
voyage, he had been excited by the constant hope of soon
arriving at the known parts of India, and by the anticipation of a triumphant return to Spain, through the
regions of the East, after circumnavigating the globe.
When disappointed in these expectations, he was yet stimulated by a conflict with incessant hardships and perils, as
he made his way back against contrary winds and storms.
The moment he was relieved from all solicitude, and beheld himself in a known and tranquil sea, the excitement
suddenly ceased, and mind and body sank exhausted by
almost superhuman exertions. The very day on which he
sailed from Mona, he was struck with a sudden malady,
which deprived him of memory, of sight, and all his faculties. He fell into a deep lethargy, resembling death itself.
His crew, alarmed at this profound torpor, feared that

[1] Muñoz, Hist. N. Mundo, lib. v. sec. 22.

death was really at hand. They abandoned, therefore, all further prosecution of the voyage; and spreading their sails to the east wind so prevalent in those seas, bore Columbus back, in a state of complete insensibility, to the harbor of Isabella.

BOOK VIII.

CHAPTER I.

ARRIVAL OF THE ADMIRAL AT ISABELLA.—CHARACTER OF BARTHOLOMEW COLUMBUS.

[1494. Sept. 4.]

THE sight of the little squadron of Columbus standing once more into the harbor was hailed with joy by such of the inhabitants of Isabella as remained faithful to him. The long time that had elapsed since his departure on this adventurous voyage, without any tidings arriving from him, had given rise to the most serious apprehensions for his safety; and it began to be feared that he had fallen a victim to his enterprising spirit in some remote part of these unknown seas.

A joyful and heartfelt surprise awaited the admiral on his arrival, in finding at his bedside his brother Bartholomew, the companion of his youth, his confidential coadjutor, and in a manner his second self, from whom he had been separated for several years. It will be recollected, that about the time of the admiral's departure from Portugal, he had commissioned Bartholomew to repair to England, and propose his project of discovery to King Henry VII. Of this application to the English court no precise particulars are known. Fernando Columbus states that his uncle, in the course of his voyage, was captured and plundered by a corsair, and reduced to such poverty, that he had for a long time to struggle for a mere subsistence by making sea-charts; so that some years elapsed before he made his ap-

plication to the English monarch. Las Casas thinks that
he did not immediately proceed to England, having found
a memorandum in his handwriting, by which it would appear that he accompanied Bartholomew Diaz in 1486, in
his voyage along the coast of Africa, in the service of the
king of Portugal, in the course of which voyage was discovered the Cape of Good Hope.[1]

[1] The memorandum cited by Las Casas (Hist. Ind. lib., i. cap. 7) is
curious, though not conclusive. He says that he found it in an old
book belonging to Christopher Columbus, containing the works of
Pedro de Aliaco. It was written in the margin of a treatise on the
form of the globe, in the handwriting of Bartholomew Columbus,
which was well known to Las Casas, as he had many of his letters
in his possession. The memorandum was in a barbarous mixture of
Latin and Spanish, and to the following effect.

In the year 1488, in December, arrived at Lisbon Bartholomew
Diaz, captain of three caravels, which the king of Portugal sent to
discover Guinea, and brought accounts that he had discovered six
hundred leagues of territory, four hundred and fifty to the south and
one hundred and fifty north, to a cape, named by him the Cape of
Good Hope; and that by the astrolabe he found the cape 45 degrees
beyond the equinoctial line. This cape was 3100 leagues distant
from Lisbon: the which the said captain says he set down, league
by league, in a chart of navigation presented by him to the king of
Portugal; in all which, adds the writer, I was present (in quibus
omnibus interfui).

Las Casas expresses a doubt whether Bartholomew wrote this note
for himself, or on the part of his brother, but infers that one, or both,
were in this expedition. The inference may be correct with respect
to Bartholomew, but Christopher, at the time specified, was at the
Spanish court.

Las Casas accounts for a difference in date between the foregoing
memorandum and the chronicles of the voyage; the former making
the return of Diaz in the year '88, the latter '87. This he observes
might be because some begin to count the year after Christmas, others at the first of January: and the expedition sailed about the end
of August '86, and returned in December '87, after an absence of
seventeen months.

NOTE.—Since publishing the first edition of this work, the author
being in Seville, and making researches in the Bibliotheca Colum-

It is but justice to the memory of Henry VII to say, that when the proposition was eventually made to him, it met with a more ready attention than from any other sov-

---

bina, the library given by Fernando Columbus to the cathedral of that city, he came accidentally upon the above-mentioned copy of the work of Pedro Aliaco. He ascertained it to be the same by finding the above-cited memorandum written on the margin, at the eighth chapter of the tract called "Imago Mundi." It is an old volume in folio, bound in parchment, published soon after the invention of printing, containing a collection in Latin of astronomical and cosmographical tracts of Pedro (or Peter) de Aliaco, archbishop of Cambray and cardinal, and of his disciple, John Gerson. Pedro de Aliaco was born in 1340, and died, according to some in 1416, according to others in 1425. He was the author of many works, and one of the most learned and scientific men of his day. Las Casas is of opinion that his writings had more effect in stimulating Columbus to his enterprise than those of any other author. "His work was so familiar to Columbus, that he had filled its whole margin with Latin notes in his handwriting; citing many things which he had read and gathered elsewhere. This book, which was very old," continues Las Casas, "I had many times in my hands; and I drew some things from it, written in Latin by the said admiral Christopher Columbus, to verify certain points appertaining to his history, of which I before was in doubt." (Hist. Ind., lib. i. cap. 11.)

It was a great satisfaction to the author, therefore, to discover this identical volume, this *Vade Mecum* of Columbus, in a state of good preservation. [It is in the cathedral library, E——G, Tab. 178, No. 21.] The notes and citations mentioned by Las Casas are in Latin, with many abbreviations, written in a very small, but neat and distinct hand, and run throughout the volume; calling attention to the most striking passages, or to those which bear most upon the theories of Columbus; occasionally containing brief comments or citing the opinions of other authors, ancient and modern, either in support or contradiction of the text. The memorandum particularly cited by Las Casas, mentioning the voyage of Bartholomew Diaz to the Cape of Good Hope, is to disprove an opinion in the text, that the torrid zone was uninhabitable. This volume is a most curious and interesting document, the only one that remains of Columbus prior to his discovery. It illustrates his researches and in a manner the current of his thoughts, while as yet his great enterprise existed but in idea, and while he was seeking means to convince the world of its practi-

ereign. An agreement was actually made with Bartholomew for the prosecution of the enterprise, and the latter
departed for Spain in search of his brother. On reaching
Paris, he first received the joyful intelligence that the discovery was already made; that his brother had returned
to Spain in triumph; and was actually at the Spanish
court, honored by the sovereigns, caressed by the nobility,
and idolized by the people. The glory of Columbus already shed its rays upon his family, and Bartholomew
found himself immediately a person of importance. He
was noticed by the French monarch, Charles VIII, who,
understanding that he was low in purse, furnished him
with one hundred crowns to defray the expenses of his
journey to Spain. He reached Seville just as his brother
had departed on his second voyage. Bartholomew immediately repaired to the court, then at Valladolid, taking
with him his two nephews, Diego and Fernando, who were
to serve in quality of pages to Prince Juan.[1] He was
received with distinguished favor by the sovereigns; who,
finding him to be an able and accomplished navigator,
gave him the command of three ships freighted with supplies for the colony, and sent him to aid his brother in his
enterprises. He had again arrived too late; reaching Isabella just after the departure of the admiral for the coast
of Cuba.

The sight of this brother was an inexpressible relief to
Columbus, overwhelmed as he was by cares, and surrounded
by strangers. His chief dependence for sympathy and
assistance had hitherto been on his brother Don Diego;
but his mild and peaceable disposition rendered him little
capable of managing the concerns of a factious colony.
Bartholomew was of a different and more efficient character. He was prompt, active, decided, and of a fearless

cability. It will be found also to contain the grounds of many of his
opinions and speculations on a variety of subjects.

[1] Hist. del Almirante, cap. 60.

spirit; whatever he determined, he carried into instant execution, without regard to difficulty or danger. His person corresponded to his mind; it was tall, muscular, vigorous, and commanding. He had an air of great authority, but somewhat stern, wanting that sweetness and benignity which tempered the authoritative demeanor of the admiral. Indeed, there was a certain asperity in his temper, and a dryness and abruptness in his manners, which made him many enemies; yet notwithstanding these external defects, he was of a generous disposition, free from all arrogance or malevolence, and as placable as he was brave.

He was a thorough seaman, understanding both the theory and practice of his profession; having been formed, in a great measure, under the eye of the admiral, and being but little inferior to him in science. He was superior to him in the exercise of the pen, according to Las Casas, who had letters and manuscripts of both in his possession. He was acquainted with Latin, but does not appear to have been highly educated; his knowledge, like that of his brother, being chiefly derived from a long course of varied experience and attentive observation. Equally vigorous and penetrating in intellect with the admiral, but less enthusiastic in spirit and soaring in imagination, and with less simplicity of heart, he surpassed him in the subtle and adroit management of business, was more attentive to his interests, and had more of that worldly wisdom which is so important in the ordinary concerns of life. His genius might never have enkindled him to the sublime speculation which ended in the discovery of a world, but his practical sagacity was calculated to turn that discovery to advantage. Such is the description of Bartholomew Columbus, as furnished by the venerable Las Casas from personal observation;[1] and it will be found to accord with his actions throughout the remaining history of the admiral, in the events of which he takes a conspicuous part.

[1] Las Casas, Hist. Ind., lib. i. cap. 29.

Anxious to relieve himself from the pressure of public business, which weighed heavily upon him during his present malady, Columbus immediately invested his brother Bartholomew with the title and authority of Adelantado, an office equivalent to that of lieutenant-governor. He considered himself entitled to do so from the articles of his arrangement with the sovereigns, but it was looked upon by King Ferdinand as an undue assumption of power, and gave great offence to that jealous monarch, who was exceedingly tenacious of the prerogatives of the crown, and considered dignities of this rank and importance as only to be conferred by royal mandate.[1] Columbus, however, was not actuated in this appointment by a mere desire to aggrandize his family. He felt the importance of his brother's assistance in the present critical state of the colony, but that this co-operation would be inefficient unless it bore the stamp of high official authority. In fact, during the few months that he had been absent, the whole island had become a scene of discord and violence, in consequence of the neglect, or rather the flagrant violation, of those rules which he had prescribed for the maintenance of its tranquillity. A brief retrospect of the recent affairs of the colony is here necessary to explain their present confusion. It will exhibit one of the many instances in which Columbus was doomed to reap the fruits of the evil seed sown by his adversaries.

CHAPTER II.

MISCONDUCT OF DON PEDRO MARGARITE AND HIS DEPARTURE FROM THE ISLAND.

[1494.]

IT will be recollected, that before departing on his voyage, Columbus had given the command of the army to

[1] Las Casas, Hist. Ind., lib. i. cap. 101.

Don Pedro Margarite, with orders to make a military tour of the island, awing the natives by a display of military force, but conciliating their good-will by equitable and amicable treatment.

The island was at this time divided into five domains, each governed by a cacique, of absolute and hereditary power, to whom a great number of inferior caciques yielded tributary allegiance. The first or most important domain comprised the middle part of the royal Vega. It was a rich, lovely country, partly cultivated after the imperfect manner of the natives, partly covered with noble forests, studded with Indian towns, and watered by numerous rivers, many of which, rolling down from the mountains of Cibao, on its southern frontier, had gold-dust mingled with their sands. The name of the cacique was Guarionex, whose ancestors had long ruled over the province.

The second, called Marien, was under the sway of Guacanagari, on whose coast Columbus had been wrecked in his first voyage. It was a large and fertile territory, extending along the northern coast from Cape St. Nicholas, at the western extremity of the Island, to the great river Yagui, afterwards called Monte Christi, and including the northern part of the royal Vega, since called the plain of Cape François, now Cape Haytien.

The third bore the name of Maguana. It extended along the southern coast from the river Ozema to the lakes, and comprised the chief part of the centre of the island lying along the southern face of the mountains of Cibao, the mineral district of Hayti. It was under the dominion of the Carib cacique Caonabo, the most fierce and puissant of the savage chieftains, and the inveterate enemy of the white men.

The fourth took its name from Xaragua, a large lake, and was the most populous and extensive of all. It comprised the whole western coast, including the long promontory of Cape Tiburon, and extended for a considerable

25

distance along the southern side of the island. The inhabitants were finely formed, had a noble air, a more agreeable elocution, and more soft and graceful manners than the natives of the other parts of the island. The sovereign was named Behechio; his sister, Anacaona, celebrated throughout the island for her beauty, was the favorite wife of the neighboring cacique Caonabo.

The fifth domain was Higuey, and occupied the whole eastern part of the island, being bounded on the north by the Bay of Samana and part of the river Yuna, and on the west by the Ozema. The inhabitants were the most active and warlike people of the island, having learnt the use of the bow and arrow from the Caribs, who made frequent descents upon their coasts; they were said also to make use of poisoned weapons. Their bravery, however, was but comparative, and was found eventually of little avail against the terror of European arms. They were governed by a cacique named Cotubanama.[1]

Such were the five territorial divisions of the island at the time of its discovery. The amount of its population has never been clearly ascertained; some have stated it at a million of souls, though this is considered an exaggeration. It must, however, have been very numerous, and sufficient, in case of any general hostility, to endanger the safety of a handful of Europeans. Columbus trusted for safety partly to the awe inspired by the weapons and horses of the Spaniards, and the idea of their superhuman nature, but chiefly to the measures he had taken to conciliate the good-will of the Indians by gentle and beneficent treatment.

Margarite set forth on his expedition with the greater part of the forces, leaving Alonzo de Ojeda in command of the fortress of St. Thomas. Instead, however, of commencing by exploring the rough mountains of Cibao, as he had been commanded, he descended into the fertile region of the Vega. Here he lingered among the populous and

[1] Charlevoix, Hist. St. Domingo, lib. i. p. 69.

hospitable Indian villages, forgetful of the object of his command, and of the instructions left him by the admiral. A commander who lapses from duty himself, is little calculated to enforce discipline. The sensual indulgences of Margarite were imitated by his followers, and his army soon became little better than a crew of riotous marauders. The Indians, for a time, supplied them with provisions with their wonted hospitality, but the scanty stores of those abstemious yet improvident people were soon exhausted by the Spaniards; one of whom they declared would consume more in a day than would support an Indian for a month. If provisions were withheld, or scantily furnished, they were taken with violence; nor was any compensation given to the natives, nor means taken to soothe their irritation. The avidity for gold also led to a thousand acts of injustice and oppression; but above all the Spaniards outraged the dearest feelings of the natives by their licentious conduct with respect to the women. In fact, instead of guests, they soon assumed the tone of imperious masters; instead of enlightened benefactors, they became sordid and sensual oppressors.

Tidings of these excesses, and of the disgust and impatience they were awakening among the natives, soon reached Don Diego Columbus. With the concurrence of the council, he wrote to Margarite reprehending his conduct, and requesting him to proceed on the military tour, according to the commands of the admiral. The pride of Margarite took fire at this reproof; he considered, or rather pretended to consider, himself independent in his command, and above all responsibility to the council for his conduct. Being of an ancient family, also, and a favorite of the king, he affected to look down with contempt upon the newly-coined nobility of Diego Columbus. His letters, in reply to the orders of the president and council, were couched in a tone either of haughty contumely or of military defiance. He continued with his followers quartered in the Vega, persisting in a course of outrages and oppressions fatal to the tranquillity of the island.

He was supported in his arrogant defiance of authority by the cavaliers and adventurers of noble birth who were in the colony, and who had been deeply wounded in the proud punctilio so jealously guarded by a Spaniard. They could not forget nor forgive the stern equity exercised by the admiral in a time of emergency, in making them submit to the privations and share the labors of the vulgar. Still less could they brook the authority of his brother Diego, destitute of his high personal claims to distinction. They formed, therefore, a kind of aristocratical faction in the colony; affecting to consider Columbus and his family as mere mercenary and upstart foreigners, building up their own fortunes at the expense of the toils and sufferings of the community, and the degradation of Spanish hidalgos and cavaliers.

In addition to these partisans, Margarite had a powerful ally in his fellow-countryman, Friar Boyle, the head of the religious fraternity, one of the members of the council, and apostolical vicar of the New World. It is not easy to ascertain the original cause of the hostility of this holy friar to the admiral, who was never wanting in respect to the clergy. Various altercations, however, had taken place between them. Some say that the friar interfered in respect to the strict measures deemed necessary by the admiral for the security of the colony; others that he resented the fancied indignity offered to himself and his household, in putting them on the same short allowance with the common people. He appears, however, to have been generally disappointed and disgusted with the sphere of action afforded by the colony, and to have looked back with regret to the Old World. He had none of that enthusiastic zeal and persevering self-devotion, which induced so many of the Spanish missionaries to brave all the hardships and privations of the New World, in the hope of converting its pagan inhabitants.

Encouraged and fortified by such powerful partisans, Margarite really began to consider himself above the temporary authorities of the island. Whenever he came to Isabella, he took no notice of Don Diego Columbus, nor paid any respect to the council, but acted as if he had paramount command. He formed a cabal of most of those who were disaffected to Columbus, and discontented with their abode in the colony. Among these the leading agitator was Friar Boyle. It was concerted among them to take possession of the ships which had brought out Don Bartholomew Columbus, and to return in them to Spain. Both Margarite and Boyle possessed the favor of the king, and they deemed it would be an easy matter to justify their abandonment of their military and religious commands by a pretended zeal for the public good; hurrying home to represent the disastrous state of the country, through the tyranny and oppression of its rulers. Some have ascribed the abrupt departure of Margarite to his fear of a severe military investigation of his conduct on the return of the admiral; others to his having, in the course of his licentious amours, contracted a malady at that time new and unknown, and which he attributed to the climate, and hoped to cure by medical assistance in Spain. Whatever may have been the cause, his measures were taken with great precipitancy, without any consultation of the proper authorities, or any regard to the consequences of his departure. Accompanied by a band of malcontents, he and Friar Boyle took possession of some ships in the harbor, and set sail for Spain; the first general and apostle of the New World thus setting the flagrant example of unauthorized abandonment of their posts.

CHAPTER III.

TROUBLES WITH THE NATIVES.—ALONZO DE OJEDA BE-
SIEGED BY CAONABO.

[1494.]

THE departure of Pedro Margarite left the army without
a head, and put an end to what little restraint or discipline
remained.   There is no rabble so licentious as soldiery left
to their own direction in a defenceless country.. They now
roved about in bands, or singly, according to their caprice,
scattering themselves among the Indian villages, and indulging in all kinds of excesses, either as prompted by
avarice or sensuality.   The natives, indignant at having
their hospitality thus requited, refused any longer to furnish them with food. In a little while the Spaniards began
to experience the pressure of hunger, and seized upon provisions wherever they could be found, accompanying these
seizures with acts of wanton violence. At length, by a
series of flagrant outrages, the gentle and pacific nature of
this people was roused to resentment, and from confiding
and hospitable hosts, they were converted into vindictive
enemies. All the precautions enjoined by Columbus having
been neglected, the evils he had apprehended came to pass.
Though the Indians, naturally timid, dared not contend
with the Spaniards while they kept up any combined and
disciplined force, yet they took sanguinary vengeance on
them whenever they met with small parties or scattered individuals, roving about in quest of food. Encouraged by
these petty triumphs, and the impunity which seemed to
attend them, their hostilities grew more and more alarming.
Guatiguana, cacique of a large town on the banks of the
Grand River, in the dominions of Guarionex, sovereign of
the Vega, put to death ten Spaniards, who had quartered
themselves in his town, and outraged the inhabitants by

their licentiousness. He followed up this massacre by setting fire to a house in which forty-six Spaniards were lodged.[1] Flushed by this success, he threatened to attack a small fortress called Magdalena, which had recently been built in his neighborhood in the Vega; so that the commander, Luis de Arriaga, having but a feeble garrison, was obliged to remain shut up within its walls until relief should arrive from Isabella.

The most formidable enemy of the Spaniards, however, was Caonabo, the Carib cacique of Maguana. With natural talents for war, and intelligence superior to the ordinary range of savage intellect, he had a proud and daring spirit to urge him on, three valiant brothers to assist him. and a numerous tribe at his command.[2] He had always felt jealous of the intrusion of the white men into the island; but particularly exasperated by the establishment of the fortress of St. Thomas, erected in the very centre of his dominions. As long as the army lay within call in the Vega, he was deterred from any attack; but when, on the departure of Margarite, it became dismembered and dispersed, the time for striking a signal blow seemed arrived. The fortress remained isolated, with a garrison of only fifty men. By a sudden and secret movement, he might overwhelm it with his forces, and repeat the horrors which he had wreaked upon La Navidad.

The wily cacique, however, had a different kind of enemy to deal with in the commander of St. Thomas. Alonzo de Ojeda had been schooled in Moorish warfare. He was versed in all kinds of feints, stratagems, lurking ambuscades, and wild assaults. No man was more fitted, therefore, to cope with Indian warriors. He had a headlong courage, arising partly from the natural heat and violence of his disposition, and, in a great measure, from religious superstition. He had been engaged in wars with Moors and Indians, in public battles and private combats, in fights,

[1] Herrera, Hist. Ind., decad. i. lib. ii. cap. 16.   [2] Ibid.

feuds, and encounters of all kinds, to which he had been
prompted by a rash and fiery spirit, and a love of adventure; yet he had never been wounded, nor lost a drop of
blood. He began to doubt whether any weapon had power
to harm him, and to consider himself under the special protection of the holy Virgin. As a kind of religious talisman,
he had a small Flemish painting of the Virgin, given him
by his patron, Fonseca, bishop of Badajoz. This he constantly carried with him, in city, camp, or field, making it
the object of his frequent orisons and invocations. In garrison or encampment, it was suspended in his chamber or
his tent; in his rough expeditions in the wilderness, he
carried it in his knapsack, and whenever leisure permitted,
would take it out, fix it against a tree, and address his
prayers to this military patroness.[1] In a word, he swore by
the Virgin, he invoked the Virgin whether in brawl or
battle, and under the favor of the Virgin he was ready for
any enterprise or adventure. Such was this Alonzo de
Ojeda; bigoted in his devotion, reckless in his life, fearless
in his spirit, like many of the roving Spanish cavaliers of
those days. Though small in size, he was a prodigy of
strength and prowess; and the chroniclers of the early
discoveries relate marvels of his valor and exploits.

Having reconnoitred the fortress, Caonabo assembled ten
thousand warriors, armed with war clubs, bows and arrows,
and lances hardened in the fire; and making his way
secretly through the forests, came suddenly in the neighborhood, expecting to surprise the garrison in a state of
careless security. He found Ojeda's forces, however, drawn
up warily within his tower, which, being built upon an almost insulated height, with a river nearly surrounding it,
and the remaining space traversed by a deep ditch, set at
defiance an attack by naked warriors.

Foiled in his attempt, Caonabo now hoped to reduce it

[1] Herrera, Hist. Ind., decad. i. lib. viii. cap. 4.   Pizarro, Varones
Ilustres, cap. 8.

by famine. For this purpose, he distributed his warriors through the adjacent forests; and waylaid every pass, so as to intercept any supplies brought by the natives, and to cut off any foraging party from the fortress. This siege, or investment, lasted for thirty days,[1] and reduced the garrison to great distress. There is a traditional anecdote, which Oviedo relates of Pedro Margarite, the former commander of this fortress, but which may with more probability be ascribed to Alonzo de Ojeda, as having occurred during this siege. At a time when the garrison was sore pressed by famine, an Indian gained access to the fort, bringing a couple of wood-pigeons for the table of the commander. The latter was in an apartment of the tower surrounded by several of his officers. Seeing them regard the birds with the wistful eyes of famishing men, "It is a pity," said he, "that here is not enough to give us all a meal; I cannot consent to feast while the rest of you are starving:" so saying, he turned loose the pigeons from a window of the tower.

During the siege, Ojeda displayed the greatest activity of spirit and fertility of resource. He baffled all the arts of the Carib chieftain, concerting stratagems of various kinds to relieve the garrison and annoy the foe. He sallied forth whenever the enemy appeared in any force, leading the van with that headlong valor for which he was noted; making great slaughter with his single arm, and, as usual, escaping unhurt from amidst showers of darts and arrows.

Caonabo saw many of his bravest warriors slain. His forces were diminishing, for the Indians, unused to any protracted operations of war, grew weary of this siege, and returned daily in numbers to their homes. He gave up all further attempt, therefore, on the fortress, and retired, filled with admiration of the prowess and achievements of Ojeda.[2]

[1] P. Martyr, decad. i. lib. iv.
[2] Oviedo, Cronica de las Indias, lib. iii. cap. 1.

The restless chieftain was not discouraged by the failure
of this enterprise, but meditated schemes of a bolder and
more extensive nature.   Prowling in secret in the vicinity
of Isabella, he noted the enfeebled state of the settlement.[1]
Many of the inhabitants were suffering under various
maladies, and most of the men capable of bearing arms
were distributed about the country.   He now conceived
the project of a general league among the caciques, to surprise and overwhelm the settlement, and massacre the
Spaniards wherever they could be found.   This handful
of intruders once exterminated, he trusted the island would
be delivered from all further molestation of the kind;
little dreaming of the hopeless nature of the contest, and
that where the civilized man once plants his foot, the
power of the savage is gone for ever.

Reports of the profligate conduct of the Spaniards had
spread throughout the island, and inspired hatred and hostility even among tribes who had never beheld them, nor
suffered from their misdeeds.   Caonabo found three of the
sovereign caciques inclined to co-operate with him, though
impressed with deep awe of the supernatural power of the
Spaniards, and of their terrific arms and animals.   The
league, however, met with unexpected opposition in the fifth
cacique, Guacanagari, the sovereign of Marien.   His conduct in this time of danger completely manifested the injustice of the suspicions which had been entertained of him by
the Spaniards.   He refused to join the other caciques with
his forces, or to violate those laws of hospitality by which
he had considered himself bound to protect and aid the
white men, ever since they had been shipwrecked on his
coast.   He remained quietly in his dominions, entertaining
at his own expense a hundred of the suffering soldiery, and
supplying all their wants with his accustomed generosity.
This conduct drew upon him the odium and hostility of his
fellow caciques, particularly of the fierce Carib, Caonabo,

[1] Hist. del Almirante, cap. 60.

and his brother-in-law, Behechio. They made irruptions into his territories, and inflicted on him various injuries and indignities. Behechio killed one of his wives, and Caonabo carried another away captive.[1] Nothing, however, could shake the devotion of Guacanagari to the Spaniards; and as his dominions lay immediately adjacent to the settlement, and those of some of the other caciques were very remote, the want of his co-operation impeded for some time the hostile designs of his confederates.[2]

Such was the critical state to which the affairs of the colony had been reduced, and such the bitter hostility engendered among the people of the island, during the absence of Columbus, and merely in consequence of violating all his regulations. Margarite and Friar Boyle had hastened to Spain to make false representations of the miseries of the island. Had they remained faithfully at their posts, and discharged zealously the trust confided to them, those miseries might have been easily remedied, if not entirely prevented.

CHAPTER IV.

MEASURES OF COLUMBUS TO RESTORE THE QUIET OF THE ISLAND.—EXPEDITION OF OJEDA TO SURPRISE CAONABO.

[1494.]

IMMEDIATELY after the return of Columbus from Cuba, while he was yet confined to his bed by indisposition, he was gratified by a voluntary visit from Guacanagari, who manifested the greatest concern at his illness, for he appears to have always entertained an affectionate reverence for the admiral. He again spoke with tears of the massacre of Fort Nativity, dwelling on the exertions he had made in defence of the Spaniards. He now informed Columbus of

[1] Hist. del Almirante, cap. 60.
[2] Herrera, Hist. Ind., decad. i. lib. ii. cap. 16.

the secret league forming among the caciques; of his opposition to it, and the consequent persecution he had suffered;
of the murder of one of his wives, and the capture of
another. He urged the admiral to be on his guard against
the designs of Caonabo, and offered to lead his subjects to
the field, to fight by the side of the Spaniards, as well out
of friendship for them, as in revenge of his own injuries.[1]

Columbus had always retained a deep sense of the ancient
kindness of Guacanagari, and was rejoiced to have all suspicion of his good faith thus effectually dispelled. Their
former amicable intercourse was renewed, with this difference, that the man whom Guacanagari had once relieved
and succored as a shipwrecked stranger, had suddenly
become the arbiter of the fate of himself and all his
countrymen.

The manner in which this peaceful island had been exasperated and embroiled by the licentious conduct of the
Europeans, was a matter of deep concern to Columbus.
He saw all his plans of deriving an immediate revenue to
the sovereigns completely impeded. To restore the island
to tranquillity required skillful management. His forces
were but small, and the awe in which the natives had stood
of the white men, as supernatural beings, had been in some
degree dispelled. He was too ill to take a personal share
in any warlike enterprise: his brother Diego was not of a
military character, and Bartholomew was yet a stranger
among the Spaniards, and regarded by the leading men
with jealousy. Still Columbus considered the threatened
combination of the caciques as but imperfectly formed; he
trusted to their want of skill and experience in warfare,
and conceived that by prompt measures, by proceeding in
detail, punishing some, conciliating others, and uniting
force, gentleness, and stratagem, he might succeed in dis-
pelling the threatened storm.

His first care was to send a body of armed men to the

[1] Herrera, Hist. Ind., decad. i. lib. ii. cap. 16.

relief of Fort Magdalena, menaced with destruction by
Guatiguana, the cacique of the Grand River, who had
massacred the Spaniards quartered in his town. Having
relieved the fortress, the troops overran the territory of
Guatiguana, killing many of his warriors, and carrying
others off captives: the chieftain himself made his escape.[1]
He was tributary to Guarionex, sovereign cacique of the
Royal Vega. As this Indian prince reigned over a great
and populous extent of country, his friendship was highly
important to the prosperity of the colony, while there was
imminent risk of his hostility, from the unbridled excesses
of the Spaniards who had been quartered in his dominions.
Columbus sent for him, therefore, and explained to him
that these excesses had been in violation of his orders, and
contrary to his good intentions towards the natives, whom
it was his wish in every way to please and benefit. He
explained, likewise, that the expedition against Guatiguana
was an act of mere individual punishment, not of hostility
against the territories of Guarionex. The cacique was of
a quiet and placable disposition, and whatever anger he
might have felt was easily soothed. To link him in some
degree to the Spanish interest, Columbus prevailed on him
to give his daughter in marriage to the Indian interpreter,
Diego Colon.[2] As a stronger precaution against any hostility on the part of the cacique, and to insure tranquillity
in the important region of the Vega, he ordered a fortress
to be erected in the midst of his territories, which he
named Fort Conception. The easy cacique agreed without
hesitation to a measure fraught with ruin to himself, and
future slavery to his subjects.

[1] Herrera, decad. i. lib. ii. cap. 16.
[2] P. Martyr, decad. i. lib. iv. Gio. Battista Spotorno, in his
Memoir of Columbus, has been led into an error by the name of
this Indian, and observes that Columbus had a brother named
Diego, of whom he seemed to be ashamed, and whom he married
to the daughter of an Indian chief.

The most formidable enemy remained to be disposed of,—
Caonabo. His territories lay in the central and mountainous parts of the island, rendered difficult of access by rugged rocks, entangled forests, and frequent rivers. To make
war upon this subtle and ferocious chieftain, in the depths
of his wild woodland territory, and among the fastnesses of
his mountains, where, at every step, there would be danger
of ambush, would be a work of time, peril, and uncertain
issue. In the meanwhile the settlements would never be
secure from his secret and daring enterprises, and the working of the mines would be subject to frequent interruption.
While perplexed on this subject, Columbus was relieved by
an offer of Alonzo de Ojeda, to take the Carib chieftain by
stratagem, and deliver him alive into his hands. The project was wild, hazardous, and romantic, characteristic of
Ojeda, who was fond of distinguishing himself by extravagant exploits and feats of desperate bravery.

Choosing ten bold and hardy followers, well armed and
well mounted, and invoking the protection of his patroness
the Virgin, whose image as usual he bore with him as a
safeguard, Ojeda plunged into the forest, and made his way
above sixty leagues into the wild territories of Caonabo,
whom he found in one of his most populous towns, the
same now called Maguana, near the town of San Juan.
Approaching the cacique with great deference as a sovereign prince, he professed to come on a friendly embassy
from the admiral, who was Guamiquina, or chief of the
Spaniards, and who had sent him an invaluable present.

Caonabo had tried Ojeda in battle; he had witnessed his
fiery prowess, and had conceived a warrior's admiration of
him. He received him with a degree of chivalrous courtesy, if such a phrase may apply to the savage state and
rude hospitality of a wild warrior of the forest. The free,
fearless deportment, the great personal strength, and the
surprising agility and adroitness of Ojeda in all manly
exercises, and in the use of all kinds of weapons, were

calculated to delight a savage, and he soon became a great favorite with Caonabo.

Ojeda now used all his influence to prevail upon the cacique to repair to Isabella, for the purpose of making a treaty with Columbus, and becoming the ally and friend of the Spaniards. It is said that he offered him, as a lure, the bell of the chapel of Isabella. This bell was the wonder of the island. When the Indians heard it ringing for mass, and beheld the Spaniards hastening toward the chapel, they imagined that it talked, and that the white men obeyed it. Regarding with superstition all things connected with the Spaniards, they looked upon this bell as something supernatural, and in their usual phrase, said it had come from "Turey," or the skies. Caonabo had heard the bell at a distance, in his prowlings about the settlement, and had longed to see it; but when it was proffered to him as a present of peace, he found it impossible to resist the temptation. He agreed, therefore, to set out for Isabella; but when the time came to depart, Ojeda beheld with surprise a powerful force of warriors assembled and ready to march. He asked the meaning of taking such an army on a mere friendly visit; the cacique proudly replied that it did not befit a great prince like himself to go forth scantily attended. Ojeda was little satisfied with this reply; he knew the warlike character of Caonabo, and his deep subtlety; he feared some sinister design; a surprise of the fortress of Isabella, or an attempt upon the person of the admiral. He knew also that it was the wish of Columbus, either to make peace with the cacique, or to get possession of his person without the alternative of open warfare. He had recourse to a stratagem, therefore, which has an air of fable and romance, but which is recorded by all the contemporary historians with trivial variations, and which, Las Casas assures us, was in current circulation in the island when he arrived there, about six years after the event. It accords too with the adventurous and extravagant character of the man, and with the wild stratagems and vaunting exploits incident to Indian warfare.

In the course of their march, having halted near the Little Yagui, a considerable branch of the Neyba, Ojeda one day produced a set of manacles of polished steel, so highly burnished that they looked like silver. These he assured Caonabo were royal ornaments which had come from heaven, or the Turey of Biscay;[1] that they were worn by the monarchs of Castile on solemn dances, and other high festivities, and were intended as presents to the cacique. He proposed that Caonabo should go to the river and bathe, after which he should be decorated with these ornaments, mounted on the horse of Ojeda, and should return in the state of a Spanish monarch, to astonish his subjects. The cacique was dazzled with the glitter of the manacles, and flattered with the idea of bestriding one of those tremendous animals so dreaded by his countrymen. He repaired to the river, and having bathed, was assisted to mount behind Ojeda, and the shackles were adjusted. Ojeda made several circuits to gain space, followed by his little band of horsemen, the Indians shrinking back from the prancing steeds. At length he made a wide sweep into the forest, until the trees concealed him from the sight of the army. His followers then closed round him, and drawing their swords, threatened Caonabo with instant death if he made the least noise or resistance. Binding him with cords to Ojeda to prevent his falling or effecting an escape, they put spurs to their horses, dashed across the river, and made off through the woods with their prize.[2]

[1] The principal iron manufactories of Spain are established in Biscay, where the ore is found in abundance.

[2] This romantic exploit of Ojeda is recorded at large by Las Casas; by his copyist Herrera (decad. i. lib. ii. cap. 16); by Fernando Pizarro, in his Varones Ilustres del Nuevo Mundo; and by Charlevoix in his History of St. Domingo. Peter Martyr and others have given it more concisely, alluding to but not inserting its romantic details.

They had now fifty or sixty leagues of wilderness to traverse on their way homewards, with here and there large Indian towns. They had borne off their captive far beyond the pursuit of his subjects; but the utmost vigilance was requisite to prevent his escape during this long and toilsome journey, and to avoid exciting the hostilities of any confederate cacique. They had to shun the populous parts of the country therefore, or to pass through the Indian towns at full gallop. They suffered greatly from fatigue, hunger, and watchfulness; encountering many perils, fording and swimming the numerous rivers of the plains, toiling through the deep tangled forests, and clambering over the high and rocky mountains. They accomplished all in safety, and Ojeda entered Isabella in triumph from this most daring and characteristic enterprise, with his wild Indian bound behind.

Columbus could not refrain from expressing his great satisfaction when this dangerous foe was delivered into his hands. The haughty Carib met him with a lofty and unsubdued air, disdaining to conciliate him by submission, or to deprecate his vengeance for the blood of white men which he had shed. He never bowed his spirit to captivity; on the contrary, though completely at the mercy of the Spaniards, he displayed that boasting defiance which is a part of Indian heroism, and which the savage maintains towards his tormentors, even amidst the agonies of the fagot and the stake. He vaunted his achievement in surprising and burning the fortress of Nativity, and slaughtering its garrison, and declared that he had secretly reconnoitred Isabella, with an intention of wreaking upon it the same desolation.

Columbus, though struck with the heroism of the chieftain, considered him a dangerous enemy, whom, for the peace of the island, it was advisable to send to Spain; in the meantime he ordered that he should be treated with kindness and respect, and lodged him in a part of his own

dwelling, where, however, he kept him a prisoner in chains.
This precaution must have been necessary, from the inse-
curity of his prison; for Las Casas observes, that the
admiral's house not being spacious, nor having many
chambers, the passers-by in the street could see the captive chieftain from the portal.[1]

Caonabo always maintained a haughty deportment towards Columbus, while he never evinced the least animosity against Ojeda. He rather admired the latter as a
consummate warrior, for having pounced upon him, and
borne him off in this hawk-like manner, from the very
midst of his fighting-men.

When Columbus entered the apartment where Caonabo
was confined, all present rose, according to custom, and
paid him reverence; the cacique alone neither moved nor
took any notice of him. On the contrary, when Ojeda
entered, though small in person and without external state,
Caonabo rose and saluted him with profound respect. On
being asked the reason of this, Columbus being Guamiquina, or great chief over all, and Ojeda but one of his
subjects, the proud Carib replied, that the admiral had
never dared to come personally to his house and seize him;
it was only through the valor of Ojeda he was his prisoner; to Ojeda, therefore, he owed reverence, not to the
admiral.[2]

The captivity of Caonabo was deeply felt by his subjects,
for the natives of this island seem generally to have been
extremely loyal, and strongly attached to their caciques.
One of the brothers of Caonabo, a warrior of great courage
and address, and very popular among the Indians, assembled an army of more than seven thousand men, and led
them secretly to the neighborhood of St. Thomas, where
Ojeda was again in command. His intention was to surprise a number of Spaniards, in hopes of obtaining his-

[1] Las Casas, Hist. Ind., lib. i. cap. 102.
[2] Las Casas, ubi sup., cap. 102.

brother in exchange for them. Ojeda, as usual, had notice of the design, but was not to be again shut up in his fortress. Having been reinforced by a detachment sent by the Adelantado, he left a sufficient force in garrison, and with the remainder, and his little troop of horse, set off boldly to meet the savages. The brother of Caonabo, when he saw the Spaniards approaching, showed some military skill, disposing his army in five battalions. The impetuous attack of Ojeda, however, with his handful of horsemen, threw the Indian warriors into sudden panic. At the furious onset of these steel-clad beings, wielding their flashing weapons, and bestriding what appeared to be ferocious beasts of prey, they threw down their weapons and took to flight: many were slain, more were taken prisoners, and among the latter was the brother of Caonabo, bravely fighting in a righteous yet desperate cause.[1]

CHAPTER V.

ARRIVAL OF ANTONIO DE TORRES WITH FOUR SHIPS FROM SPAIN.—HIS RETURN WITH INDIAN SLAVES.

[1494.]

THE colony was still suffering greatly from want of provisions; the European stock was nearly exhausted, and such was the idleness and improvidence of the colonists, or the confusion into which they had been thrown by the hostilities of the natives; or such was their exclusive eagerness after the precious metals, that they seem to have neglected the true wealth of the island, its quick and productive soil, and to have been in constant danger of famine, though in the midst of fertility.

At length they were relieved by the arrival of four ships,

[1] Oviedo, Cronica de las Indias, lib. iii. cap. 1. Charlevoix, Hist. St. Domingo, lib. ii. p. 131.

commanded by Antonio Torres, which brought an ample supply of provisions. There were also a physician and an apothecary, whose aid was greatly needed in the sickly state of the colony; but above all, there were mechanics, millers, fishermen, gardeners, and husbandmen,—the true kind of population for a colony.

Torres brought letters from the sovereigns (dated August 16, 1494,) of the most gratifying kind, expressing the highest satisfaction at the accounts sent home by the admiral, and acknowledging that every thing in the course of his discoveries had turned out as he had predicted. They evinced the liveliest interest in the affairs of the colony, and a desire of receiving frequent intelligence as to his situation, proposing that a caravel should sail each month from Isabella and Spain. They informed him that all differences with Portugal were amicably adjusted, and acquainted him with the conventional agreement with that power relative to a geographical line, separating their newly-discovered possessions; requesting him to respect this agreement in the course of his discoveries. As in adjusting the arrangement with Portugal, and in drawing the proposed line, it was important to have the best advice, the sovereigns requested Columbus to return and be present at the convention; or, in case that should be inconvenient, to send his brother Bartholomew, or any other person whom he should consider fully competent, furnished with such maps, charts, and designs, as might be of service in the negotiation.[1]

There was another letter, addressed generally to the inhabitants of the colony, and to all who should proceed on voyages of discovery, commanding them to obey Columbus as implicitly as they would the sovereigns themselves, under pain of their high displeasure, and a fine of ten thousand maravedies, for each offence.

Such was the well-merited confidence reposed at this mo-

[1] Herrera, decad. i. lib. ii. cap. 17.

ment by the sovereigns in Columbus, but which was soon to be blighted by the insidious reports of worthless men. He was already aware of the complaints and misrepresentations which had been sent home from the colony, and which would be enforced by Margarite and Friar Boyle. He was aware that his standing in Spain was of that uncertain kind which a stranger always possesses in the service of a foreign country, where he has no friends nor connections to support him, and where ēven his very merits increase the eagerness of envy to cast him down. His efforts to promote the working of the mines, and to explore the resources of the island, had been impeded by the misconduct of Margarite and the disorderly life of the Spaniards in general, yet he apprehended that the very evils which they had produced would be alleged against him, and the want of profitable returns be cited to discredit and embarrass his expeditions.

To counteract any misrepresentations of the kind, Columbus hastened the return of the ships, and would have returned with them, not merely to comply with the wishes of the sovereigns in being present at the settlement of the geographical line, but to vindicate himself and his enterprises from the aspersions of his enemies. The malady, however, which confined him to his bed prevented his departure; and his brother Bartholomew was required to aid, with his practical good sense, and his resolute spirit, in regulating the disordered affairs of the island. It was determined, therefore, to send home his brother Diego, to attend to the wishes of the sovereigns, and to take care of his interests at court. At the same time, he exerted himself to the utmost to send by the ships satisfactory proofs of the value of his discoveries. He remitted by them all the gold that he could collect, with specimens of other metals, and of various fruits and valuable plants, which he had collected either in Hispaniola or in the course of his voyage. In his eagerness to produce immediate profit, and to indemnify the

sovereigns for those expenses which bore hard upon the
royal treasury, he sent, likewise, above five hundred Indian
prisoners, who, he suggested, might be sold as slaves at
Seville.

It is painful to find the brilliant renown of Columbus
sullied by so foul a stain. The customs of the times, however, must be pleaded in his apology. The precedent had
been given long before, by both Spaniards and Portuguese,
in their African discoveries, wherein the traffic in slaves
had formed one of the greatest sources of profit. In fact,
the practice had been sanctioned by the Church itself, and
the most learned theologians had pronounced all barbarous
and infidel nations, who shut their ears to the truths of
Christianity, fair objects of war and rapine, of captivity and
slavery. If Columbus needed any practical illustration of
this doctrine, he had it in the conduct of Ferdinand himself,
in his late wars with the Moors of Granada, in which he
had always been surrounded by a crowd of ghostly advisers,
and had professed to do every thing for the glory and advancement of the faith. In this holy war, as it was termed, it
was a common practice to make inroads into the Moorish
territories and carry off *cavalgadas*, not merely of flocks and
herds, but of human beings, and those not warriors taken
with weapons in their hands, but quiet villagers, laboring
peasantry, and helpless women and children. These were
carried to the mart at Seville, or to other populous towns,
and sold into slavery. The capture of Malaga was a
memorable instance, where, as a punishment for an obstinate and brave defence, which should have excited admiration rather than revenge, eleven thousand people of both
sexes, and of all ranks and ages, many of them highly cultivated and delicately reared, were suddenly torn from their
homes, severed from each other, and swept into menial
slavery, even though half of their ransoms had been paid.
These circumstances are not advanced to vindicate, but to
palliate, the conduct of Columbus. He acted but in con-

formity to the customs of the times, and was sanctioned by the example of the sovereign under whom he served. Las Casas, the zealous and enthusiastic advocate of the Indians, who suffers no opportunity to escape him of exclaiming in vehement terms against their slavery, speaks with indulgence of Columbus on this head. If those pious and learned men, he observes, whom the sovereigns took for guides and instructors, were so ignorant of the injustice of this practice, it is no wonder that the unlettered admiral should not be conscious of its impropriety.[1]

CHAPTER VI.

EXPEDITION OF COLUMBUS AGAINST THE INDIANS OF THE VEGA.—BATTLE.

[1494.]

NOTWITHSTANDING the defeat of the Indians by Ojeda, they still retained hostile intentions against the Spaniards. The idea of their cacique being a prisoner, and in chains, enraged the natives of Maguana; and the general sympathy manifested by other tribes of the island shows how widely that intelligent savage had extended his influence, and how greatly he was admired. He had still active and powerful relatives remaining, to attempt his rescue, or revenge his fall. One of his brothers, Manicaotex by name, a Carib, bold and warlike as himself, succeeded to the sway over his subjects. His favorite wife also, Anacaona, so famous for her charms, had great influence over her brother Behechio, cacique of the populous province of Xaragua. Through these means a violent and general hostility to the Spaniards was excited throughout the island, and the formidable league of the caciques, which Caonabo had in vain attempted to accomplish when at large, was produced by his

[1] Las Casas, Hist. Ind., tom. i. cap. 122, MS.

captivity. Guacanagari, the cacique of Marien, alone remained friendly to the Spaniards, giving them timely information of the gathering storm, and offering to take the field
with them as a faithful ally.

The protracted illness of Columbus, the scantiness of his
military force, and the wretched state of the colonists in
general, reduced by sickness and scarcity to great bodily
weakness, had hitherto induced him to try every means of
conciliation and stratagem to avert and dissolve the confederacy. He had at length recovered his health, and his
followers were in some degree refreshed and invigorated by
the supplies brought by the ships. At this time, he received
intelligence that the allied caciques were actually assembled
in great force in the Vega, within two days' march of Isabella, with an intention of making a general assault upon
the settlement, and overwhelming it by numbers. Columbus
resolved to take the field at once, and to carry the war into
the territories of the enemy, rather than suffer it to be
brought to his own door.

The whole sound and effective force that he could muster,
in the present infirm state of the colony, did not exceed two
hundred infantry and twenty horse. They were armed with
cross-bows, swords, lances, and espingardas, or heavy arquebuses, which in those days were used with rests, and sometimes mounted on wheels. With these formidable weapons,
a handful of European warriors, cased in steel and covered
with bucklers, were able to cope with thousands of naked
savages. They had aid of another kind, however, consisting of twenty blood-hounds, animals scarcely less terrible
to the Indians than the horses, and infinitely more fatal.
They were fearless and ferocious; nothing daunted them,
nor when they had once seized upon their prey, could any
thing compel them to relinquish their hold. The naked
bodies of the Indians offered no defence against their
attacks. They sprang on them, dragged them to the earth,
and tore them to pieces.

The admiral was accompanied in the expedition by his brother Bartholomew, whose counsel and aid he sought on all occasions, and who had not merely great personal force and undaunted courage, but also a decidedly military turn of mind. Guacanagari also brought his people into the field : neither he nor his subjects, however, were of a warlike character, nor calculated to render much assistance. The chief advantage of his co-operation was, that it completely severed him from the other caciques, and insured the dependence of himself and his subjects upon the Spaniards. In the present infant state of the colony its chief security depended upon jealousies and dissensions sown among the native powers of the island.

On the 27th of March, 1495, Columbus issued forth from Isabella with his little army, and advanced by marches of ten leagues a day in quest of the enemy. He ascended again to the mountain-pass of the Cavaliers, whence he had first looked down upon the Vega. With what different feelings did he now contemplate it ! The vile passions of the white men had already converted this smiling, beautiful, and once peaceful and hospitable region, into a land of wrath and hostility. Wherever the smoke of an Indian town rose from among the trees, it marked a horde of exasperated enemies, and the deep rich forests below him swarmed with lurking warriors. In the picture which his imagination had drawn of the peaceful and inoffensive nature of this people, he had flattered himself with the idea of ruling over them as a patron and benefactor, but now he found himself compelled to assume the odious character of a conqueror.

The Indians had notice, by their scouts, of his approach, but though they had already had some slight experience of the warfare of the white men, they were confident from the vast superiority of their numbers, which, it is said, amounted to one hundred thousand men.[1] This is probably an exag-

[1] Las Casas, Hist. Ind., lib. i. cap. 104, MS.

geration : as Indians never draw out into the open field in
order of battle, but lurk among the forests, it is difficult to
ascertain their force, and their rapid movements and sudden
sallies and retreats from various parts, together with the
wild shouts and yells from opposite quarters of the woodlands, are calculated to give an exaggerated idea of their
number. The army must, however, have been great, as it
consisted of the combined forces of several caciques of this
populous island. It was commanded by Manicaotex, the
brother of Caonabo. The Indians, who were little skilled
in numeration and incapable of reckoning beyond ten, had
a simple mode of ascertaining and describing the force of an
enemy, by counting out a grain of maize or Indian corn for
every warrior. When, therefore, the spies, who had watched
from rocks and thickets the march of Columbus, came back
with a mere handful of corn as the amount of his army, the
caciques scoffed at the idea of so scanty a number making
head against their countless multitude.[1]

Columbus drew near to the enemy about the place where
the town of St. Jago has since been built.   The Indian
army, under Manicaotex, was posted on a plain interspersed
with clusters of forest-trees, now known as the Savanna of
Matanza. Having ascertained the great force of the enemy,
Don Bartholomew advised that their little army should be
divided into detachments, and should attack the Indians at
the same moment from several quarters : this plan was
adopted. The infantry, separating into different bodies,
advanced suddenly from various directions with great din
of drums and trumpets, and a destructive discharge of firearms from the covert of the trees. The Indians were thrown
into complete confusion. An army seemed pressing upon
them from every quarter, their fellow-warriors to be laid
low with thunder and lightning from the forests. While
driven together and confounded by these attacks, Alonzo de
Ojeda charged their main body impetuously with his troop

[1] Las Casas, ubi sup.

of cavalry, cutting his way with lance and sabre. The horses bore down the terrified Indians, while their riders dealt their blows on all sides unopposed. The blood-hounds at the same time rushed upon the naked savages, seizing them by the throat, dragging them to the earth, and tearing out their bowels. The Indians, unaccustomed to large and fierce quadrupeds of any kind, were struck with horror when assailed by these ferocious animals. They thought the horses equally fierce and devouring. The contest, if such it might be called, was of short duration.

The Indians fled in every direction with yells and howlings; some clambered to the top of rocks and precipices, whence they made piteous supplications, and offers of complete submission; many were killed, many made prisoners, and the confederacy was for the time completely broken up and dispersed.

Guacanagari had accompanied the Spaniards into the field according to his promise, but he was little more than a spectator of this battle, or rather rout. He was not of a martial spirit, and both he and his subjects must have shrunk with awe at this unusual and terrific burst of war, even though on the part of their allies. His participation in the hostilities of the white men was never forgiven by the other caciques, and he returned to his dominions, followed by the hatred and execrations of all the islanders.

CHAPTER VII.

SUBJUGATION OF THE NATIVES.—IMPOSITION OF TRIBUTE.

[1494.]

COLUMBUS followed up his victory by making a military tour through various parts of the island, and reducing them to obedience. The natives made occasional attempts at opposition, but were easily checked. Ojeda's troop of cavalry was of great efficacy from the rapidity of its movements, the active intrepidity of its commander, and the terror inspired by the horses. There was no service too wild and hazardous for Ojeda. If any appearance of war arose in a distant part of the country, he would penetrate with his little squadron of cavalry through the depths of the forests, and fall like a thunderbolt upon the enemy, disconcerting all their combinations and enforcing implicit submission.

The Royal Vega was soon brought into subjection. Being an immense plain, perfectly level, it was easily overrun by the horsemen, whose appearance overawed the most populous villages. Guarionex, its sovereign cacique, was of a mild and placable character, and though he had been roused to war by the instigation of the neighboring chieftains, he readily submitted to the domination of the Spaniards. Manicaotex, the brother of Caonabo, was also obliged to sue for peace; and being the prime mover of the confederacy, the other caciques followed his example. Behechio alone, the cacique of Xaragua, and brother-in-law of Caonabo, made no overtures of submission. His territories lay remote from Isabella, at the western extremity of the island, around the deep bay called the Bight of Leogan, and the long peninsula called Cape Tiburon. They were difficult of access, and had not as yet been visited by the white men. He retired into his domains, taking with him his sister, the beautiful Anacaona, wife of Caonabo, whom he cherished with fraternal affection under her misfortunes, who soon acquired almost equal sway over his subjects with himself, and was destined subsequently to make some figure in the events of the island.

Having been forced to take the field by the confederacy of the caciques, Columbus now asserted the right of a conqueror, and considered how he might turn his conquest to most profit. His constant anxiety was to make wealthy returns to Spain, for the purpose of indemnifying the sovereigns for their great expenses; of meeting the public expectations, so extravagantly excited; and, above all, of silencing the calumnies of those who had gone home determined to make the most discouraging representations of his discoveries. He endeavored, therefore, to raise a large and immediate revenue, by imposing heavy tributes on the subjected provinces. In those of the Vega, Cibao, and all the region of the mines, each individual above the age of fourteen years was required to pay, every three months, the measure of a Flemish hawk's-bell of gold dust.[1] The caciques had to pay a much larger amount for their personal tribute. Manicaotex, the brother of Caonabo, was obliged individually to render in, every three months, half a calabash of gold, amounting to one hundred and fifty pesos. In those districts which were distant from the mines, and produced no gold, each individual was required to furnish an arroba (twenty-five pounds) of cotton every three months. Each Indian, on rendering this tribute, received a copper medal as a certificate of payment, which he was to wear suspended round his neck; those who were found without such documents were liable to arrest and punishment.

The taxes and tributes thus imposed bore hard upon the spirit of the natives, accustomed to be but lightly tasked by their caciques; and the caciques themselves found the exactions intolerably grievous. Guarionex, the sovereign of the Royal Vega, represented to Columbus the difficulty he had in complying with the terms of his tribute. His richly fertile plain yielded no gold; and though the mountains on his borders contained mines, and their brooks and

---

[1] A hawk's-bell, according to Las Casas (Hist. Ind., lib. i. cap. 105), contains about three castellanos' worth of gold dust, equal to five dollars, and in estimating the superior value of gold in those days, equivalent to fifteen dollars of our time. A quantity of gold worth one hundred and fifty castellanos was equivalent to seven hundred and ninety-eight dollars of the present day.

torrents washed down gold dust into the sands of the rivers,
yet his subjects were not skilled in the art of collecting it..
He proffered, therefore, instead of the tribute required, to
cultivate with grain a band of country stretching across the
island from sea to sea, enough, says Las Casas, to have furnished all Castile with bread for ten years.[1]

His offer was rejected. Columbus knew that gold alone
would satisfy the avaricious dreams excited in Spain, and
insure the popularity and success of his enterprises. Seeing, however, the difficulty that many of the Indians had
in furnishing the amount of gold dust required, he lowered
the demand to the measure of one-half of a hawk's-bell.

To enforce the payment of these tributes, and to maintain the subjection of the island, Columbus put the fortress
already built in a strong state of defence, and erected
others. Besides those of Isabella, and of St. Thomas, in
the mountains of Cibao, there were now the fortress of
Magdalena, in the Royal Vega, near the site of the old
town of Santiago, on the river Jalaqua, two leagues from
the place where the new town was afterwards built; another called Santa Catalina, the site of which is near the
Estencia Yaqui; another called Esperanza, on the banks
of the river Yaqui, facing the outlet of the mountain pass
La Puerta de los Hidalgos, now the pass of Marney; but
the most important of those recently erected was Fort
Conception, in one of the most fruitful and beautiful parts
of the Vega, about fifteen leagues to the east of Esperanza,
controlling the extensive and populous domains of Guarionex.[2]

In this way was the yoke of servitude fixed upon the
island, and its thraldom effectually insured. Deep despair now fell upon the natives when they found a perpetual task inflicted upon them, enforced at stated and
frequently recurring periods. Weak and indolent by

[1] Las Casas, Hist. Ind., lib. i. cap. 105.
[2] Ibid., ubi sup., cap. 110.

nature, unused to labor of any kind, and brought up in the untasked idleness of their soft climate and their fruitful groves, death itself seemed preferable to a life of toil and anxiety. They saw no end to this harassing evil, which had so suddenly fallen upon them; no escape from its all-pervading influence; no prospect of return to that roving independence and ample leisure, so dear to the wild inhabitants of the forest. The pleasant life of the island was at an end : the dream in the shade by day ; the slumber during the sultry noontide heat by the fountain or the stream, or under the spreading palm-tree; and the song, the dance, and the game in the mellow evening, when summoned to their simple amusements by the rude Indian drum. They were now obliged to grope day by day, with bending body and anxious eye, along the borders of their rivers, sifting the sands for the grains of gold which every day grew more scanty ; or to labor in their fields beneath the fervor of a tropical sun, to raise food for their taskmasters, or to produce the vegetable tribute imposed upon them. They sank to sleep weary and exhausted at night, with the certainty that the next day was but to be a repetition of the same toil and suffering. Or if they occasionally indulged in their national dances, the ballads to which they kept time were of a melancholy and plaintive character. They spoke of the times that were past before the white men had introduced sorrow, and slavery, and weary labor among them; and they rehearsed pretended prophecies, handed down from their ancestors, foretelling the invasion of the Spaniards; that strangers should come into their island, clothed in apparel, with swords capable of cleaving a man asunder at a blow, under whose yoke their posterity should be subdued. These ballads, or areytos, they sang with mournful tunes and doleful voices, bewailing the loss of their liberty, and their painful servitude.[1]

They had flattered themselves, for a time, that the visit

[1] Peter Martyr, decad. iii. lib. ix.

of the strangers would be but temporary, and that, spreading their ample sails, their ships would once more bear them back to their home in the sky. In their simplicity, they had repeatedly inquired when they intended to return to Turey, or the heavens. They now beheld them taking root, as it were, in the island. They beheld their vessels lying idle and rotting in the harbor, while the crews, scattered about the country, were building habitations and fortresses, the solid construction of which, unlike their own slight cabins, gave evidence of permanent abode.[1]

Finding how vain was all attempt to deliver themselves by warlike means from these invincible intruders, they now concerted a forlorn and desperate mode of annoyance. They perceived that the settlement suffered greatly from shortness of provisions, and depended, in a considerable degree, upon the supplies furnished by the natives. The fortresses in the interior, also, and the Spaniards quartered in the villages, looked almost entirely to them for subsistence. They agreed among themselves, therefore, not to cultivate the fruits, the roots and maize, their chief articles of food, and to destroy those already growing; hoping, by producing a famine, to starve the strangers from the island. They little knew, observes Las Casas, one of the characteristics of the Spaniards, who the more hungry they are, the more inflexible they become, and the more hardened to endure suffering.[2] They carried their plan generally into effect, abandoning their habitations, laying waste their fields and groves, and retiring to the mountains, where there were roots and herbs and abundance of utias for their subsistence.

This measure did indeed produce much distress among the Spaniards, but they had foreign resources, and were

---

[1] Las Casas, Hist. Ind., lib. i. cap. 106.

[2] No conociendo la propriedad de los Espanoles, los cuales cuanto mas hambrientos, tanto mayor teson tienen y mas duros son de sufrir y para sufrir. Las Casas, Hist. Ind., lib. i. cap. 106.

enabled to endure it by husbanding the partial supplies brought by their ships; the most disastrous effects fell upon the natives themselves. The Spaniards stationed in the various fortresses, finding that there was not only no hope of tribute, but a danger of famine from this wanton waste and sudden desertion, pursued the natives to their retreats, to compel them to return to labor. The Indians took refuge in the most sterile and dreary heights; flying from one wild retreat to another, the women with their children in their arms or at their backs, and all worn out with fatigue and hunger, and harassed by perpetual alarms. In every noise of the forest or the mountain they fancied they heard the sound of their pursuers; they hid themselves in damp and dismal caverns, or in the rocky banks and margins of the torrents, and not daring to hunt, or fish, or even to venture forth in quest of nourishing roots and vegetables, they had to satisfy their raging hunger with unwholesome food. In this way, many thousands of them perished miserably, through famine, fatigue, terror, and various contagious maladies engendered by their sufferings. All spirit of opposition was at length completely quelled. The surviving Indians returned in despair to their habitations, and submitted humbly to the yoke. So deep an awe did they conceive of their conquerors, that it is said a Spaniard might go singly and securely all over the island, and the natives would even transport him from place to place on their shoulders.[1]

Before passing on to other events, it may be proper here to notice the fate of Guacanagari, as he makes no further appearance in the course of this history. His friendship for the Spaniards had severed him from his countrymen, but did not exonerate him from the general woes of the island. His territories, like those of the other caciques, were subjected to a tribute, which his people, with the common repugnance to labor, found it difficult to pay. Columbus, who

---

[1] Las Casas, Hist. Ind., lib. i. c. 106. Hist. del Almirante, cap. 60,

27

knew his worth, and could have protected him, was long
absent either in the interior of the island, or detained in
Europe by his own wrongs.   In the interval, the Spaniards
forgot the hospitality and services of Guacanagari, and his
tribute was harshly exacted.   He found himself overwhelmed with opprobrium from his countrymen at large,
and assailed by the clamors and lamentations of his suffering subjects.   The strangers whom he had succored in distress, and taken as it were to the bosom of his native island,
had become its tyrants and oppressors.   Care, and toil, and
poverty, and strong-handed violence, had spread their
curses over the land, and he felt as if he had invoked them
on his race.   Unable to bear the hostilities of his fellow
caciques, the woes of his subjects, and the extortions of his
ungrateful allies, he took refuge at last in the mountains,
where he died obscurely and in misery.[1]

An attempt has been made by Oviedo to defame the
character of this Indian prince: it is not for Spaniards,
however, to excuse their own ingratitude by casting a
stigma on his name.   He appears to have always manifested towards them that true friendship which shines
brightest in the dark days of adversity.   He might have
played a nobler part, in making a stand, with his brother
caciques, to drive these intruders from his native soil; but
he appears to have been fascinated by his admiration of
the strangers, and his personal attachment to Columbus.
He was bountiful, hospitable, affectionate, and kind-hearted;
competent to rule a gentle and unwarlike people in the
happier days of the island, but unfitted, through the softness
of his nature, for the stern turmoil which followed the arrival of the white men.

[1] Charlevoix, Hist. de St. Domingo, lib. ii.

CHAPTER VIII.

INTRIGUES AGAINST COLUMBUS IN THE COURT OF SPAIN.
—AGUADO SENT TO INVESTIGATE THE AFFAIRS OF HIS-
PANIOLA.

[1495.]

WHILE Columbus was endeavoring to remedy the evils produced by the misconduct of Margarite, that recreant commander and his political coadjutor, Friar Boyle, were busily undermining his reputation in the court of Castile. They accused him of deceiving the sovereigns and the public by extravagant descriptions of the countries he had discovered; they pronounced the island of Hispaniola a source of expense rather than profit, and they drew a dismal picture of the sufferings of the colony, occasioned, as they said, by the oppressions of Columbus and his brothers. They charged them with tasking the community with excessive labor during a time of general sickness and debility; with stopping the rations of individuals on the most trifling pretext, to the great detriment of their health; with wantonly inflicting severe corporal punishments on the common people, and with heaping indignities on Spanish gentlemen of rank. They said nothing, however, of the exigencies which had called for unusual labor; nor of the idleness and profligacy which required coercion and chastisement; nor of the seditious cabals of the Spanish cavaliers, who had been treated with indulgence rather than severity. In addition to these complaints, they represented the state of confusion of the island, in consequence of the absence of the admiral, and the uncertainty which prevailed concerning his fate, intimating the probability of his having perished in his foolhardy attempts to explore unknown seas, and discover unprofitable lands.

These prejudiced and exaggerated representations derived much weight from the official situations of Margarite and Friar Boyle. They were supported by the testimony of many discontented and factious idlers, who had returned with them to Spain. Some of these persons had connections of rank, who were ready to resent, with Spanish haughtiness, what they considered the arrogant assumptions of an ignoble foreigner. Thus the popularity of Columbus received a vital blow, and immediately began to decline. The confidence of the sovereigns also was impaired, and precautions were adopted which savor strongly of the cautious and suspicious policy of Ferdinand.

It was determined to send some person of trust and confidence, who should take upon himself the government of the island in case of the continued absence of the admiral, and who, even in the event of his return, should inquire into the alleged evils and abuses, and remedy such as should appear really in existence. The person proposed for this difficult office was Diego Carillo, a commander of a military order; but as he was not immediately prepared to sail with the fleet of caravels about to depart with supplies, the sovereigns wrote to Fonseca, the superintendent of Indian affairs, to send some trusty person with the vessels, to take charge of the provisions with which they were freighted. These he was to distribute among the colonists, under the supervision of the admiral, or, in case of his absence, in presence of those in authority. He was also to collect information concerning the manner in which the island had been governed, the conduct of persons in office, the causes and authors of existing grievances, and the measures by which they were to be remedied. Having collected such information, he was to return and make report to the sovereigns; but in case he should find the admiral at the island, every thing was to remain subject to his control.

There was another measure adopted by the sovereigns about this time, which likewise shows the declining favor of Columbus. On the 10th of April, 1495, a proclamation was issued, giving general permission to native-born subjects to settle in the island of Hispaniola, and to go on private voyages of discovery and traffic to the New World. This was granted, subject to certain conditions.

All vessels were to sail exclusively from the port of Cadiz, and under the inspection of officers appointed by the crown. Those who embarked for Hispaniola without pay, and at their own expense, were to have lands assigned them, and to be provisioned for one year, with a right to retain such lands, and all houses they might erect upon them. Of all gold which they might collect, they were to retain one-third for themselves, and pay two-thirds to the crown. Of all other articles of merchandise, the produce of the island, they were to pay merely one-tenth to the crown. Their purchases were to be made in the presence of officers appointed by the sovereigns, and the royal duties paid into the hands of the king's receiver.

Each ship sailing on private enterprise was to take one or two persons named by the royal officers at Cadiz. One-tenth of the tonnage of the ship was to be at the service of the crown, free of charge. One-tenth of whatever such ships should procure in the newly-discovered countries was to be paid to the crown on their return. These regulations included private ships trading to Hispaniola with provisions.

For every vessel thus fitted out on private adventure, Columbus, in consideration of his privilege of an eighth of tonnage, was to have the right to freight one on his own account.

This general license for voyages of discovery was made in consequence of the earnest applications of Vincent Yañes Pinzon, and other able and intrepid navigators, most of whom had sailed with Columbus. They offered to make voyages at their own cost and hazard. The offer was tempting and well-timed. The government was poor, the expeditions of Columbus were expensive, yet their object was too important to be neglected. Here was an opportunity of attaining all the ends proposed, not merely without expense, but with a certainty of gain. The permission, therefore, was granted, without consulting the opinion or the wishes of the admiral. It was loudly complained of by him, as an infringement of his privileges, and as disturbing the career of regular and well-organized discovery, by the licentious and sometimes predatory enterprises of reckless adventurers. Doubtless, much of the odium that has attached itself to the Spanish discoveries in the New World has arisen from the grasping avidity of private individuals.

Just at this juncture, in the early part of April, while the interests of Columbus were in such a critical situation, the ships commanded by Torres arrived in Spain. They brought intelligence of the safe return of the admiral to Hispaniola, from his voyage along the southern coast of Cuba, with the evidence which he had collected to prove that it was the extremity of the Asiatic continent, and that he had penetrated to the borders of the wealthiest countries of the East. Specimens were likewise brought of the gold, and the various animal and vegetable curiosities, which he had procured in the course of his voyage. No arrival could have been more timely. It at once removed all doubts respecting his safety, and obviated the necessity of part of the precautionary measures then on the point of being taken. The supposed discovery of the rich coast of Asia, also, threw a temporary splendor about his expedition, and again awakened the gratitude of the sovereigns. The effect was immediately apparent in their measures. Instead of leaving it to the discretion of Juan Rodriguez de Fonseca to appoint whom he pleased to the commission of inquiry about to be sent out, they retracted that power, and nominated Juan Aguado.

He was chosen, because, on returning from Hispaniola, he had been strongly recommended to royal favor by Columbus. It was intended, therefore, as a mark of consideration to the latter, to appoint as commissioner a person of whom he had expressed so high an opinion, and who, it was to be presumed, entertained for him a grateful regard.

Fonseca, in virtue of his official station as superintendent of the affairs of the Indies, and probably to gratify his growing animosity for Columbus, had detained a quantity of gold which Don Diego, brother to the admiral, had brought on his own private account. The sovereigns wrote to him repeatedly, ordering him not to demand the gold, or if he had seized it, to return it immediately, with satisfactory explanations, and to write to Columbus in terms calculated to soothe any angry feelings which he might have excited. He was ordered, also, to consult the persons recently arrived from Hispaniola, in what manner he could yield satisfaction to the admiral, and to act accordingly. Fonseca thus suffered one of the severest humiliations of an arrogant spirit, that of being obliged to make atonement for its arrogance. It quickened, however, the malice which he had conceived against the admiral and his family. Unfortunately his official situation, and the royal confidence which he enjoyed, gave him opportunities of gratifying it subsequently in a thousand insidious ways.

While the sovereigns thus endeavored to avoid any act which might give umbrage to Columbus, they took certain measures to provide for the tranquillity of the colony. In a letter to the admiral, they directed that the number of persons in the settlement should be limited to five hundred, a greater number being considered unnecessary for the service of the island, and a burdensome expense to the crown. To prevent further discontents about provisions, they ordered that the rations of individuals should be dealt out in portions every fifteen days; and that all punishment by short allowance, or the stoppage of rations, should be discontinued, as tending to injure the health of the colonists, who required every assistance of nourishing diet, to fortify them against the maladies incident to a strange climate.

An able and experienced metallurgist, named Pablo
Belvis, was sent out in place of the wrong-headed Firmin
Cedo. He was furnished with all the necessary engines
and implements for mining, assaying, and purifying the
precious metals, and with liberal pay and privileges. Ecclesiastics were also sent to supply the place of Friar
Boyle, and of certain of his brethren, who desired to leave
the island. The instruction and conversion of the natives
awakened more and more the solicitude of the queen. In
the ships of Torres a large number of Indians arrived, who
had been captured in the recent wars with the caciques.
Royal orders had been issued, that they should be sold as
slaves in the markets of Andalusia, as had been the custom with respect to negroes taken on the coast of Africa,
and to Moorish prisoners captured in the war with Granada. Isabella, however, had been deeply interested by
the accounts given of the gentle and hospitable character
of these islanders, and of their great docility. The discovery had been made under her immediate auspices; she
looked upon these people as under her peculiar care, and
she anticipated, with pious enthusiasm, the glory of leading them from darkness into the paths of light. Her compassionate spirit revolted at the idea of treating them as
slaves, even though sanctioned by the customs of the time.
Within five days after the royal order for the sale, a letter
was written by the sovereigns to Bishop Fonseca, suspending that order, until they could inquire into the cause
for which the Indians had been made prisoners, and consult learned and pious theologians, whether their sale would
be justifiable in the eyes of God.[1] Much difference of opinion took place among divines, on this important question,
the queen eventually decided it according to the dictates
of her own pure conscience and charitable heart. She
ordered that the Indians should be sent back to their na-

[1] Letter of the Sovereigns to Fonseca. Navarrete, Coleccion de
los Viages, i. 11, Doc. 92.

tive country, and enjoined that the islanders should be conciliated by the gentlest means, instead of being treated
with severity. Unfortunately her orders came too late to
Hispaniola to have the desired effect. The scenes of warfare and violence, produced by the bad passions of the colonists and the vengeance of the natives, were not to be forgotten, and mutual distrust and rankling animosity had
grown up between them, which no after exertions could
eradicate.

CHAPTER IX.

ARRIVAL OF AGUADO AT ISABELLA.—HIS ARROGANT CON-
DUCT.—TEMPEST IN THE HARBOR.

[1495.]

JUAN AGUADO set sail from Spain towards the end of
August, with four caravels, well freighted with supplies of
all kinds. Don Diego Columbus returned in this squadron
to Hispaniola, and arrived at Isabella in the month of
October, while the admiral was absent, occupied in re-estab-
lishing the tranquillity of the interior. Aguado, as has
already been shown, was under obligations to Columbus,
who had distinguished him from among his companions,
and had recommended him to the favor of the sovereigns.
He was, however, one of those weak men, whose heads are
turned by the least elevation. Puffed up by a little temporary power, he lost sight, not merely of the respect and
gratitude due to Columbus, but of the nature and extent
of his own commission. Instead of acting as an agent
employed to collect information, he assumed a tone of
authority, as though the reins of government had been
transferred into his hands. He interfered in public affairs;
ordered various persons to be arrested; called to account
the officers employed by the admiral; and paid no respect

to Don Bartholomew Columbus, who remained in command
during the absence of his brother. The Adelantado, astonished at this presumption, demanded a sight of the commission under which he acted; but Aguado treated him
with great haughtiness, replying that he would show it only
to the admiral. On second thoughts, however, lest there
should be doubts in the public mind of his right to interfere in the affairs of the colony, he ordered his letter of
credence from the sovereigns to be pompously proclaimed
by sound of trumpet. It was brief but comprehensive, to
the following purport:—"Cavaliers, Esquires, and other
persons, who by our orders are in the Indies, we send to
you Juan Aguado, our groom of the chambers, who will
speak to you on our part. We command you to give him
faith and credit."

The report now circulated, that the downfall of Columbus
and his family was at hand, and that an auditor had arrived,
empowered to hear and to redress the grievances of the public. This rumor originated with Aguado himself, who threw
out menaces of rigid investigations and signal punishments.
It was a time of jubilee for offenders. Every culprit
started up into an accuser; every one who by negligence
or crime had incurred the wholesome penalties of the laws,
was loud in his clamors against the oppression of Columbus. There were ills enough in the colony, some incident
to its situation, others produced by the misdeeds of the
colonists, but all were ascribed to the mal-administration
of the admiral. He was made responsible alike for the
evils produced by others, and for his own stern remedies.
All the old complaints were reiterated against him and his
brothers, and the usual and illiberal cause given for their
oppressions, that they were foreigners, who sought merely
their own interest and aggrandizement, at the expense of
the sufferings and the indignities of Spaniards.

Destitute of discrimination to perceive what was true
and what false in these complaints, and anxious only to

condemn, Aguado saw in every thing conclusive testimony of the culpability of Columbus. He intimated, and perhaps thought, that the admiral was keeping at a distance from Isabella, through fear of encountering his investigations. In the fullness of his presumption, he even set out with a body of horse to go in quest of him. A vain and weak man in power is prone to employ satellites of his own description. The arrogant and boasting followers of Aguado, wherever they went, spread rumors among the natives of the might and importance of their chief, and of the punishment he intended to inflict upon Columbus. In a little while the report circulated through the island, that a new admiral had arrived to administer the government, and that the former one was to be put to death.

The news of the arrival and of the insolent conduct of Aguado reached Columbus in the interior of the island; he immediately hastened to Isabella to give him a meeting. Aguado, hearing of his approach, also returned there. As every one knew the lofty spirit of Columbus, his high sense of his services, and his jealous maintenance of his official dignity, a violent explosion was anticipated at the impending interview. Aguado also expected something of the kind, but, secure in his royal letter of credence, he looked forward with the ignorant audacity of a little mind to the result. The sequel showed how difficult it is for petty spirits to anticipate the conduct of a man like Columbus in an extraordinary situation. His natural heat and impetuosity had been subdued by a life of trials; he had learned to bring his passions into subjection to his judgment; he had too true an estimate of his own dignity to enter into a contest with a shallow boaster like Aguado; above all, he had a profound respect for the authority of his sovereigns; for in his enthusiastic spirit, prone to deep feelings of reverence, his loyalty was inferior only to his religion. He received Aguado, therefore, with grave and punctilious courtesy; and retorted upon him his own ostentatious ceremonial,

ordering that the letter of credence should be again proclaimed by sound of trumpet in presence of the populace.
He listened to it with solemn deference, and assured
Aguado of his readiness to acquiesce in whatever might
be the pleasure of his sovereigns.

This unexpected moderation, while it astonished the beholders, foiled and disappointed Aguado. He had come
prepared for a scene of altercation, and had hoped that
Columbus, in the heat and impatience of the moment,
would have said or done something that might be construed into disrespect for the authority of the sovereigns.
He endeavored, in fact, some months afterwards, to procure
from the public notaries present a prejudicial statement
of the interview; but the deference of the admiral for the
royal letter of credence had been too marked to be disputed;
and all the testimonials were highly in his favor.[1]

Aguado continued to intermeddle in public affairs, and
the respect and forbearance with which he was uniformly
treated by Columbus, and the mildness of the latter in all
his measures to appease the discontents of the colony, were
regarded as proofs of his loss of moral courage. He was
looked upon as a declining man, and Aguado hailed as the
lord of the ascendant. Every dastard spirit who had any
lurking ill-will, any real or imaginary cause of complaint,
now hastened to give it utterance; perceiving that, in gratifying his malice, he was promoting his interest, and that
in villifying the admiral he was gaining the friendship of
Aguado.

The poor Indians, too, harassed by the domination of the
white men, rejoiced in the prospect of a change of rulers;
vainly hoping that it might produce a mitigation of their
sufferings. Many of the caciques who had promised allegiance to the admiral after their defeat in the Vega, now
assembled at the house of Manicaotex, the brother of Caonabo, near the river Yagui, where they joined in a formal

[1] Herrera, Hist. Ind., decad. i. lib. ii. cap. 18.

complaint against Columbus, whom they considered the cause of all the evils which had sprung from the disobedience and the vices of his followers.

Aguado now considered the great object of his mission fulfilled. He had collected information sufficient, as he thought, to insure the ruin of the admiral and his brothers, and he prepared to return to Spain. Columbus resolved to do the same. He felt that it was time to appear at court, and dispel the cloud of calumny gathering against him. He had active enemies, of standing and influence, who were seeking every occasion to throw discredit upon himself and his enterprises; and, stranger and foreigner as he was, he had no active friends at court to oppose their machinations. He feared that they might eventually produce an effect upon the royal mind, fatal to the progress of discovery: he was anxious to return, therefore, and explain the real causes of the repeated disappointments with respect to profits anticipated from his enterprises. It is not one of the least singular traits in this history, that, after having been so many years in persuading mankind that there was a new world to be discovered, he had almost equal trouble in proving to them the advantage of its discovery.

When the ships were ready to depart, a terrible storm swept the island. It was one of those awful whirlwinds which occasionally rage within the tropics, and were called by the Indians " furicanes," or " uricans," a name they still retain with trifling variation. About mid-day a furious wind sprang up from the east, driving before it dense volumes of cloud and vapor. Encountering another tempest of wind from the west, it appeared as if a violent conflict ensued. The clouds were rent by incessant flashes, or rather streams of lightning. At one time they were piled up high in the sky, at another they swept to the earth, filling the air with a baleful darkness more dismal than the obscurity of midnight. Wherever the whirlwind passed, whole tracts of forests were shivered and stripped of their

leaves and branches: those of gigantic size, which resisted
the blast, were torn up by the roots, and hurled to a great
distance.   Groves were rent from the mountain precipices,
with vast masses of earth and rock, tumbling into the valleys with terrific noise, and choking the course of rivers.
The fearful sounds in the air and on the earth, the pealing
thunder, the vivid lightning, the howling of the wind, the
crash of falling trees and rocks, filled every one with affright; and many thought that the end of the world was at
hand. Some fled to caverns for safety, for their frail houses
were blown down, and the air was filled with the trunks and
branches of trees, and even with fragments of rocks, carried along by the fury of the tempest. When the hurricane
reached the harbor, it whirled the ships round as they lay
at anchor, snapped their cables, and sank three of them
with all who were on board. Others were driven about,
dashed against each other, and tossed mere wrecks upon
the shore by the swelling surges of the sea, which in some
places rolled for three or four miles upon the land.   The
tempest lasted for three hours.   When it had passed away,
and the sun again appeared, the Indians regarded each
other in mute astonishment and dismay. Never in their
memory, nor in the traditions of their ancestors, had their
island been visited by such a storm. They believed that
the Deity had sent this fearful ruin to punish the cruelties
and crimes of the white men; and declared that this people
had moved the very air, the water, and the earth, to disturb
their tranquil life, and to desolate their island.[1]

[1] Ramusio, tom. iii. p. 7.   Peter Martyr, decad. i. lib. iv.

CHAPTER X.

DISCOVERY OF THE MINES OF HAYNA.

[1496.]

In the recent hurricane, the four caravels of Aguado had been destroyed, together with two others which were in the harbor. The only vessel which survived was the Niña, and that in a very shattered condition. Columbus gave orders to have her immediately repaired, and another caravel constructed out of the wreck of those which had been destroyed. While waiting until they should be ready for sea, he was cheered by tidings of rich mines in the interior of the island, the discovery of which is attributed to an incident of a somewhat romantic nature.[1] A young Arragonian, named Miguel Diaz, in the service of the Adelantado, having a quarrel with another Spaniard, fought with him, and wounded him dangerously. Fearful of the consequences, he fled from the settlement, accompanied by five or six comrades, who had either been engaged in the affray, or were personally attached to him. Wandering about the island, they came to an Indian village on the southern coast, near the mouth of the river Ozema, where the city of San Domingo is at present situated. They were received with kindness by the natives, and resided for some time among them. The village was governed by a female cacique, who soon conceived a strong attachment for the young Arragonian. Diaz was not insensible to her tenderness, a connection was formed between them, and they lived for some time very happily together.

The recollection of his country and his friends began at length to steal upon the thoughts of the young Spaniard. It was a melancholy lot to be exiled from civilized life, and an outcast from among his countrymen. He longed to re-

---

[1] Oviedo, Cronica de las Indias, lib. ii. cap. 13.

turn to the settlement, but dreaded the punishment that
awaited him, from the austere justice of the Adelantado.
His Indian bride, observing him frequently melancholy and
lost in thought, penetrated the cause, with the quick intelligence of female affection.   Fearful that he would abandon
her, and return to his countrymen, she endeavored to devise
some means of drawing the Spaniards to that part of the
island.   Knowing that gold was their sovereign attraction,
she informed Diaz of certain rich mines in the neighborhood, and urged him to persuade his countrymen to abandon the comparatively sterile and unhealthy vicinity of Isabella, and settle upon the fertile banks of the Ozema;
promising they should be received with the utmost kindness
and hospitality by her nation.

Struck with the suggestion, Diaz made particular inquiries about the mines, and was convinced that they
abounded in gold.   He noticed the superior fruitfulness
and beauty of the country, the excellence of the river, and
the security of the harbor at its entrance.   He flattered
himself that the communication of such valuable intelligence would make his peace at Isabella, and obtain his
pardon from the Adelantado.   Full of these hopes, he procured guides from among the natives, and taking a
temporary leave of his Indian bride, set out with his comrades through the wilderness for the settlement, which was
about fifty leagues distant.   Arriving there secretly, he
learnt, to his great joy, that the man whom he had wounded
had recovered.   He now presented himself boldly before
the Adelantado, relying that his tidings would earn his forgiveness.   He was not mistaken.   No news could have
come more opportunely.   The admiral had been anxious to
remove the settlement to a more healthy and advantageous
situation.   He was desirous also of carrying home some conclusive proof of the riches of the island, as the most effectual
means of silencing the cavils of his enemies.   If the representations of Miguel Diaz were correct, here was a means of

effecting both these purposes. Measures were immediately taken to ascertain the truth. The Adelantado set forth in person to visit the river Ozema, accompanied by Miguel Diaz, Francisco de Garay, and the Indian guides, and attended by a number of men well armed. They proceeded from Isabella to Magdalena, and thence across the Royal Vega to the fortress of Conception. Continuing on to the south, they came to a range of mountains, which they traversed by a defile two leagues in length, and descended into another beautiful plain, which was called Bonao. Proceeding hence for some distance, they came to a great river called Hayna, running through a fertile country, all the streams of which abounded in gold. On the western bank of this river, and about eight leagues from its mouth, they found gold in greater quantities and in larger particles than had yet been met with in any part of the island, not even excepting the province of Cibao. They made experiments in various places within the compass of six miles, and always with success. The soil seemed to be generally impregnated with that metal, so that a common laborer, with little trouble, might find the amount of three drachms in the course of a day.[1] In several places they observed deep excavations in the form of pits, which looked as if the mines had been worked in ancient times; a circumstance which caused much speculation among the Spaniards, the natives having no idea of mining, but contenting themselves with the particles found on the surface of the soil, or in the beds of the rivers.

The Indians of the neighborhood received the white men with their promised friendship, and in every respect the representations of Miguel Diaz were fully justified. He was not only pardoned, but received into great favor, and was subsequently employed in various capacities in the island, in all which he acquitted himself with great fidelity.

[1] Herrera, Hist. Ind., decad. i. lib. ii. cap. 18. Peter Martyr, decad. i. lib. iv.

He kept his faith with his Indian bride, by whom, according to Oviedo, he had two children. Charlevoix supposes that they were regularly married, as the female cacique appears to have been baptized, being always mentioned by the Christian name of Catalina.[1]

When the Adelantado returned with this favorable report, and with specimens of ore, the anxious heart of the admiral was greatly elated. He gave orders that a fortress should be immediately erected on the banks of the Hayna, in the vicinity of the mines, and that they should be diligently worked. The fancied traces of ancient excavations gave rise to one of his usual veins of golden conjectures. He had already surmised that Hispaniola might be the ancient Ophir. He now flattered himself that he had discovered the identical mines whence King Solomon had procured his gold for the building of the temple of Jerusalem. He supposed that his ships must have sailed by the gulf of Persia, and round Trapoban to this island,[2] which, according to his idea, lay opposite to the extreme end of Asia, for such he firmly believed the island of Cuba.

It is probable that Columbus gave free license to his imagination in these conjectures, which tended to throw a splendor about his enterprises, and to revive the languishing interest of the public. Granting, however, the correctness of his opinion, that he was in the vicinity of Asia, an error by no means surprising in the imperfect state of geographical knowledge, all his consequent suppositions were far from extravagant. The ancient Ophir was believed to lie somewhere in the East, but its situation was a matter of controversy among the learned, and remains one of those conjectural questions about which too much has been written for it ever to be satisfactorily decided.

[1] Oviedo, Cronica de las Ind., lib. ii. cap. 13. Charlevoix, Hist. St. Domingo, lib. ii. p. 146.
[2] Peter Martyr, decad. i. lib. iv.

BOOK IX.

CHAPTER I.

[1496.]

THE new caravel, the Santa Cruz, being finished, and the Niña repaired, Columbus made every arrangement for immediate departure, anxious to be freed from the growing arrogance of Aguado, and to relieve the colony from a crew of factious and discontented men. He appointed his brother, Don Bartholomew, to the command of the island, with the title, which he had already given him, of Adelantado: in case of his death, he was to be succeeded by his brother Don Diego.

On the 10th of March the two caravels set sail for Spain, in one of which Çolumbùs embarked, and in the other Aguado. In consequence of the orders of the sovereigns, all those who could be spared from the island, and some who had wives and relatives in Spain whom they wished to visit, returned in these caravels, which were crowded with two hundred and twenty-five passengers, the sick, the idle, the profligate, and the factious. Never did a more miserable and disappointed crew return from a land of promise.

There were thirty Indians also on board of the caravels, among whom were the once redoubtable cacique Caonabo, one of his brothers, and a nephew. The curate of Los Palacios observes that Columbus had promised the cacique and his brother to restore them to their country and their power, after he had taken them to visit the King and Queen of Castile.[1] It is probable that by kind treatment and by a display of the wonders of Spain and the grandeur and might of its sovereigns, he hoped to conquer their enmity to the Spaniards, and convert them into important instruments towards obtaining a secure and peaceable dominion over the island. Caonabo, however, was of that proud nature, of wild but vigorous growth, which can never be tamed. He remained a moody and dejected captive. He had too much intelligence not to perceive that his power was for ever blasted, but he retained his haughtiness, even in the midst of his despair.

Being, as yet, but little experienced in the navigation of these seas, Columbus, instead of working up to the northward, so as to fall in with the tract of westerly winds, took an easterly course on leaving the island. The consequence was, that almost the whole of his voyage was a toilsome and tedious struggle against the trade-winds and calms which prevail between the tropics. On the 6th of April he found himself still in the vicinity of the Caribbee Islands, with his crews fatigued and sickly, and his provisions rapidly diminishing. He bore away to the southward, therefore, to touch at the most important of those islands, in search of supplies.

On Saturday the 9th, he anchored at Marigalante, whence, on the following day, he made sail for Guadaloupe. It was contrary to the custom of Columbus to weigh anchor on Sunday when in port, but the people murmured, and observed, that when in quest of food, it was no time to stand on scruples as to holy days.[2]

Anchoring off the island of Guadaloupe, the boat was sent on shore well armed. Before it could reach the land,

---

[1] Cura de los Palacios, cap. 131.
[2] Hist. del Almirante, cap. 62.

a large number of females issued from the woods, armed
with bows and arrows, and decorated with tufts of feathers,
preparing to oppose any descent upon their shores. As
the sea was somewhat rough, and a surf broke upon the
beach, the boats remained at a distance, and two of the
Indians from Hispaniola swam to shore. Having explained to these Amazons that the Spaniards only sought
provisions, in exchange for which they would give articles
of great value, the women referred them to their husbands,
who were at the northern end of the island. As the boats
proceeded thither, numbers of the natives were seen on the
beach, who manifested great ferocity, shouting, and yelling,
and discharging flights of arrows, which, however, fell far
short in the water. Seeing the boats approach the land,
they hid themselves in the adjacent forest, and rushed
forth with hideous cries as the Spaniards were landing.
A discharge of firearms drove them to the woods and
mountains, and the boats met with no further opposition.
Entering the deserted habitations, the Spaniards began to
plunder and destroy, contrary to the invariable injunctions
of the admiral. Among other articles found in these
houses, were honey and wax, which Herrera supposes had
been brought from Terra Firma, as these roving people
collected the productions of distant regions in the course
of their expeditions. Fernando Columbus mentions likewise that there were hatchets of iron in their houses; these,
however, must have been made of a species of hard and
heavy stone, already mentioned, which resembled iron; or
they must have been procured from places which the Spaniards had previously visited, as it is fully admitted that no
iron was in use among the natives prior to the discovery.
The sailors also reported that in one of the houses they
found the arm of a man roasting on a spit before a fire;
but these facts, so repugnant to humanity, require more
solid authority to be credited; the sailors had committed
wanton devastations in these dwellings, and may have

sought a pretext with which to justify their maraudings
to the admiral.

While some of the people were getting wood and water,
and making cassava bread, Columbus dispatched forty men,
well armed, to explore the interior of the island. They
returned on the following day with ten women and three
boys. The women were of large and powerful form, yet
of great agility. They were naked, and wore their long
hair flowing loose upon their shoulders; some decorated
their heads with plumes of various colors. Among them
was the wife of a cacique, a woman of great strength and
proud spirit. On the approach of the Spaniards, she
had fled with an agility which soon left all her pursuers
far behind, excepting a native of the Canary Islands
remarkable for swiftness of foot. She would have escaped
even from him, but, perceiving that he was alone, and far
from his companions, she turned suddenly upon him, seized
him with astonishing force, and would have strangled him,
had not the Spaniards arrived and taken her entangled like
a hawk with her prey. The warlike spirit of these Carib
women, and the circumstance of finding them in armed
bands, defending their shores, during the absence of their
husbands, led Columbus repeatedly into the erroneous idea,
that certain of these islands were inhabited entirely by
women; for which error, as has already been observed, he
was prepared by the stories of Marco Polo concerning an
island of Amazons near the coast of Asia.

Having remained several days at the island, and prepared three weeks' supply of bread, Columbus prepared to
make sail. As Guadaloupe was the most important of the
Caribbee Islands, and in a manner the portal or entrance to
all the rest, he wished to secure the friendship of the inhabitants. He dismissed, therefore, all the prisoners, with many
presents, to compensate for the spoil and injury which had
been done. The female cacique, however, declined going on
shore, preferring to remain and accompany the natives of

Hispaniola who were on board, keeping with her also a young daughter. She had conceived a passion for Caonabo, having found out that he was a native of the Caribbee Islands. His character and story, gathered from the other Indians, had won the sympathy and admiration of this intrepid woman.[1]

Leaving Guadaloupe on the 20th of April, and keeping in about the twenty-second degree of latitude, the caravels again worked their way against the whole current of the trade-winds, insomuch, that, on the 20th of May, after a month of great fatigue and toil, they had yet a great part of their voyage to make. The provisions were already so reduced, that Columbus had to put every one on a daily allowance of six ounces of bread and a pint and a half of water: as they advanced, the scarcity grew more and more severe, and was rendered more appalling from the uncertainty which prevailed on board the vessels as to their situation. There were several pilots in the caravels; but being chiefly accustomed to the navigation of the Mediterranean, or the Atlantic coasts, they were utterly confounded, and lost all reckoning when traversing the broad ocean. Every one had a separate opinion, and none heeded that of the admiral. By the beginning of June there was an absolute famine on board of the ships. In the extremity of their sufferings, while death stared them in the face, it was proposed by some of the Spaniards, as a desperate alternative, that they should kill and eat their Indian prisoners; others suggested that they should throw them into the sea, as so many expensive and useless mouths. Nothing but the absolute authority of Columbus prevented this last counsel from being adopted. He represented that the Indians were their fellow-beings, some of them Christians like themselves, and all entitled to similar treatment. He exhorted them to a little patience, assuring them that they would soon make land, for that, according to his reckoning, they were

[1] Hist. del Almirante, cap. 63.

not far from Cape St. Vincent. At this all scoffed, for they believed themselves yet far from their desired haven; some affirming that they were in the English channel, others that they were approaching Gallicia; when Columbus, therefore, confident in his opinion, ordered that sail should be taken in at night, lest they should come upon the land in the dark, there was a general murmur; the men exclaiming that it was better to be cast on shore, than to starve at sea. The next morning, however, to their great joy, they came in sight of the very land which Columbus had predicted. From this time, he was regarded by the seamen as deeply versed in the mysteries of the ocean, and almost oracular in matters of navigation.[1]

On the 11th of June, the vessels anchored in the bay of Cadiz, after a weary voyage of about three months. In the course of this voyage, the unfortunate Caonabo expired. It is by the mere casual mention of contemporary writers, that we have any notice of this circumstance, which appears to have been passed over as a matter of but little moment. He maintained his haughty nature to the last, for his death is principally ascribed to the morbid melancholy of a proud but broken spirit.[2] He was an extraordinary character in savage life. From being a simple Carib warrior, he had risen, by his enterprise and courage, to be the most powerful cacique, and the dominant spirit of the populous island of Hayti. He was the only chieftain that appeared to have had sagacity sufficient to foresee the fatal effects of Spanish ascendency, or military talent to combine any resistence to its inroads. Had his warriors been of his own

[1] Hist. del Almirante, cap. 63.

[2] Cura de los Palacios, cap. 131. Peter Martyr, decad. i. lib. iv. Some have affirmed that Caonabo perished in one of the caravels which foundered in the harbor of Isabella during the hurricane, but the united testimony of the curate of Los Palacios, Peter Martyr, and Fernando Columbus proves that he sailed with the admiral in his return voyage.

intrepid nature, the war which he raised would have been formidable in the extreme. His fate furnishes, on a narrow scale, a lesson to human greatness. When the Spaniards first arrived on the coast of Hayti, their imaginations were inflamed with rumors of a magnificent prince in the interior, the lord of the Golden House, the sovereign of the mines of Cibao, who reigned in splendid state among the mountains; but a short time had elapsed, and this fancied potentate of the East, stripped of every illusion, was a naked and dejected prisoner on the deck of one of their caravels, with none but one of his own wild native heroines to sympathize in his misfortunes. All his importance vanished with his freedom; scarce any mention is made of him during his captivity, and with innate qualities of a high and heroic nature, he perished with the obscurity of one of the vulgar.

CHAPTER II

DECLINE OF THE POPULARITY OF COLUMBUS IN SPAIN.—
HIS RECEPTION BY THE SOVEREIGNS AT BURGOS.—HE
PROPOSES A THIRD VOYAGE.

ENVY and malice had been but too successful in undermining the popularity of Columbus. It is impossible to keep up a state of excitement for any length of time, even by miracles. The world, at first, is prompt and lavish in its admiration, but soon grows cool, distrusts its late enthusiasm, and fancies it has been defrauded of what it bestowed with such prodigality. It is then that the caviler who had been silenced by the general applause puts in his insidious suggestion, detracts from the merit of the declining favorite, and succeeds in rendering him an object of doubt and censure, if not of absolute aversion. In three short years, the public had become familiar with the stupendous wonder of a newly-discovered world, and was now open to every insinuation derogatory to the fame of the discoverer and the importance of his enterprises.

The circumstances which attended the present arrival of Columbus were little calculated to diminish the growing prejudices of the populace. When the motley crowd of mariners and adventurers who had embarked with such sanguine expectations landed from the vessels in the port of Cadiz, instead of a joyous crew, bounding on shore, flushed with success, and laden with the spoils of the golden Indies, a feeble train of wretched men crawled forth, emaciated by the diseases of the colony and the hardships of the voyage, who carried in their yellow countenances, says an old writer, a mockery of that gold which had been the object of their search, and who had nothing to relate of the New World, but tales of sickness, poverty, and disappointment.

Columbus endeavored, as much as possible, to counteract these unfavorable appearances, and to revive the languishing enthusiasm of the public. He dwelt upon the importance of his recent discoveries along the coast of Cuba, where, he supposed, he had arrived nearly to the Aurea Chersonesus of the ancients, bordering on some of the richest provinces of Asia. Above all, he boasted of his discovery of the abundant mines on the south side of Hispaniola, which he persuaded himself were those of the ancient Ophir. The public listened to these accounts with sneering incredulity; or if for a moment a little excitement was occasioned, it was quickly destroyed by gloomy pictures drawn by disappointed adventurers.

In the harbor of Cadiz Columbus found three caravels, commanded by Pedro Alonzo Niño, on the point of sailing with supplies for the colony. Nearly a year had elapsed without any relief of the kind; four caravels which had sailed in the preceding January having been lost on the coast of the Peninsula.[1] Having read the royal letters and

[1] Muñoz, Hist. N. Mundo, lib. vi.

dispatches of which Niño was the bearer, and being informed of the wishes of the sovereigns, as well as of the state of the public mind, Columbus wrote by this opportunity, urging the Adelantado to endeavor, by every means, to bring the island into a peaceful and productive state, appeasing all discontents and commotions, and seizing and sending to Spain all caciques, or their subjects, who should be concerned in the deaths of any of the colonists. He recommended the most unremitting diligence in exploring and working the mines recently discovered on the river Hayna, and that a place should be chosen in the neighborhood, and a sea-port founded. Pedro Alonzo Niño set sail with the three caravels on the 17th of June.

Tidings of the arrival of Columbus having reached the sovereigns, he received a gracious letter from them, dated at Almazen, 12th July, 1496; congratulating him on his safe return, and inviting him to court when he should have recovered from the fatigues of his voyage. The kind terms in which this letter was couched were calculated to reassure the heart of Columbus, who, ever since the mission of the arrogant Aguado, had considered himself out of favor with the sovereigns, and fallen into disgrace. As a proof of the dejection of his spirits, we are told that when he made his appearance this time in Spain, he was clad in a humble garb, resembling in form and color the habit of a Franciscan monk, simply girded with a cord, and that he had suffered his beard to grow like the brethren of that order.[1] This was probably in fulfillment of some penitential vow made in a moment of danger or despondency,—a custom prevalent in those days, and frequently observed by Columbus. It betokened, however, much humility and depression of spirit, and afforded a striking contrast to his appearance on his former triumphant return. He was doomed, in fact, to yield repeated examples of the reverses to which those are subject who have once launched from

[1] Cura de los Palacios, cap. 131. Oviedo, lib. ii: cap. 13.

the safe shores of obscurity on the fluctuating waves of popular opinion.

However indifferent Columbus might be to his own personal appearance, he was anxious to keep alive the interest in his discoveries, fearing continually that the indifference awakening towards him might impede their accomplishment. On his way to Burgos, therefore, where the sovereigns were expected, he made a studious display of the curiosities and treasures which he had brought from the New World. Among these were collars, bracelets, anklets, and coronets of gold, the spoils of various caciques, and which were considered as trophies won from barbaric princes of the rich coasts of Asia, or the islands of the Indian seas. It is a proof of the petty standard by which the sublime discovery of Columbus was already estimated, that he had to resort to this management to dazzle the gross perceptions of the multitude by the mere glare of gold.

He carried with him several Indians also, decorated after their savage fashion, and glittering with golden ornaments ; among whom were the brother and nephew of Caonabo, the former about thirty years of age, the latter only ten. They were brought merely to visit the king and queen, that they might be impressed with an idea of the grandeur and power of the Spanish sovereigns, after which they were to be restored in safety to their country. Whenever they passed through any principal place, Columbus put a massive collar and chain of gold upon the brother of Caonabo, as being cacique of the golden country of Cibao. The curate of Los Palacios, who entertained the discoverer and his Indian captives for several days in his house, says that he had this chain of gold in his hands, and that it weighed six hundred castellanos.[1] The worthy curate likewise makes mention of various Indian masks and images of wood or cotton, wrought with fantastic faces of animals, all

---

[1] Equivalent to the value of three thousand one hundred and ninety-five dollars of the present time.

of which he supposed were representations of the devil, who he concludes must be the object of adoration of these islanders.[1]

The reception of Columbus by the sovereigns was different from what he had anticipated; for he was treated with distinguished favor, nor was any mention made either of the complaints of Margarite and Boyle, or the judicial inquiries conducted by Aguado. However these may have had a transient effect on the minds of the sovereigns, they were too conscious of the great deserts of Columbus, and the extraordinary difficulties of his situation, not to tolerate what they may have considered errors on his part.

Encouraged by the favorable countenance he experienced, and by the interest with which the sovereigns listened to his account of his recent voyage along the coast of Cuba, and the discovery of the mines of Hayna, which he failed not to represent as the Ophir of the ancients, Columbus now proposed a further enterprise, by which he promised to make yet more extensive discoveries, and to annex Terra Firma to their dominions. For this purpose he asked eight ships; two to be dispatched to the island of Hispaniola with supplies, the remaining six to be put under his command for a voyage of discovery. The sovereigns readily promised to comply with his request, and were probably sincere in their intentions to do so, but in the performance of their promise Columbus was doomed to meet with intolerable delay; partly in consequence of the operation of public events, partly in consequence of the intrigues of men of office, the two great influences which are continually diverting and defeating the designs of princes.

The resources of Spain were, at this moment, tasked to the utmost by the ambition of Ferdinand, who lavished all his revenues in warlike expenses and in subsidies. While maintaining a contest of deep and artful policy with France, with the ultimate aim of grasping the sceptre of Naples, he

[1] Cura de los Palacios, cap. 131 .

was laying the foundation of a wide and powerful connection by the marriages of the royal children, who were now maturing in years. At this time arose that family alliance which afterwards consolidated such an immense empire under his grandson and successor, Charles V.

While a large army was maintained in Italy, under Gonsalvo of Cordova, to assist the king of Naples in recovering his throne, of which he had been suddenly dispossessed by Charles VIII of France, other armies were required on the frontiers of Spain, which were menaced with a French invasion. Squadrons also had to be employed for the safeguard of the Mediterranean and Atlantic coasts of the Peninsula, while a magnificent armada of upwards of a hundred ships, having on board twenty thousand persons, many of them of the first nobility, was dispatched to convoy the Princess Juana to Flanders, to be married to Philip, Archduke of Austria, and to bring back his sister Margarita, the destined bride of Prince Juan.

These widely-extended operations, both of war and amity, put all the land and naval forces into requisition. They drained the royal treasury, and engrossed the thoughts of the sovereigns, obliging them also to journey from place to place in their dominions. With such cares of an immediate and homefelt nature pressing upon their minds, the distant enterprises of Columbus were easily neglected or postponed. They had hitherto been sources of expense instead of profit; and there were artful counselors ever ready to whisper in the royal ear, that they were likely to continue so. What, in the ambitious eyes of Ferdinand, was the acquisition of a number of wild, uncultivated, and distant islands, to that of the brilliant domain of Naples; or the intercourse with naked and barbaric princes, to that of an alliance with the most potent sovereigns of Christendom? Columbus had the mortification, therefore, to see armies levied and squadrons employed in idle contests about a little point of territory in Europe, and a vast armada of upwards of a hundred sail destined to the ostentatious service of convoying a royal bride; while he vainly solicited a few caravels to prosecute his discovery of a world..

At length, in the autumn, six millions of maravedies were ordered to be advanced to Columbus for the equipment of his promised squadron.[1] Just as the sum was about to be delivered, a letter was received from Pedro Alonzo Niño, who had arrived at Cadiz with his three caravels, on his return from the island of Hispaniola. Instead of proceeding to court in person, or forwarding the dispatches of the Adelantado, he had gone to visit his family at Huelva, taking the dispatches with him, and merely writing, in a vaunting style, that he had a great amount of gold on board of his ships.[2]

This was triumphant intelligence to Columbus, who immediately concluded that the new mines were in operation, and the treasures of Ophir about to be realized. The letter of Niño, however, was fated to have a most injurious effect on his concerns.

The king at that moment was in immediate want of money, to repair the fortress of Salza, in Rousillon, which had been sacked by the French; the six millions of maravedies about to be advanced to Columbus were forthwith appropriated to patch up the shattered castle, and an order was given for the amount to be paid out of the gold brought by Niño. It was not until the end of December, when Niño arrived at court, and delivered the dispatches of the Adelantado, that his boast of gold was discovered to be a mere figure of speech, and that his caravels were, in fact, freighted with Indian prisoners, from the sale of whom the vaunted gold was to arise.

It is difficult to describe the vexatious effects of this absurd hyperbole. The hopes of Columbus, of great and

---

[1] Equivalent to 86,956 dollars of the present day.

[2] Las Casas, Hist. Ind., lib. i. cap. 123, MS.

immediate profit from the mines, were suddenly cast down; the zeal of his few advocates was cooled; an air of empty exaggeration was given to his enterprises; and his enemies pointed with scorn and ridicule to the wretched cargoes of the caravels, as the boasted treasures of the New World. The report brought by Niño and his crew represented the colony as in a disastrous condition, and the dispatches of the Adelantado pointed out the importance of immediate supplies; but in proportion as the necessity of the case was urgent, the measure of relief was tardy. All the unfavorable representations hitherto made seemed corroborated, and the invidious cry of "great cost and little gain" was revived by those politicians of petty sagacity and microscopic eye, who, in all great undertakings, can discern the immediate expense, without having scope of vision to embrace the future profit.

CHAPTER III.

PREPARATIONS FOR A THIRD VOYAGE.—DISAPPOINTMENTS AND DELAYS.

[1497.]

It was not until the following spring of 1497 that the concerns of Columbus and of the New World began to receive serious attention from the sovereigns. The fleet had returned from Flanders with the Princess Margarita of Austria. Her nuptials with Prince Juan, the heir-apparent, had been celebrated at Burgos, the capital of Old Castile, with extraordinary splendor. All the grandees, the dignitaries, and chivalry of Spain, together with ambassadors from the principal potentates of Christendom, were assembled on the occasion. Burgos was for some time a scene of chivalrous pageant and courtly revel, and the whole kingdom celebrated with great rejoicings this powerful alliance, which seemed to insure to the Spanish sovereigns a continuance of their extraordinary prosperity.

In the midst of these festivities, Isabella, whose maternal heart had recently been engrossed by the marriages of her children, now that she was relieved from these concerns of a tender and domestic nature, entered into the affairs of the New World with a spirit that showed she was determined to place them upon a substantial foundation, as well as clearly to define the powers, and reward the services of Columbus. To her protecting zeal all the provisions in favor of Columbus must be attributed; for the king began to look coldly on him, and the royal counselors, who had most influence in the affairs of the Indies, were his enemies.

Various royal ordinances dated about this time manifest the generous and considerate disposition of the queen. The rights, privileges, and dignities granted to Columbus at Santa Fé were again confirmed; a tract of land in Hispaniola, fifty leagues in length, and twenty-five in breadth, was offered to him, with the title of duke or marquess. This, however, Columbus had the forbearance to decline; he observed that it would only increase the envy which was already so virulent against him, and would cause new misrepresentations; as he should be accused of paying more attention to the settlement and improvement of his own possessions, than of any other part of the island.[1]

As the expenses of the expeditions had hitherto far exceeded the returns, Columbus had incurred debt rather than reaped profit from the share he had been permitted to take in them; he was relieved, therefore, from his obligation to bear an eighth part of the cost of the past enterprises, excepting the sum which he had advanced towards the first voyage; at the same time, however, he was not to claim any share of what had hitherto been brought from the island. For three ensuing years he was to be allowed an eighth of the gross proceeds of every voyage, and an

[1] Las Casas, Hist. Ind., lib. i. cap. 123.

additional tenth after the costs had been deducted. After
the expiration of the three years, the original terms of
agreement were to be resumed.

To gratify his honorable ambition also, and to perpetuate
in his family the distinction gained by his illustrious deeds,
he was allowed the right of establishing a mayorazgo, or
perpetual entail of his estates, so that they might always
descend with his titles of nobility. This he shortly after
exercised in a solemn testament executed at Seville in the
early part of 1498, by which he devised his estates to his
own male descendants, and on their failure to the male
descendants of his brothers, and in default of male heirs
to the females of his lineage.

The heir was always to bear the arms of the admiral, to
seal with them, to sign with his signature, and in signing,
never to use any other title than simply "The Admiral,"
whatever other titles might be given him by the king, and
used by him on other occasions. Such was the noble pride
with which he valued this title of his real greatness.

In this testament he made ample provision for his brother,
the Adelantado, his son Fernando, and his brother Don
Diego, the last of whom, he intimates, had a desire to enter
into ecclesiastical life. He ordered that a tenth part of
the revenues arising from the mayorazgo should be devoted
to pious and charitable purposes, and in relieving all poor
persons of his lineage. He made provisions for the giving
of marriage-portions to the poor females of his family. He
ordered that a married person of his kindred who had
been born in his native city of Genoa should be maintained
there in competence and respectability, by way of keeping
a domicile for the family there; and he commanded whoever should inherit the mayorazgo, always to do every
thing in his power for the honor, prosperity, and increase
of the city of Genoa, provided it should not be contrary to
the service of the church, and the interests of the Spanish
crown. Among various other provisions in this will, he

solemnly provides for his favorite scheme, the recovery of
the holy sepulchre. He orders his son Diego, or whoever
else may inherit his estate, to invest from time to time as
much money as he can spare, in stock in the bank of St.
George at Genoa, to form a permanent fund, with which he
is to stand ready at any time to follow and serve the king
in the conquest of Jerusalem. Or should the king not
undertake such enterprise, then, when the funds have
accumulated to sufficient amount, to set on foot a crusade
at his own charge and risk, in hopes that, seeing his determination, the sovereigns may be induced either to adopt
the undertaking, or to authorize him to pursue it in their
name.

Beside this special undertaking for the Catholic faith, he
charges his heir in case there should arise any schism in
the church, or any violence menacing its prosperity, to
throw himself at the feet of the pope, and devote his person
and property to defend the church from all insult and
spoliation. Next to the service of God, he enjoins loyalty
to the throne; commanding him at all times to serve the
sovereigns and their heirs, faithfully and zealously, even to
the loss of life and estate. To insure the constant remembrance of this testament, he orders his heir that, before he
confesses, he shall give it to his father confessor to read,
who is to examine him upon his faithful fulfillment of its
conditions.[1]

As Columbus had felt aggrieved by the general license
granted in April, 1495, to make discoveries in the New
World, considering it as interfering with his prerogatives, a
royal edict was issued on the 2d of June, 1497, retracting
whatever might be prejudicial to his interests, or to the
previous grants made him by the crown. " It never was
our intention," said the sovereigns in their edict, " in any
way to affect the rights of the said Don Christopher Columbus, nor to allow the conventions, privileges, and favors

[1] This testament is inserted at large in the Appendix.

which we have granted him to be encroached upon or
violated; but on the contrary, in consequence of the services which he has rendered us, we intend to confer still
further favors on him." Such, there is every reason to believe, was the sincere intention of the magnanimous Isabella; but the stream of her royal bounty was poisoned
or diverted by the base channels through which it flowed.

The favor shown to Columbus was extended likewise to
his family. The titles and prerogatives of Adelantado with
which he had invested his brother Don Bartholomew had
at first awakened the displeasure of the king, who jealously
reserved all high dignities of the kind to be granted exclusively by the crown. By a royal letter, the office was
now conferred upon Don Bartholomew, as if through spontaneous favor of the sovereigns, no allusion being made to
his having previously enjoyed it.

While all these measures were taken for the immediate
gratification of Columbus, others were adopted for the interests of the colony. Permission was granted him to take
out three hundred and thirty persons in royal pay, of whom
forty were to be escuderos or servants, one hundred foot-
soldiers, thirty sailors, thirty ship-boys, twenty miners, fifty
husbandmen, ten gardeners, twenty mechanics of various
kinds, and thirty females. He was subsequently permitted
to increase the number, if he thought proper, to five
hundred; but the additional individuals were to be paid
out of the produce and merchandise of the colony. He was
likewise authorized to grant lands to all such as were disposed to cultivate vineyards, orchards, sugar plantations, or
to form any other rural establishments, on condition that
they should reside as householders on the island for four years
after such grant, and that all the brazil-wood and precious
metals, found on their lands, should be reserved to the crown.

Nor were the interests of the unhappy natives forgotten
by the compassionate heart of Isabella. Notwithstanding
the sophisms by which their subjection and servitude were

made matters of civil and divine right, and sanctioned by the political prelates of the day, Isabella always consented with the greatest reluctance to the slavery even of those who were taken in open warfare; while her utmost solicitude was exerted to protect the unoffending part of this helpless and devoted race. She ordered that the greatest care should be taken of their religious instruction, and the greatest leniency shown in collecting the tributes imposed upon them, with all possible indulgence to defalcators. In fact, the injunctions given with respect to the treatment both of Indians and Spaniards, are the only indications, in the royal edicts, of any impression having been made by the complaints against Columbus of severity in his government. It was generally recommended by the sovereigns, that, whenever the public safety did not require stern measures, there should be manifested a disposition to lenity and easy rule.

When every intention was thus shown on the part of the crown to dispatch the expedition to the colony, unexpected difficulties arose on the part of the public. The charm was dispelled which in the preceding voyage had made every adventurer crowd into the service of Columbus. An odium had been industriously thrown upon his enterprises; and his new-found world, instead of a region of wealth and delight, was considered a land of poverty and disaster. There was a difficulty in procuring either ships or men for the voyage. To remedy the first of these deficiencies, one of those arbitrary orders was issued, so opposite to our present ideas of commercial policy, empowering the officers of the crown to press into the service whatever ships they might judge suitable for the purposed expedition, together with their masters and pilots; and to fix such price for their remuneration, as the officers should deem just and reasonable. To supply the want of voluntary recruits, a measure was adopted at the suggestion of Columbus,[1] which

[1] Las Casas, Hist. Ind., lib. i. cap. 112, MS.

shows the desperate alternatives to which he was reduced by the great reaction of public sentiment. This was, to commute the sentences of criminals condemned to banishment, to the galleys, or to the mines, into transportation to the new settlements, where they were to labor in the public service without pay. Those whose sentence was banishment for life, to be transported for ten years; those banished for a specific term, to be transported for half that time. A general pardon was published for all malefactors at large, who within a certain time should surrender themselves to the admiral, and embark for the colonies; those who had committed offences meriting death, to serve for two years, those whose misdeeds were of a lighter nature, to serve for one year.[1] Those only were excepted from this indulgence who had committed heresy, treason, coining, murder, and certain other specific crimes. This pernicious measure, calculated to poison the population of an infant community at its very source, was a fruitful cause of trouble to Columbus, and of misery and detriment to the colony. It has been frequently adopted by various nations, whose superior experience should have taught them better, and has proved the bane of many a rising settlement. It is assuredly as unnatural for a metropolis to cast forth its crimes and vices upon its colonies, as it would be for a parent willfully to ingraft disease upon his children. In both instances the obligation of nature is vitiated; nor should it be matter of surprise, if the seeds of evil thus sown should bring forth bitter retribution.

Notwithstanding all these violent expedients, there was still a ruinous delay in fitting out the expedition. This is partly accounted for by changes which took place in the persons appointed to superintend the affairs of the Indies. These concerns had for a time been consigned to Antonio de Torres, in whose name, conjointly with that of Columbus, many of the official documents had been made out.

[1] Muñoz, lib. vi. § 19.

In consequence of high and unreasonable demands on the part of Torres, he was removed from office, and Juan Rodriguez de Fonseca, Bishop of Badajos, reinstated. The papers had, therefore, to be made out anew, and fresh contracts formed. While these concerns were tardily attended to, the queen was suddenly overwhelmed with affliction by the death of her only son Prince Juan, whose nuptials had been celebrated with such splendor in the spring. It was the first of a series of domestic calamities which assailed her affectionate heart, and overwhelmed her with affliction for the remainder of her days. In the midst of her distress, however, she still thought of Columbus. In consequence of his urgent representations of the misery to which the colony must be reduced, two ships were dispatched in the beginning of 1498, under the command of Pedro Fernandez Coronel, freighted with supplies. The necessary funds were advanced by the queen herself, out of the moneys intended to form the endowment of her daughter Isabella, then betrothed to Emanuel, King of Portugal. An instance of her kind feeling toward Columbus was also evinced in the time of her affliction: his two sons, Diego and Fernando, had been pages to the deceased prince; the queen now took them, in the same capacity, into her own service.

With all this zealous disposition on the part of the queen, Columbus still met with the most injurious and discouraging delays in preparing the six remaining vessels for his voyage. His cold-blooded enemy Fonseca, having the superintendence of Indian affairs, was enabled to impede and retard all his plans. The various petty officers and agents employed in the concerns of the armament were many of them minions of the bishop, and knew that they were gratifying him in annoying Columbus. They looked upon the latter as a man declining in popularity, who might be offended with impunity; they scrupled not, therefore, to throw all kinds of difficulties in his path, and to treat him occasionally with that arrogance which petty and ignoble men in place are prone to exercise.

It seems almost incredible at the present day that such important and glorious enterprises should have been subject to such despicable molestations. Columbus bore them all with silent indignation. He was a stranger in the land he was benefiting; he felt that the popular tide was setting against him, and that it was necessary to tolerate many present grievances for the sake of effecting his great purposes. So wearied and disheartened, however, did he become by the impediments artfully thrown in his way, and so disgusted by the prejudices of the fickle public, that he at one time thought of abandoning his discoveries altogether. He was chiefly induced to persevere by his grateful attachment to the queen, and his desire to achieve something that might cheer and animate her under her afflictions.[1]

At length, after all kinds of irritating delays, the six vessels were fitted for sea, though it was impossible to conquer the popular repugnance to the service sufficiently to enlist the allotted number of men. In addition to the persons in employ already enumerated, a physician, surgeon, and apothecary were sent out for the relief of the colony, and several priests to replace Friar Boyle and certain of his discontented brethren; while a number of musicians were embarked by the admiral, to cheer and enliven the colonists.

The insolence which Columbus had suffered from the minions of Fonseca throughout this long protracted time of preparation, harassed him to the last moment of his sojourn in Spain, and followed him to the very water's edge. Among the worthless hirelings who had annoyed him, the most noisy and presuming was one Ximeno Breviesca, treasurer or accountant of Fonseca. He was not an old Christian, observes the venerable Las Casas; by which it is

---

[1] Letter of Columbus to the nurse of Prince Juan.

to be understood that he was either a Jew or a Moor converted to the Catholic faith.   He had an impudent front and an unbridled tongue, and, echoing the sentiments of his patron the bishop, had been loud in his abuse of the admiral and his enterprises.   The very day when the squadron was on the point of weighing anchor, Columbus was assailed by the insolence of this Ximeno, either on the shore when about to embark, or on board of his ship where he had just entered.   In the hurry of the moment, he forgot his usual self-command; his indignation, hitherto repressed, suddenly burst forth; he struck the despicable minion to the ground, and kicked him repeatedly, venting in this unguarded paroxysm the accumulated griefs and vexations which had long rankled in his mind.[1]

Nothing could demonstrate more strongly what Columbus had previously suffered from the machinations of unworthy men, than this transport of passion, so unusual in his well-governed temper.   He deeply regretted it, and in a letter written some time afterwards to the sovereigns, he endeavored to obviate the injury it might do him in their opinion, through the exaggeration and false coloring of his enemies.   His apprehensions were not ill-founded, for Las Casas attributes the humiliating measures shortly after adopted by the sovereigns toward Columbus, to the unfavorable impression produced by this affair.   It had happened near at home, as it were, under the very eye of the sovereigns; it spoke, therefore, more quickly to their feelings than more important allegations from a distance.   The personal castigation of a public officer was represented as a flagrant instance of the vindictive temper of Columbus, and a corroboration of the charges of cruelty and oppression sent from the colony.   As Ximeno was a creature of the invidious Fonseca, the affair was represented to the sovereigns in the most odious point of view.   Thus the generous intentions of princes, and the exalted services of their sub-

[1] Las Casas, Hist. Ind., lib. i. cap. 126, MS.

jécts, are apt to be defeated by the intervention of cold and crafty men in place. By his implacable hostility to Columbus, and the secret obstructions which he threw in the way of the most illustrious of human enterprises, Fonseca has insured perpetuity to his name, coupled with the contempt of every generous mind.

BOOK X.

CHAPTER I.

[1498.]

On the 30th of May, 1498, Columbus set sail from the port of San Lucar de Barrameda, with his squadron of six vessels, on his third voyage of discovery. The route he proposed to take was different from that pursued in his former voyages. He intended to depart from the Cape de Verde Islands, sailing to the southwest until he should come under the equinoctial line, then to steer directly westward with the favor of the trade-winds, until he should arrive at land, or find himself in the longitude of Hispaniola. Various considerations induced him to adopt this course. In his preceding voyage, when he coasted the southern side of Cuba, under the belief that it was the continent of Asia, he had observed that it swept off toward the south. From this circumstance, and from information gathered among the natives of the Caribbee Islands, he was induced to believe that a great tract of the main land lay to the south of the countries he had already discovered. King John II of Portugal appears to have entertained a similar idea; as Herrera records an opinion expressed by that monarch, that there was a continent in the southern ocean.[1] If this were the case, it was supposed by Columbus, that, in proportion as he approached the equator, and ex-

[1] Herrera, Hist. Ind., decad. i. lib. iii. cap. 9.

459

tended his discoveries to climates more and more under the torrid influence of the sun, he should find the productions of nature sublimated by its rays to more perfect and precious qualities. He was strengthened in this belief by a letter written to him at the command of the queen, by one Jayme Ferrer, an eminent and learned lapidary, who, in the course of his trading for precious stones and metals, had been in the Levant and in various parts of the East; had conversed with the merchants of the remote parts of Asia and Africa, and the natives of India, Arabia, and Ethiopia, and was considered deeply versed in geography generally, but especially in the natural histories of those countries whence the valuable merchandise in which he dealt was procured. In this letter Ferrer assured Columbus, that, according to his experience, the rarest objects of commerce, such as gold, precious stones, drugs, and spices, were chiefly to be found in the regions about the equinoctial line, where the inhabitants were black, or darkly colored; and that until the admiral should arrive among people of such complexions, he did not think he would find those articles in great abundance.[1]

Columbus expected to find such people more to the south. He recollected that the natives of Hispaniola had spoken of black men who had once come to their island from the south and southeast, the heads of whose javelins were of a sort of metal which they called Guanin. They had given the admiral specimens of this metal, which, on being assayed in Spain, proved to be a mixture of eighteen parts gold, six silver, and eight copper, a proof of valuable mines in the country whence they came. Charlevoix conjectures that these black people may have come from the Canaries, or the western coast of Africa, and been driven by tempest to the shores of Hispaniola.[2] It is probable, however, that Columbus had been misinformed as to their color, or had

[1] Navarrete, Colec., tom. ii. doc. 68.
[2] Charlevoix, Hist. St. Domingo, lib. iii. p. 162.

misunderstood his informants. It is difficult to believe that the natives of Africa, or the Canaries, could have performed a voyage of such magnitude, in the frail and scantily provided barks they were accustomed to use.

It was to ascertain the truth of all these suppositions, and, if correct, to arrive at the favored and opulent countries about the equator, inhabited by people of similar complexions with those of the Africans under the line, that Columbus in his present voyage to the New World took a course much farther to the south than that which he had hitherto pursued.

Having heard that a French squadron was cruising off Cape St. Vincent, he stood to the southwest after leaving St. Lucar, touching at the islands of Porto Santo and Madeira, where he remained a few days taking in wood and water and other supplies, and then continued his course to the Canary Islands. On the 19th of June, he arrived at Gomara, where there lay at anchor a French cruiser with two Spanish prizes. On seeing the squadron of Columbus standing into the harbor, the captain of the privateer put to sea in all haste, followed by his prizes; one of which, in the hurry of the moment, left part of her crew on shore, making sail with only four of her armament, and six Spanish prisoners. The admiral at first mistook them for merchant ships alarmed by his warlike appearance; when informed of the truth, however, he sent three of his vessels in pursuit, but they were too distant to be overtaken. The six Spaniards, however, on board of one of the prizes, seeing assistance at hand, rose on their captors, and the admiral's vessel coming up, the prize was retaken, and brought back in triumph to the port. The admiral relinquished the ship to the captain, and gave up the prisoners to the governor of the island, to be exchanged for six Spaniards carried off by the cruiser.[1]

Leaving Gomara on the 21st of June, Columbus divided

---

[1] Hist. del Almirante, cap. 65.

his squadron off the island of Ferro : three of his ships he
dispatched direct for Hispaniola, to carry supplies to the
colony. One of these ships was commanded by Alonzo
Sanchez de Caravajal, native of Baeza, a man of much
worth and integrity; the second by Pedro de Arana of
Cordovo, brother of Doña Beatrix Henriquez, the mother
of the admiral's second son Fernando. He was cousin also
of the unfortunate officer who commanded the fortress of
La Navidad at the time of the massacre. The third was
commanded by Juan Antonio Columbus (or Colombo), a
Genoese, related to the admiral, and a man of much judgment and capacity. These captains were alternately to
have the command, and bear the signal light a week at a
time. The admiral carefully pointed out their course.
When they came in sight of Hispaniola, they were to steer
for the south side, for the new port and town, which he supposed to be by this time established in the mouth of the
Ozema, according to royal orders sent out by Coronel.
With the three remaining vessels, the admiral prosecuted
his voyage towards the Cape de Verde Islands. The ship
in which he sailed was decked, the other two were merchant caravels.[1] As he advanced within the tropics, the
change of climate, and the close and sultry weather,
brought on a severe attack of the gout, followed by a
violent fever. Notwithstanding his painful illness, he enjoyed the full possession of his faculties, and continued to
keep his reckoning, and make his observations, with his
usual vigilance and minuteness.

On the 27th of June, he arrived among the Cape de
Verde Islands, which, instead of the freshness and verdure
which their name would betoken, presented an aspect of the
most cheerless sterility. He remained among these islands
but a very few days, being disappointed in his expectation
of obtaining goats' flesh for ships' provisions, and cattle for
stock for the island of Hispaniola. To procure them would

[1] P. Martyr, decad. i. lib. vi.

require some delay; in the meantime the health of himself and of his people suffered under the influence of the weather. The atmosphere was loaded with clouds and vapors; neither sun nor star was to be seen; a sultry, depressing temperature prevailed; and the livid looks of the inhabitants bore witness to the insalubrity of the climate.[1]

Leaving the island of Buena Vista on the 5th of July, Columbus stood to the southwest, intending to continue on until he found himself under the equinoctial line. The currents, however, which ran to the north and northwest among these islands impeded his progress, and kept him for two days in sight of the Island del Fuego. The volcanic summit of this island, which, seen at a distance, resembled a church with a lofty steeple, and which was said at times to emit smoke and flames, was the last point discerned of the Old World.

Continuing to the southwest about one hundred and twenty leagues, he found himself, on the 13th of July, according to his observations, in the fifth degree of north latitude. He had entered that region which extends for eight or ten degrees on each side of the line, and is known among seamen by the name of the calm latitudes. The trade-winds from the southeast and northeast, meeting in the neighborhood of the equator, neutralize each other, and a steady calmness of the elements is produced. The whole sea is like a mirror, and vessels remain almost motionless, with flapping sails; the crews panting under the heat of a vertical sun, unmitigated by any refreshing breeze. Weeks are sometimes employed in crossing this torpid tract of the ocean.

The weather for some time past had been cloudy and oppressive; but on the 13th there was a bright and burning sun. The wind suddenly fell, and a dead sultry calm commenced, which lasted for eight days. The air was like a furnace; the tar melted, the seams of the ship yawned; the

[1] Hist. del Almirante, cap. 65.

salt meat became putrid; the wheat was parched as if with fire; the hóops shrank from the wine and water-casks, some of which leaked, and others burst; while the heat in the holds of the vessels was so suffocating, that no one could remain below a sufficient time to prevent the damage that was taking place. The mariners lost all strength and spirits, and sank under the oppressive heat. It seemed as if the old fable of the torrid zone was about to be realized; and that they were approaching a fiery region, where it would be impossible to exist. It is true the heavens were, for a great part of the time, overcast, and there were drizzling showers; but the atmosphere was close and stifling, and there was that combination of heat and moisture which relaxes all the energies of the human frame.

During this time, the admiral suffered extremely from the gout, but, as usual, the activity of his mind, heightened by his anxiety, allowed him no indulgence nor repose. He was in an unknown part of the ocean, where every thing depended upon his vigilance and sagacity; and was continually watching the phenomena of the elements, and looking out for signs of land. Finding the heat so intolerable, he altered his course, and steered to the southwest, hoping to find a milder temperature farther on, even under the same parallel. He had observed, in his previous voyages, that after sailing westward a hundred leagues from the Azores, a wonderful change took place in the sea and sky, both becoming serene and bland, and the air temperate and refreshing. He imagined that a peculiar mildness and suavity prevailed over a great tract of ocean extending from north to south, into which the navigator, sailing from east to west, would suddenly enter, as if crossing a line. The event seemed to justify his theory, for after making their way slowly for some time to the westward, through an ordeal of heats and calms, with a murky, stifling atmosphere, the ships all at once emerged into a genial region, a pleasant cooling breeze played over the surface of the sea, and gently filled their sails, the close and drizzling clouds broke away, the sky became serene and clear, and the sun shone forth with all its splendor, but no longer with a burning heat.

Columbus had intended, on reaching this temperate tract, to have stood once more to the south and then westward; but the late parching weather had opened the seams of his ships, and caused them to leak excessively, so that it was necessary to seek a harbor as soon as possible, where they might be refitted. Much of the provisions also was spoiled, and the water nearly exhausted. He kept on therefore directly to the west, trusting, from the flights of birds and other favorable indications, he should soon arrive at land. Day after day passed away without his expectations being realized. The distresses of his men became continually more urgent; wherefore, supposing himself in the longitude of the Caribbee Islands, he bore away towards the northward in search of them.[1]

On the 31st of July, there was not above one cask of water remaining in each ship, when, about mid-day, a mariner at the mast-head beheld the summits of three mountains rising above the horizon, and gave the joyful cry of land. As the ships drew nearer, it was seen that these mountains were united at the base. Columbus had determined to give the first land he should behold the name of the Trinity. The appearance of these three mountains united into one struck him as a singular coincidence; and, with a solemn feeling of devotion, he gave the island the name of La Trinidad, which it bears at the present day.[2]

[1] Hist. del Almirante, cap. 67.   Ibid., ubi sup.

30

CHAPTER II.

VOYAGE THROUGH THE GULF OF PARIA.

[1498.]

SHAPING his course for the island, Columbus approached its eastern extremity, to which he gave the name of Punta de la Galera, from a rock in the sea, which resembled a galley under sail. He was obliged to coast for five leagues along the southern shore, before he could find safe anchorage. On the following day, (August 1,) he continued coasting westward, in search of water and a convenient harbor where the vessels might be careened. He was surprised at the verdure and fertility of the country, having expected to find it more parched and sterile as he approached the equator; whereas he beheld groves of palm-trees, and luxuriant forests, sweeping down to the sea-side, with fountains and running streams. The shores were low and uninhabited, but the country rose in the interior, was cultivated in many places, and enlivened by hamlets and scattered habitations. In a word, the softness and purity of the climate, and the verdure, freshness, and sweetness of the country, appeared to him to equal the delights of early spring in the beautiful province of Valencia.[1]

Anchoring at a point to which he gave the name of Punta de la Playa, he sent the boats on shore for water. They found an abundant and limpid brook, at which they filled their casks, but there was no safe harbor for the vessels, nor could they meet with any of the islanders, though they found prints of footsteps, and various fishing implements, left behind in the hurry of flight. There were tracks also of animals, which they supposed to be goats,

[1] Letter of Columbus to the Sovereigns from Hispaniola, Navarrete, Colec., tom. i.

but which must have been deer, with which, as it was after-wards ascertained, the island abounded.

While coasting the island, Columbus beheld land to the south, stretching to the distance of more than twenty leagues. It was that low tract of coast intersected by the numerous branches of the Oronoco, but the admiral, supposing it to be an island, gave it the name of La Isla Santa; little imagining that he now, for the first time, beheld that conti-nent, that Terra Firma, which had been the object of his earnest search.

On the 2d of August he continued on to the southwest point of Trinidad, which he called Point Arenal. It stretched towards a corresponding point of Terra Firma, making a narrow pass, with a high rock in the centre, to which he gave the name of El Gallo. Near this pass the ships cast anchor. As they were approaching this place, a large canoe, with five-and-twenty Indians, put off from the shore, but paused on coming within bow-shot, and hailed the ships in a language which no one on board understood. Columbus tried to allure the savages on board, by friendly signs, by the display of looking-glasses, basins of polished metal, and various glittering trinkets, but all in vain. They remained gazing in mute wonder for above two hours, with their paddles in their hands, ready to take to flight on the least attempt to approach them. They were all young men, well formed, and naked, excepting bands and fillets of cotton about their heads, and colored cloths of the same about their loins. They were armed with bows and arrows, the latter feathered and tipped with bone, and they had bucklers, an article of armor seen for the first time among the inhabitants of the New World.

Finding all other means to attract them ineffectual, Columbus now tried the power of music. He knew the fondness of the Indians for dances performed to the sound of their rude drums, and the chant of their traditional ballads. He ordered something similar to be executed on

the deck of his ship, where, while one man sang to the
beat of the tabor, and the sound of other musical instruments, the ship-boys danced, after the popular Spanish
fashion.   No sooner, however, did this symphony strike up,
than the Indians, mistaking it for a signal of hostilities,
put their bucklers on their arms, seized their bows, and let
fly a shower of arrows.   This rude salutation was immediately answered by the discharge of a couple of cross-bows,
which put the auditors to flight, and concluded this singular
entertainment.

Though thus shy of the admiral's vessel, they approached
one of the caravels without hesitation, and, running under
the stern, had a parley with the pilot, who gave a cap and
a mantle to the one who appeared to be the chieftain.   He
received the presents with great delight, inviting the pilot
by signs to come to land, where he should be well entertained, and receive great presents in return.   On his
appearing to consent, they went to shore to wait for him.
The pilot put off in the boat of the caravel to ask permission of the admiral; but the Indians, seeing him go on
board of the hostile ship, suspected some treachery, and
springing into their canoe, darted away, nor was any thing
more seen of them.[1]

The complexion and other physical characteristics of
these savages caused much surprise and speculation in the
mind of Columbus.   Supposing himself in the seventh degree of latitude, though actually in the tenth, he expected
to find the inhabitants similar to the natives of Africa
under the same parallel, who were black and ill-shaped,
with crisped hair, or rather wool; whereas these were well
formed, had long hair, and were even fairer than those
more distant from the equator.   The climate, also, instead
of being hotter as he approached the equinoctial, appeared

[1] Hist. del Almirante, cap. 88.   P. Martyr, decad. i. lib. vi.   Las
Casas, Hist. Ind., lib. i. cap. 138.   MS. Letter of Columbus to the
Castilian Sovereigns, Navarrete, Colec., tom. i.

more temperate. He was now in the dog-days, yet the nights and mornings were so cool that it was necessary to use covering as in winter. This is the case in many parts of the torrid zone, especially in calm weather, when there is no wind, for nature, by heavy dews, in the long nights of those latitudes, cools and refreshes the earth after the great heats of the day. Columbus was at first greatly perplexed by these contradictions to the course of nature, as observed in the Old World; they were in opposition also to the expectations he had founded on the theory of Ferrer the lapidary, but they gradually contributed to the formation of a theory which was springing up in his active imagination, and which will be presently shown.

After anchoring at Point Arenal, the crews were permitted to land and refresh themselves. There were no runs of water, but by sinking pits in the sand they soon obtained sufficient to fill the casks. The anchorage at this place, however, was extremely insecure. A rapid current set from the eastward through the strait formed by the mainland and the island of Trinidad, flowing, as Columbus observed, night and day, with as much fury as the Guadalquiver, when swollen by floods. In the pass between Point Arenal and its correspondent point, the confined current boiled and raged to such a degree, that he thought it was crossed by a reef of rocks and shoals, preventing all entrance, with others extending beyond, over which the waters roared like breakers on a rocky shore. To this pass, from its angry and dangerous appearance, he gave the name of Boca del Sierpe (the Mouth of the Serpent). He thus found himself placed between two difficulties. The continual current from the east seemed to prevent all return, while the rocks which appeared to beset the pass threatened destruction if he should proceed. Being on board of his ship, late at night, kept awake by painful illness and an anxious and watchful spirit, he heard a terrible roaring from the south, and beheld the sea heaped up, as it were,

into a great ridge or hill, the height of the ship, covered
with foam, and rolling towards him with a tremendous up-
roar. As this furious surge approached, rendered more
terrible in appearance by the obscurity of night, he
trembled for the safety of his vessels. His own ship was
suddenly lifted up to such a height that he dreaded lest it
should be overturned or cast upon the rocks, while another
of the ships was torn violently from her anchorage. The
crews were for a time in great consternation, fearing they
should be swallowed up; but the mountainous surge passed
on, and gradually subsided, after a violent contest with the
counter-current of the strait.[1] This sudden rush of water,
it is supposed, was caused by the swelling of one of the
rivers which flow into the Gulf of Paria, and which were
as yet unknown to Columbus.

Anxious to extricate himself from this dangerous neighborhood, he sent the boats on the following morning to
sound the depth of water at the Boca del Sierpe, and to
ascertain whether it was possible for ships to pass through
to the northward. To his great joy, they returned with a
report that there were several fathoms of water, and currents and eddies setting both ways, either to enter or return. A favorable breeze prevailing, he immediately made
sail, and passing through the formidable strait in safety,
found himself in a tranquil expanse beyond.

He was now on the inner side of Trinidad. To his left
spread the broad gulf since known by the name of Paria,
which he supposed to be the open sea, but was surprised,
on tasting it, to find the water fresh. He continued northward, towards a mountain at the northwest point of the
island, about fourteen leagues from Point Arenal. Here he
beheld two lofty capes opposite each other, one on the
island of Trinidad, the other to the west, on the long prom-

---

[1] Letter of Columbus to the Castilian Sovereigns, Navarrete,
Colec., tom. i. Herrera, Hist. Ind. decad. i. lib. iii. cap. 10. Hist.
del Almirante, cap. 69.

ontory of Paria, which stretches from the main-land and forms the northern side of the gulf, but which Columbus mistook for an island, and named Isla de Gracia.

Between these capes there was another pass, which appeared even more dangerous than the Boca del Sierpe, - being beset with rocks, among which the current forced its way with roaring turbulence. To this pass Columbus gave the name of Boca del Dragon. Not choosing to encounter its apparent dangers, he turned northward, on Sunday, the 5th of August, and steered along the inner side of the supposed island of Gracia, intending to keep on until he came to the end of it, and then to strike northward into the free and open ocean, and shape his course for Hispaniola.

It was a fair and beautiful coast, indented with fine harbors lying close to each other; the country cultivated in many places, in others covered with fruit trees and stately forests, and watered by frequent streams. What greatly astonished Columbus was still to find the water fresh, and that it grew more and more so the farther he proceeded; it being that season of the year when the various rivers which empty themselves into this gulf are swollen by rains, and pour forth such quantities of fresh water as to conquer the saltness of the ocean. He was also surprised at the placidity of the sea, which appeared as tranquil and safe as one vast harbor, so that there was no need of seeking a port to anchor in.

As yet he had not been able to hold any communication with the people of this part of the New World. The shores which he had visited, though occasionally cultivated, were silent and deserted, and, excepting the fugitive party in the canoe at Point Arenal, he had seen nothing of the natives. After sailing several leagues along the coast, he anchored on Monday, the 6th of August, at a place where there appeared signs of cultivation, and sent the boats on

' They found recent traces of people, but not an

individual was to be seen. The coast was hilly, covered with beautiful and fruitful groves, and abounding with monkeys. Continuing further westward, to where the country was more level, Columbus anchored in a river.

Immediately a canoe, with three or four Indians, came off to the caravel nearest to the shore, the captain of which, pretending a desire to accompany them to land, sprang into their canoe, overturned it, and, with the assistance of his seamen, secured the Indians as they were swimming. When brought to the admiral, he gave them beads, hawks'-bells, and sugar, and sent them highly gratified on shore, where many of their countrymen were assembled. This kind treatment had the usual effect. Such of the natives as had canoes came off to the ships with the fullest confidence. They were tall of stature, finely formed, and free and graceful in their movements. Their hair was long and straight; some wore it cut short, but none of them braided it, as was the custom among the natives of Hispaniola. They were armed with bows, arrows, and targets; the men wore cotton cloths about their heads and loins, beautifully wrought with various colors, so as at a distance to look like silk; but the women were entirely naked. They brought bread, maize, and other eatables, with different kinds of beverage, some white, made from maize, and resembling beer, and others green, of a vinous flavor, and expressed from various fruits. They appeared to judge of every thing by the sense of smell, as others examine objects by the sight or touch. When they approached a boat, they smelt to it, and then to the people. In like manner every thing that was given them was tried. They set but little value upon beads, but were extravagantly delighted with hawks'-bells. Brass was also held in high estimation; they appeared to find something extremely grateful in the smell of it, and called it Turey, signifying that it was from the skies.[1]

[1] Herrera, Hist. Ind., decad. i. lib. iii. cap. 11.

From these Indians Columbus understood that the name of their country was Paria, and that farther to the west he would find it more populous. Taking several of them to serve as guides and mediators, he proceeded eight leagues westward to a point which he called Aguja, or the Needle. Here he arrived at three o'clock in the morning. When the day dawned he was delighted with the beauty of the country. It was cultivated in many places, highly populous, and adorned with magnificent vegetation; habitations were interspersed among groves laden with fruits and flowers; grape-vines entwined themselves among the trees, and birds of brilliant plumage fluttered from branch to branch. The air was temperate and bland, and sweetened by the fragrance of flowers and blossoms; and numerous fountains and limpid streams kept up a universal verdure and freshness. Columbus was so much charmed with the beauty and amenity of this part of the coast, that he gave it the name of The Gardens.

The natives came off in great numbers, in canoes, of superior construction to those hitherto seen, being very large and light, with a cabin in the centre for the accommodation of the owner and his family. They invited Columbus, in the name of their king, to come to land. Many of them had collars and burnished plates about their necks, of that inferior kind of gold called by the Indians Guanin. They said that it came from a high land, which they pointed out, at no great distance to the west, but intimated that it was dangerous to go there, either because the inhabitants were cannibals, or the place infested by venomous animals.[1] But what aroused the attention and awakened the cupidity of the Spaniards, was the sight of strings of pearls round the arms of some of the natives. These, they informed Columbus, were procured on the sea-coast, on the northern side of Paria, which he still supposed

[1] Letter of Columbus to the Castilian Sovereigns, Navarrete, Colec., tom. i. p. 252.

to be an island; and they showed the mother-of-pearl shells
whence they had been taken. Anxious for further information, and to procure specimens of these pearls to send to
Spain, he dispatched the boats to shore. A multitude of
the natives came to the beach to receive them, headed by
the chief cacique and his son. They treated the Spaniards
with profound reverence, as beings descended from heaven,
and conducted them to a spacious house, the residence of
the cacique, where they were regaled with bread and various fruits of excellent flavor, and the different kinds of beverage already mentioned. While they were in the house, the
men remained together at one end of it, and the women at
the other. After they had finished their collation at the
house of the cacique, they were taken to that of his son,
where a like repast was set before them. These people
were remarkably affable, though, at the same time, they
possessed a more intrepid and martial air and spirit than
the natives of Cuba and Hispaniola. They were fairer,
Columbus observes, than any he had yet seen, though so
near to the equinoctial line, where he had expected to find
them of the color of Ethiopians. Many ornaments of gold
were seen among them, but all of an inferior quality; one
Indian had a piece of the size of an apple. They had
various kinds of domesticated parrots, one of a light-green
color, with a yellow neck, and the tips of the wings of a
bright red; others of the size of domestic fowls, and of a
vivid scarlet, excepting some azure feathers in the wings.
These they readily gave to the Spaniards; but what the
latter most coveted were the pearls, of which they saw
many necklaces and bracelets among the Indian women.
The latter gladly gave them in exchange for hawks'-bells
or any article of brass, and several specimens of fine pearls
were procured for the admiral to send to the sovereigns.[1]

The kindness and amity of this people were heightened

[1] Letter of Columbus. Herrera, Hist. Ind., decad. i. lib. iii. cap.
11. Hist. del Almirante, cap. 70.

by an intelligent demeanor and a martial frankness. They seemed worthy of the beautiful country they inhabited. It was a cause of great concern both to them and the Spaniards, that they could not understand each other's language. They conversed, however, by signs; mutual good-will made their intercourse easy and pleasant; and at the hour of vespers the Spaniards returned on board of their ships, highly gratified with their entertainment.

CHAPTER III.

CONTINUATION OF THE VOYAGE THROUGH THE GULF OF PARIA.—RETURN TO HISPANIOLA.

[1498.]

THE quantity of fine pearls found among the natives of Paria was sufficient to arouse the sanguine anticipations of Columbus. It appeared to corroborate the theory of Ferrer, the learned jeweler, that, as he approached the equator, he would find the most rare and precious productions of nature. His active imagination, with its intuitive rapidity, seized upon every circumstance in unison with his wishes, and, combining them, drew thence the most brilliant inferences. He had read in Pliny that pearls are generated from drops of dew which fall into the mouths of oysters: if so, what place could be more propitious to their growth and multiplication than the coast of Paria? The dew in those parts was heavy and abundant, and the oysters were so plentiful that they clustered about the roots and pendant branches of the mangrove trees, which grew within the margin of the tranquil sea. When a branch which had drooped for a time in the water was drawn forth, it was found covered with oysters. Las Casas, noticing this sanguine conclusion of Columbus, observes, that the shell-fish here spoken of are not of the kind which produce pearl, for that those by a natural instinct, as if conscious of their precious charge, hide themselves in the deepest water.[1]

Still imagining the coast of Paria to be an island, and anxious to circumnavigate it, and arrive at the place where these pearls were said by the Indians to abound, Columbus left the Gardens on the 10th of August, and continued coasting westward within the gulf, in search of an outlet to the north. He observed portions of Terra Firma appearing towards the bottom of the gulf, which he supposed to be islands, and called them Isabeta and Tramontana, and fancied that the desired outlet to the sea must lie between them. As he advanced, however, he found the water continually growing shallower and fresher, until he did not dare to venture any farther with his ship, which, he observed, was of too great a size for expeditions of this kind, being of an hundred tons burden, and requiring three fathoms of water. He came to anchor, therefore, and sent a light caravel called the Correo, to ascertain whether there was an outlet to the ocean between the supposed islands. The caravel returned on the following day, reporting that at the western end of the gulf there was an opening of two leagues, which led into an inner and circular gulf, surrounded by four openings, apparently smaller gulfs, or rather mouths of rivers, from which flowed the great quantity of fresh water that sweetened the neighboring sea. In fact, from one of these mouths issued the great river the Cuparipari, or, as it is now called, the Paria. To this inner and circular gulf Columbus gave the name of the Gulf of Pearls, through a mistaken idea that they abounded in its waters, though none, in fact, are found there. He still imagined that the four openings of which the mariners spoke, might be intervals between islands, though they affirmed that all the land he saw was connected.[2] As it

---

[1] Las Casas, Hist. Ind., cap. 136.
[2] Hist. del Almirante, cap. 78.

was impossible to proceed further westward with his ships, he had no alternative but to retrace his course, and seek an exit to the north by the Boca del Dragon. He would gladly have continued for some time to explore this coast, for he considered himself in one of those opulent regions described as the most favored upon earth, and which increase in riches towards the equator. Imperious considerations, however, compelled him to shorten his voyage, and hasten to San Domingo. The sea-stores of his ships were almost exhausted, and the various supplies for the colony, with which they were freighted, were in danger of spoiling. He was suffering, also, extremely in his health. Besides the gout, which had rendered him a cripple for the greater part of the voyage, he was afflicted by a complaint in his eyes, caused by fatigue and over-watching, which almost deprived him of sight. Even the voyage along the coast of Cuba, he observes, in which he was three and thirty days almost without sleep, had not so injured his eyes and disordered his frame, or caused him so much painful suffering, as at present.[1]

On the 11th of August, therefore, he set sail eastward for the Boca del Dragon, and was borne along with great velocity by the currents, which, however, prevented him from landing again at his favorite spot, the Gardens. On Sunday the 13th, he anchored near to the Boca, in a fine harbor, to which he gave the name of Puerto de Gatos, from a species of monkey called gato paulo, with which the neighborhood abounded. On the margin of the sea he perceived many trees which, as he thought, produced the mirabolane, a fruit only found in the countries of the East. There were great numbers also of mangroves growing within the water, with oysters clinging to their branches, their mouths open, as he supposed, to receive the dew, which was afterwards to be transformed to pearls.[2]

[1] Letter of Columbus to the Sovereigns, Navarrete, tom. i. p. 252.
[2] Herrera, Hist. Ind., decad. i. lib. iii. cap. 10.

On the following morning, the 14th of August, towards
noon, the ships approached the Boca del Dragon, and prepared to venture through that formidable pass.   The
distance from Cape Boto at the end of Paria, and Cape
Lapa the extremity of Trinidad, is about five leagues;
but in the interval there were two islands, which Columbus
named Caracol and Delphin.   The impetuous body of
fresh water which flows through the gulf, particularly in
the rainy months of July and August, is confined at the
narrow outlets between these islands, where it causes a turbulent sea, foaming and roaring as if breaking over rocks,
and rendering the entrance and exit of the gulf extremely
dangerous.   The horrors and perils of such places are
always tenfold to discoverers, who have no chart, nor pilot,
nor advice of previous voyager, to guide them.   Columbus,
at first, apprehended sunken rocks and shoals; but on
attentively considering the commotion of the strait, he
attributed it to the conflict between the prodigious body of
fresh water setting through the gulf and struggling for an
outlet, and the tide of salt water struggling to enter.   The
ships had scarcely ventured into the fearful channel when
the wind died away, and they were in danger every moment
of being thrown upon the rocks or sands.   The current of
fresh water, however, gained the victory, and carried them
safely through.   The admiral, when once more safe in the
open sea, congratulated himself upon his escape from this
perilous strait, which, he observes, might well be called
the Mouth of the Dragon.[1]

He now stood to the westward, running along the outer
coast of Paria, still supposing it an island, and intending to
visit the Gulf of Pearls, which he imagined to be at the
end of it, opening to the sea.   He wished to ascertain
whether this great body of fresh water proceeded from
rivers, as the crew of the caravel Correo had affirmed; for
it appeared to him impossible that the streams of mere

[1] Herrera, Hist. Ind., decad. i. lib. ii. cap. 11.

islands, as he supposed the surrounding lands, could furnish such a prodigious volume of water.

On leaving the Boca del Dragon, he saw to the northeast, many leagues distant, two islands, which he called Assumption and Conception; probably those now known as Tobago and Granada. In his course along the northern coast of Paria he saw several other small islands, and many fine harbors, to some of which he gave names, but they have ceased to be known by them. On the 15th he discovered the islands of Margarita and Cubagua, afterwards famous for their pearl fishery. The island of Margarita, about fifteen leagues in length, and six in breadth, was well peopled. The little island of Cubagua, lying between it and the main-land, and only about four leagues from the latter, was dry and sterile, without either wood or fresh water, but possessing a good harbor. On approaching this island, the admiral beheld a number of Indians fishing for pearls, who made for the land. A boat being sent to communicate with them, one of the sailors noticed many strings of pearls round the neck of a female. Having a plate of Valencia ware, a kind of porcelain painted and varnished with gaudy colors, he broke it, and presented the pieces to the Indian woman, who gave him in exchange a considerable number of her pearls. These he carried to the admiral, who immediately sent persons on shore, well provided with Valencian plates and hawks'-bells, for which in a little time he procured about three pounds' weight of pearls, some of which were of a very large size, and were sent by him afterwards to the sovereigns as specimens.[1]

There was great temptation to visit other spots, which the Indians mentioned as abounding in pearls. The coast of Paria also continued extending to the westward as far as the eye could reach, rising into a range of mountains, and provoking examination to ascertain whether, as he began to think, it was a part of the Asiatic continent. Columbus

[1] Charlevoix, Hist. St. Domingo, lib. iii. p. 169.

was compelled, however, though with the greatest reluctance, to forego this most interesting investigation.

The malady of his eyes had now grown so virulent, that
he could no longer take observations or keep a look-out,
but had to trust to the reports of the pilots and mariners.
He bore away, therefore, for Hispaniola, intending to repose there from the toils of his voyage, and to recruit his
health, while he should send his brother, the Adelantado,
to complete the discovery of this important country. After
sailing for five days to the northwest, he made the island
of Hispaniola on the 19th of August, fifty leagues to the
westward of the river Ozema, the place of his destination;
and anchored on the following morning under the little
island of Beata.

He was astonished to find himself so mistaken in his calculations, and so far below his destined port; but he attributed it correctly to the force of the current setting out
of the Boca del Dragon, which, while he had lain to at
nights, to avoid running on rocks and shoals, had borne his
ship insensibly to the west. This current, which sets across
the Caribbean sea, and the continuation of which now
bears the name of the Gulf Stream, was so rapid, that on
the 15th, though the wind was but moderate, the ships had
made seventy-five leagues in four-and-twenty hours. Columbus attributed to the violence of this current the formation of that pass called the Boca del Dragon, where he supposed it had forced its way through a narrow isthmus that
formerly connected Trinidad with the extremity of Paria.
He imagined, also, that its constant operation had worn
away and inundated the borders of the main-land, gradually producing that fringe of islands which stretches from
Trinidad to the Lucayos or Bahamas, and which, according
to his idea, had originally been part of the solid continent.
In corroboration of this opinion, he notices the form of
those islands: narrow from north to south, and extending

in length from east to west, in the direction of the current.[1]

The island of Beata, where he had anchored, is about thirty leagues to the west of the river Ozema, where he expected to find the new sea-port which his brother had been instructed to establish. The strong and steady current from the east, however, and the prevalence of winds from that quarter, might detain him for a long time at the island, and render the remainder of his voyage slow and precarious. He sent a boat on shore, therefore, to procure an Indian messenger to take a letter to his brother, the Adelantado. Six of the natives came off to the ships, one of whom was armed with a Spanish cross-bow. The admiral was alarmed at seeing a weapon of the kind in the possession of an Indian. It was not an article of traffic, and he feared could only have fallen into his hands by the death of some Spaniard.[2] He apprehended that further evils had befallen the settlement during his long absence, and that there had again been troubles with the natives.

Having dispatched his messenger, he made sail, and arrived off the mouth of the river on the 30th of August. He was met on the way by a caravel, on board of which was the Adelantado, who, having received his letter, had hastened forth with affectionate ardor to welcome his arrival. The meeting of the brothers was a cause of mutual joy; they were strongly attached to each other, each had had his trials and sufferings during their long separation, and each looked with confidence to the other for comfort and relief. Don Bartholomew appears to have always had great deference for the brilliant genius, the enlarged mind, and the commanding reputation of his brother; while the latter placed great reliance, in times of difficulty, on the worldly knowledge, the indefatigable activity, and the lion-hearted courage of the Adelantado.

[1] Letter to the King and Queen, Navarrete, Colec., tom. i.
[2] Las Casas, Hist. Ind., lib. i. cap. 148.

31

. Columbus arrived almost the wreck of himself. His voyages were always of a nature to wear out the human frame, having to navigate amidst unknown dangers, and to keep anxious watch, at all hours, and in all weathers. As age and infirmity increased upon him, these trials became the more severe. His constitution must originally have been wonderfully vigorous; but constitutions of this powerful kind, if exposed to severe hardships at an advanced period of life, when the frame has become somewhat rigid and unaccommodating, are apt to be suddenly broken up, and to be a prey to violent aches and maladies. In this last voyage Columbus had been parched and consumed by fever, racked by gout, and his whole system disordered by incessant watchfulness; he came into port haggard, emaciated, and almost blind. His spirit, however, was, as usual, superior to all bodily affliction or decay, and he looked forward with magnificent anticipations to the result of his recent discoveries, which he intended should be immediately prosecuted by his hardy and enterprising brother.

CHAPTER IV.

SPECULATIONS OF COLUMBUS CONCERNING THE COAST OF PARIA.

[1498.]

THE natural phenomena of a great and striking nature presented to the ardent mind of Columbus in the course of this voyage, led to certain sound deductions and imaginative speculations. The immense body of fresh water flowing into the Gulf of Paria, and thence rushing into the ocean, was too vast to be produced by an island or by islands. It must be the congregated streams of a great extent of country pouring forth in one mighty river, and the land necessary to furnish such a river must be a continent.

He now supposed that most of the tracts of land which he had seen about the Gulf were connected; that the coast of Paria extended westward far beyond a chain of mountains which he had beheld afar off from Margarita; and that the land opposite to Trinidad, instead of being an island, continued to the south, far beyond the equator, into that hemisphere hitherto unknown to civilized man. He considered all this an extension of the Asiatic continent; thus presuming that the greater part of the surface of the globe was firm land. In this last opinion he found himself supported by authors of the highest name, both ancient and modern; among whom he cites Aristotle and Seneca, St. Augustine and Cardinal Pedro de Aliaco. He lays particular stress also on the assertion of the apocryphal Esdras, that of seven parts of the world, six are dry land, and one part only is covered with water.

The land, therefore, surrounding the Gulf of Paria was but the border of an almost boundless continent, stretching far to the west and to the south, including the most precious regions of the earth, lying under the most auspicious stars and benignant skies, but as yet unknown and uncivilized, free to be discovered and appropriated by any Christian nation. "May it please our Lord," he exclaims in his letter to the sovereigns, "to give long life and health to your highnesses, that you may prosecute this noble enterprise, in which, methinks, God will receive great service, Spain vast increase of grandeur, and all Christians much consolation and delight, since the name of our Saviour will be divulged throughout these lands."

Thus far the deductions of Columbus, though sanguine, admit of little cavil; but he carried them still farther, until they ended in what may appear to some mere chimerical reveries. In his letter to the sovereigns, he stated that, on his former voyages, when he steered westward from the Azores, he had observed, after sailing about a hundred leagues, a sudden and great change in the sky and the stars,

the temperature of the air, and the calmness of the ocean.
It seemed as if a line ran from north to south, beyond
which every thing became different. The needle, which had
previously inclined towards the northeast, now varied a
whole point to the northwest. The sea, hitherto clear, was
covered with weeds, so dense, that in his first voyage he had
expected to run aground upon shoals. A universal tranquillity reigned throughout the elements, and the climate
was mild and genial whether in summer or winter. On
taking his astronomical observations at night, after crossing
that imaginary line, the north star appeared to him to describe a diurnal circle in the heavens, of five degrees in
diameter.

On his present voyage he had varied his route, and had
run southward from the Cape de Verde Islands for the
equinoctial line. Before reaching it, however, the heat had
become insupportable, and, a wind springing up from the
east, he had been induced to strike westward, when in the
parallel of Sierra Leone in Guinea. For several days he
had been almost consumed by scorching and stifling heat
under a sultry yet clouded sky, and in a drizzling atmosphere, until he arrived at the ideal line already mentioned,
extending from north to south. Here suddenly, to his
great relief, he had emerged into serene weather, with a
clear blue sky and a sweet and temperate atmosphere. The
farther he had proceeded west, the more pure and genial he
had found the climate; the sea tranquil, the breezes soft
and balmy. All these phenomena coincided with those he
had remarked at the same line, though farther north, in his
former voyages; excepting that here there was no herbage
in the sea, and the movements of stars were different. The
polar star appeared to him here to describe a diurnal circle
of ten degrees instead of five; an augmentation which
struck him with astonishment, but which he says he ascertained by observations taken in different nights, with his
quadrant. Its greatest altitude at the former place, in the

parallel of the Azores, he had found to be ten degrees, and in the present place fifteen.

From these and other circumstances, he was inclined to doubt the received theory with respect to the form of the earth. Philosophers had described it as spherical; but they knew nothing of the part of the world which he had discovered. The ancient part, known to them, he had no doubt was spherical, but he now supposed the real form of the earth to be that of a pear, one part much more elevated than the rest, and tapering upward towards the skies. This part he supposed to be in the interior of this newly-found continent, and immediately under the equator. All the phenomena which he had previously noticed, appeared to corroborate this theory. The variations which he had observed in passing the imaginary line running from north to south, he concluded to be caused by the ships having arrived at this supposed swelling of the earth, where they began gently to mount towards the skies into a purer and more celestial atmosphere.[1] The variation of the needle he ascribed to the same cause, being affected by the cool-ness and mildness of the climate; varying to the northwest in proportion as the ships continued onward in their ascent.[2] So also the altitude of the north-star, and the circle it described in the heavens, appeared to be greater, in conse-

[1] Peter Martyr mentions that the admiral told him, that, from the climate of great heat and unwholesome air, he had ascended the back of the sea, as it were ascending a high mountain towards heaven. Decad. i. lib. vi.

[2] Columbus, in his attempts to account for the variation of the needle, supposed that the north star possessed the quality of the four cardinal points, as did likewise the loadstone. That if the needle were touched with one part of the loadstone, it would point east, with another west, and so on. Wherefore, he adds, those who pre-pare or magnetize the needles, cover the loadstone with a cloth, so that the north part only remains out; that is to say, the part which possesses the virtue of causing the needle to point to the north. Hist. del Almirante. cap, 66.

quence of being regarded from a greater elevation, less
obliquely, and through a purer medium of atmosphere;
and these phenomena would be found to increase the more
the navigator approached the equator, from the still increasing eminence of this part of the earth.

He noticed, also, the difference of climate, vegetation,
and people, of this part of the New World, from those
under the same parallel in Africa. There the heat was
insupportable, the land parched and sterile, the inhabitants
were black, with crisped wool, ill-shapen in their forms,
and dull and brutal in their natures. Here, on the contrary, although the sun was in Leo, he found the noontide
heat moderate, the mornings and evenings fresh and cool,
the country green and fruitful, and covered with beautiful
forests, the people fairer even than those in the lands he
had discovered farther north, having long hair, with well-
proportioned and graceful forms, lively minds, and cour-
ageous dispositions. All this, in a latitude so near to the
equator, he attributed to the superior altitude of this part
of the world, by which it was raised into a more celestial
region of the air. On turning northward, through the
Gulf of Paria, he had found the circle described by the
north star again to diminish. The current of the sea also
increased in velocity, wearing away, as has already been
remarked, the borders of the continent, and producing by
its incessant operation the adjacent islands. This was a
further confirmation of the idea that he ascended in going
southward, and descended in returning northward.

Aristotle had imagined that the highest part of the
earth, and nearest to the skies, was under the antarctic
pole. Other sages had maintained that it was under the
arctic. Hence it was apparent that both conceived one
part of the earth to be more elevated, and noble, and
nearer to the heavens than the rest. They did not think
of this eminence being under the equinoctial line, observed
Columbus, because they had no certain knowledge of this

hemisphere, but only spoke of it theoretically and from conjecture.

As usual, he assisted his theory by Holy Writ. " The sun, when God created it," he observes, " was in the first point of the Orient, or the first light was there." That place, according to his idea, must be here, in the remotest part of the East, where the ocean and the extreme part of India meet under the equinoctial line, and where the highest point of the earth is situated.

He supposed this apex of the world, though of immense height, to be neither rugged nor precipitous, but that the land rose to it by gentle and imperceptible degrees. The beautiful and fertile shores of Paria were situated on its remote borders, abounding of course with those precious articles which are congenial with the most favored and excellent climates. As one penetrated the interior and gradually ascended, the land would be found to increase in beauty and luxuriance, and in the exquisite nature of its productions, until one arrived at the summit under the equator. This he imagined to be the noblest and most perfect place on earth, enjoying, from its position, an equality of nights and days, and a uniformity of seasons; and being elevated into a serene and heavenly temperature, above the heats and colds, the clouds and vapors, the storms and tempests which deform and disturb the lower regions. In a word, here he supposed to be situated the original abode of our first parents, the primitive seat of human innocence and bliss, the Garden of Eden, or terrestrial paradise !   .

He imagined this place, according to the opinion of the most eminent fathers of the church, to be still flourishing, possessed of all its blissful delights, but inaccessible to mortal feet, excepting by divine permission. From this height he presumed, though of course from a great distance, proceeded the mighty stream of fresh water which filled the Gulf of Paria, and sweetened the salt ocean in its

vicinity, being supplied by the fountain mentioned in
Genesis, as springing from the tree of life in the Garden
of Eden.

Such was the singular speculation of Columbus, which
he details at full length in a letter to the Castilian sovereigns,[1] citing various authorities for his opinions, among
which were St. Augustine, St. Isidor, and St. Ambrosius,
and fortifying his theory with much of that curious and
speculative erudition in which he was deeply versed.[2] It
shows how his ardent mind was heated by the magnificence
of his discoveries. Shrewd men, in the coolness and quie-
tude of ordinary life, and in these modern days of cautious
and sober fact, may smile at such a revery, but it was
countenanced by the speculations of the most sage and
learned of those times; and if this had not been the case,
could we wonder at any sally of the imagination in a man
placed in the situation of Columbus? He beheld a vast
world, rising, as it were, into existence before him, its
nature and extent unknown and undefined, as yet a mere
region for conjecture. Every day displayed some new feature of beauty and sublimity; island after island, where the
rocks, he was told, were veined with gold, the groves teemed
with spices, or the shores abounded with pearls. Interminable ranges of coast; promontory beyond promontory,
stretching as far as the eye could reach; luxuriant valleys
sweeping away into a vast interior, whose distant mountains, he was told, concealed still happier lands, and realms

---

[1] Navarrete, Colec. de Viages, tom. i. p. 242.

[2] See Illustrations, article " Situation of the Terrestrial Paradise."

NOTE.—A great part of these speculations appear to have been
founded on the treatise of the Cardinal Pedro de Aliaco, in which
Columbus found a compendium of the opinions of various eminent
authors on the subject; though it is very probable he consulted many
of their works likewise. In the volume of Pedro de Aliaco, existing
in the library of the Cathedral at Seville, I have traced the germs of
these ideas in various passages of the text, opposite to which marginal
notes have been made in the handwriting of Columbus.

of greater opulence.   When he looked upon all this region of golden promise, it was with the glorious conviction that his genius had called it into existence ; he regarded it with the triumphant eye of a discoverer.   Had not Columbus been capable of these enthusiastic soarings of the imagination, he might, with other sages, have reasoned calmly and coldly in his closet about the probability of a continent existing in the west ; but he would never have had the daring enterprise to adventure in search of it into the unknown realms of ocean.

Still, in the midst of his fanciful speculations, we find that sagacity which formed the basis of his character. The conclusion which he drew from the great flow of the Oronoco, that it must be the outpouring of a continent, was acute and striking. A learned Spanish historian has also ingeniously excused other parts of his theory. " He suspected," observes he, " a certain elevation of the globe at one part of the equator ; philosophers have since determined the world to be a spheroid, slightly elevated in its equatorial circumference. He suspected that the diversity of temperatures influenced the needle, not being able to penetrate the cause of its inconstant variations ; the successive series of voyages and experiments have made this inconstancy more manifest, and have shown that extreme cold sometimes divests the needle of all its virtue. Perhaps new observations may justify the surmise of Columbus. Even his error concerning the circle described by the polar star, which he thought augmented by an optical illusion in proportion as the observer approached the equinox, manifests him a philosopher superior to the time in which he lived." [1]

[1] Muñoz, Hist. N. Mundo, lib. vi. § 32.

END OF VOL.

Printed in the USA
CPSIA information can be obtained
at www.ICGtesting.com
LVHW080430071123
763186LV00005B/485